LAND, RIGHTS AND INNOVATION
Improving Tenure Security for the Urban Poor

Edited by

Geoffrey Payne

Practical
ACTION
PUBLISHING

Practical Action Publishing Ltd
27a Albert Street, Rugby, CV21 2SG, Warwickshire, UK
www.practicalactionpublishing.org

© Intermediate Technology Publications 2002

First published 2002
Reprinted in the UK, 2018

ISBN 13 Paperback: 9781853395444
ISBN Library Ebook: 9781780441207
Book DOI: http://dx.doi.org/10.3362/ 9781780441207

Since 1974, Practical Action Publishing has published and disseminated
books and information in support of international development work
throughout the world. Practical Action Publishing is a trading name
of Practical Action Publishing Ltd (Company Reg. No. 1159018), the
wholly owned publishing company of Practical Action. Practical Action
Publishing trades only in support of its parent charity objectives and any
profits are covenanted back to Practical Action (Charity Reg. No. 247257,
Group VAT Registration No. 880 9924 76).

Contents

Foreword

This book is about people; it is also about place. It is about enabling each of us to find a recognizable space within human settlements in which to live and work. Such places are now increasingly in the towns and cities of the world, and in particular in the towns and cities of developing countries. Over the next 30 years or so – within a single generation – the urban population of the world will double in size. Thus space for over two billion new urban residents will be required, with secure and accepted rights, so that all residents, no matter what their background or reason to be there, can be incorporated into the city domain.

What is a city? A city should, I believe, be a place of cooperation where people work together to create collectively a dynamic economy from a diversity of operations, skills, resources, knowledge, personal drive, leadership and political will. In this way, cities provide the stimulus for national economies, and, in many countries, the sheer majority of the national economic product. This ethos of cooperation – the civic ethos – naturally works best when organized efficiently with a combination of spatial and resource planning, together with a respect for the component parts and contributors to the economic processes – primary and supportive, creative and enabling, producer and consumer.

There is therefore the economic argument that all households are contributors to the city economy whether or not formally employed. The wealth of the city is built up from every single house and resident household – be it a villa employing dozens, a row house, a multi-storey flat, a humble structure of mud, cardboard or plastic sheets with perhaps a corrugated iron roof, a hovel – all of which form a continuum of the placement of people in the urban area context, and thus have the potential to be economically active.

The lowest income worker is the gold dust of the city economy. But such an existence is a fragile one, all too easily blown away. To capture its effect, and to sustain and nurture it, requires the certainty of security and options for growth. To ensure a process whereby each worker is not only protected – able to remain healthy, eat sufficiently and be free from exploitation – but also able to progress – through access to information, or education or training – the lowest income worker must be enabled to develop as part of the city's own dynamic progress. This is essential for a successful city to develop. Every household thus contributes to the city economy. Remove any part of this continuum, or restrict its growth, and everyone in the city feels the loss of some of its potential.

So how do people participate in this continuum, in this economic dynamic? First they need to be assured of their place in society, and secondly, their physical spatial existence. They need a degree of security for this space: some form of tenure security or property rights is vital for the system to work effectively. Only by being inclusive, so that all parts of society can exercise their right to a place in the productive economy and thus be a benefit to all others in society, will the economic continuum be effective.

As this book demonstrates, tenure systems can take many forms, including statutory, customary, religious and informal. The inability of the statutory systems to provide access at the scale required has led to informal tenure systems expanding in most cities of developing countries and as these systems have expanded, so a continuum of tenure systems has evolved to parallel the economic continuum, making policies for providing security a complex process.

This book addresses this complexity and the various ways in which tenure security can be achieved. It draws on real life – on case studies from seventeen example countries. The book will be a valuable resource for those who have the awesome responsibility to ensure that all who want to can participate in the economy of nations through a process of establishing their space and place in productive settlements, with the necessary degree of security for them to be effective.

Michael Mutter
Senior Urban Planning Adviser
Department for International Development

Acknowledgements

Most books are a team effort. However, this one involved a particularly large number of contributors from all parts of the world. I should therefore like to place on record my appreciation and gratitude for the commitment and patience of all the contributors in responding to many requests for additions and changes to their chapters, so that the volume could amount to more than merely a collection of individual papers.

In addition, I should like to thank Ahmereen Reza and Andrew Richardson, research assistants, and Sara Thurman, Tania Payne and Silva Ferretti for help with editing chapters. Michael Mutter and Andrew Preston at the Department for International Development (DFID) gave unstintingly of their time and support, while Farouk Tebbal, Sylvie Lacroux and Chris Williams at UN-HABITAT, and Billy Cobbett at Cities Alliance, provided regular advice and feedback based on work with the United Nations Global Campaign for Secure Tenure. The research on which the book is based could not have been undertaken without the financial support provided by DFID and the Lincoln Institute of Land Policy in Cambridge, Massachusetts. Finally, Helen Marsden at ITDG Publishing gave invaluable help and guidance in preparing the material for publication.

Geoffrey Payne, Editor

The authors of individual chapters also wish to make the following acknowledgements.

Chapter 4. The process of urban land tenure formalization in Peru

Ayako Kagawa and Jan Turkstra

This chapter was made possible thanks to DFID funding for primary data collection. However, the study is also built on earlier research sponsored by PromPeru (Promocion Perú). Our sincere gratitude goes to COFOPRI, whose staff gave time and internal documents despite the difficult circumstances they were facing at the time of our investigation. Special thanks go to Ivette Raffo for co-ordinating the institutional interviews. PlandeMetru, Municipality of Trujillo, has also been very resourceful in providing data on Alto Trujillo. Silvia Mendoza, Gina Chambi, Jenny Leon and Pocho Rojas assisted with fieldwork, and community leaders and households in both Metropolitan Lima and Trujillo co-operated fully. Other institutions, such as IMP (Instituto Metropolitano de Planificacion, Municipalidad

Metropolitana de Lima), INADUR (Instituto Nacional de Desarollo Urbano), Banco de Materiales, RPU, RPI (Registro de la Propiedad Inmueble), CENCA (Centro de Estudios y Promoción del Desarrollo) and PEGUP (Programa de Educación en Gestión Urbana para el Perú) have been very generous in providing time and sharing opinions. Last but not least, we appreciate the interest of ITC (International Institute for Aerospace Survey and Earth Sciences) in the investigation.

Chapter 7. Current changes and trends: Benin, Burkina Faso and Senegal

Alain Durand-Lasserve, in collaboration with Alain Bagré, Moussa Gueye and José Tonato
Alain Durand-Lasserve would like to thank his collaborators for their contributions in preparing this chapter.

Chapter 8. Tenure security, housing investment and environmental improvement: the cases of Delhi and Ahmedabad, India

Amitabh Kundu
This chapter was prepared with the assistance of Mr Bal Paritosh and Mr Sohel Firdos. Grateful thanks to Professor Nilima Risbud for helpful discussion.

Chapter 9. Legality and legitimacy of tenure in Turkey

Murat Balamir
I am most grateful to Aslı Kayıket and Saygın Can Oğuz for their patient and professional help in interviewing the sampled households and taking photographs in Ankara.

Chapter 12. Combining tenure policies, urban planning and city management in Brazil

Edesio Fernandes
I wish to thank Betania de Moraes Alfonsin for her contribution to the research in Porte Alegre.

Chapter 13. Community Land Trusts and other tenure innovations in Kenya

Saad S Yahya
I wish to thank Dr Mohammed Swazuri, Hannah Kamau and David Mshilla for their assistance with data collection and analysis. The Nairobi Informal Settlements Coordination Committee facilitated access to data at City Hall and in the field.

Chapter 14. Going against the grain: alternatives to individual ownership in South Africa

Lauren Royston and Cecile Ambert

The participation of the residents of Everest Court and the Newtown Housing Co-operative, staff at Cope Housing Association and other social housing institutions, provincial and national government officials, and other NGO role-players in the research process is gratefully acknowledged.

Chapter 15. A level playing field: security of tenure and the urban poor in Bangkok, Thailand

Radhika Savant Mohit

I wish to thank Khun Kampong and the Samakee Pattana community, the Nong Chok and Rom Poon community members, Khun Pramul, Khun Nath and other staff of NHA, Khun Reum and staff of the Clergy Foundation, Khun Somchai of Building Together Association, Khun Kaek and the staff of Women's Slum Networking, Khun Maw, Khun Song, Khun Vichai and the staff of the Urban Management Centre for their contributions. I am also indebted to Dr Yap Kioe Sheng for sharing his vast experience and resources on housing and security of tenure in the developing world.

Figures

Tables

Boxes

Acronyms and abbreviations

ACS	Azad Camp in Sarita Vihar
AEC	Ahmedabad Electricity Corporation
AEIS	Special Areas of Social Interest
AMC	Ahmedabad Municipal Corporation
ANL	Agentia Nationala pentru Locuinte
BMA	Bangkok Metropolitan Administration
CBO	community-based organization
CEC	Casa de Economii si Consemnatiuni
CLT	Community Land Trust
CODI	Community Organisation Development Institute
COFOPRI	Comisión de Formalización de la Propiedad Informal
COR	Certificate of Rights
CPA	Communal Property Association
CRRU	Concession of the Real Right to Use
DCHFC	Delhi Co-operative Housing Finance Corporation
DDA	Delhi Development Authority
DFID	Department for International Development
EBRD	European Bank for Reconstruction and Development
FPSG	Fixed Period State Grant
GDP	gross domestic product
GNP	gross national product
GPA	Global Plan of Action
GTZ	German Technical Cooperation Agency
ICH	Indira Camp behind Safdarjung Hospital
ICS	Indira Camp in Srinivashpuri
ILD	Institute of Liberty and Democracy
IMP	Institute of Metropolitan Planning
INADUR	National Institute for Urban Research
IUDP	Integrated Urban Development Project
JCK	Jawahar Camp in Kirti Nagar
KfW	German Bank for Reconstruction and Development
LBC	land-buying company

LD	Ley de Descentralizacion Administrativa
LDO	land development objective
LNC	Laxminagar Camp
LPP	Ley de Participacion Popular
MCD	Municipal Corporation of Delhi
MWA	Metropolitan Water Authority
NACHU	National Co-operative Housing Union
NCC	Nairobi City Council
NGO	non-government organization
NHA	National Housing Administration
NLP	National Land Policy
NRC	Narela Resettlement Colony
NSS	National Sample Survey
PGN	Pravinnagar-Guptanagar
PROFAM	Programa de Lotes Familiares
PT	Workers' Party (Partido dos Trabalhadores)
PUPRP	Peru Urban Property Rights Project
PWD	public works department
ROSCA	Rotating Saving Credit Associations
RP	Registro Predial
RPI	Registro de la Propiedad Inmueble
RPU	Registro Predial Urbano
RUC	Contributors Unique Registration
SCS	Sonia Gandhi Camp at Smalkha
SCT	V.P. Singh Camp in Tughlakabad
SHHA	Self Help Housing Agency
SHN	Sinheshwarinagar
SJN	Sanjaynagar
SNP	Slum Networking Project
STDP	Small Towns Development Project
TOL	Temporary occupation licence
UCDO	Urban Community Development Office
UMP	Urban Master Plan
UNCHS	United Nations Centre for Human Settlements (now UN-HABITAT)
UPIS	Urbanizaciones Populares de Interés Social
USAID	United States Agency for International Development
ZEIS	Special Zones of Social Interest

ISSUES AND CONTEXT

Introduction[1]

Geoffrey Payne

Every day, millions of people around the world spend their hard-earned cash improving houses that they do not legally or officially own. The vast majority of them are poor households in the urban areas of the South or transition economies of Eastern Europe. In some cities, more than half the entire population live in various types of unauthorized housing and the numbers are increasing faster than other forms of development. This book reviews some of these non-formal or non-statutory tenure and property rights systems and the extent to which they can contribute to improved urban management and living conditions for the urban poor.

Why do people risk investing in an activity that many urban authorities seek to prevent or remove? The answer is partly that most have little choice. Land in urban areas tends to be expensive, especially in areas near employment centres where the very poor need to live. Globalization has accelerated the commercialization of urban land markets in developing countries to the point that in the mid-1990s land in Mumbai (Bombay), India, was among the most expensive in the world, despite the fact that a large proportion of the population live below the official poverty line. The only practical answer for many people was therefore to occupy unused government land or purchase agricultural land from farmers and build a house without permission to meet their immediate needs, improving it over time as resources permitted.

For all these diverse groups, access to secure shelter is a precondition for access to other benefits, such as livelihood opportunities, public services and credit. Tenure therefore forms the foundation on which any effort to improve living conditions for the poor has to be built. However, the subject is not one that can easily be defined or delivered according to universally agreed norms. This is because tenure has many historical, cultural, legal and economic associations that affect people's perceptions and behaviour. It therefore needs to be seen as part of a package of measures in which tenure status is related to location, the nature and distribution of employment centres, transportation systems and the distribution of public service networks. For each subcategory of demand, the balance of needs and resources will vary. For example, the priority for the very poor is invariably to obtain access to livelihood opportunities, which are usually in prime, central urban locations where competition for land is greatest and prices correspondingly high. Tenure for them is important insofar as it provides access to street trading and related income-generating activities. For more established low-income households, the ability to cover transport costs may open up opportunities in less central areas and priorities may extend to the need for a secure plot of land or dwelling in which to raise children. For this group, long-term tenure security becomes more important as a means of improving access to services and credit. The home itself may well be a place for income generation. However, land prices, high planning and building standards, together with cumbersome administrative procedures, all conspire to raise land and housing costs to levels that preclude access to formal housing with formal titles. For all such households, access to land and housing is dependent on non-formal and non-statutory tenure systems.

In some cases, people do not consider that they are acting illegally, even though they do not possess a title deed to their property. In many parts of Africa, for example, customary tenure systems have existed for centuries before colonialization introduced the notion of private property in the new urban settlements (Payne, 2001). Similarly, throughout the Middle East, Islamic systems of land tenure have enabled cities to evolve unique forms appropriate to social, cultural and climatic conditions (United Nations, 1973). Both customary and religious tenure systems enabled low-income households to obtain land on terms and conditions that they were generally able and willing to meet. In many countries, these tenure systems continue unchallenged in the rural areas. After independence, however, migrants swelled urban populations causing them to spread into areas of customary tenure. This led to ambiguity and conflict over the role of local chiefs, who traditionally allocate land to members of their community under well-established and officially recognized arrangements. People living in such areas understandably object to being considered illegal occupants of their land. The inability of the state and the unwillingness of the formal market to increase the supply of planned residential land at prices that the poor can afford has perpetuated dependence on these traditional practices and introduced new ones.

In yet other cases, people may act in ways that are based on historical precedents that have not been repealed and can therefore claim a degree of legitimacy. The Ottoman Land Law of 1858, for example, entitled any citizen to claim unused state land and occupy it for as long as they used it. Naturally, when migrants from rural areas arrived in the big cities, they did not consider they were acting outside the law by applying this traditional approach, though the local authorities responsible for implementing an urban master plan saw things very differently.

LEGITIMACY VERSUS LEGALITY

These examples demonstrate that urban land tenure issues in the South are highly complex. It is not a subject that can be defined in terms of legal or illegal, formal or informal. Tenure systems are also the outcome of historical and cultural forces and reflect the relationships between people and society and between people and the land on which they live. In this sense, tenure can be defined as 'the mode by which land is held or owned, or the set of relationships among people concerning land or its product'. Property rights can also be defined as 'a recognized interest in land or property vested in an individual or group and can apply separately to land or development on it'. Naturally, societies that place a great deal of emphasis on communal interests will reflect this in the forms of tenure which are officially recognized, while those that give priority to the interests of individuals will encourage private tenure systems. Thus most communist countries and half of sub-Saharan African countries (Mabogunje, 1990) brought all land under public ownership, and others imposed severe constraints on individual rights. In customary systems, land is regarded as sacred and man's role is considered to be one of stewardship, to protect the interests of future generations. Allocation, use, transfer, etc., are determined by the leaders of the community according to its needs, rather than through payment, though some form of token amount (e.g. beer money or cattle) is often extracted as a sign of agreement. Private tenure systems are intended to ensure the most intense and efficient use of land and are favoured by societies that place priority on the rights of individuals.

Each of these systems has advantages and limitations. Land nationalization all too often resulted in bureaucratic inertia, clientelism and corruption, while customary tenure has become subject to commercial pressures that have eroded the social cohesion from which it derived its legitimacy. Private tenure systems have the benefit of transparency and efficiency, but have proved singularly weak in enabling the poor to obtain land and shelter. While no single tenure system provides advantages without some major limitations, it is clear that globalization has tended to reinforce statutory tenure systems based on Western preoccupations with the rights of the individual. Those unable to meet the terms and conditions imposed by commercial land markets offering individual titles are therefore forced into various non-formal solutions. Ground-breaking studies of these unauthorized settlements by Abrams (1966), Turner (1965, 1967) and Mangin (1970) showed that they consisted almost completely of organized mass invasions of peri-urban, often state-owned, land. In cities where empty state-owned land was limited, people purchased plots on the urban fringe from farmers and developed land that was legally theirs, but was not in locations approved for residential development. Later still, these processes became commercialized and entry was only possible at a cost determined by the informal market.

The co-existence of these different tenure systems and submarkets within most cities creates a complex series of relationships in which policy related to any one has major, and often unintended, repercussions on the others. To further complicate matters, many settlements and even dwellings within settlements, move between one category and another, yet subtle differences between categories, which may be invisible to outsiders, can be critical to those living in them. In some cases, several forms of tenure may co-exist on the same plot, as in Calcutta, where '*thika*' tenants rent plots and then sublet rooms to others who sublet beds on a shift system, with each party entitled to certain rights. The tenure status of individual plots and settlements may also change over time.

By the late 1980s, non-formal tenure categories had become one of the largest single forms of land development in cities of the South and are increasing more rapidly than any other (Payne, 1989). The result is their increasing diversification. In fact, most people now live at some point on a continuum, in which they may be the recognized owners of the land, but have constructed a house in areas not zoned for residential use, or they may simply have failed to conform initially to official regulations or procedures. In some cases, there may even be more than one legally acceptable system operating, such as statutory, customary and religious systems (as in Islamic countries).

The literature on land tenure and property rights was slow to reflect these changes. Apart from a landmark review by Charles Abrams in 1953 and a later global review by the United Nations (1973), urban land tenure received scant attention as a subject in its own right until the 1980s. At that point, Angel (1983), Barnes (1985), Baross (1983) and Doebele (1983, 1987) noted that at a time of increasing demand and therefore prices, speculative tendencies demanded increasing public sector intervention, though they acknowledged that governments had generally failed to respond effectively. Doebele also produced a useful typology of tenure systems that sought to explain the myriad forms found in urbanizing countries. Another major contributor to understanding on tenure issues is McAuslan (1985, 1989). He emphasized the need to consider cultural and historical traditions in assessing tenure options and noted that countries continued to pursue approaches developed during colonial periods, rather than developing more appropriate local options. The impact of cultural and historical factors demonstrates that land and property, while increasingly seen as exclusively economic resources, are more complex in that they also attract strong emotional attachments. In addition, each piece of land is unique in terms of its location, quality and other attributes, so that generalizing about it is more difficult, yet effective urban land tenure policies can only be developed if these factors are taken into account. For this purpose, any attempt to understand the role that a given tenure category plays in the overall land and housing market must first identify the full range of tenure categories, formal and non-formal, existing in a town or city. In this respect, the typology presented in the United Nations urban indicators list (see www.unchs.org/guo/gui/guide.html/#ind1) is fundamentally limited as it reduces the range of non-formal tenure categories to two: 'squatter owner' and 'squatter tenant'. Even superficial evidence demonstrates that a wider range of categories exists in most cities and needs to be acknowledged. While this will inevitably increase the range of categories and make international comparisons more difficult, the important objective should be to reflect local realities as a basis for policy. International comparisons of tenure may, in any case, be of little value, especially if they encourage authorities to present information in ways that project favourable impressions and do not reflect the nature of local tenure systems. By creating a typology that reflects the full range of non-formal and formal tenure categories, the degree of de facto security that residents consider is provided by each can be assessed and the likely consequences of a policy intervention estimated.

However, identifying and classifying the full range of tenure categories existing in a city and the degrees of security they afford is not sufficient in itself to provide a proper understanding of the issues involved. It is also important to assess the rights associated with them. As Malpezzi (2001) has noted, it is possible for one person to enjoy absolute zero probability of removal without due process, but no ability to sell or mortgage their property, and face removal through an eminent domain action, while another may suffer low, but non-zero, probability of summary eviction, but be free to sell, upgrade or sublet their property, albeit at a price discounted for the risk. Although the first person is 'secure' and the second is not, the volume of the second person's property rights could, in fact, be greater.

How can the full range of tenure types, their degree of security and the rights associated with them be identified and presented? One option is shown in Figure 1.1, although this omits customary and religious categories for reasons of simplicity. It is important to note that the tenure categories shown are indicative; the number of categories and the proportion of the total represented by each will vary from one time and place to another. This is reflected in the varied widths of each column. The degree of tenure security and the rights they provide may also fluctuate. When recording rights, it is important to identify if they are available to women as well as men, and this should be recorded for each category.

The widespread existence of various non-statutory tenure systems is partly a response to the failure of statutory and customary tenure systems to meet the needs of lower-income groups, which invariably represent the majority of increasing urban populations. It may also reflect the persistence of traditional practices for obtaining and developing land that are not officially recognized. Given that the lower levels of security provided by non-formal categories are likely to be reflected in the cost of entry to such land and housing, it can be assumed that these alternative forms may enable the poor to obtain land and housing in areas that would otherwise not be affordable or available. Where official mechanisms deny the poor legal access to land and shelter, such alternatives can claim to provide a degree of social and moral legitimacy. The larger the proportion of people unable to conform to official norms and procedures, the more they are undermined, risking a reduction in respect for the law in general.

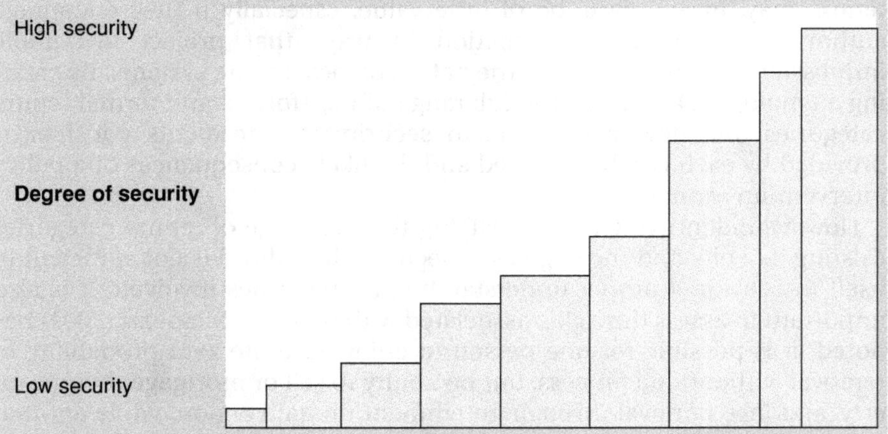

Tenure category / Property rights	Pavement dweller	Squatter tenant	Squatter 'owner'	Tenant in unauthorized subdivision	Owner–unauthorized subdivision	Legal owner–unauthorized construction	Tenant with contract	Leaseholder	Freeholder
Occupy/use/enjoy									
Restrict[2]									
Dispose, buy, inherit									
Develop/improve									
Cultivate/produce									
Sublet									
Sublet and fix rent									
Pecuniary[3]									
To access services									
To access formal credit									

Degree of security: High security ... Low security (bar chart ascending from left to right)

0%   Distribution of tenure types   100%

Notation: The availability of rights by gender can be shown as:
\   Right available to men only
/   Right available to women only
X   Right available equally to men and women

Figure 1.1   Notional typology of urban tenure categories, degrees of security and associated property rights.

POLICY RESPONSES AND THE MYTH OF PROPERTY OWNERSHIP

Unfortunately, the response of many authorities has been to act without understanding this complexity. In Delhi in the mid-1970s, and to some extent also today, the authorities have conducted a campaign of removing residents whom they consider illegal occupants, even though many claim rights dating from Mughal times. Such draconian responses to massive informal development may be understandable, but they do not resolve the problems of enabling people to obtain access to secure land in which they can build their lives and contribute to society. They simply move the problem somewhere else.

The most common single approach adopted to date in addressing this problem is to provide settlers with land titles. This approach has several objectives:

- To provide settlers with the most secure form of tenure available.
- To enable households to use their property titles as collateral in obtaining loans from formal-sector finance institutions in order to improve their homes or develop businesses.
- To help local authorities increase the proportion of planned urban land and provide services more efficiently.
- To enable local governments to integrate informal settlements into the tax system.
- To improve the efficiency of urban land and property markets.

Recent reviews of urban land tenure policy (e.g. Angel, 2001; Fernandes, 2001; Payne, 1997, 2001) suggest that titling has not achieved these objectives and is of doubtful benefit to the poor. Angel, for example, expresses concern that the new urban poor may confront a pattern of land ownership that is more rigid, more regulated, better enforced and hence considerably less affordable than before. Land titling programmes have been implemented in many countries during the past two or three decades, although usually on a highly selective basis rather than at the wider urban scale. The approach received a major boost in the early 1990s through the work of Hernando de Soto (1989), who advocated the formalization of informal settlements, based on empirical research in Peru. His arguments were reflected in the World Bank's housing policy paper (1993), entitled 'Housing: enabling markets to work', a title that harnessed the social concept of enablement to the market bandwagon. The paper listed improvements to property rights as the first priority in terms of demand-side instruments (World Bank, 1993: iii). Furthermore, tenure security and property rights are listed (World Bank, 1993: 10) as among the most important factors influencing housing demand and it is claimed that insecure tenure leads to underinvestment in housing and reduced housing quality. For lower-income countries, the paper recommended developing market-oriented systems of property rights and allocated priority to upgrading systems of land titling and regularizing tenure in squatter settlements. The form of tenure proposed, as a long-term objective, is individual freehold titles or private ownership (World Bank, 1993: 34, 71 and 82), although it is accepted that other forms of title which can be upgraded to full freehold title over time, may be appropriate.

This approach is softened considerably in the World Bank's recent draft urban strategy paper (2000), which makes limited reference to urban land tenure except to emphasize the need for 'stronger property rights' in real estate markets and 'secure and clear' tenure in upgrading projects. However, the momentum in favour of a land titling approach has recently been given a boost by the publication of de Soto's second book (de Soto, 2000). This takes his earlier argument in favour of formalizing informal settlements one step further by advocating that property ownership has been the foundation on which capitalism itself has flourished and that if the Third World is to develop it will need to follow the path laid out by the West. De Soto claims that the major stumbling block that keeps the rest of the world from benefiting from capitalism is its inability to produce capital, and that while the poor already possess the assets they need to make capitalism work for them, they hold these assets in defective forms. By this he means that they lack titles to their properties which they can use to invest in businesses, rendering their assets as 'dead' capital. He estimates the total value of such 'dead' capital is at least US$9.3 trillion.

De Soto then claims (de Soto, 2000: 65) that the 'substantial increase of capital in the West over the past two centuries is the consequence of gradually improving property systems'. The implication of his analysis is that if only the governments of developing countries could get their act together and provide universal property ownership with clear titles and rights enforceable in law, then capitalism would enable countries to lever themselves, and their poor majorities, out of poverty and into the promised land of capitalist affluence.

To what extent are de Soto's claims supported by evidence? He is surprisingly coy in discussing the methods by which he arrived at the estimated scale of 'dead' capital, apart from 'surveying the cost of the building and observing the selling prices of comparable buildings'. He omits to say how he extrapolated from the case studies in five countries where he was conducting such surveys to the rest of the world in order to obtain his global estimate. Of more interest than the sum, however, is its significance. If one accepts the figure as reasonable, this would confirm his conclusion that the poor have amassed vast assets despite their poverty. Yet he chooses to overlook that such assets were invariably developed through access to credit, albeit not normally from formal institutions. His assertion that property cannot easily be traded on the open market without titles overlooks evidence that residential mobility within the large cities of Latin America is very limited (Persaud, 1992 in Gilbert, 2001), and in Bogota and Santiago is equally low for those with and without titles (Gilbert, 2001: 7). In South Africa, it appears that many households who obtain titles are selling their subsidized housing units for less than their face value, simply because they cannot afford the service charges, let alone the costs of servicing additional loans. There is even anecdotal evidence in many countries that the poor are as suspicious of borrowing from banks as the banks are of lending to the poor. His claim suggests that extra-legal property is sleeping (rather than dead) and only needs a kiss from the Prince Charming of the formal banking sector to awaken it to prosperity. However, this overlooks the manifest failure of banks to lend to the poor even when they possess titles. After all, what self-respecting bank manager would lend to a household without first checking that their incomes were sufficient to service the debt, before checking what collateral is being offered to secure it?

De Soto's comparison between the experiences of the US and the Third World has two major flaws. First, and most important, while he provides fascinating material on the development of property rights and increasing affluence of the West, he fails to provide any empirical evidence in support of a causal relationship between the two. He also conveniently overlooks the role of colonialism and slavery in building the economies of the West. Neither is it difficult to refute his notion of the link between property ownership and affluence in the UK. In 1914, when Britain was at the apex of its economic and political power, only 10 per cent of its population were property owners (Malpas and Murie,1999). The remaining 90 per cent were tenants and therefore not in a position to use the property they occupied as collateral in obtaining credit.

The relationship between property ownership and economic development is central to de Soto's hypothesis. However, the proportion of home owners in Munich, Germany, is 17 per cent, in Stockholm, Sweden, 11 per cent and in Zurich, Switzerland, a mere 7 per cent (United Nations, 1996: 212), compared to 55 per cent in Jakarta, Indonesia, and 53 per cent in Delhi, India. At national levels, Bulgaria has more than twice the proportion of households (87 per cent) in owner-occupied housing than Germany (40 per cent), yet few would consider Bulgaria more developed or affluent (United Nations, 1996: 221).

Recent evidence goes so far as to suggest that high levels of home ownership may even have detrimental impacts on economic development. In a recent paper comparing European countries, Oswald (1999, 2001) argues that the higher a nation's level of home ownership, the higher its level of unemployment. For example, Switzerland has the lowest rate of home ownership of any industrialized nation and only 1 per cent unemployment, while in Spain, 80 per cent of the population own their homes and unemployment is at 13 per cent, the worst of any advanced country. Even in the US, it seems that the pattern is repeated over long periods of time and Oswald cites West Virginia as having both the highest proportion of home owners *and* the highest levels of unemployment in the country. Oswald concludes that the reason for this direct relationship throughout the industrialized countries is that high home ownership levels restrict labour market mobility and thereby increase unemployment.

A final concern over property ownership is the way in which many multinationals are extending the concept to *intellectual* property rights, to the increasing concern of farmers and governments in developing countries.

None of this criticism is intended to deny that individual property ownership represents an attractive option for many people and deserves a place in the tenure policy of any government. What it *is* intended to demonstrate is that it is highly dangerous to place all one's eggs in one basket, especially at the present time, when land registries are so incomplete and inaccurate that moves to provide titles in urban or peri-urban areas may encourage or intensify disputes over who has the primary claim. Even Tiger Woods would be unlikely to win tournaments if he was restricted to using a single club to play every shot. In Peru, where de Soto's approach has been taken up wholeheartedly by his brainchild COFOPRI (Comisión de Formalización de la Propiedad Informal), the vast majority of titles have been allocated on government-owned desert land well outside the urban areas. Once the programme moved into areas held under private tenure, and the situation became more typical of other cities around the world, claims and counterclaims have slowed down delivery dramatically.

Where de Soto is undoubtedly correct is in his insistence that legal systems cannot aspire to legitimacy if they cut out 80 per cent of their people (de Soto, 2000: 151). He claims (de Soto, 2000: 171) that 'any attempt to create a unified property system that does not take into account the collective contracts that underpin existing property arrangements will crash into the very roots of the rights most people rely on for holding onto their assets'. He continues, 'to be legitimate, a right does not necessarily have to be defined by formal law; that a group of people strongly supports a particular convention is enough for it to be upheld as a right and defended against formal law. That is why property law and titles imposed without reference to existing social contracts continually fail. They lack legitimacy'. The focus of this book is to identify and review forms of tenure and property rights that enjoy such social legitimacy and provide the basis for pro-poor urban development.

DIVERSITY AND CHOICE

Under conditions of rapid urbanization, competition for secure, serviced land is increasing in all developing countries. This places greater pressure on existing tenure systems and requires governments to formulate policies that encourage efficient land use and improve accessibility to it, especially for the urban poor. The central issue is therefore what forms of land tenure are most likely to achieve the objectives of improved efficiency and equity in different contexts? In addressing this issue, it is necessary to recognize that although land tenure raises important technical and procedural questions, it is ultimately a political issue, since rights over land cannot be isolated from packages of rights in general.

Perhaps the first point to make is that there are no absolute standards by which security of tenure can be defined. For squatters who have lived in a settlement for many years, their *perceived* security of tenure may be indistinguishable in practice from households living in legal housing. They may also be more able to buy and sell such rights than residents in more formal tenure categories. It is therefore important to distinguish between de facto and de jure tenure status, and such distinctions can only be assessed through participatory studies and surveys of local investment in environmental improvements.

It has also been suggested above that the policy objectives outlined above can be achieved in many other ways than through the provision of land titles. For example, a radical review and sustained reform of the regulatory frameworks by which urban land markets are managed may well be able to achieve considerable progress in meeting these objectives. High building and planning standards, restrictive regulations on land use and development, plus cumbersome administrative procedures raise entry costs to land markets and legal shelter that inhibit access to planned development by low-income households. Permitting modest initial development and incremental development, together with the introduction of streamlined administrative systems, such as 'one-stop-shops', for processing land transfers and development proposals could generate major improvements in the efficiency and equity of urban economies and land markets. Measures to strengthen finance institutions which offer loans without requiring title deeds as collateral can also stimulate rapid improvements in housing conditions.

The evidence suggests that there is no silver bullet that can solve all urban land tenure problems and that caution is advisable. This is partly because titles and rights, once granted, cannot easily be withdrawn, unless occupants fail to meet agreed obligations, and because the wider implications of specific tenure policy changes are presently difficult to predict. A starting point may therefore be to regard every step along the continuum from complete illegality to formal tenure and full property rights as a move in the right direction, to be carried out incrementally. This not only follows the pattern of incremental physical improvements adopted in most unauthorized settlements, but would minimize further distortion of land markets and the risk of undesirable social consequences, such as the eviction of squatter tenants. It also provides time for land registries and other elements of urban land administration to update and verify records, establish systems for resolving land disputes and develop the capability to manage more formal tenure systems.

Until more information and experience are acquired on the impacts of tenure changes, one option is to increase the rights of residents within existing tenure arrangements, rather than changing their formal tenure status (Payne, 2001). Such options might involve granting enhanced rights to women, making it easier to develop livelihood-generating economic activities within residential areas and accepting community-based methods for resolving land disputes wherever possible. Simply registering land sub-divisions and the details of occupants may improve residents' security and rights of access to services and credit. For local authorities, it could increase their ability to manage urban land and provide a basis for generating tax revenues. Such an approach would serve to reduce exposure to forced eviction without further distorting urban land markets or committing urban authorities to a specific tenure category. Figure 1.2 indicates how such a rights-based approach may be able to increase tenure security (and therefore equity) at the bottom end of the continuum accommodating the most vulnerable social groups.

For example, if residents in the lowest categories of tenure (1–3 in Figure 1.2) are protected from eviction through the provision of occupancy permits, etc., their security will increase, although the commercial value of their property will remain relatively low, thereby making it easier for the urban poor to afford it. Initial efforts at policy formulation should therefore focus on identifying existing statutory, customary, religious and non-formal tenure systems to assess the extent to which they enjoy a degree of social legitimacy and provide the basis for building a more integrated and consensual legal framework.

Consideration should also be given to increasing the range of tenure options available, possibly by adapting existing indigenous tenure systems or innovations from other countries. Diversity of tenure options will help to minimize short-term fluctuations in land prices and other indirect consequences and enable households – and governments – to learn from experience and adjust to change at an acceptable pace. As more and more households are forced into living in various types of unauthorized settlement, they have acquired strength in numbers and the authorities are increasingly reluctant to undertake forced evictions. As such, perceptions of de facto security have increased, irrespective of de jure tenure status. What concerns households more, therefore, is access to services and, to a lesser extent, credit. For this reason, a major consideration of tenure policy should be the ways in which it can facilitate improved access to these benefits for both the residents of existing unauthorized settlements and the millions of households that projections indicate will need land and housing within urban areas in the near future.[4] In the meantime, strengthening the administrative capacity of land registers is a precondition to establishing efficient land markets and systems of property rights. It is also important to remember that social and cultural needs have an important place in maintaining the way that tenure systems operate.

THE CASE STUDIES

In February 2000, the UK Department for International Development (DFID) funded a research project to identify and review examples of innovative approaches to providing secure tenure for the urban poor. The

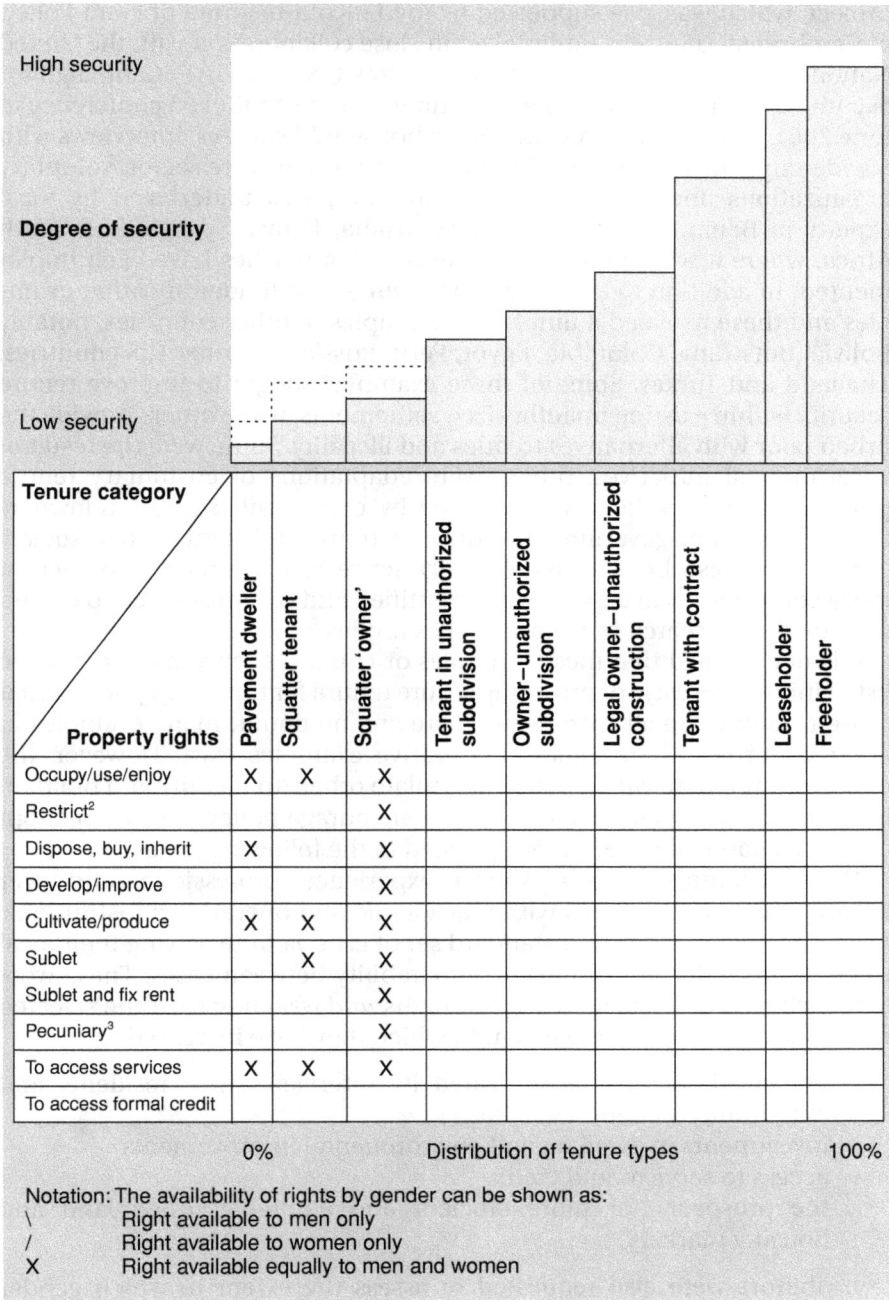

Property rights	Pavement dweller	Squatter tenant	Squatter 'owner'[1]	Tenant in unauthorized subdivision	Owner–unauthorized subdivision	Legal owner–unauthorized construction	Tenant with contract	Leaseholder	Freeholder
Occupy/use/enjoy	X	X	X						
Restrict[2]			X						
Dispose, buy, inherit	X		X						
Develop/improve			X						
Cultivate/produce	X	X	X						
Sublet		X	X						
Sublet and fix rent			X						
Pecuniary[3]			X						
To access services	X	X	X						
To access formal credit									

0%   Distribution of tenure types   100%

Notation: The availability of rights by gender can be shown as:
\   Right available to men only
/   Right available to women only
X   Right available equally to men and women

Figure 1.2   Likely consequences of improving tenure rights and security in unauthorized settlements

project, which was also supported by the Lincoln Institute of Land Policy, in Cambridge, USA, was undertaken in close collaboration with the United Nations Centre for Human Settlements (now UN-HABITAT) Campaign for Secure Tenure and was completed in time for the Istanbul+5 conference in June 2001. Primary research, involving household surveys, interviews with a wide range of stakeholders in government, the private sector, voluntary organizations and low-income communities, was undertaken by local experts in Benin, Burkina Faso, Brazil, India, Kenya, Senegal and South Africa, where it was known that innovative approaches have been implemented. In addition to these, searches were made to identify other examples and these revealed a number of examples in other countries, notably Bolivia, Botswana, Colombia, Egypt, Peru, Russia and other CIS countries, Thailand and Turkey. Some of these examples sought to improve tenure security within existing unauthorized settlements, while others provide the urban poor with alternatives to titles and illegality. Some were the result of governmental initiatives, others were adaptations of customary tenure practices and yet others were evolved by communities and landowners themselves. Non-governmental organizations and other civil society groups have also become increasingly active in this process. In each of these countries, local experts were identified and commissioned to extend their existing research to review local examples.

It is not claimed that these examples or countries represent a definitive list of innovative ways of providing secure tenure for the urban poor, or that those reviewed are all successful. There are, no doubt, many examples in other countries where equally innovative examples exist. However, the ones reviewed here will hopefully stimulate others to identify and build on local tenure arrangements. It may also encourage policy makers to adopt and adapt some of the approaches listed in the following pages.

The contributors to this book are all experienced professionals and cover a wide range of disciplines within academic and operational institutions. Each was invited to apply a standard set of criteria in reviewing their local examples in order to maximize comparability between cases. These were that each case should assess the strengths *and* weaknesses of the selected case studies in terms of the extent to which they have increased:

- perceived security as indicated by interviews with residents and community leaders
- investments in dwelling and environmental improvements
- access to services and credit
- the prospects for more efficient and equitable urban land and housing markets.

Contributors were also requested to assess the extent to which gender issues have been addressed and if women have benefited more from the non-statutory approaches than has often been the case under either statutory or customary systems. Finally, contributors were invited to assess policy implications of their case studies and to indicate if they would recommend the selected example of innovation elsewhere and, if so, under what conditions? In particular, what changes would make the examples more effective in helping the poor?

The book is organized into four main parts. Part I consists of this introductory chapter and an analysis of the legal aspects of tenure issues by Patrick McAuslan. On the basis of extensive international experience, McAuslan identifies blockages to the formulation of appropriate laws for secure tenure. He argues that at present the law is framed by and for the interests of the political elite and against the majority of the poor, thereby driving them into the very illegality that the law is supposed to prevent. He draws attention to attempts at reform and notes that greater reliance is increasingly being placed on open market oriented decision-making systems. In addition, he observes a move away from a centralized state-dominated approach to more local systems of land allocation and use as well as moves to consult with and take into account the views of the users of the system, including the urban poor.

Part II comprises two chapters, which review conventional approaches to increasing security of tenure for the urban poor. Both involve the large-scale allocation of individual titles to low-income households, but are shown to have limits within their own context and even more limited applicability to other countries. In Chapter 3, Richard Grover, Paul Munro-Faure and Mikhail Soloviev review the privatization of property in the transitional economies of Eastern Europe. The emphasis of government policy has been to privatize public housing and create levels of home ownership that in some cases exceed those of Western Europe. While this has transformed housing and land markets, the authors express concern that the emerging markets will transfer responsibility for maintaining often substandard housing from the state which built it, to the residents. In many cases, the communal areas have not been privatized, so that obtaining loans even for the better properties is not easy, especially since housing finance mechanisms to offer credit have not been established on the scale required. They also express concern that the emphasis on privatization has reduced options for vulnerable groups in need of social housing or the mobility offered by rental tenure systems. As a result, the benefits of owner occupation may not be widely distributed.

The limitations of the conventional land titling approach are also made apparent by Ayako Kagawa and Jan Turkstra, who assess the massive land titling programme initiated in Peru in 1996 by COFOPRI, with financial support from the World Bank. Today, COFOPRI claims to have achieved its objective of allocating one million titles, a major achievement by any standards. However, most of these are on government-owned desert land surrounding major urban centres. Now that COFOPRI has started to regularize informal settlements on private land, staff are finding that numerous claims to individual parcels of land are slowing the allocation process dramatically. This suggests that the Peruvian approach may not be an appropriate model for other developing countries.

Improving security of tenure for the large numbers of urban populations living in various types of unauthorized settlements is a priority concern not just for governments, international agencies and professionals, but for the residents themselves. Part III therefore presents examples from different parts of the world that demonstrate more innovative ways of improving tenure security for the urban poor in existing settlements. In Chapter 5, David Sims shows that tenure security in Greater Cairo, Egypt, is achieved by the accretion of various rights over time. These may include receipts for the payment of property taxes or service charges and the cultivation of good relations with local politicians. Over 60 per cent of all urban housing in Egypt is provided in this way, so the critical mass now reached ensures that residents enjoy de facto security of tenure and can lobby effectively for the installation of services. The state usually obliges, especially before elections.

Formal tenure systems are often considered essential in influencing access to basic services. However, in Chapter 6, Nora Aristazabal and Andrés Ortíz Gomez show that in Colombia, legislation entitles all citizens to obtain public services such as water supply, sewage disposal, electricity, circulation, storm drainage, garbage recollection, telephone and gas for their homes. The only thing required to achieve this right is to prove that they live in the housing unit. A range of intermediate tenure systems, such as 'Declarations of Possession', 'buying and selling rights for future use' and 'communal tenancy', all provide stepping stones with increasing rights and levels of protection from eviction, which enable poor households to obtain secure housing at affordable costs. In such cases, land tenure is not even a subject of concern to the majority of poor households since they are protected by law from forced evictions without due legal process and are entitled to receive all essential services irrespective of their tenure status.

In Chapter 7, Alain Durand-Lasserve, with Alan Bagré, Moussa Gueye and Jose Tonato, shows that in the Francophone sub-Saharan African countries of Benin, Burkina Faso and Senegal, popular reinterpretation or adaptation of customary practices enable the urban poor to acquire de facto and eventually de jure tenure rights. For example, land in urban Benin is characterized by the existence of a very dynamic informal land delivery system that is tolerated, and to some extent partly controlled by, the state. This attempts to integrate customary tenure practices into the sphere of modern law and planning regulations and involves procedures that combine land readjustment, or replotting, the reallocation of plots and the provision of 'housing permits' to occupants. This land delivery system has two main advantages. First, the state does not intervene in the allocation of land, at least in the initial stage. Instead, customary owners play a key role in the provision of land for housing in all urban and suburban areas and negotiate directly with households seeking a plot. Second, the system offers reasonably good security of tenure after the land readjustment and redevelopment process has been completed. In Burkina Faso, civil society groups have upgraded Occupancy Permits into more stable titles, while in

Senegal, a similar approach was initiated at national level by the government as a basis for improving the physical environment of informal settlements.

In Chapter 8, Amitabh Kundu reviews government tenure policies and provides examples in New Delhi and Ahmedabad, India, which provide a degree of tenure security to the urban poor. In Ahmedabad, the Slum Networking Programme granted residents of unauthorized settlements ten-year licences to their land, enabling them to improve both their houses and the local environment. In Delhi, he found that 80 per cent of slum dwellers had improved their dwellings without receiving any formal tenure status, demonstrating that even the poor are willing to invest providing they *feel* secure. Unfortunately, the situation in Delhi, Ahmedabad and other Indian cities has changed dramatically at the turn of the millennium. Court orders favouring the land-owning agencies, together with large-scale evictions, have shattered the perceived security of tenure of the slum dwellers who suddenly realized that their social and political connections or a host of semi-legal documents are not of much use. Many of the industrial and commercial enterprises in both cities have been closed down and their occupants evicted, despite their having approvals from a number of departments of the local government and paying normal fees. This is likely to discourage further investment in housing and amenities. The fact that such measures rarely succeed in creating the orderly growth of urban areas as envisaged by the authorities is of little consolation to the masses of poor people who suffer major social and economic dislocation as a result.

The final chapter in Part III provides a review of the Turkish approach to urban tenure issues by Murat Balamir. This case study reflects a highly pragmatic response to the need for large numbers of largely poor people to obtain access to land and shelter on terms and conditions they can accept. He reviews three different processes in Ankara, whereby households obtain land or housing either by appropriating and building on state land (*gecekondus*), purchasing a share in a land subdivision, or obtaining a unit in an apartment developed on land which was originally appropriated but has been gradually absorbed into a planned residential area. Balamir considers that these processes have enjoyed a high degree of social legitimacy in the absence of affordable formal options. However, he raises concerns that the benefits are not equally shared and that *gecekondu* tenants are often evicted by owners seeking to realize the commercial value of their plots by replacing houses with apartment blocks.

Meeting the tenure needs of existing urban populations is, however, only part of the problem. Given the massive projected increase of urban populations in developing countries, ensuring access to land and shelter on terms and conditions acceptable to all social groups, especially the poor and vulnerable groups including women, presents an even greater challenge. If titles demand a premium that the poor cannot afford, then providing alternatives to titles and illegality has to become a key feature of tenure policy. Part IV therefore contains examples of alternatives to titles and illegality for households seeking a plot or dwelling in new urban areas. Some of these offer the possibility of obtaining full individual titles in the medium to longer terms, while others are considered as long-term alternatives to titles. The important point is that they offer entry points to land and housing markets which avoid the social, economic and environmental penalties of illegality. Providing secure tenure options on affordable terms at the scale required for the increasing number of urban households is unlikely to be solved in the near future by government action alone. Since few poor households are able to obtain access to a legal plot or a dwelling that conforms to all official norms and procedures, these examples show that there are many ways of meeting the primary need for security on terms and conditions which the poor can afford and which need not impede the development of efficient urban land and housing markets.

In Chapter 10, Fabian Farfan Espinoza describes how the need to put existing housing to full use and also increase access for those in need of housing in Bolivia, led to the development of the 'anticretico' tenure system. This was a response to massive rural–urban migration, which resulted in the rapid growth of informal settlements around the major cities. The 'anticretico' contract means 'against a normal credit', and is now recognized by national legislation, due to its importance for peoples' livelihoods. It is a mechanism involving two parties, the owner of a house on one side and the potential occupant on the other. They make a legal contract, in which the former receives a lump sum from the latter for the right of using the property, normally for a period of two years. What makes the 'anticretico' tenure system different from simple rental agreements is that at the end of the contract period, the owner returns *the full amount* deposited to the property user. For the property owner, this is an effective way of raising capital sums without incurring high interest rates from the banks, while for the user, it represents an effective way of living at low cost for those able to raise the deposit. 'Anticretico' tenure also encourages people to maintain the property, due to the possibility of purchasing it when the contract period expires. Although the system enjoys widespread social acceptance, it depends on both parties fulfilling their obligations. Government attempts to formalize the system and extract revenues from a transfer tax have recently made the approach more bureaucratic.

Saad Yahya notes in Chapter 11 that Certificates of Rights were adopted in Botswana in the 1970s in recognition of the need to provide a measure of tenure security to households unable to afford formal shelter, and to encourage them to maintain and improve their houses when and as they could afford it. The system provided housing to two-thirds of all urban households and has effectively averted the incidence of squatter development in urban centres. The system could be upgraded to the more formal Fixed Period State Grant tenure, although there is presently a freeze on further allocations, due to the degree of administration involved and alternatives provided by the Tribal Land Boards.

In Chapter 12, Edesio Fernandes reviews the Concession of the Real Right to Use (CRRU) land, which has been adopted in several Brazilian cities, notably Porte Alegre and Recife. It has stimulated the regularization of *favelas* and has been based on the notion that public land should not, and need not, be privatized for the recognition of housing rights to take place. In fact, he argues that the unqualified privatization of public land might undermine the other main objective of tenure regularization programmes, namely to guarantee that the original residents are able to remain in the areas where they live. Being a recognized right to land, the CRRU cannot easily be revoked. As it is a form of property rights, it does not imply the full transfer of freehold titles, but provides legal security of tenure, thus pre-empting eviction measures. In Porto Alegre, the local legislation only accepts transfers of rights in cases of death. Whereas in Recife, they can be transferred when the original beneficiaries wish to move out, subject to control by both the state and the local communities, so that public investment is not capitalized upon by land subdividers. The CRRU can be used in an individual or a collective manner, in this sense recognizing group rights. It also gives women the same rights as men and should a domestic conflict exist, women have even been given priority treatment for the recognition of titles.

Chapter 13 provides a review by Saad Yahya of the Community Land Trusts (CLTs), Temporary Occupation Licences (TOLs) and land-buying companies in Kenya's cities. CLTs were introduced in the 1990s to combine the advantages of communal tenure with the virtues of market-oriented individual ownership. By retaining ownership of the land in the hands of a group and allowing members to hold leases from the group title, it is designed to control transfers and discourage speculation. However, in spite of numerous advantages, CLTs have some limitations. For example, they are new and not yet well understood. Not only politicians but also administrators at the local level are not well versed in their precise intent and mechanics. They also require lengthy and complex documentation, although the task is made slightly easier by the prototypes already developed. For some people, the communal ownership of the land could also be a disincentive, since restrictions on sale in the open market discourage speculation and the rapid realization of capital appreciation.

In Chapter 14, Lauren Royston and Cecile Ambert note that in South Africa, tenure policy is dominated by the need to reverse a strong sense of deprivation and denial of the right by the black majority to own property. This has led to a demand for freehold titles as the only form of tenure to provide both security and a sense of equality. However, other options are being explored and they review examples of co-operative housing in Johannesburg, which provide households with ample security of tenure and communal ownership of the land in ways intended to discourage speculation. The high level of institutional support required, plus popular prejudice, has constrained the expansion of alternatives to titles so far.

Finally, in Chapter 15, Radhika Savant Mohit reviews the land rental system in Thailand, by which low-income communities come to an arrangement with private landowners in central areas near employment centres where they would not be able to afford to buy a plot or apartment. They find landowners who are waiting for the market price of their land to rise even higher before developing it and offer to rent the land on a short- to medium-term lease, paying what they can afford. In recent years, communities and authorities have been looking at arrangements and mechanisms by which to provide basic services, though if a longer lease is agreed they may provide higher standards. This arrangement depends on the residents agreeing to move out when required and reflects a deferential approach to those higher up the social pecking order than applies in many other countries. However, it has enabled large numbers of poor households to live in areas that would otherwise be well beyond their reach. When and if the land market expands, they can move to other locations that offer similar advantages.

The book concludes with a short summary by the editor of issues raised in the case studies and some policy implications. This emphasizes the need to create and maintain a wide range of statutory, customary and non-statutory tenure options, so that all households, especially the poor and vulnerable, can obtain access to land, shelter, services and livelihood opportunities in ways that meet their short- and longer-term needs. Improving security for existing low-income urban households represents a major challenge. Ensuring that options exist for new households in the future will prove even greater. The examples reviewed in this book demonstrate that such options already exist in many countries. However, if any appear appropriate for application in other contexts it will be necessary to ensure that they are compatible with local conditions. Alternatively, it may be possible to identify and develop tenure options that already exist locally.

CHAPTER TWO

Tenure and the law: the legality of illegality and the illegality of legality

Patrick McAuslan

INTRODUCTION

The principal aim of this chapter is to explore the role and place of the law in developing or confirming 'informal' systems of urban tenure. This subject is not very much discussed in the literature, but is mentioned in passing. In the select bibliography of Durand-Lasserve and Clerc's 1996 study on the regularization of tenure in irregular settlements, of 171 references, only seven (six of them by two authors) are to writings about law and informal settlements. Since then, the immensely useful book *Illegal Cities* (Fernandes and Varley, 1998) has been published. But even there, ten of the 17 contributors were non-lawyers, and while the case studies concentrated on the legal and illegal aspects of city development, there was no work which took as its central focus the practical aspects of law in urban development: the 'how to' questions. Such questions are now being addressed, not least in the wealth of literature on urban law being published in Brazil and in practice in some countries – India, Brazil, Namibia, Peru and Tanzania to name just a few – and it is these issues which this chapter addresses.

THE HABITAT AGENDA

My starting point here is the same one I take in my work as a consultant on these issues: the Istanbul Declaration and Habitat Agenda, and the Global Plan of Action adopted at the City Summit in June 1996. Interestingly, these statements also occupy a central position in the recently published DFID consultative document on urban development and poverty (DFID, 2001). They provide the international policy and legal context for any review of the policies, laws and practices relating to urban land tenure. In the eyes of international lawyers, these documents are examples of 'soft' international law, which give rise to what might be called quasi-legal obligations which cannot be enforced by any international law enforcement agency. Nevertheless, by agreeing to these documents, all governments represented at that Summit put themselves under an obligation – part legal, part moral – to begin the process of reviewing their policies, laws and practices to bring them into line with the principles enshrined in the Declaration and the Agenda. At the outset of this chapter, therefore, it is essential to set out the principal provisions of both the Declaration and the Agenda that relate to land, so that the international legal benchmarks against which the existing provisions may be assessed and any proposals for change may be judged are there for all to see.

It is readily acknowledged that these benchmarks cannot be the only criteria against which existing and possible future policies and laws on urban land tenure must be measured. It may be suggested, however, that significant departures from the principles agreed to in Istanbul will need to have a clear and reasoned justification, since these principles have behind them the aim of advancing the welfare of the people by making 'cities . . . places where human beings lead fulfilling lives in dignity, good health, safety, happiness and hope'. Any significant departure from these principles then would need to show that the same ultimate goal would be achieved, notwithstanding these departures.

We may start from the Istanbul Declaration. Two principles relating to land are set out:

8. We reaffirm our commitment to the full and progressive realisation of the right to adequate housing as provided for in international instruments. To that end, we shall seek the active participation of our public, private and non-governmental partners at all levels to *ensure legal security of tenure, protection from discrimination and equal access to affordable adequate housing for all persons and their families.*
9. We shall work to expand the supply of affordable housing by *enabling markets to perform efficiently and in a socially and environmentally responsible manner, enhancing access to land and credit and assisting those who are unable to participate in housing markets.* (italics added)

The Habitat Agenda is in three parts: Goals and Principles; Commitments; and the Global Plan of Action (GPA). Under Commitments, governments commit themselves to:

Providing legal security of tenure and equal access to land to all people, including women and those living in poverty. . .

Ensuring transparent, comprehensive and accessible systems in transferring land rights and legal security of tenure.

Protecting all people from and providing legal protection and redress for forced evictions that are contrary to law, taking human rights into consideration and when evictions are unavoidable, ensuring, as appropriate, that alternative suitable solutions are provided.

Turning to the GPA, the Commitments are fleshed out in a series of specific actions based on the strategy of 'enablement, transparency and participation', which will in turn assist governments to establish, *inter alia*, legislative frameworks to enable the achievement of adequate shelter for all. A range of actions are proposed for ensuring access to land and security of tenure. These are stated to be 'strategic prerequisites for the provision of adequate shelter for all and for the development of sustainable human settlements. . .'. While recognizing the existence of different systems of land tenure and national laws, governments are enjoined to:

> *strive to remove all possible obstacles that may hamper equitable access to land and ensure that equal rights of women and men related to land and property are protected under the law. The failure to adopt, at all levels, appropriate rural and urban land policies and land management practices remains a primary cause of inequity and poverty. (para. 75)*

Thirty-two specific actions are then proposed in respect of land. Among the most pertinent to the subject matter of this chapter, the following may be highlighted:

- Recognise and legitimize the diversity of land delivery mechanisms.
- Consider the adoption of innovative instruments for the efficient and sustainable assembly and delivery of land, including, where appropriate, land readjustment and consolidation.
- Develop appropriate cadastral systems and streamline land registration procedures in order to facilitate the regularization of informal settlements, where appropriate, and simplify land transactions.
- Develop land codes and legal frameworks that define the nature of land and real property and the rights that are formally recognized
- Support the development of land markets by means of effective legal frameworks, and develop flexible and varied mechanisms aimed at mobilizing lands with diverse juridical status.
- Review restrictive, exclusionary and costly legal and regulatory processes, planning systems, standards and development regulations.
- Adopt an enabling legal and regulatory framework based on an enhanced knowledge, understanding and acceptance of existing practices and land delivery mechanisms so as to stimulate partnerships with the private business and community sectors, specifying recognized types of land tenure and prescribing procedures for the regularization of tenure, where needed.
- Provide institutional support, accountability and transparency of land management, and accurate information on land ownership, land transactions and current and planned land use.
- Explore innovative arrangements to enhance security of tenure, other than full legalization which may be too costly and time-consuming in certain situations, including access to credit, as appropriate, in the absence of a conventional title to land.

Four other actions from the heading 'Popular participation and civic engagement' may be noted, as these have a very direct bearing on the development and implementation of land management in accordance with the principles and actions set out above:

- Facilitate the legal recognition of organized communities and their consolidation.
- Provide access to effective judicial and administrative channels for affected individuals and groups so that they can challenge or seek redress from decisions and actions that are socially and environmentally harmful or violate human rights.
- Broaden the procedural right of individuals and civil society organizations to take legal action on behalf of affected communities or groups that do not have the resources or skills to take action themselves.
- Facilitate access to decision-making and planning structures and legal services by people living in poverty and other low-income groups through the provision of such facilities as legal aid and free legal advice centres.

If one were to sum up the principal message of these provisions, it is that while a strategy of enablement is to be the preferred mechanism for providing access to land and ensuring security of tenure, the role of governments does not stop at enabling land markets to operate efficiently and transparently, important though these matters are. Governments must also direct their attention to considerations of equity in the operation of land markets – land markets must be enabled to work for the benefit of all, and all must be enabled to participate on an equal and fair footing in the land market. To this end, government at all levels and civil society must be involved in working with the disadvantaged and the poor, removing obstacles to their obtaining land, and developing innovative mechanisms, instruments and institutions to help them obtain access to land and security of tenure via the market. Governments must also desist from actions that penalize such persons and lessen their opportunities to obtain and hold on to land.

Both the Agenda and the GPA place considerable stress on the use of the law to develop appropriate systems of land management, if for no other reason – and there are other reasons, as will be developed in this chapter – than that we cannot ignore the legal framework in our discussions on these issues. The Habitat Agenda takes the position that a legal framework must be developed that accommodates the needs of the urban poor; leaving them out and continuing the dual city – the legal and the illegal – is not an option.

BLOCKAGES TO MEETING THE HABITAT AGENDA PRECEPTS

These then are the standards that must be aimed for. What have been the blockages hitherto which have prevented governments adopting these standards and developing appropriate laws for secure tenure, especially in relation to informal settlements? A summary of main blockages may be given.

The present systems of allocation and use of land for development in the city may be objectively – and judged by criteria of efficiency or equity – inefficient and inequitable, but it would be a mistake not to realize that these systems confer benefits on those who operate them and that is why they are as they are. Senior politicians and public servants in cities all over the world manipulate or ignore the law and administration relating to land allocation and development so as to line their own pockets and those of their families, friends and political allies. A process of land allocation based on secretive administrative criteria as opposed to open market criteria lends itself to corrupt behaviour, and those in charge of such systems have not been slow to take advantage of that fact. Lower down the scale of the bureaucracy, where the actual acquisition of land may be more difficult to achieve, there are plenty of opportunities for illicit gain. A file can only be located out of the disorganized heap and thereafter processed if money is paid. An 'illegal' structure can be left undisturbed if money is paid. An invasion of land by squatters can succeed if money is paid, and services can be acquired – water, electricity, etc. – if money is paid.

What this adds up to is a system which if not designed then at least is adapted to facilitate the exploitation of the poor. It is the poor who live in 'illegal' structures, who squat and who cannot afford lawful connections to services. But the present system goes further in its facilitation of the exploitation of the poor. By being weighed so heavily towards those who have the financial or political power – the latter often precedes the former, but the two are usually ultimately linked – the system facilitates the development of the exploitative relationship of landlords and tenants in the cities of the developing world, rather than that of owner-occupiers. Much research has shown that, contrary to the ideal put forward by many commentators and supposedly facilitated by international aid programmes, what is happening in cities in the developing world is the commodification of shelter; shelter as a scarce good sold to the highest bidder without any effective restrictions or controls on the transactions. The urban poor in such circumstances are forced into less and less salubrious accommodation with fewer and fewer rights. The fact that their accommodation does not measure up to legal public health standards triply disadvantages them: first, the inferior accommodation affects their health and welfare; second, at any point in time their landlord can evict them in the interests of 'complying with the law'; and third, if their landlord falls foul of the authorities, demolition may follow, again 'to comply with the law'.

Indeed there is evidence in some cities to suggest that demolition is in fact used to facilitate the growth of landlordism. The bulldozing of squatter settlements inhabited by owner-occupiers of houses both forces such persons into rented accommodation and frees land for the development of further rented accommodation. Even where the demolition is done with the best of intentions – that is, there is a genuine belief that 'slums' are being demolished so that their inhabitants can be rehoused in something better – too often the 'something better' is unaffordable to the 'slum dwellers', who finish up in worse conditions further from where they can earn a livelihood, while the 'something better' finishes up in the possession of the better off.

This then is the crux of the matter: present systems of land allocation and use in the cities benefit the urban elite. The urban elite either run or have influence over the government of the cities and indeed the national governments, which usually have a significant role in urban land management. The law is manipulated by the elites for their benefit, often with the most spurious justification. At a workshop to consider a report I had written on urban land tenure and law reform in Bangladesh (McAuslan 2002b), there was a mixed reaction to the call for land law reform. While urban non-government organizations (NGOs) and some lawyers supported the call, a senior official opined that the urban poor would resist reform as they welcomed being exploited; laws that facilitated their being exploited also allowed them to exploit each other. Where there is an absence of any external or internal stimulus to urban land reform, in too many countries reform doesn't happen, or where it happens on paper, reform consists of yet more bureaucracy, and loopholes in the law and its administration are quickly discovered and remain unplugged.

THE 'PROBLEM' OF ILLEGALITY

An important issue here is the whole notion of 'illegality', for it is this concept which is used as the basic justification of city governments for the demolition of informal settlements. Too many countries, particularly, it must be said, in Africa, still approach issues of urban land management in these terms and it is distinctly unhelpful. As noted earlier, use of these terms and action taken in pursuance of them is much more of a sociopolitical than a legal matter – it benefits the urban elite who wield the law. But the point needs to be made that policies and their implementation, which are predicated on the basis that the majority of urban dwellers are in some way living 'illegally', have not succeeded in dealing with the problems of urban land in the past and are very unlikely to succeed in the future.

There are in fact two intellectual problems to overcome in respect of notions of 'illegal' land occupation and use. The first, which is the more obvious one, is the basic principle seized on by lawyers, administrators and landowners that to tolerate the illegal occupation and use of land is contrary to all precepts of good government – adherence to the rule of law, protection of property, compliance with lawful authority – and it really should make no difference whether the illegality is being perpetrated by a few people or by many, perhaps the majority of urban dwellers. The counter-argument to this formalistic position is that the social context of 'illegality' must be considered. For the vast majority of 'illegal' occupants and users of land in the cities of the developing world, there is no alternative. The official legal system of land allocation and use is beyond their reach, either because they cannot afford it, or because they lack the political influence and connections to obtain access to it. There is nothing contrary to the principles of good government or the rule of law to address the issues giving rise to illegality rather than attempting to 'put an end' to the illegality by, in this case, such means as forcible removal, demolition, criminal charges, etc.

The second intellectual problem is this. The characterization of popular or informal settlements as 'illegal' or 'unauthorized' or 'slum' leads those who use such terms to assume that the inhabitants of these settlements are, if not all criminals, then certainly living an inferior lawless kind of existence which needs to be contained rather than encouraged. Nothing could be further from the truth, as increasing numbers of studies have shown. First, informal settlements, even those which start as wholly illegal, do not exist in a Hobbesian state of nature; some system of ordering interpersonal relations in respect of tenurial issues and other matters quickly comes into being. Indeed, studies from around the world show that these 'systems of ordering' are usually modelled on the official land laws of the state. Official documents are copied and used; contracts have to be in writing (an interesting study from Tanzania shows how this has slowly developed in the informal sector; Kombe, 2000); dispute settlement processes model themselves on the formal system.

Second, the institutions involved in such a system come from both inside and outside the informal settlement; those outside the settlement being part of the official formal system of governance. In practice, they may be:

- local government institutions, as shown by Fernandes in his study of favelas in Belo Horizonte (Fernandes, 1995) and as occurs in land-sharing operations in Bangkok
- party officials, as is the case in informal settlements in Lusaka, Dar es Salaam and many Indian cities
- organizations of lawyers, either official as in Caracas, quasi-official, i.e. a legal aid society formally registered in accordance with governmental regulations (e.g. the Legal Advice Centre in Nairobi) or unofficial – groups of lawyers willing to give their time free or for a fee to persons within the informal settlements (e.g. in Bangalore)
- NGOs
- in areas where customary law applies, those with authority over land and people within the customary system (e.g. in Douala, Bamako, Accra).

Third, while there may be some, perhaps inevitable, reference to formal legal terminology – concepts, forms, etc. – within the informal systems, their development and operation is eclectic and consumer-orientated. They aim to satisfy their clientele, keep the peace and uphold legitimate claims and interests to land and housing – legitimate within the informal settlement, that is. Fourth, assuming that some official involvement in ordering informal tenurial relations betokens official tolerance of the informal settlement, for whatever reason, a fair degree of security of tenure from external forces, i.e. eviction, demolition, is or may be obtained. Even security of tenure from internal forces, i.e. landlords, may be strengthened by the existence of official involvement.

These factors then lead to this fundamental point: acceptance of the reality of life in the informal settlements is a necessary prelude to addressing the legal problems that arise from it. Concepts of legality and illegality obfuscate rather than illuminate. Rather than legal and illegal, it might be better to think of urban land laws as having two intersecting circuits: the formal and the informal. This approach will be used throughout this chapter.

LESSONS LEARNED

So far, I have addressed problems and what we should avoid. I now want to turn to the positive. First, from the various attempts that have been made to tackle informal settlements, what can we learn that may be relevant to developing legal frameworks? Second, I want to draw attention to some recent examples of the use of the law in creating a framework for tackling tenure problems in informal settlements. In doing so, I shall not refer to countries that are covered elsewhere in this book.

What general themes seem to run through successful, or at least not wholly unsuccessful, attempts at informal tenure reform? First, in place of politico-bureaucratic decisions about land taken in secret, greater reliance is placed on open and market-oriented decisions. Market-oriented means not only decisions determined by price, but also decisions determined by criteria such as: the facilitation of transactions; the perception of land as being an economic no less than a social asset; the desirability, perhaps the normality, of attempting to meet demand, i.e. to pay attention to the wishes of consumers and the irrelevance of personal factors – political, clientelism, favours, etc. – in determining who gets what.

Second, there is a clear move away from the centralized state-dominated approach to the development of more local systems of land allocations and use. Political factors in the decision-making process over land are, if not eliminated – it would be unrealistic to suppose that that would be achieved overnight – then reduced and subjected to more local involvement. This too is an aspect of a more market-oriented approach to land, where decisions are made by many individuals and organizations and not just by one centralized agency. Decentralization also helps bring the decision-making process closer to the people, and assists in its accountability.

Third, a notable feature of the more successful cases is the care taken by governments to consult with and take account of the views of the users of the system – land developers, residents' associations, customary title holders, squatters, etc. It is abundantly clear that these consultative processes were not a mere formality. Governments were not 'consulting' some handpicked group of sycophants or organizations dependent on a government licence to continue in existence, who could be relied on to produce the answers the government wanted to hear. In three cases I examined in the early 1990s in Thailand, the land developers were and are an independent economic force. Indeed, in Peru, the NGO, the Institute for Liberty and Democracy, took over the process of preparing the basic legislation and consulting the consumers, with the government happy to follow in its wake. And in Botswana, great attention was paid both to traditional concerns and the views of modern economic entities (McAuslan, 2002a)

In a chapter focusing on the role of law in urban land tenure reform, it seems worthwhile to devote a little more space to the issue of consultation. In considering legal frameworks for public action – and at least in the initial stages of land reform, public action is required – probably the single most significant difference between authoritarian administration and democratic governance is the willingness of public officials to listen and respond in their actions to the uncensored and uninhibited views of the people – the electorate, the consumers and producers of national wealth. Thus in constructing new or reforming old legal frameworks, in developing new policies or implementing existing ones, lawyers should be prepared to focus on the process of consultation and ensure that that is a reality in the administrative process.

A fourth general theme is that of flexibility in implementation. This covers a variety of matters. In Botswana, it refers to the willingness to develop new and adapt old forms of tenure to suit the new urban needs of the Botswana. In Thailand, it refers to the willingness to adjust regulations to facilitate the better operation of the market; to the whole concept of land sharing and negotiated settlements of land disputes; and to the eclectic mixture of laws that make up the Thai legal framework of land management. In Peru, it refers to the willingness of government to allow an NGO to take the lead in law reform and to accept an alternative, simpler system of title registration to that which had existed for 100 years. In Trinidad and Tobago, it refers to the willingness of government to work with an NGO to develop more realistic standards of subdivision and development to cater for the urban poor and landless. This flexibility may be contrasted with the rigidity of centralized statutory urban planning systems – a particular deficiency in countries in the British Commonwealth which adhere to variants of the English town and country planning legislation and often treat the relevant laws as if they were variants of the Law of the Medes and Persians which altereth not.

Fifth, as noted above, a strong characteristic of informal settlements is their reproduction within their settlements of basic elements of the formal legal systems which have, in a sense, rejected them. They have a legal system and, perhaps not surprisingly, it copies the only legal system that the inhabitants of the informal settlements know – the existing system. This more than anything else should dispose of the canard of the legal and the 'illegal' city. Rather we can see the two intersecting circuits of legality within the city, and the task for urban policy makers and managers is to try to bring these two circuits closer together.

LATE 20TH-CENTURY EXAMPLES OF INNOVATIVE LAWS

In the last few years of the 20th century, there were encouraging signs that urban planners and policy makers had begun to bite the bullet and develop, with inputs from those concerned with developing national land policies, legal regimes at the formal national level that aimed to develop, on the basis of an acceptance of informal tenure systems, urban land tenure systems which would provide security of tenure for the urban poor, thus meeting a key requirement of the Habitat Agenda. Some of these are discussed and highlighted in the UMP Working Paper prepared by Durand-Lasserve and Clerc (1996) as a contribution to Habitat II, and need not be repeated here. I shall draw attention to some Anglophone developments made since then, or not mentioned in that paper. Two examples in particular may be discussed, South Africa and Tanzania.

South Africa

Although South Africa is one of the countries featured in this book, it is worth drawing attention to one of the most innovative approaches to informal urban settlements that has been provided for by national legislation. This is the Development Facilitation Act 1995. The Act is designed to overcome the bottlenecks in obtaining permission to develop and the discriminatory practices of local authorities which operated to the disadvantage of the black community in South Africa. Provinces and local governments are required to set land development objectives (LDOs), the content of which is set out in the Act through a participatory procedure. These LDOs in effect take precedence over existing plans – master plans, structure plans, etc. – which might already exist. They are, as the name implies, directed to setting out how the land is to be developed, adopting national standards and principles to overcome the inherited practices of the past.

Two specific innovative aspects of the Act may be looked at in a little more detail. The first is the setting out of the General Principles of Land Development at the commencement of the Act. These principles are to apply throughout the country; to the actions of the State and a local government body; and to serve as guides to the administration of any physical plan, transport plan, structure plan, zoning scheme or other similar plan or scheme. They are also to serve as guidelines by reference to which any competent authority shall exercise discretion or take a decision on any matter concerned with land development. These principles set out an inspiring vision of the desired urban future of South Africa and enshrine a new approach to planning law.[1] They provide, *inter alia*, that:

> (a) *Policy, administrative practice and law should . . . facilitate the development of formal and informal, existing and new settlements. . .;*

(c) *Policy, administrative practice and law should promote efficient and integrated land development in that they*

   (iii) *promote the availability of residential and employment opportunities in close proximity to or integrated with each other;*
   (iv) *promote a diverse combination of land uses, also at the level of individual erven [plots of land] and subdivisions of land. . .*

(d) *Members of communities affected by land development should actively participate in the process of land development. . .;*

(f) *Policy, administrative practice and laws should encourage and optimise the contributions of all sectors of the economy (government and non-government) to land development...*

(g) *Laws, procedures and administrative practice relating to land development should:*

   (i)   *be clear and generally available to those likely to be affected thereby;*
   (iii) *be calculated to promote trust and acceptance on the part of those likely to be affected thereby;*
   (iv) *give further content to the fundamental rights set out in the Constitution. . .*

(i)   *Policy, administrative practice and laws should promote speedy land development;*

(k) *Land development should result in security of tenure, provide for the widest possible range of tenure alternatives, including individual and communal tenure, and in cases where land development takes the form of upgrading an existing settlement, not deprive beneficial occupiers[2] of homes or land or, where it is necessary for land or homes occupied by them to be utilised for other purposes, their interests in such land or homes should be reasonably accommodated in some other manner;*

(m) *Policy, administrative practice and laws relating to land development should stimulate the effective functioning of a land development market based on open competition between suppliers of goods and services.*

These principles are very much in line with the principles enshrined in the GPA and so have an application beyond South Africa.

The second innovation concerns the upgradation of informal settlements. Two specific LDOs are:

(i)   *the integration of areas of low-income communities into the relevant area as a whole [relevant area being the area of the local authority to which the LDOs apply];*

(v)   *the overall density of settlements, with due regard to the interests of beneficial occupiers. . .*

This enjoins local authorities to treat low-income settlements occupied by persons with no valid title to the land they are occupying as full members of the local community and as such entitled to proper planning and the provision of adequate infrastructure. Even more interesting, however, is section 63 of the Act:

> *(1)   Whenever land development takes the form of the upgrading of an existing settlement, informal or unregistered tenure arrangements existing among occupants of the settlement may, subject to any conditions [in other sections], be converted into ownership in the manner prescribed.*

Subsection (2) sets out the matters that may be provided for by regulations and these make plain that the whole process is to be a participatory one, with members of the communities concerned playing an active role in the process of upgrading. Upgrading leads to formal layout plans, followed by registration of those plans and the new titles in the Deeds Registry.

This brief summary cannot do full justice to a law which is clearly inspired by a vision that urgent action must be taken to rectify the grievous land development wrongs of the past, and that this can be, and indeed must be, driven by the twin imperatives of advancing human rights and democratic participation on the one hand, and developing an effective land market on the other. Furthermore, and this is very much in keeping with governance traditions in South Africa, implementation of this vision is through the legal process – through detailed laws, procedures and formal judicial and quasi-judicial processes and hearings. Notwithstanding that this Act has not worked wholly satisfactorily in South Africa and is going to be repealed and replaced by provincial legislation, the principles enshrined in the law remain a valid model and are worth careful consideration by countries considering replacing their top-down Anglophone models of planning legislation.

Tanzania

The second example comes from the Tanzanian Land Act, 1999. The National Land Policy (NLP), approved by Parliament in 1995, accorded recognition to tenure rights in unplanned urban settlements as follows.

- Residents in unplanned urban settlements shall have their rights recorded and maintained by the relevant land allocating authority and that record will be registered.
- All interests on land, including customary land rights that exist in the planning areas, shall be identified and recorded.
- The land rights of peri-urban dwellers will be fully recognized and Right of Occupancy issued.
- Upgrading plans will be prepared and implemented by local authorities with the participation of residents and their local community organizations. Local resources will be mobilized to finance the plans through appropriate cost recovery systems.

Sections 56 to 60 of the Land Act set out a framework for a process of regularization designed to facilitate the implementation of these policies.

Section 56 sets out the land – in urban and peri-urban areas – to which the provisions apply. Section 57 explains the purpose and criteria to be used in deciding whether to declare a scheme of regularization. While the scheme is concerned with tenure issues, it will be important to form a judgement as to whether a potential scheme area is one which is a settled residential area where the residents are committed to improving the area and their homes. That will be the best kind of area in which to commence a scheme of regularization. Section 58 sets out the procedures for determining whether to declare an area to be a regularization area. The minister may act on his own motion or at the request of an urban authority. He may request the Commissioner of Lands to compile a report on the area under consideration, or some other body or person: an independent research organization, consultancy or NGO. Consultation with the target population must be undertaken. The report forms the basis of the minister's decision on whether to proceed to the stage of preparing a draft scheme.

Section 59 sets out the procedures for declaring a scheme of regularization. A draft scheme is prepared, discussed with the target population in the proposed scheme area and the local authorities in the area, and submitted to the minister, who decides whether to approve the scheme with or without amendments or refer it back to the Commissioner. Persons likely to lose land in any scheme must be given notice of the draft scheme so they can make representations thereon. Section 60 sets out the content of a scheme of regularization. The centrepiece of any scheme will be adjudication of interests in land. The area of a scheme could be a ward, smaller than a ward or more than one ward. In addition to adjudication, a scheme may make provision for boundary readjustment and for redistribution and sharing of rights in land. This is where urban adjudication is likely to be different to adjudication of village land in rural areas. Informal settlements tend to be densely packed together and any regularization scheme should take the opportunity to try to provide a better arrangement of plots at the same time as validating the occupation rights of residents. As the NLP makes clear, residents must be involved in any such schemes and this too must be provided for in a scheme.

Towards the end of 2000, draft Land (Regularization) Regulations were prepared to enable these provisions to be activated, though these have not yet been approved.

Three further examples may be noted.

Uganda

The 1995 Constitution of Uganda brought about a revolution of land tenure in that country, and the Land Act, 1998 fleshed out the details of the constitutional principles. The Constitution conferred security of tenure via either ownership rights (including customary law ownership) or perpetual lease rights on lawful and *bona fide* occupiers of land – the overwhelming majority of land occupiers in the country. This includes occupiers of land in urban areas who, along with all other occupiers, now have the right to obtain either freehold or leasehold rights to their land, or a certificate of occupancy to the land. Administrative problems have delayed the implementation of the Act (McAuslan, 2002b) so it is too early to say whether it will facilitate security of tenure for persons in unauthorized urban settlements.

Trinidad and Tobago

In Trinidad and Tobago, the Regularization of Tenure Act, 1998 creates a 'Certificate of Comfort', which confers security of tenure on squatters as the first step in a process designed to give a full legal title to such persons. However, the way in which the legislation has been constructed does not provide any incentive to move from the provisional title conferred by a Certificate. Indeed the reverse is the case because Certificates are free, while moving to full title must be paid for, so, not surprisingly few residents in unauthorized settlements are taking the necessary steps to acquire full title. The 'error' of the government is to assume that people will want the full legal title to the land. What they actually want is security of tenure, and if that is achieved, paying money for a full legal title is not seen to be a priority by the urban poor.

Namibia

Namibia has for some time been developing proposals for a more flexible tenure system designed to provide tenure rights for the persons in informal settlement areas. A report was produced in mid-1998 suggesting two new tenure forms in Namibia, a *starter title* and *landhold title*, and a draft Recognition of Starter Title Tenure Rights and Landhold Title Tenure Rights Bill was published for general comment in early 1999. What follows is taken from the draft Bill, which was based on the report of a consultant. The Bill is still with the Government draftsperson.

A community, non-governmental organisation, body or other person who wishes to upgrade or develop an informal settlement area may apply to a local or regional authority for approval for same. After a feasibility study has been undertaken and approved the area shall be surveyed and registered in the Deeds Registry as a block erf (a specific tract of land). Within the block erf, individuals may apply for and obtain either a starter title tenure right or a landhold title tenure right. The first form of title is subject to the constitution and rules of the community or other organisation that has applied for the block erf (including rules of customary law) and confers on the holder a right in perpetuity to occupy a site within the block erf and deal with it subject to the rules etc. of the community. The second form of title confers on the holder a right in perpetuity to occupy a defined site or piece of land within the block erf and undertake the full range of commercial and family transactions with the land. The formalities for obtaining a landhold title are considerable and approximate to the formalities for obtaining a freehold title. Each form of title is registrable in the Deeds Register. A community or a person within a community may upgrade a starter tenure title to a landhold tenure title.

There was considerable opposition among the surveying and legal professions in Namibia to more flexible title systems. Part of the proposals – reflected in the draft Bill – involved the introduction of simplified systems of surveying and registration with a new para-professional, termed a landmeasurer, who would undertake the simplified land surveying, and local property offices, which would be the locus of the registered block erfs and new rights obtainable within the block erfs. The Bill reflects the tensions inherent in the proposals. A more simplified system is to be introduced but the procedures involved in getting the new systems up and running may inhibit its development. It is not known whether professional opposition to the proposals is the cause of the continued delay to their enactment.

CONCLUSIONS

What these examples show is that the bringing together of the two circuits of urban land law is both possible and practical. It is a step-by-step process.

There must be a recognition of the legitimacy of the informal sector and informal systems of land tenure. This is best achieved at the national level by a national policy prescription or constitutional provisions. Here, South Africa with both, Uganda with constitutional provisions, and Tanzania with a national land policy, point the way forward. Bangladesh, which continues to resist conferring any form of secure tenure on residents in informal settlements, and Lesotho, which is proposing to tackle informal settlements with the full rigour of the law, are not examples to be emulated.

There needs to be primary legislation either at the national level or in a federal system where land is either a state responsibility or a concurrent responsibility at the state level as well. Alongside any proposed national legislation there must be a fully costed budget for implementation. It was the failure to cost out the new legislation in Uganda that has been a factor in delayed implementation.

Primary legislation will need to be followed up by secondary legislation and governmental policy guidance to provide the detailed arrangements for implementation. Given the delays in developing and giving legal effect to the necessary secondary legislation, which seems to affect so many countries, it might be desirable to try to develop the whole package of primary and secondary legislation at the same time.

A programme of capacity building for officials and public education for the residents of the informal settlements must be developed and undertaken *before* the process of implementation can be commenced. Literature, radio and TV programmes on the new systems must be produced in languages that the intended beneficiaries of the programmes will understand. The Ugandan programmes of public education and awareness raising and the South African programme of education and training for officials are models that are worth close study.

Only when all that has been completed can action on the ground begin. Both the secondary legislation and the programmes of public education and training should involve participatory processes. Equally, as the Tanzanian draft regulations and the South African Development Facilitation Act show, the process of regularization (which is what the integration of the two circuits of urban land tenure law amount to) can only proceed on the basis of a participatory process throughout. This seems to be a deficiency of the draft Namibian law, which lays stress of official action but has few provisions on participation.

PART II

THE LIMITATIONS OF CONVENTIONAL APPROACHES

CHAPTER THREE

Housing tenure change in the transitional economies

Richard Grover, Paul Munro-Faure and Mikhail Soloviev

INTRODUCTION

Since the opening of the Berlin Wall, the 413 million people of transitional economies of Central and Eastern Europe and the former USSR have been the subject of a social experiment in housing provision, with potentially far-reaching consequences. During the period of Communist rule, the state played the major role in housing, both through direct provision of accommodation and, indirectly, through credit from state banks to housing co-operatives and individuals. Housing construction and the maintenance and management of blocks of apartments were mainly done by state organizations. Since 1990, significant parts of the housing stock, which were in state hands, have passed into the private sector as a result of privatization and restitution. Private housing markets have developed, including those concerned with housing development, renting and housing finance.

New housing tenures have been created which have granted rights over property that could not previously have been enjoyed. These include enhanced rights to acquire property and to alienate it by sale, bequest and gift, and the right to let property to tenants. However, with the new rights have come new liabilities and responsibilities. As the 1995 Slovak Republic policy document *The Concept of State Housing Policy by the Year 2000* put it, in a market economy, the responsibility for procuring their own housing is shifted on to the citizens (Slovak Republic, 2000: 4). Responsibilities for maintenance and upkeep tend to fall on the new owners rather than on the state or municipalities. Failure to meet obligations such as rents, mortgages, service charges or property taxes brings the right to become insolvent and the potential loss of the property. The construction industry in the new climate of increased individual responsibility for housing has become more oriented towards the building of properties for those with effective demand. There has been a decline in the construction of social and affordable housing and the safety net for those unable to make their own housing provision has shrunk. Greater freedom in housing has been accompanied by the transfer of risk from the state to the individual.

This chapter examines the issues that have arisen during the course of this process, and what lessons can be learned from the way in which the transformation of housing provision took place. There are problems that result from the growth of private housing markets in the transitional economies not having come about organically, but as the result of sudden enfranchisement as the state retreated from its role in housing. The change has brought increased security of tenure for those who have taken advantage of privatization and restitution to acquire the freeholds of their properties. In principle, this should have given them greater control over their housing. In practice, the infrastructure to support the markets has not developed at the same rate as the tenure changes. For example, mortgage markets have been slow to develop, so that there is limited access to affordable long-term credit to enable households to purchase residential property. The privatization of individual apartments has raised issues about who is to assume responsibility for the care and maintenance of common areas and the common parts of the fabric. This case study suggests that just creating freeholds does not by itself result in either an efficient housing market or in the mobilization of the capital tied up in real estate. Rather, appropriate legal and financial infrastructure must be developed as well. The creation of secure tenures, like freehold, may be necessary, but is not a sufficient condition for bringing about efficient housing and capital markets.

As the transitional economies were not uniform in their approach to the role of the state in housing during the Communist period, this chapter focuses particularly on three countries at either end of a continuum. The Russian Federation inherited from the USSR a situation in which the state was a near-monopoly provider of housing. By contrast, Bulgaria and Romania under Communism had greater individual involvement in housing provision and a lesser role for the state and municipalities. Each has adopted contrasting policies since 1990 and has encountered different issues.

THE DECLINE OF THE STATE IN HOUSING

As noted above, the role of the state in housing provision varied between the transitional countries while they were under Communist rule. In the USSR, the state, in principle, dominated housing provision; there was no legal market for state housing and an almost complete prohibition of market relations in the co-operative and private sectors. Accommodation tended to be allocated to those on waiting lists at work or place of residence. The right to be included on the waiting list was principally determined by the quality of current accommodation, particularly whether there was overcrowding compared to official norms; the date of *propiska* (official residence permit); the health and social characteristics of the household; and any privileges to which individuals were entitled. The *propiska* system of residential occupancy permits restricted the ability of citizens to live where they would wish. In particular, it acted to control migration to the more attractive urban areas. It also limited the succession of tenancies within families, restricting rights of inheritance of tenancies to those with *propiska*.

State enterprises and organizations were the main source of capital investment in housing construction. In practice, there was also a small, private self-build provision in urban as well as rural areas, officially approved housing exchanges and shadow private renting markets (Bessonova, 1992). Individuals could not own land but personal property could include housing. This was largely to be found in rural areas and was almost non-existent in the major urban areas. Mass construction in the 1950s and 1960s substantially met the physical accommodation needs of the population and ensured that the overwhelming majority of households had separate flats. Some communal flats did remain and the quality of post-war construction tended to be low. There were centralized budgets for building, maintenance and communal services, with only symbolic payments by residents. The population was not encouraged to solve its own residential problems or to develop understanding of the obligations of proprietors. Queuing for free state provision of housing was the norm. This raises questions as to how well prepared the population was to cope with the requirements of private markets when they developed after 1990.

In countries like Bulgaria and Romania, there was considerably more private provision of housing, both by individuals and through housing co-operatives. However, funding tended to come through credits from state banks, so that the state was able to exercise financial control over housing provision. In Bulgaria in 1985, approximately 85 per cent of the total housing stock and 78 per cent of that in urban areas was privately owned. Until 1989, the State Savings Bank (now the DSK Bank) was the only institution authorized to engage in housing finance. In Romania, the CEC (Casa de Economii si Consemnatiuni) performed a similar function to the Bulgarian State Savings Bank.

The processes by which private housing markets were created varied between transitional countries as each has adopted its own laws. The main processes have been privatization and restitution. With privatization, housing is transferred from a state or municipal body to private owners, usually the sitting tenants. With restitution, those with a claim to title have been able to recover property that had previously been expropriated, or which they or their predecessors in title had been forced to sell.

In Russia, there has been no significant restitution, so that the creation of private housing markets has been largely driven by privatization. State housing has been privatized through free and voluntary transfers from the state or municipalities to those occupiers with *propiska* renting under social contracts. By 1996, 41 per cent of flats in Moscow had been privatized and 59 per cent of those in the Russian Federation as a whole, with the Moscow proportion rising to 49 per cent in 1998 (Grover and Soloviev, 2000). The main period of privatization was 1991–93, with a subsequent reduction in the rate. In the first half of 1993, 10.8 per cent of the properties in the Russian Federation were privatized and 18.2 per cent of those in Moscow, compared with 5.6 per cent and 3.9 per cent respectively in the first half of 1994 (Centre of Economic Analysis, 1994). A rental market developed with privatization. It is believed that approximately 20 per cent of the new private owners in Moscow derive their principal income from rents. The development and opening up of the Russian economy since 1990 has created a demand for quality housing for rent by Russian and foreign employees of the sectors that have enjoyed growth, such as financial services.

Almost all the housing stock that was privatized took the form of flats rather than individual houses. Privatization did not transfer obligations and rights over common areas, common services or the maintenance of the fabric. The final target of transferring responsibility for the maintenance of the stock and the provision of communal services has not yet been met. Privatization has not ended the *propiska* system. In principle, the owner of a dwelling may not necessarily possess residence rights. The private housing markets remain subject to regulation through the *propiska*. This has prevented mass migration of populations from areas where industry has collapsed to areas of relative prosperity, as those who might wish to move must obtain the necessary residence permits.

In Romania, state housing was sold to the tenants and, if unoccupied, to the public. A 1990 decree that governed the latter had prohibitions on resale and purchase for renting. Prices of these properties were governed by the characteristics of the properties, such as the number of rooms, size, grade of comfort, seismic strength and other attributes. The market price was not the basis for the sales, although many of the attributes would have an influence on this. The prices at which Romanian state housing was sold to its tenants was determined by the historic cost of its construction, updated by a price index. It is believed that this resulted in many of the properties being sold to their occupiers at values below the market price. The proportion of the housing stock in public ownership fell from 11.2 per cent in 1992 to 5.7 per cent in 1997 (National Commission for Statistics, 1998). It had been 37 per cent in urban areas under the Communist regime. In Bulgaria, it is believed that half of the rental units in the larger towns and cities were sold in 1990 and 1991, as those renting municipal units took advantage of their right to purchase their units at the old prices and loan terms, in anticipation of the abolition of subsidized housing (Hoffman and Koleva, 1993). In some of the other transitional economies, the decline in the public sector has been even more rapid. In Estonia, the public sector housing stock declined from 51 per cent of the total in 1995 to just 7 per cent in 1999 (Jakobson, 2000: 8).

Restitution has been an important influence on the formation of private housing markets in some of the transitional economies. In Romania, a 1995 law permits the restitution of dwellings. Former landlords and their heirs can recover property that is not occupied or of which they are tenants. A law passed in 2000 provides for financial compensation from state budgets where property cannot be recovered, but the criteria for determining the compensation to be paid has not yet been finalized. The Czech Republic has allowed the original owners and their heirs to regain property that belonged to them prior to February 1948 (Grabmullerova, 2000). In 1991, the Czech government transferred all rental housing that was not subject to restitution to municipalities. This has resulted in the retention of a larger rental sector (33 per cent of the total) than has been the case with many of the other transitional countries. However, many countries in the region have the potential problem of resolving restitution issues of multiple claimants of properties. Successive waves of expropriation and forced sales under the Nazis in the post-war population migrations and under Communism have resulted in subsequent owners believing that they had acquired properties in good faith with good title, when others may also have claims. Ethnic cleansing in areas of conflict, such as the former Yugoslavia, has also produced problems of restitution, with refugees settling in the properties of the dispossessed (Rose et al., 2000).

THE GROWTH OF OWNER OCCUPATION

The effect of privatization and restitution on housing tenure in the transitional economies has been enormous. Many of them now have levels of owner occupation that are in excess of those generally to be found in Western Europe. Bulgaria, Estonia, Hungary, Kyrgyzstan, Romania and Slovenia have owner occupation levels in excess of 80 per cent. Within the European Union, no country has such a high level of owner occupation, although Greece, Ireland and Spain approach this level (McCrone and Stephens, 1995; Yasui, 2000).

On the face of it, the changes ought to be welcomed. They have provided the population with a degree of control over its housing that it did not previously enjoy. They are no longer 'enserfed' by the housing committees of enterprises and local soviets (Andrusz, 1992: 238). Individual households are free to invest in improving the quality of their accommodation, rather than having to accept the conditions and standards of maintenance and repair determined by public bodies. There is quite a backlog of maintenance and construction defects to make good. In Bulgaria, it is reported that:

> There is hardly a prefab apartment building which does not have cracked walls, leaking pipes, damaged water insulation and a leaking roof (Bulgaria, 2000: 13).

In Latvia, similar problems exist:

> As there was very little or virtually no maintenance of housing stock carried out during the soviet era, the level of deterioration of buildings is tremendous (Vecvagare, 2000: 6).

Restitution for those lucky enough to reclaim residential properties in business districts has enabled them to establish businesses, or to rent out premises for business use. This has transformed the central areas of cities like Sofia, as new restaurants, bars and shops have opened in what were formerly residential properties. Economic benefits should come from the enhanced ability of households to respond to changes in employment by seeking to migrate to where jobs are being created. Households also have better opportunities to alter their housing in response to lifetime events, such as the birth of children and retirement.

However, for a significant proportion of the population, these changes have brought difficulties and insecurity in housing. Alongside the growth in owner occupation there has been the decline of social housing and the rented sector. In Romania in 1992, 49.8 per cent of dwellings completed were financed from public funds, but by 1998 this had fallen to 9.8 per cent. The number of dwellings completed with public funding in 1997 was only 25.5 per cent of the number completed with public funding in 1992 (National Commission for Statistics, 1998). This raises questions about whether the current systems of housing provision are making adequate provision for low income and vulnerable groups. The rented sector in market economies is important for labour mobility, as well as providing a stepping stone to other tenures. Its decline in the transitional economies as a result of the decline in social housing raises questions as to whether there is adequate provision of housing for those who are geographically or occupationally mobile (Romania, 2000: 6).

Certain groups seem to be particularly vulnerable as new housing markets develop. The cases coming before the courts in Moscow, for example, indicate three particular problem areas concerning children, the elderly and dwellings in co-ownership. Children in dysfunctional families can be vulnerable where their parents decide to sell or trade down the family home. It has proved necessary in Moscow to take steps to support children's rights, such as requiring municipal consent for any bargain concerning a flat where a child has *propiska*. The elderly have become vulnerable as state pensions have failed to keep pace with inflation and public services have been subjected to budgetary restraint. In Russia, the elderly can enter into official contracts under which they receive additional financial support in return for bequeathing their flat. This is a traditional form of de facto inheritance and is confirmed by judicial and municipal bodies. Although this arrangement may be within an extended family, charitable bodies and realtor firms may also enter into these contracts. There is clearly scope for abuse and there are press reports of criminal uses of the process, including the fraudulent posing as a charitable body. Such abuses have led Moscow City Government to develop a contract between it and elderly citizens under which the flat will pass to the City and the City will provide for the individual, either in their own flat or in special flats for the elderly. Disputes over flats in co-ownership can occur after the death of one of the co-owners, when new owners inherit and move into the accommodation.

MORTGAGES AND HOUSING FINANCE

The mortgage market plays an important part in ensuring that housing markets dominated by owner-occupiers function efficiently. A mortgage can be defined as a loan secured against an asset. Mortgages are usually used to finance the purchase of real estate, although they can also be used to release capital tied up in it. The existence of a mortgage market facilitates the purchase of housing for owner occupation. It enables owner-occupiers to change dwellings as their lifetime circumstances dictate. Thus, households can migrate to larger dwellings to accommodate additional children, or to smaller ones on retirement or after the death of a partner. A functioning mortgage market is essential for an efficient labour market, as there needs to be opportunity for geographical mobility of owner-occupying households to places of employment. Owner-occupiers need to be able to sell their current properties and purchase alternatives in locations where they can obtain employment. Mortgages also enable households to realize some of the wealth they have tied up in housing and to mobilize it for other purposes, for example to supplement inadequate state pensions.

The mortgage provides a source of finance for home improvements and refurbishment. Given the historic problems with the construction and maintenance of the housing stock, and defects such as poor energy insulation in the transitional economies, the ability to raise funds for housing improvement is important. In Latvia, Price Waterhouse has estimated major renovations at $2 billion (Vecvagare, 2000: 7). The new owners may lack the resources to finance major repairs and investment unless they are able to draw on the wealth in their dwellings.

Housing privatization has led to the situation where the majority of apartment owners are not able to invest enough to carry out the first priority works in their housing units to ensure that their technical quality is maintained (Jakobson, 2000: 8).

Where the mortgage market does not function efficiently, alternative sources of finance have to be used instead, such as the mobilization of family savings. Although the better-connected and more astute were able to move at least some resources into hard currencies, the majority of family savings have been fundamentally undermined by the effects of very high levels of inflation during the 1990s. Family savings are in any case neither as flexible nor as easy to raise in the short term as a mortgage. They do not overcome the front-end loading problem of financing housing purchase by enabling the cost to be spread over the occupancy of the property in the way that a mortgage does.

The mortgage market can also be an important source of funding for social housing. In the UK, the voluntary housing movement, in the form of charitable housing associations, borrows finance for housing development from banks and the money markets to supplement government development grants. These mortgages are secured against the social housing they are used to develop. There is an implied government guarantee for such loans, as those housing associations in receipt of state funding are regulated by the government's Housing Corporation. Lenders tend to regard housing associations as being of low risk and they pay comparatively low interest rates on their borrowings, of the order of 0.5–0.6 per cent above base rates (Lawson, 2000). In this way, private funding can be brought into social housing through the mortgage market. Such development depends on the existence of an efficient mortgage market.

Housing loans in the transitional economies are very low relative to their gross domestic products (GDPs) compared with the European Union. Within the EU, only Austria and Italy have housing loans that are less than 10 per cent of their GDPs. For Denmark, the Netherlands, UK, Germany and Sweden, housing loans amount to more than 40 per cent of the GDP. By contrast, none of the transitional economies has housing loans that exceed 5 per cent of the GDP. Only in the Czech Republic and Estonia does the proportion exceed 3 per cent, while in Poland, the Slovak Republic and Slovenia, the proportion is around 2 per cent (Yasui, 2000). Data on the extent of the mortgage market in Russia are difficult to obtain, but there is evidence that mortgages have been slow to develop and are used in only a limited way. For example, the Russian Federation Savings Bank granted just 500 mortgages in 2000 with an average credit of $20 000. The income required by borrowers was in excess of 15 000 roubles per month, which is approximately triple the monthly income of a university lecturer. Moscow has established building savings schemes, which guarantee credits that can be combined with grants for those in the municipal housing queue and commercial mortgages. The construction programme for these consists of 16 blocks of flats (183 000 m^2) in 2000 and 12 blocks (114 000 m^2) in 2001. To put this in perspective, this programme in 2000 amounted to 11 per cent of the space constructed by the City Government as part of the programme to tackle building obsolescence.

These figures may, however, underestimate the extent to which the mortgage markets are developing. In Bulgaria, where outstanding housing loans are less than 1 per cent of GDP, 30 per cent of residential property sales in 1999 were combined with a credit from a bank (Munro-Faure and Evtimov, 2000: 30). Recently, there has been rapid growth in the mortgage markets of some of the transitional economies, although from a very low base, particularly in Estonia, Latvia and the Slovak Republic. In Estonia, over half of the dwellings purchased in 1997 were bought using housing loans (Jakobson, 2000: 10).

The transitional economies can be said to be characterized by high levels of owner occupation, with limited tenure choice and restricted access to mortgage credit, a situation Stephens characterizes as the 'Southern European Model' of housing finance (Stephens, 2000; McCrone and Stephens, 1995). In the absence of mortgage finance, informal lending, particularly within extended families, becomes a feature of housing finance. This can restrict access to housing and result in the postponement of marriage and having children. This, in turn, can have adverse implications for the demographic structure, contributing to an ageing population.

A number of reasons can be advanced for the limited development of mortgage markets in the transitional economies. The banking systems in the transitional economies are less developed than for market economies with comparable incomes per capita. The European Bank for Reconstruction and Development (EBRD, 1999: 93–4) examined relationships between broad money in the GDP and the gross national product (GNP) per capita and private sector credit in GDP and the GNP per capita. It found that transitional countries have ratios below those normally found at comparable GNP per capita levels for market economies. In the EU, the amount of financial institutions' credit to the private sector is typically around 90 per cent of GDP. In the transitional economies, the typical proportion is 10 per cent, with only the Czech and Slovak Republics having a proportion in excess of 40 per cent.

Until recently, state banks dominated the banking systems in the transitional economies. Not only were the banks state owned, but their small numbers restricted competition and innovation. In Romania in 1994, four state banks controlled 80 per cent of bank assets and in 1998 this was still 75 per cent. In Bulgaria, the two largest banks are state owned, including the DSK Bank, which holds 90 per cent of the housing finance market (Bulgaria, 2000: 8). Figure 3.1 shows how state banks dominated the banking systems in a number of the transitional countries as recently as 1997.

Even with the privatization of state banks, there is still often a high degree of concentration in the banking system, which could be argued to limit competition and innovation. Entry into the mortgage market may be subject to restraints that may discourage or restrict the number of entrants. For example, in the Czech Republic, the granting of a mortgage licence to banks is on the condition that they offer fixed interest loans (Grabmullerova, 2000).

While greater competition ought to encourage innovation, this may not help housing finance. In Hungary, the state banks' share of assets fell from 63 per cent in 1994 to 12 per cent in 1998 (EBRD, 1999). However, the more competitive banking system, together with falls in property values and high interest rates, have contributed to a decline in housing loans. In 1991, housing loans amounted to 27.8 per cent of retail and corporate loans but only 6.5 per cent in 1997 (Hegedus and Varhegyi, 1999). As a proportion of total assets, mortgage loans fell from 4.6 per cent in 1995 to 1.8 per cent in 1999 (Szilagyi, 2000: 23).

Financial and liquidity pressures as a result of bad debts have restricted the development of the banking systems of some of the transitional countries, with adverse consequences for the development of their mortgage markets. For example, in Romania bad loans amounted to 34 per cent of total loans in 1998. In September 1997, overdue credits amounted to 26 per cent of non-governmental credit, and in December 1997 provisions were 18 per cent of bank gross portfolios (OECD, 1998; IMF, 1998). In Bulgaria, the banking sector developed very quickly in the early 1990s, with banks starting to offer mortgages on urban properties. Due to problems in regulation,

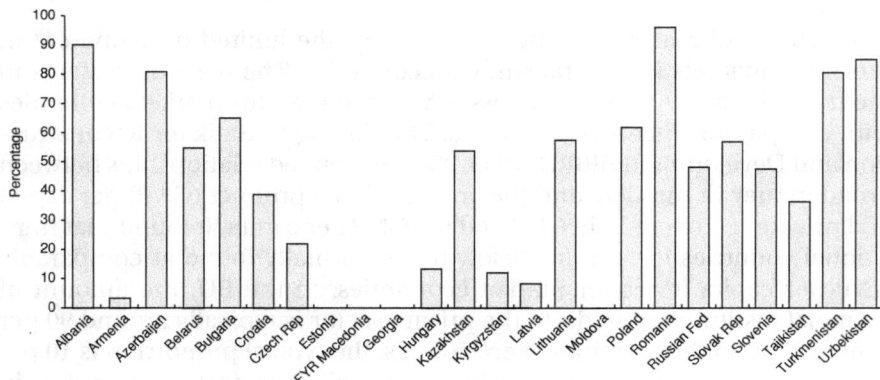

Figure 3.1   Asset share of state-owned banks 1997 (%).

confidence in the banking system was severely eroded following the banking crisis of 1994. Subsequently, Bulgarian banks have been very conservative in setting norms for mortgage lending, which has limited the development of the market (Munro-Faure and Evtimov, 2000). Progress in banking reform has varied markedly between the transitional economies. For example, Hungary scored 4 in 1999 on the EBRD scale of banking reform, which is close to Bank of International Settlement standards. Bulgaria and Romania scored 3, which indicates substantial progress in the establishment of bank solvency and a framework of prudential regulation. Russia scored 2, which indicates liberalization of interest rates and credit allocation, but limited development of the prudential framework.

The approach to prudential regulation adopted towards mortgage lending can be argued to be over-cautious when compared with the risks inherent in loans backed by real estate assets. The Basle Agreement places mortgages on residential property that is occupied by the borrower, or rented, in the risk class that carries a 50 per cent weight. This is half the weight given to claims against the private sector because of the low record of loss in most countries for such loans. The target standard ratio of capital to weighted risk assets is 8 per cent. Therefore, the Basle Agreement implies that banks will hold a 4 per cent reserve ratio for residential mortgages (Basle Committee, 1988). In Romania, the Agreement was implemented in the 1994 rules on credit classifications. However, banks voluntarily make higher provisions. We have found examples of three major Romanian banks that made provisions of up to 125 per cent for mortgages, that is a 10 per cent reserve ratio. This makes mortgage finance very capital-intensive for the banks.

Reserve ratios for mortgages in Europe tend to be higher than in the USA, as American banks tend to remove mortgages from their balance sheets by means of securitization. This can take the form of mortgage bonds, which are sold to investors rather than remaining in the ownership of the banks. However, there are also problems in developing mortgage-backed securities. The experience of the German mortgage banks in the early 1990s suggests that investors are unwilling to accept such securities unless they have confidence in the quality of the valuations of the properties against which the loans are secured. The German mortgage banks were obliged to seek the help of the British Royal Institution of Chartered Surveyors to set up a professional body for mortgage surveyors, together with examination and education systems, to improve market acceptance of their securities. A few of the transitional economies, such as Bulgaria, the Czech Republic, Hungary, Poland and Russia, have good courses for the training of valuers, but in most countries such programmes do not exist. Even where such courses do exist, the numbers of graduates produced each year are relatively small. In Bulgaria, licensed valuers, approved to undertake privatization work, are expected to undertake mortgage valuations (Bulgaria, 2000).

Capital adequacy requirements may encourage banks to pursue other forms of lending with fewer capital adequacy demands, or ones that are potentially more profitable than residential mortgages, such as commercial mortgages (Munro-Faure and Evtimov, 2000). A survey we undertook in 1999 of seven major Romanian banks, with 77 per cent of the net Romanian banking assets, found that residential mortgages were not a very important part of lending activity, typically accounting for not more than 5 per cent of loans. Interest rates were high at 2–14 per cent above a base rate of 45–55 per cent. The high level of interest rates meant that the level of loans advanced was low, as banks expect the security to be sufficient to cover the annual interest charge in the first year of the loan as well as the principal.

Banks in transitional economies appear to be having difficulty in developing deposit bases that are suitable for major mortgage lending. Successful mortgage banks can draw their funds in two main ways – from retail deposits and from the money markets. The traditional approach is to draw on a broad retail base and take deposits in the form of long-term savings. Some 62 per cent of mortgage lending in the EU is financed by retail deposits (Hardt and Manning, 2000: 10). This is the approach of the CEC in Romania: in 1998, 32 per cent of the sums it loaned were for construction or the purchase or refurbishment of dwellings. The balance was mainly consumer loans. Some 82 per cent of its deposits in 1998 were term deposits and only 17 per cent were sight deposits. However, the average size of deposit with the CEC was very low at about $50 per fixed-term saving book. In the UK, by way of comparison, the balance between savers and borrowers for mortgage banks is typically five to eight savers per mortgage account. The figures indicate that the CEC needs to operate with ratios of savers to mortgage accounts of ten times or more these levels. The development of the mortgage market will probably require much greater levels of individual savings with banks.

An alternative approach is to draw funds from the money markets and place them through agents rather than a branch network. This is the approach of the central lender and is the business plan behind the

Romanian ANL (Agentia Nationala pentru Locuinte), which was formed with government backing in order to expand the mortgage market. This plans to raise $300 million by an international tender. It received state funds of $15 million in 1999/2000 and has been placing its loans through the Banca Comerciala Romana. It made approximately 1000 loans during 1999/2000. Its approach has been to lend to the more creditworthy households. Such a restricted approach, coupled with the small scale of its activities, means that its impact on the market has been limited. Mortgage markets tend to be the preserve of the higher-income group. In Latvia, which is one of the transitional economies in which the mortgage market is developing most rapidly, it is estimated that only 10–20 per cent of the population at the top end of the income distribution can obtain mortgage loans from banks (Vecvagare, 2000: 11).

THE MANAGEMENT OF APARTMENT BLOCKS

The properties that have been privatized include a significant proportion in the form of flats or apartments rather than individual family houses. This raises questions as to who is to assume responsibility for the management, maintenance and servicing of common areas, such as lifts and lobbies, and the maintenance of common parts of the structure, such as roofs. Maintenance is an important issue in view of the dominance of panel construction in the apartment blocks and the relatively poor standards of construction and maintenance of the housing stock that private owners have inherited. Before privatization, this tended to be the responsibility of state construction or management companies. After privatization, this could continue to be done by a state company or by a mutual organization created by the owners of the flats or by a company that they employ for this purpose.

When Russia's housing was first privatized, municipalities retained responsibility for the management of apartment blocks. In many blocks, there is a mixture of tenures, with both privatized flats and those remaining in the ownership of municipalities present. A small proportion of the flats are owned by state bodies. The apportionment of costs and responsibilities between private and public sector owners is potentially fraught with problems. The blocks can also contain non-residential properties, usually belonging to the municipality. A 1998 Moscow Government Decree allows such properties to be let or sold to condominiums without competition, providing that the premises are free of other claims, for example contracts with an external company. This can enable the management of the block to be united. A complication has been the incomplete enactment of the Land Code, which means that significant pillars of the legal infrastructure have still to come into force. Land boundaries for blocks of flats are also unclear.

The Law on Associations of Homeowners 1996 gave apartment owners in residential blocks the choice as to whether to manage the properties themselves or to leave this task to the municipal authorities. It provides for the registration of condominiums and associations of home owners. An association can set a budget, maintain common areas and undertake capital repairs. It can collect charges and fees from the owners of flats and pursue them in the event of default. Registration procedures are complex, requiring approval from 22 municipal and other official committees and departments, with 106 forms and 238 copies. The procedure usually takes between seven and nine months, instead of the one to three months set as the norm. Setting up a home owners' association can be regarded as an activity for an enthusiast.

Historically, home owners' associations existed in Moscow during the New Economic Policy period. There were 8400 in Moscow in 1923 and 11 200 in 1927. However, with the commencement of the five-year plans, private residential forms of ownership were abolished. Moscow has approximately 38 700 blocks of flats. In December 1998, there were 384 home owners' associations of all kinds, of which fewer than 100 were condominiums. By May 2000, this had risen to 395, of which 132 were condominiums (Moscow Government). Therefore, only about 1 per cent of the potential blocks are covered by home owners' associations of any type, including co-operatives as well as condominiums. Russia is not alone in experiencing problems with home owners' associations. Estonia has also experienced problems because the owners of restituted properties with sitting tenants lack funds for maintenance and because of the legal complexities in establishing associations (Jakobson, 2000: 9). In Lithuania, home ownership associations are responsible for only 10–15 per cent of the stock (Lithuania, 2000: 21).

A survey by Moscow City Government indicated that about half of respondents preferred the traditional municipal management to establishing condominiums (Moscow Government). They appeared to prefer to live in privately owned flats under municipal management. This shifts the risks of management and maintenance on to the municipality. Municipal service charges are lower than the true costs. In Moscow, citizens pay only 40 per cent of the true costs, and those in the Russian Federation as a whole only 70 per cent (Moscow Government). Private owners could be concerned that in the future the municipality may withdraw subsidies from the blocks that it does not manage. There is evidence that municipal and state payments and transfers to private associations are irregular, while utility companies take payments from home owners associations' accounts when payment is due. Fears that service charges will rise to commercial levels for private dwellings may also be responsible for occupiers being reluctant to exercise their rights to privatize their properties, in the belief that social housing will continue to be subsidized. If service charges rise to commercial levels, this would certainly raise issues of affordability, as have been encountered in other transitional countries. The elderly, being reliant on state pensions, may be unable to meet unsubsidized service charges. Service charges in Moscow are mainly for the collective provision of utilities. Heating and hot water account for 55 per cent of the total charges, and electricity, water, sewerage and gas for 37 per cent. Maintenance and cleaning are responsible for only 8 per cent of the total. Individuals have relatively little ability to control their payments through limiting their consumption.

THE ORIENTATION OF THE CONSTRUCTION INDUSTRY

With the decline of state and social housing development, the construction industries have become more oriented towards satisfying the demands of those groups with purchasing power. This has brought about some significant changes in the types of dwelling being constructed. In Romania, for example, the level of housing construction has been stable during the 1990s with 1.2 units per 1000 persons being constructed in 1992, 1.6 in 1995 and 1.3 in 1998. The type of housing being constructed has changed. Whereas in 1991 75 per cent of new dwellings were in apartment blocks of three or more storeys and 17 per cent were single family houses, in 1998 the proportions were 17 per cent and 58 per cent respectively. Larger units have tended to be built. In 1990, the average dwelling constructed was 33.75 m^2 and contained 2.46 rooms. In 1994, this had increased to 47.03 m^2 and 2.88 rooms (Romania 2000). These trends have resulted in the development of new upmarket residential areas, such as the Baneasa Lake district in northern Bucharest. This is a low-density suburb with extensive parks. It is close to upmarket office areas, out-of-town supermarkets and the international airport.

While private construction companies have become more oriented towards the provision of housing for higher-income groups, Moscow City Government has sought to pursue policies aimed at improving the standards of housing for the mass of its citizens. Mass construction in the 1950s and 1960s has raised questions about the obsolescence of the housing stock. This is put at 40–55 per cent of the housing stock in Moscow and 50–70 per cent of that in the historic centre of the city. The obsolete stock is mainly five- and nine-storey concrete panel blocks. These were built with an expected life of 50–60 years and are therefore approaching the point at which they need to be extensively refurbished or replaced. Since their construction, standards of space per person and for common areas have increased. Moscow City Government has developed a strategy, known as the Wave, for tackling the problem of obsolescence, which involves systematic demolition and reconstruction. The blocks were built in groups, making micro-area regeneration possible. The occupants of one block are resettled and the block demolished. As it is reconstructed, so the occupants of the next block can be resettled in it and so on. Utilizing areas between blocks can increase space standards so that the replacement blocks are larger than those demolished. In 2000, 0.5 million square metres of blocks were demolished and replaced by 1.7 million square metres.

Moscow also has 151 000 communal flats housing 318 000 households. These amount to 4.6 per cent of flats. There is a policy of supporting real estate firms in resettling their residents into single-family flats. Realtors will offer flats in exchange for vacant possession. Achieving the move can be a lengthy process, and the main risk to the resident concerns the reliability of the realtor firm. The communal flats thus released are sought after as single-family residences because of their size and location. A programme of new building by the City Government also enables properties to be made available to those on municipal waiting lists. Moscow is bucking the trend in construction in the Russian Federation. Whereas in the Federation as a whole, residential construction in 2000 was 40 per cent of the level in 1993, that in Moscow has been more stable.

CONCLUSIONS

Privatization and restitution have radically altered the housing markets of the transitional economies since 1990. Many households have gained greater control over their housing through the acquisition of tenures with similar rights to freehold. There has been substantial growth in owner occupation, but a decline in the availability of social housing. The financial and legal infrastructure to support private housing markets has not developed at the same rate as the markets themselves. In particular, housing finance markets to support the purchase of owner-occupied housing are still in an embryonic state. The legal framework for the management of large blocks of flats in multiple and mixed private and public ownership has been slow to develop in a number of the economies. While the construction industry has developed to meet the demands of high-income groups, the construction of social housing has declined and there has been limited progress in tackling the legacy of poor construction and maintenance. These problems suggest that the creation of legal tenures akin to freehold is not sufficient either to create an efficient housing market or to enable the mobilization of capital tied up in real estate assets. Rather, tenure changes need to be accompanied by measures to create appropriate financial and legal infrastructure. Tenure change by itself does not overcome the problems of dead capital (de Soto, 2000), although it may be a necessary condition to enable this to be mobilized.

The net and ongoing results of these trends is to reduce housing access, qualitatively and quantitatively, for the poor and vulnerable in society. As noted, this is compounding already disturbing demographic trends in many of the transitional economies. Although there have been important responses that have aimed to alleviate this in some countries, the ongoing deterioration of structures of limited life span will be a considerable challenge to most of these economies. It is therefore of critical importance that innovative approaches to addressing the problem, effectively of under-capitalization of housing, should be developed in these countries.

The responses to change have varied between countries. Many of the transitional countries have adopted policies of liberalizing their housing markets by reducing government intervention and pursuing measures aimed at supporting the private ownership of real estate, such as land registration. The Russian Federation, and Moscow in particular, has retained many of the controls from before 1990, for example the *propiska* system of residence permits. This could be argued to act as a restraint on individual freedoms. However, the authorities have been able to take a more interventionist approach, for example towards replacing obsolete housing, which has enabled them to direct resources towards improving the housing conditions of middle- and lower-income groups. It remains to be seen which approach will prove the more effective. However, the policies of liberalizing housing markets need more support through the development of appropriate legal and financial infrastructures, and social housing for those for whom market solutions are not possible, before they can be regarded as being successful.

CHAPTER FOUR

The process of urban land tenure formalization in Peru

Ayako Kagawa and Jan Turkstra

INTRODUCTION

Rapid urbanization and poverty in Peru have resulted in the development of informal settlements. These *pueblos jóvenes* are organized land invasions with de facto security of tenure based on an incremental development process and are a phenomenon found in many other developing countries. What distinguishes Peru is the existence since 1961 of a legal framework that permits the legalisation of these informal neighbourhoods, introduced at a time when many countries were still evicting and bulldozing their dwellings. However, many legalization initiatives, especially land titling, are considered to be of an ad hoc or electoral character, both at national and local levels, while legal, technical and physical problems of cities continue to grow.

Many Peruvians will agree that without Hernando de Soto's vision, the formalization policy of land titling and registration would never have been implemented at today's scale. In his widely acclaimed book *The Other Path* (1989), he claims that due to the inefficient Peruvian bureaucratic system, it took an average of 3 years and 7 months to register property and this did not give greater access to urban services. He suggested the need for a faster, simpler process of formalization as he considered that land titles derived from formalization would increase the value of both land and property and consequently allow further consolidation. Furthermore, he stressed that this process would allow greater accessibility to credit from the private financial sector as land titles could be used as collateral. This would then stimulate economic development, since there would be more production in the construction sector and create a dynamic financial and real estate market.

The formalization project, PROFORM, conducted by de Soto's NGO, the Institute of Liberty and Democracy (ILD), received financial backing from USAID and the World Bank in the late 1980s and early 1990s (McLaughlin and de Soto, 1994). De Soto's criticisms on the shortcomings of public policies also led to the creation of Registro Predial (RP) in 1988, a separate registry system from the traditional Registro de la Propiedad Inmueble (RPI). The PROFORM project between 1990 and 1993 claims to have formalized 150 000 properties in selected urban and rural areas.

There are criticisms of de Soto's theory being more ideological than theoretical (Calderón, 1990) or that the pilot project by ILD does not sufficiently prove the theory by the selection of pilot project areas and the analysis of the statistics (Riofrio, 1991). Whatever the reservations, it is true to state that his book and the pilot projects encouraged the government of Peru to implement a national regularization policy as part of their poverty alleviation strategy.

The initiative led to the setting up of COFOPRI in 1996 and co-ordination with RPU (Registro Predial Urbano), which had existed since 1988. The major aim is to create a mortgage-based credit and real estate market that supports development through formal land ownership. Massive land titling and registration in metropolitan Lima and, later on, in other cities throughout the country began with the aim of formalizing 1 million urban land parcels. The World Bank was interested from the initial stage and began its loan in 1999. Today, COFOPRI claims to have achieved its objective of providing 1 million titles.

This chapter provides an overview of Peruvian informal settlements and illustrates a typical process of land tenure formalization of a low-income settlement in Trujillo, Peru, to illustrate how Peruvians have been able to access urban land since the 1960s. It outlines how COFOPRI operates and has influenced the speed and quality of the land tenure formalization process. Based on interviews with staff at COFOPRI and with community leaders and households, an analysis of its operation is given and a conceptual framework is proposed, which includes the main elements for a successful formalization process.

INFORMAL SETTLEMENTS AND LAND TENURE FORMALIZATION

The rapid urbanization process has led many developing countries to shift from a rural to an urban society in just a couple of decades. Legislation and institutions could not cope with this process. Unstable employment and low wages meant that many were unable to afford formal housing.

Informal settlements are more the norm than the exception in many cities of developing countries (Baross, 1990), with the majority of the inhabitants living in informal areas. The term 'parallel markets' has been used to indicate that there are different market realities in urban development processes (Siembieda, 1994). The increasing population in informal areas made it necessary to change policies towards these settlements.

In the early phase of the rapid urbanization process, formal alternatives have been sought through subsidized social housing and, later, site-and-services projects. Current thinking is more towards accepting informal settlements as part of a solution, instead of a considering it as a problem. Two aspects are of importance: legality (security of land and housing tenure) and physical consolidation (dwelling and infrastructure development).

While in many countries physical upgrading in informal settlements has been practised through the installation of infrastructure, it is sometimes argued (Werlin, 1999) that without land titles physical improvement will not be sustainable. An informal land tenure situation is thought to make it more difficult for people to access mortgages to invest in dwelling construction or obtain loans for the development of employment opportunities. However, these informal land tenure arrangements might be the only feasible option as existing systems of formally registering land titles through conventional procedures are time consuming, difficult and expensive, and the benefits are not very clear for the inhabitants. In such a situation, we cannot speak of being within or outside a legal system (legal apartheid) but indeed of parallel systems, each with its positive and negatives sides.

The growth of Lima and other cities in Peru was slow until the 1940s; in 1940, Lima had a population of some 600 000 inhabitants, while current figures estimate a population of 7 million. Most of the rural–urban migrants could find only informal shelter solutions (see Figure 4.1). The increasing numbers of people living in informal settlements meant that the state could no longer repress these settlements or turn a blind eye and it has gradually become involved in these settlements to gain political support. Military governments were afraid of left-wing support within these areas and started to develop populist strategies, such as relocation and de facto acceptance of land invasions.

In 1961, the first legislative recognition took place with Law 13517, Ley de Barrios Marginales. The ideas behind this law were rather innovative. Much of the experience developed in Peru has later been 'marketed' by the writings of John Turner. Publications by him (e.g. Turner, 1976) and others (Mangin,

Figure 4.1   Informal settlements surround most of Peru's major urban centres. Credit: Ayako Kagawa

1967) have influenced international development agencies such as the United Nations and World Bank to adapt strategies such as site-and-services schemes and settlement upgrading, clearly reflected in the declarations of the first UN Habitat conference in Vancouver in 1976. Twenty years later, the Habitat II conference in Istanbul promoted shelter for all where 'legal and bureaucratic hindrances should be reduced, promotion of efficient and accessible land markets is part of this strategy' (UNCHS, 1996).

Law 13517 considered informal settlements as a given fact and proposed that these areas should legally be integrated into formal methods of urban development. The law consisted of two aspects:

- Legalization, with individual property titles, and physical improvement of existing informal settlements, those established before 20 September 1960.
- To avoid new informal settlements a social housing programme was created (Urbanizaciones Populares de Interés Social, UPIS). These UPIS consisted of core-dwellings incorporating the concept of self-help housing.

Law 13517 created the feeling among the population that properly planned land invasions had a de facto land tenure ownership without fear of eviction and that land titles with formal registered ownership could be obtained in the future. Land invasions therefore became much more planned with clear demarcation of parcels (*lotes tizados*), rectangular building blocks, street pattern and space reserved for social facilities. In Peru, land invasions were tolerated, which meant that squatters on state land held informal property rights.

Since 1961, a number of other laws have been developed to accept new invasions. In the case of Lima, some 200 000 municipal titles were issued in the 1980s (Calderón, 1998). Municipal land titling continued at the discretion of each local government's initiatives and capacities throughout the 1980s.

In 1996, the COFOPRI was set up to formalize informal settlements on a national scale. Details of their operation are discussed below.

Informal and guided land developments: El Porvenir and Alto Trujillo

Urban development consists of macro planning at the city scale and micro planning for specific sites. The urban development process can be divided into land assembly, trunk service provision and zoning, while the site development process is divided into planning (P), servicing (S), building (B) and occupation (O) (Baross, 1990). What matters is the sequence of these activities; while formal developments with finished housing units have the sequence P–S–B–O, informal developments have a reversed development sequence, O–B–S–P.

The major problem of informally developed areas is the slow consolidation process. It can take many years to have basic services installed, while little or no space is reserved for schools, playgrounds, etc. An important advantage of the sequence O–B in informal areas, instead of B–O, is that it improves its affordability; this change in the sequence of development is used in self-help housing schemes such as site-and-services projects.

Alternatives to compete with land invasions and private developments were developed in Bogotá in the 1980s, with the so-called *normas minimas* concept (Molina, 1990), which are basically sites *without* services and the sequence is then P–O–B–S. These schemes are planned urban developments on land acquired by the local housing agency. However, political priorities were more with middle-income social housing and the *normas minimas* as a housing concept for the lower-income groups was never implemented on a large scale. However, similar developments can be seen in Peru, such as the 1970s' development of Villa El Salvador in Lima, and more recently in Trujillo (the third biggest city in Peru), with initiatives labelled as 'guided land developments'.

The development and legalization processes of two different low-income neighbourhoods of Trujillo are briefly described (see Boxes 4.1 and 4.2) using the P–S–B–O model and focusing on land tenure. These cases illustrate that land tenure is a complicated process, which cannot be divided into formal and informal or legal and illegal. While El Porvenir can be classified as informal, in reality land tenure is a process that goes from a completely illegal and insecure land tenure situation (initial stage) to, eventually, registration of individual land titles. If we turn to formally developed low-income neighbourhoods, such as Alto Trujillo, people first received possession certificates and later, after demonstrating that they lived permanently in the area and developed the initial stage of their dwelling, the municipality issued them with individual titles. These titles could then be registered, against a small fee, in the Public Registry. The whole process can take several years.

Box 4.1   El Porvenir, a popular settlement in the urban–rural fringe of Trujillo
Occupation and building: 1934–1960

In 1934, four families invaded some desert land on the outskirts of Trujillo and built their modest dwellings with straw mats, which were gradually replaced with adobe. Growth was initially very slow and by 1945 only 11 families occupied the area. Both municipal councillors and members of the adjacent shooting club started to collect possession fees, while the inhabitants argued that the land belonged to the state. Layout plans were made by the families to accommodate the requests for parcels by low-income families. By 1951, the area was occupied by 2500 inhabitants. Violent clashes took place with the Guardia Civil (military police) as the people refused to pay the fees asked for by the shooting club and the municipality of Simbal. The area was forbidden to consolidate dwellings but growth continued and, in 1955, the population had expanded to around 6000 people and a community organization was founded. In 1958, the population had grown to 9000 and the area received the status of municipal district from the municipality of Trujillo.

Servicing and planning: 1961–2000
With the national law 13517, Porvenir was recognized as a marginal settlement on 15 September 1961. On 8 January 1965, the status of El Porvenir was raised to municipal district through a presidential order. On 13 May 1970, the boundaries were established (the district currently has 29 neighbourhoods and is some 16 km² in size) and official surveying of parcel boundaries and development of layout plans led the informal settlement to meet requirements of urbanization and construction regulations and standards.

On 31 May 1970, Peru was hit by a strong earthquake, which resulted in a massive wave of rural–urban migration and subsequently to new land invasions. Consolidation continued with the issuing of possession certificates.

For several decades the delivery of electricity, water and sewerage services was provisional and it was only in 1979 that piped systems started to be installed. The local community put the local water and electricity company under pressure and the possession titles gave enough security for the infrastructure companies to build the networks.

In 1983, the provincial municipality of Trujillo started issuing land titles, and currently most people of El Porvenir have registered their titles in the Public Registry. According to one of the districts' leaders, this registration is relatively simple.

Land tenure
The land tenure situation in El Porvenir is typical for many land invasions in Peruvian cities. From an initial insecure situation, security is gradually obtained through the possession of certificates and finally individual titles that then can be registered in the Public Registry.

A key factor in the process of land tenure legalization is the level of community organization that will assist in developing the relationship with the municipality for legal and technological consultation and implementation.

The recognition of the neighbourhood and individual tenure security (certificate of possession) is important for the consolidation process and to obtain services. Although it is possible to sell and buy land with possession certificates only, individual registered titles are important in case residents need a loan or mortgage.

Box 4.2   Guided land development in the neighbourhood of 'Alto Trujillo'
The municipality of Trujillo decided in 1995 to adopt a new strategy to deal with the large demand for housing of lower-income groups. The strategy was named 'accessibility and planned occupation with community participation of land' or 'guided land development'. The objective was to offer an alternative to land invasions and illegal subdivisions of agricultural land. In July 1995, the municipality agreed to reserve 580 hectares of land for this guided land development. Within four years (July 1999), Alto Trujillo consisted of seven neighbourhoods accommodating around 5000 households and an estimated population of 22 000 inhabitants. When fully developed, the area can accommodate some 14 000 households with over 60 000 inhabitants on an area of 467 hectares.

Planning and occupation

The municipal master plan indicates various areas suitable for urban expansion. The 'Alto Trujillo' neighbourhood is one of these. The approval of the limits of the neighbourhood is a first step in this guided land development process.

The area is mainly reserved for residential development and norms are set for plot and road size and a simple layout plan is made. Areas are reserved for facilities such as schools, playgrounds and other facilities. The (desert) land originally belonging to the national government will be registered in the Public Registry in the name of the municipality. This phase also consists of the demarcation of parcels and procedures for registration of households interested to obtain a parcel in the area. A standard plot is 140 m^2 (7 × 20) and the area has a gross population density of 192 persons/ha, which is considerable higher than the city average of 116 persons/ha. Households without ownership of a property can obtain a parcel free of charge and receive temporary titles (adjudication).

Building and servicing

Building is an incremental process and most people start with cheap materials such as straw mats, which they later replace with adobe and bricks. Through neighbourhood committees and with support from the municipality, people start to organize themselves to facilitate the consolidation process. The initial development phase is a period of hardship due to the lack of infrastructure and the peripheral location. Gradually, latrines are built, water tanks installed, earth roads developed and soon requests are made to install electricity. Households can obtain loans from the Banco de Materiales to improve and expand their dwellings.

Land tenure

To obtain formal land titles from the municipality, households should show their interest to live in the area, which can be demonstrated through the consolidation of the dwelling with permanent building materials. The experience so far is that most households obtain titles from the municipality within a period of two years. These titles are registered at the Public Registry individually and later on transferred to RPU due to the COFORPI project. Although the land is given free by the municipality, it is through the investment of the households themselves that these areas acquire an economic value.

COMISIÓN DE FORMALIZACIÓN DE LA PROPIEDAD INFORMAL (COFOPRI)

COFOPRI was established in 1996, through a legislative decree, as an autonomous agency under the Ministry of Presidency[1] and was to work in parallel with Registro Predial (RP), which was renamed Registro Predial Urbano (RPU). The law also meant the ending of local government jurisdiction on land tenure formalization.

COFOPRI was to be responsible for the legal and physical verification of informal settlements and their parcels, and issuing its land titles, while

RPU was to be responsible for registering these land titles. The objective of COFOPRI was thus, 'to create a system assuring formal and sustainable rights to real property in selected, predominantly poor settlements in larger urban areas' (World Bank, 1998). Under the name of the Peru Urban Property Rights Project (PUPRP), the World Bank set aside a $38 million loan, and $19 million was to be from the Peruvian national budget, to carry out national-scale formalization. Therefore, it is important to note that while this formalization process was to be a policy for the Peruvian government, it was also to be a project for the World Bank.

The Peruvian government and the World Bank identified three major components: a legal and institutional framework, new organizational arrangements, and a national formalization programme (World Bank, 1998). This chapter will focus on the third component, which was a national formalization programme for issuing and registering land titles to the residents of informal settlements. The formalization process was divided into three stages, shown in Figure 4.2. Process 0 (strategic planning phase) concentrates on collecting all the relevant information. The second step, Process 1 establishes and registers the ownership rights for the settlements. This in fact means possession rights and perimeter plans are developed and recorded in the COFOPRI and RPU database. This is also the stage where informal settlements located in archaeological areas or hazard risk areas and those settlements with land ownership conflicts are identified. The third stage, Process 2, is when the field officers from COFOPRI have the most contact with the community. This involves meetings and individual visits to the dwellings to verify the documents and issuance of land titles and registration.

At the initial stage of its operation, COFOPRI focused on three types of informal settlements, as they estimated 4 million people to be living in these areas. These are *asentamientos humanos* (AAHH), housing associations (UUPP) and co-operatives. The AAHH are mainly characterized as settlements that have developed from the invasion of state land, while UUPP and co-operatives have been developed through the purchase of either state or private land via legal or illegal forms. According to the 1993 Peruvian Census, the AAHH accounted for 72 per cent of the target population (World Bank, 1997). Some AAHH have previously received municipal

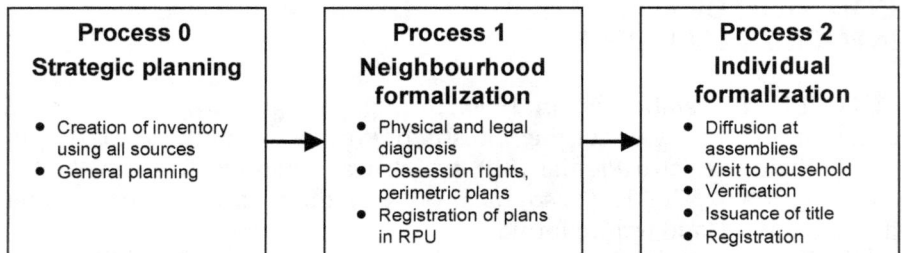

Process 0 Strategic planning	Process 1 Neighbourhood formalization	Process 2 Individual formalization
• Creation of inventory using all sources • General planning	• Physical and legal diagnosis • Possession rights, perimetric plans • Registration of plans in RPU	• Diffusion at assemblies • Visit to household • Verification • Issuance of title • Registration

Figure 4.2   The formalization process.

titles in the 1980s and some have possession certificates. In the case of UUPP and co-operatives, there are no individual titles distributed among the community, since they have purchased the land in a group. What COFOPRI aims to do is to standardize all the documents for these settlements.

The main criteria used to formalize the informal properties initially were:

- Those AAHH, UUPP and co-operatives invaded or recognized prior to March 1996.
- The individual households showed evidence that they are in need of this parcel for dwelling purposes.
- The individual households have been living for more than a year on the parcel and can prove the permanency of their residence.

It is important to note that if a household is composed of a couple and their children, both the man's and woman's names are recorded on the land title to ensure the equal rights to the property. If the household is composed of several siblings, all are recorded. Using this recording system, COFOPRI has been trying to ensure that women and minorities enjoy equal rights to property.

Informal settlements developed on public state land were seen to require fewer legal procedures to be conducted than those settlements on private land. In the latter case, COFOPRI was to play the role of facilitator between the original owner and the de facto residents in order to reach an agreement, whether on physical or financial terms.

COFOPRI and RPU's activities have been prioritized in metropolitan Lima, as the 1993 Census data identified that out of the 914 000 possible informal properties, 478 000 existed in metropolitan Lima. Later, COFOPRI selected several cities outside Lima in which to operate. Table 4.1 illustrates the number of parcels formalized and titled between August 1996 and November 2000. In a presidential speech, Alberto Fujimori promised that 1 million land titles were to be issued nationally before July 2000. One million has since become the magic number for both COFOPRI and RPU, as they saw that this number was large enough to convince the residents in formalized settlements to see themselves as potential clients for the private financial markets.

In Table 4.1, properties are those registered at COFOPRI and individual titles are those that were later registered by RPU. COFOPRI claims that it has been able to deliver the promised quantity and that the operational strategy has been extremely fast and efficient.[2]

Table 4.1   Number of parcels and titles formalized and registered by COFOPRI and RPU

	1996	1997	1998	1999	2000	Total
Properties	50 000	178 000	166 000	509 500	497 000	1 400 500
Individual titles	34 000	129 000	150 000	322 000	398 000	1 033 000

Source: COFOPRI Annual Report (1998), COFOPRI Internal Statistics (November 2000).

The peak of its formalization process was between 1999 and 2000 when a maximum of 2455 personnel[3] were employed. The professional background of the selected personnel have been diverse and included bankers, lawyers, sociologists, economists, architects, civil engineers, programmers and cartographers. What is important is that all management-level personnel have been recruited from the private sector and thus have no working experience in a public sector entity, which may explain the rapid speed of formalization.

During the four years of operation, COFOPRI has been continuously introducing laws, and changing its organizational structure and its operational strategies in order to improve its activities. COFOPRI has also been pressured to solve the problems of invasions after March 1996. This has led it to create a special section within the organization, called the Programa de Lotes Familiares (PROFAM), to deal with the prevention of further invasions. What they identified was a programme that allowed the identification and reservation of areas for urban expansion and adjudication prior to issuing titles. PROFAM's activities started in March 2000 by relocating 10 000 families in Pachacutec, originally military and desert land. These newly relocated residents are then expected to gradually improve their dwellings and environment. In effect, the stance PROFAM takes is one similar to Alto Trujillo as parcels are planned. A demand for 800 000 parcels has been identified nationally and three criteria were established to select those households that were in real need of a parcel:

- The applicant is a family.
- The family shows real necessity for a parcel.
- Currently living with other members of family and in need of a dwelling for own family.

While it is premature to offer a definitive assessment of COFOPRI's activities, it is hard to deny that its existence has been drawn to the attention of Peruvian society. The following review of COFOPRI's achievements and limitations considers its impact so far on the urban landscape.

REFLECTIONS

Fieldwork for this analysis involved a range of stakeholders, including community leaders and household interviews in informal settlements and was structured as a SWOT analysis (Strengths, Weaknesses, Opportunities and Threats).

Strengths

The strengths that can be identified with COFOPRI are extensive. The institutional framework of being an autonomous institution has been an advantage, as it has been able to introduce changes relatively quickly and modify them if they did not suit its activities. This can be reflected in the 24 legislative laws that have been passed since its establishment.

Autonomy and the combination of being a project financially backed by the World Bank have also helped COFOPRI to be independent in its operation. Investment in personnel, facilities (ranging from office space to computers) and mobility in the field have been extensive, and have facilitated quick implementation of operational activities. The investment in personnel has also contributed to both COFOPRI and RPU having a rather dynamic institutional culture compared to traditional public entities, and those involved are proud and satisfied to be involved in treating the problem of poverty and see that their objective is clear. The investment in information technology includes a parcel-based system and linking the graphical information with the data of the property owner.

The mass scale of titling has also achieved a standard formalization process that, once established, can be turned into a routine operation. The specialization and distribution of these tasks to specific personnel has also improved operational inefficiency.

Weaknesses

The centralized and authoritarian approach has been criticized from its initiation, especially from municipalities, as the formalization functions which they had in the 1980s have been taken away. COFOPRI argues that while there have been transparent, conscientious and active municipalities that did see formalization as important, they also claim that there have been municipalities that gave municipal titles to informal settlements without clarifying both the legal tenure and physical cadastre or registering their records in RPI. The irony is that both central and local governments accuse each other of using formalization as part of electoral campaigns.

There have been criticisms that land titles have been duplicated and Calderón (1998) states that there is an issue of redundancy as COFOPRI is retitling what was titled in former times by municipalities. However, from COFOPRI's point of view, these municipal titles are legally ambiguous and there was a need for verification.

Land titling has been concentrated in the so-called AAHH informal settlements, where invasions on public state land have been dominant. In these cases, legal tenure is not a difficult issue as it can transfer the state ownership into the name of COFOPRI and then distribute individual titles when all the residents are identified. Physical occupation is also a relatively minor problem, as often the land is arid, non-productive desert land and there are no major competitions for land use. However, COFOPRI has yet to enter into settlements where there are conflicts because of unclear legal tenure status or the invasion of private property. In this sense, COFOPRI has been criticized for starting from the relatively easier areas in order to increase production.

It was assumed that land titles would facilitate access to credit. However, the major entity that was prepared to give credits to formalized informal settlements was the Banco de Materiales, a public sector entity that is under the Ministry of Presidency. It is important to note that Banco de Materiales does not necessarily give priority to those households that have land titles from COFOPRI. The capacity to pay and permanency of residence are important criteria to access their credit. Of those residents who currently have loans from Banco de Materiales, 25 per cent are said to have defaulted, since they are either unable or unwilling to repay. Banco de Materiales identifies the latter reason as due to COFOPRI because it and RPU have given land for free, giving the beneficiaries the illusion that anything given by the state is for free and therefore there is no need to pay back.

There have been criticisms from the beginning that individual titling would decrease community cohesion and organization, since the moment an individual gains a title, he or she will no longer be interested in developing the neighbourhood, but would focus on consolidating his or her dwelling. Many informal settlements have experienced members of the community who left their parcel as soon as they gained title to the parcel. This poses difficulties for the remaining households who want to develop the neighbourhood by installing infrastructure, such as water and sewerage, for which installation costs are distributed between them. This problem was foreseen by the World Bank, which stressed the fact that 'formalisation is part of a broader process of modernisation' (World Bank, 1998: 11).

There are also doubts about the quality of the verification some of COFOPRI's field officers have been carrying out. A community leader in Lima gave several examples in which somebody other than the de facto residents of particular parcels received the titles.

Limitations in the transparency of the formalization procedure were also identified once it became clear that there are residents in the older consolidated informal settlements who registered their dwellings with RPI prior to 1996, but did not realize that their registration record has now been transferred to the RPU. A resident in El Porvenir, Trujillo, assumed that her land title would be registered in RPI as her dwelling was already titled in the mid-1970s. She stated that COFOPRI had come to the area in the late 1990s, but has not returned since. What is understood, however, is that her dwelling is already transferred from RPI to RPU and a land title by COFOPRI should be issued to her.

Opportunities

While the present political climate will most likely transform from a centralist to a decentralized approach, it is important to note the achievements of COFOPRI and identify the future role COFOPRI could have on a smaller scale than at present. While there are some voices that call for the deactivation of COFOPRI and its formalization programme, COFOPRI and entities such as RPU, the Institute of Metropolitan Planning (IMP), the National Institute for Urban Research (INADUR) and various NGOs see that there are still many options that COFOPRI can take.

COFOPRI itself sees that in the future, as major mass titling has been accomplished in the larger urban areas of Peru, its strategy will be geared more towards capacity building in smaller municipalities to carry out formalization using the COFOPRI formula. This activity has already begun, as a decree was passed in March 2001 to create a Commission at the local level (Government of Peru, 2001).

COFOPRI wants to keep the quality and the process of formalization they have developed in the past four years. Its director feels that COFOPRI has the 'know-how' and therefore would like to apply this experience throughout Peru, so that there is a universal guarantee on the quality of the formalization process. This can be seen as an opportunity for Peru from the land administration perspective, as it means they are able to rely on one standard procedure. COFOPRI and RPU are also starting to develop a strategy where they are trying to link their clients and the private sector banks. The banks are beginning to show an interest in the residents of formalized settlements. COFOPRI and RPU claim that out of the 1 million households, 10 per cent do have the potential to pay back as they are employed and the level of consolidation of their dwellings is relatively high. For example, an agreement has been reached between COFOPRI, RPU and Banco de Wiese Sudameris, which allows the bank to access the database the two public entities have been developing in order to select or check their potential clients' portfolio. The databases include positive portfolios of potential clients in terms of whether they pay their taxes, water and electricity bills regularly, have a social security number and are employed, etc.

What COFOPRI and RPU have learnt is that, ironically, there is no such thing as the formal city and the problem of urban tenure also exists in those areas recognized to be formal. There are superimpositions of registration, and informal tenure arrangements are even more complicated in the city proper than in the informal settlements. This is also reflected in a comment given by the director of RPI in the Trujillo office, who thinks that 40 per cent of the historical colonial centre of Trujillo has duplicated land registration.

There is a consensus among entities related to formalization and registration that the current environment of parallel registries cannot continue. There have been preparatory movements between the two registries discussing how the two registry systems could be integrated. RPI has been established longer but has increasing problems of information management, while RPU has a shorter history and a modern cadastre-based registration system. The technology for integration is there and it is possible to carry it out within a decade. However, the greatest barrier to the integration process is how two different registries with different institutional cultures can be integrated with minimum friction.

Threats

One of the biggest threats COFOPRI is facing currently is that of dependency on political stability. As this policy was introduced under the Fujimori administration, opposition parties see COFOPRI as an entity established for a political campaign. What may relieve this uncertainty a little is the fact that it is also a World Bank project, which has so far been very well received and is proposed to continue until 2003. There is an urgent need for COFO-PRI and RPU to develop a strategy to avoid being pulled into political manoeuvring, both at national and local levels, and to state their position on how they want to continue their operation.

There is a danger that a new administration may not have the objective capacity to judge both the benefits and limitations of COFOPRI and thus eliminate all the achievements. Even if operations may not be deactivated but decentralized, it is possible that municipalities have an allergy towards the norms and frameworks that COFOPRI has developed and will refuse to apply them, claiming that they will be able to develop a better model.

Another threat COFOPRI will face is the issue of cost recovery. As the PUPRP is a loan project, there is a need for the Peruvian government to establish a mechanism in which it does not have to rely on additional financial flows in the future, but can be self-sustaining. In this respect, the option of integration with RPU and RPI would allow formalization to be financially accountable. Unfortunately for COFOPRI, the macro-economic climate of Peru has not been favourable for testing whether land titles trigger access to credit. Under the current economic crisis, even residents of the formal city are unable to access credit as banks are afraid of default. Yet it is also true that had the economic situation not degenerated to its present state, private banks may never have talked with COFOPRI and RPU to discuss possibilities for their property owners to be clients in the future.

It is important to question what the necessary conditions are in order to have a successful land tenure formalization process. To do this, the urban land tenure issue must be seen as part of a wider development process.

Figure 4.3 demonstrates that in order to develop a land tenure policy framework, two key elements need to be satisfied. These are: first, political stability that supports formalization as an important policy; and second, institutional stability that allows technocratic implementation with minimum political interference. Within such an environment, land tenure formalization can be implemented with efficiency and effectiveness. While Hernando de Soto claimed that formalization will automatically create an environment that facilitates access to credit, and physical consolidation can follow later, from the current investigation it is possible to state that this does not occur as directly and simply as he had speculated. In reality, legal consolidation can only be effective when social interactions and economic opportunities occur in parallel. Economic opportunities means

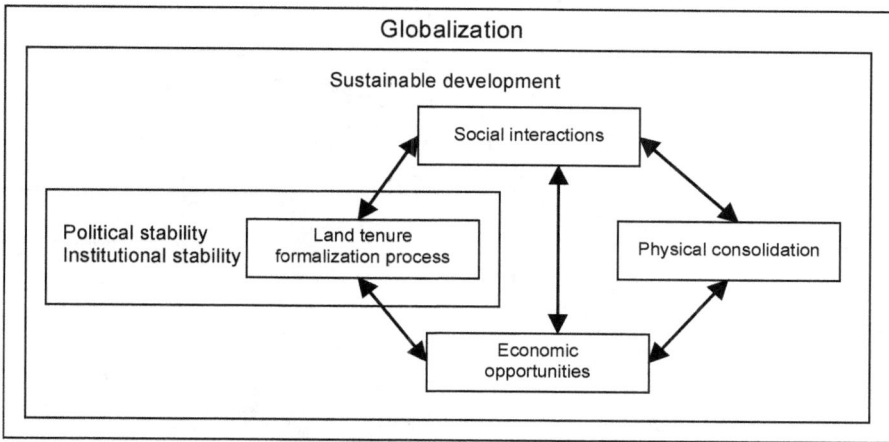

Figure 4.3 Conceptual framework of a land tenure formalization process.

making use of land titles as collateral and accessing credits both for physical consolidation of the dwelling and improving their economic activities. In cases where employment opportunities are limited, there is a need to establish interaction with the social environment both at household and settlement level in order to increase the opportunities for physical consolidation and employment. COFOPRI and RPU are now developing methods to increase the chances of economic consolidation by guaranteeing private banks that their titles and registration are viable. As stated above, only 10 per cent of formalized residents are potential clients for the private sector finance institutions.

On the other hand, COFOPRI expects that 90 per cent of the households in formalized settlements will not be eligible for loans from private banks. These people will depend on social networks to develop both their dwelling and neighbourhood. These social networks (de Souza, 1999) can help to make the community realize that legal consolidation is not an end, but a means to an end. Comments by community leaders in the informal settlements illustrate that group- or community-based applications for infrastructure services are much more effective than applications representing an individual interest. In this sense, development is based on 'socially created value' developed by the initiatives of the residents.

It is interesting to question and analyse what the impact of COFOPRI is, and to see whether it is only the legal and physical consolidation that is crucial, or whether the element of time influences this consolidation process.

Figure 4.4 illustrates schematically the impact and the role of COFOPRI for informal settlements. C1 illustrates the process of development in invaded settlements. C2 illustrates de Soto's theory, where physical consolidation increases soon after the property receives legality. However, while legal consolidation is important, it is not able to accelerate physical

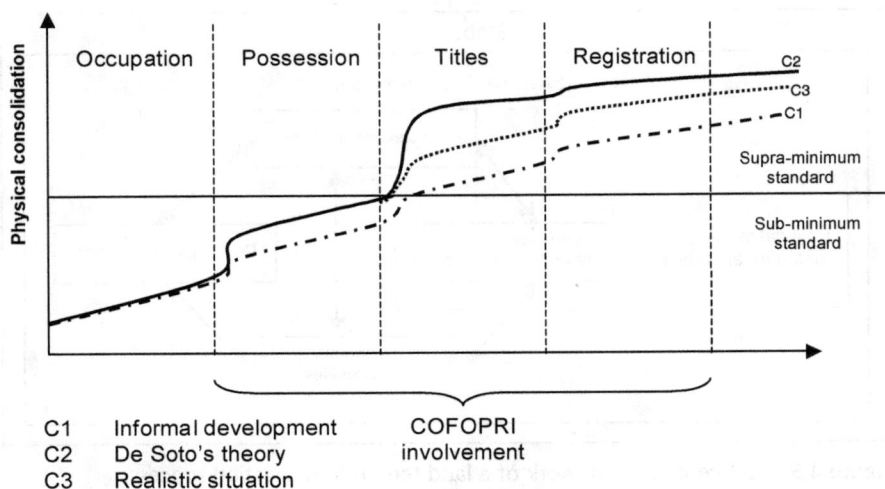

Figure 4.4   Impact of COFOPRI.

consolidation, as factors such as time and socioeconomic interaction between the owner and the neighbourhood are also important. Therefore, C3 is the realistic curve whereby the upgrading of legality by COFOPRI has stimulated a certain extent of physical consolidation, but not at the scale or rate that de Soto projected.

POLICY IMPLICATIONS

To issue and register 1 million land titles affecting some 5 million urban residents (25 per cent of the total Peruvian urban population) within a few years is a major political and project management achievement. Some concluding remarks can be made regarding the costs and benefits of the COFOPRI approach, whether its operation has improved access to secure tenure, and whether it has had an impact on the wider urban land and housing market. The future of the land tenure formalization process and urban development, as well as the importance of the Peruvian experience for other countries that are in an earlier phase of urban land tenure formalization or considering starting such programmes, are also important points to consider.

The technocratic and dynamic approach of COFOPRI has made other public entities aware that to achieve efficiency, institutional culture matters a great deal. The disadvantage of its approach has been the lack of integration with other public entities, resulting in a normative framework that others did not comply with.

COFOPRI has increased legal and perceived security of tenure. All households interviewed felt that a title is important, as it is a legal guarantee that nobody can remove. However, many households felt that there are other elements, such as the dwelling itself, the ability to repay the loan and improve their dwelling, the length of residence, neighbourhood recognition that you are the resident and owner, that also influence their sense of security. In COFOPRI's mass titling, distortion of the land market is minimal, since most of the land formalized is on unproductive public state land that has never been on the formal urban land market. The housing market is also not disturbed as all invasions have occurred because of the limited supply of housing in the first place.

When considering the exportability of COFOPRI's approach, the head of COFOPRI has been clear that 'it is important to decide what type of land tenure a country wants' (COFOPRI institutional interview, 2000). While COFOPRI has been successful in Peru, 'it is only the vision, but not the system' that should be exported, as every country has to develop its own model.

Land tenure, land titling and registration

Theoretically, land tenure should not be an issue as it should be clear, transparent and reliable for everybody. The major driving force behind the massive land titling project in Peru is to create this stability as a 'conditio sine qua non' for development. An unambiguous land tenure situation is supposed to create an environment in which development will flourish.

Peru has been fortunate in its urban development from a land tenure perspective. Since the 1960s, cities have expanded mainly through 'planned invasions' on peripheral state-owned, unproductive, sandy land, with de facto property ownership. In such cases, formalization of land is relatively easy; it is a matter of stepping up formalization of informal property rights, through simplified procedures and converting the long-standing practice of locally issued titles into registered titles. This has been the case for COFOPRI, as the dominant land used for the informal settlements has been on unproductive desert land owned by the state. For COFOPRI, it is much more difficult to formalize land tenure in those areas with private, and frequently conflicting, land-ownership claims that they are currently entering, but with much caution.

Central or local?

In the 1980s, formalization was a municipal responsibility and this role was taken over by COFOPRI in 1996. The driving force to centralize land titling is mainly political. The central issue is how such a project, after its current sponsored phase, will be embedded into existing local or central institutions.

The status of COFOPRI changed in March 2001, as a decree to establish a Commission of Formalizing Informal Property at the local level was passed. Considering local governments have closer links to the communities,

NGOs, infrastructure companies, etc., they will not only reduce overhead costs, but also facilitate involvement in crucial social interactions. What is important to develop is the institutional capacity at all levels, in order to maintain both the quality of land titles and institutional accountability. In this sense, whether it is national or local government that has created the basis should not be an issue, as long as it has been able to deliver the products.

Political stability and commitment

COFOPRI was established in the first year of the second term of Alberto Fujimori's administration (1990–2000), in an environment in which it was easy to implement changes suited to its political taste. Political stability and institutional continuity are needed not only to develop ideas, but also to implement them. The disadvantage of COFOPRI is that projects such as PUPRP, with a limited project period, special funding and closely related to political interest, are not a guarantee for continuity and maintenance.

Within the political context, *simple and transparent* processes to avoid bribery and other unnecessary costs are crucial. The formalization process in Peru has done much to create the legal framework and technical specifications to simplify procedures and inform the people.

Community organization

The involvement of grass-roots organizations has facilitated the formalization process of COFOPRI. This is seen as crucial in both the land titling project and guided land development projects. Consolidation of the neighbourhood, dwelling improvement, development of facilities such as schools, playgrounds, etc., needs an organized community that can negotiate with all kinds of institutions. Honest and elected neighbourhood representatives living in the area are important success factors for titling and consolidation.

Credit

Credit for dwelling improvements should be within the economic capacities of the people. The (low) income situation of many households is much more critical compared to having a registered legal title. Commercial credit providers and banks are not yet interested in taking a significant step into this mortgage market due to the relatively small and risky loans involved. This theme needs more investigation in the next few years to evaluate the amount of credit in formalized settlements, as this is one of the major justifications for the titling project.

Institutional and inter-institutional capacity building

The success of land tenure formalization is dependent on institutional accountability. COFOPRI's model has shown that it is possible to have such institutions as long as there is a positive commitment at all institutional levels. Capacity building by COFOPRI in smaller municipalities is starting because both can benefit from the formalization process using the COFO-PRI formula and municipal initiatives. There are also movements by private banks to use the database from COFOPRI to create a portfolio for prospective credit clients.

Monitoring and evaluation

There is a need for continuous critical assessment of the development of land tenure formalization. If a one-off assessment is made, there are neither archives nor future records when urban tenure issue is a dynamic process. In this respect, there is a need for a longitudinal study to be implemented.

The Peruvian experience highlights a case in which the informal city is rapidly becoming part of the formal city in its legal framework and slowly in its economic framework. COFOPRI has been able to implement a formalization process proactively, due to the fact that many informal settlements are located on unproductive desert land already in public ownership. It is part of its future challenge to deal with those settlements that are located on private land and carry out their formalization process in a decentralized environment with greater local government involvement. What is ironic is that the existence of COFOPRI has revealed, through the formalization process, that the formal city's tenure discrepancies are becoming increasingly exposed. This has led Peruvian land-related organizations to realize that they need to deal with the urban land tenure issue in a more integrated manner.

PART III

IMPROVING SECURITY BY INCREASING RIGHTS

CHAPTER FIVE

What is secure tenure in urban Egypt?

David Sims

INTRODUCTION

This chapter assesses the extent to which various land tenure systems provide adequate security of tenure in urban Egypt's vast and growing informal settlements, with a particular emphasis on how these systems benefit or protect the poor and disadvantaged. 'Adequate' security of tenure is measured by the same five criteria as other case studies in this book, namely the extent to which it:

1 protects against arbitrary eviction/demolition
2 encourages investment and house improvement
3 allows for the provision of infrastructure and public services
4 permits market values to apply to property
5 allows owners to leverage equity for credit.

The information used to support the discussion comes from a number of sources.[1] The chapter begins with a short background to certain aspects of informal urban tenure which are particular to Egypt. It is important that the Egyptian context is understood, since in many ways Egypt does not conform to generally perceived notions of urban informality, poverty and the extents of state power in developing countries.

CONTEXT

The extent and nature of informal settlements

It is only a slight exaggeration to say that informality is *the* defining characteristic of the modern Egyptian city. Starting in the 1950s and 1960s, significant desert areas on the urban fringes began to be squatted. In parallel, even larger areas of fringe private agricultural holdings began to be subdivided and built upon in contravention of laws regulating planning, construction, the registration of property and the preservation of agricultural resources. By the late 1970s, the phenomenon had outstripped formal urban expansion. For example, in 1981, it was estimated that over 80 per cent of new housing units in Greater Cairo were being produced by the informal sector (Abt Associates Inc. and Dames and Moore Inc. 1982). By

1996, in spite of increasingly strict legislation proscribing illegal construction, in many cities informal areas represented more than half of all residential areas. A recent study estimates that in Greater Cairo 52 per cent of residential districts are informal (as measured by net surface area), and that 62 per cent of the metropolitan population live in these areas (Sims, 2000: 8). The same study identifies several typologies of residential informality, as shown in Table 5.1.

Table 5.1   Extent of informal residential areas in Greater Cairo

Typology/subtypology		Net surface area (km²)	Percentage
A1	On private agricultural land	105.5	81.6
A2	On core village land	3.5	3.0
A3	On government agricultural land	4.2	3.3
B1	On local administration (desert) land	4.3	3.3
B2	On reclaimed (desert) land	3.9	3.0
B3	On decree (desert) land	7.8	6.0
	Total	129.2	100.0

As the table shows, the vast majority (81 per cent) of informal settlements are on private agricultural land, with informal development on desert (state) lands limited to about 10 per cent of the total. The remainder of informal settlements are on agricultural land nominally controlled by the state. These figures for Greater Cairo reflect more or less the situation in other towns. In some cities, such as Alexandria, the portion of informal areas on desert lands is significantly higher, and local variations are common (for example settlements on religious endowment land (*awqaf*) and on desert land where Bedouin have customary rights).

Unlike many developing countries, in Egypt there is virtually no squatting on, or invasion of, private land. Moreover, private landowners practically never allow – under any formal or informal leasing arrangements – the occupation of their vacant lands by settlers.

Quality of informal construction

The quality of most construction in informal areas in Egypt is remarkably good, with the most common type being three- to six-storey apartment blocks of reinforced concrete frame and slab construction with brick infill walls. Quality tends to be slightly better in informal areas on agricultural land than those on desert land. Only in small pockets (usually on public rights of ways and in just-squatted desert areas) does one find precarious construction that begins to evoke the images of informal settlements standard in many parts of the developing world.

The nature of urban poverty

Although poverty and unemployment is pervasive in urban Egypt – studies suggest that as many as 40 per cent of urban households are below the official poverty line (Government of Egypt, 2000) – it is important to understand three aspects of this poverty:

- Many urban families may be income-poor, but possess significant assets, usually in the form of property acquired or built in the past, most commonly as a result of savings generated from work in the neighbouring oil-rich countries and appreciation of land values.
- Urban poverty is not, as a rule, geographically segregated or particularly concentrated. Within and around higher-income residential districts, poor residents are common and, conversely, within even the poorest informal areas a significant number of professionals, traders, contractors, etc., can be found, as well as lower-middle-class families.
- The phenomenon of pavement dwellers and other absolutely precarious forms of clustering of the ultra-poor, such as hutments along railway tracks, is not common in urban Egypt. Nor is squatting in public buildings or on privately owned land.

Legal options for tenure

In Egypt, where the legal system is heavily influenced by the Napoleonic Code, stress is placed on the inalienable right of an individual to use and benefit from his private property, and freehold tenure is the focus of the bulk of the civil code, criminal code and executive legislation dealing with property rights. Except for a couple of minor land/property rental systems discussed below, there are no specific provisions in law for leasehold urban land tenure. (Only in the past decade have laws been passed regulating the contractual, time-bound leasing of agricultural land and of housing units.) There has been no legislation introduced to provide innovative tenure frameworks which aim to address the needs of informal areas. And as a unified republic, in Egypt, neither governorates nor municipalities have any significant authority to introduce local tenure variations.

Security of housing tenancies

Well over half of urban families in Egypt rent their dwelling units. The vast majority of these – those renting before 1996 – enjoy extremely secure tenancies based on successive laws dealing with the relations of landlord and tenant. There is no time limit to the rental period (and contracts pass to offspring on the death of the tenant), rents cannot be raised and grounds for eviction are very few. This secure rental system exists in informal settlements as well as formal residential areas. In poorer areas, even if a renter cannot show a written document, his tenancy is sanctioned by community pressure, and local police stations, who rely on the testimony of neighbours, inevitably favour the tenant over the landlord in disputes. Such security of tenure even extends to business premises. There are cases of tricks to force tenant eviction (the most popular of which is to 'encourage' the collapse of old structures for the land value), but these are exceptions to the norm.

Police power and evictions

Both by law and by local authority policy, there is little arbitrary eviction and demolition of residential property in Egypt, no matter how dubious its tenure status. If the property is occupied, physical demolition is impossible, unless alternative housing is offered by the concerned governorate. (This alternative housing may be in a remote and shoddy public housing block without connected utilities, and the allocation of this housing may be chaotic, but this is another story.) Local governments have backlogs of thousands of 'demolition orders' because a particular building has transgressed some law, but the payment of a small fine (and sometimes a larger bribe) usually closes the case.[2] In effect, local authorities in Egypt see demolition and eviction as no-win headaches, to be avoided if at all possible. Authorities usually act only when they uncover actual construction in progress and before occupation, thus explaining the frenzied building activity common in informal areas on Fridays, during holidays and even at night, when government inspectors are unlikely to appear.

THE ARRAY OF TENURE POSSIBILITIES ON DESERT (STATE) LAND

There is a range of formal, semi-formal and informal tenure possibilities for informal settlements built on state land, practically all of which is desert land. Such desert land is by law state domain land, which, by executive law or presidential decree, can be transferred to the authority/ownership of local authorities (governorates), the military, the land reclamation authority, the antiquities authorities, the new settlements authority (Ministry of Housing, Utilities and New Communities) or specialized state development agencies. Within the Civil Code and by executive legislation there are mechanisms by which the tenure of parcels of such land may be sold to or claimed by private entities (individuals and companies), both before and after such land has been occupied. The intent of these mechanisms is to encourage the productive development of Egypt's vast desert areas. As can be imagined, the distribution of such land is subject to considerable pressure from various private interests.

Urban squatting has historically occurred on the desert fringes of existing towns where the land was largely under the authority of governorates or state enterprises. The success of such squatting and its extent have always depended on particular local factors, but until recently it was largely condoned or allowed to occur as long as the land in question was of little value or had not already been assigned to institutions that had the power or influence to protect it.[3] Property owners in these squatted areas can enjoy various degrees of tenure security that are usually combinations of official documentation and de facto recognition of the existing situation. The array of such tenure possibilities are briefly noted in the following paragraphs, starting with the most secure and working down.

Registered freehold tenure

Various laws prescribe the conditions and procedures under which a squatter (a condition called *wada' yed* or 'hand claim') can apply for freehold ownership of the land he or she occupies (most recently, Law 31 of 1984). In all cases, the process (*tamlik*) must first be sanctioned by a local governor's decree opening the *tamlik* in a particular area. In addition, a government committee must be formed to set the price of the land, which must be purchased from the state, usually a schedule of nominal values based on the width of the street on which the property is located. Also, at least in the past few years, the area designated for *tamlik* must first have been planned, and the detailed plans (street widths, building lines and public land uses) approved. The process of *tamlik* starts with the claimant submitting a standard application to the local administration with a down payment and accompanied by various proofs of occupation/ownership (see the various types of recognized hand claims described below). There are a bewildering number of surveying and administrative steps that must be taken, and the burden is always on the claimant to pursue the trajectory of paperwork through various offices and cover the fees (and sometimes bribes) involved. At the end of the process, a claimant receives a preliminary title (*aqd ibtida'i*) and, assuming he or she follows a schedule of instalment payments normally lasting five to 15 years, final title (*aqd niha'i*) is issued. Only at this point can the ownership title be registered officially at the property registry (*shahr el aaqari*), normally a prerequisite for a building licence to be issued should the owner wish to rebuild.

This *tamlik* process has been applied only selectively in Egypt and with varied success, almost always in older and mature settlements (as the state does not want to reward squatting). Some *tamlik* has been associated with external assistance projects (Hay el Salam and Abou Atwa in Ismailia, Nasseriya in Aswan and Helwan Community Upgrading) and others have been initiated due to local political pressures (Agami and Ameriya in Alexandria, Manshiet el Shohada' in Ismailia, etc.).

In theory, the Civil Code allows a squatter to apply for land ownership if he proves that he has 'improved' it and resided for at least 15 years.[4] A lengthy procedure with the public registry is specified. In practice, such a mechanism is almost never successful and is rarely attempted, but it can generate documentation, which in itself gives the claimant a certain security.

Freehold tenure under process

The above system in pursuit of registered freehold tenure may be initiated but suspended for various reasons. The claimant himself may give up at some point along the way (usually out of frustration at the hassles and costs) or the local administration may officially freeze *tamlik* in an area, or simply kill it by benign neglect. Although by law no property rights accrue to the claimant until he receives the preliminary contract, those who have initiated the process usually feel a bit more secure than neighbours who have not, i.e. another piece of paper always helps.

El Hekr land rent system

The *hekr* land rent (*hekr* means ground rent or quitrent in Arabic) is set out in the Civil Code (articles 999 to 1012). It allows the renting of land for a set period but with a maximum of 60 years. The leaseholder can dispose of his right, the contract can be registered and the leaseholder owns outright all improvements he/she introduced on the land (plantings, buildings). The ground rent, payable annually, should not be less than the rent of equivalent premises.

Local authorities sometimes resort to the *hekr* system to control and gain revenues from encroachments on desert public land (usually in the case of individual land reclamation efforts), and the rents are collected by the concerned governorate's *amlak* (properties) departments. Theoretically, such a system gives squatters considerable rights, but it is rarely applied for urban encroachments. In the few urban expansion cases known (Ismailia, Alexandria, Aswan), nominal *hekr* rents are simply imposed without contracts, maps or a set period, and its main value is that it provides a paper basis for launching the *tamlik* process in areas where no other proofs of occupation exist. The *hekr* system is also used by specialized state authorities (e.g. the Religious Endowments Authority and the Suez Canal Authority) to regulate and gain income from their (mostly agricultural) lands.

Hand claim with property taxes

In established squatter areas, the Ministry of Finance, through its revenue branches in local administrative units (*idarat el iradat*), will identify and record buildings and assess the 'owner' with an annual property tax (*aawayid*) regardless of the status of claims on the land. The tax rate on residences is usually small and is calculated on the theoretic rental revenues such units should render. Every ten years the properties in a particular revenue district are reassessed through property-by-property field surveys, from which are produced detailed descriptions of the property (*kashf el mushtemalat*), which are entered in the tax rolls. The existence of this description and payment of the associated taxes is a prerequisite (at least

Box 5.1 Manshiet Nasser – a massive informal settlement on state land

Figure 5.1 Building in progress in Manshiet Nasser.

Extensive limestone quarries abutting the Muqattam Hills, owned by Cairo Governorate, started to be settled in the 1960s. The first inhabitants had been pushed out of huts in nearby inner-city locations and told by authorities to relocate in the abandoned quarries which, at the time, were on the extreme eastern limits of the city. By the end of the 1960s the population had reached several thousand and, on hearing about the settlement, President Gamal Abdel Nasser ordered that water and power be extended to it. Hence the name of the settlement. In 1972, Cairo Governorate ordered the relocation of the mainly Christian garbage collector community (*zabaaliin*) to one part of Manshiet Nasser. By the end of the 1970s the area had over 100 000 inhabitants and was growing rapidly, with most people coming originally from Upper Egyptian villages. Its relatively central location within the metropolis, plus its range of cheap rental accommodation, made it particularly attractive to poor families.

This encroachment on state land was illegal, but although there were no official documents to prove otherwise, settlers perceived that they had rights derived from the fact that: (i) it was the state that first told them to settle there, and (ii) the state recognized their existence by providing services (however minimal). A first attempt at regularizing the area came in the late 1970s as part of the World Bank's First Urban Project in Egypt, with a scheme for titling existing plots and using the land revenues to finance needed infrastructure. Due to a number of factors, the project came to nothing. Except for the introduction of some schools and health facilities (and foreign NGO initiatives in the *zabaaliin* community), the area was left by the government to develop under a kind of benign neglect. In the mid-1990s, with the population exceeding 400 000 (at average net residential densities exceeding 2000 persons per hectare) and an increased government concern about informal areas as hotbeds of fundamentalism, Cairo Governorate allowed building owners to apply for freehold title. Fixing the price of the land proved problematic, with residents arguing that it was they who had made the land inhabitable and had created any real estate value that could be assigned to the land. In any event, the land titling was never undertaken seriously, and it was frozen in 1998. At the same time, the minister of housing announced a totally unrealistic scheme of wholesale demolition of Manshiet Nasser and the rehousing of inhabitants in public housing blocks, the first-phase construction of which was started in 1999 with much fanfare. This created more confusion and distrust, a situation which has only been remedied with the commitment of government during the November 2000 parliamentary elections to replan and upgrade the area and record and title all land holdings, rehousing only a small fraction of families.

in squatter areas where the system applies) for applying for *tamlik*, and it is also now a prerequisite for obtaining metered electricity connections.

The *aawayid* tax system is generally poorly administered at the local level (lack of maps and addresses, manpower shortages for field work and faulty record keeping), but it bestows hand claim squatters with considerable legitimacy. It also serves as a documentary base for property transfers, a feature on which the market puts a premium.

Hand claim with usufruct rent

The usufruct rent system *(haq el intifaa)* is briefly defined in the Civil Code. It is intended to grant usufruct over real property; with the stipulation that such property should be maintained in the condition in which it was handed over. The period of rent may be limited or unlimited, but in all cases expires with the death of the leaseholder. In practice, local authorities frequently use it to rent out space in buildings and markets and for stalls and kiosks. It is occasionally applied to occupied public land, and it is an additional rent that must be paid (dated from the time the structure was built) as part of the *tamlik* process. Under usufruct rent of public land, the state reserves the right to acquire the land for public purposes without compensation to the leaseholder. In practice, the usufruct system seems to be rarely used for informal settlements on desert land and does not bestow any significant rights to the occupiers other than another slip of paper.

Hand claim with electricity/water connections

Gaining metered electricity connections (and to a lesser extent water connections) is an important step for a squatter to gain legitimacy for his/her encroachment. In the absence of the tenure situations described above, it is practically the only way to have a contractual relationship with the state. Although in itself it gives no rights, the proof of monthly electricity bills in the squatter's name bestows a certain security and proof of occupation, something that can be important either for the *tamlik* process or to be assigned public housing should (in rare cases) the dwelling need removal.

Recently, in Cairo Governorate at least, to obtain an electricity connection requires: (a) a certification from an engineer that the dwelling is sound and was built before 1996, and (b) proof of payment of the *aawayid* (property tax). Yet there is no law *per se* that prevents utilities authorities from providing service connections to unauthorized developments, and most mature informal settlements are provided with basic utilities services. For example, in Cairo Governorate, 87 per cent of all families have piped water connections and 98 per cent have access to electricity.[5]

Documented transfer of hand claims

Almost all sales of squatter properties are at least based on simple *aurfi* contracts (signed by the two parties as well as two male witnesses), considered by the judiciary as a primary contract. It is not uncommon, should the parties wish stronger documentation, for these to be endorsed by a relatively simple and inexpensive court procedure called *dawa saha wa towqia*. This process does not, however, represent in any way an acknowledgement of ownership.

Traditional Bedouin rights

Although not specifically referred to in law, in practice, local authorities respect the traditional rights of Bedouin tribes, at least in the sense that they have a 'first claim' in certain desert areas coming under encroachment/development. The most striking example is found west of Alexandria, where Bedouin are the virtual arbiters of initial development. They act as land brokers, define parcellation, guard encroachments and set informal market prices. Those wishing to purchase land in these areas find they must pay for the land twice, once to the Bedouin and again to the Alexandria Amlak Department. Bucking this system is not advised.

According to the 1996 Census, the population of Ezbet el Haggana (see Box 5.2) stood at 35 000 inhabitants on an area of 220 hectares, representing a gross density of only 160 persons per hectare. Recently Cairo Governorate has attempted to regularize the land tenure situation by sanctioning trilateral negotiations between residents (land claimers), the Medinet Nasser company, and the military. Sewerage works have started, but most utilities and public services are still seriously deficient.

Box 5.2   Ezbet el Haggana – an extensive low-density settlement
on state desert land

Figure 5.2   Layout of Ezbet el Haggana.

Ezbet el Haggana first started in the late 1950s as an informal settlement at K4.5 on the Suez Road (about 16 km from downtown Cairo) set up by members of the frontier/desert corps (thus the name 'haggana'). These policemen were allowed by their superiors to erect housing for their families, although no official written permission was given. This constituted the core of informal development in an area which was, at the time, extremely remote from Cairo and of virtually no real estate value. In 1958, the Medinet Nasser Public Housing Company Concession was issued, which included, at least nominally, the whole of what is now Ezbet el Haggana, but until the early 1980s the company had no interest in such a remote site.

In the 1960s and 1970s a number of public sector company factories (most notably the Arab Automotive factories north of the Suez road just one kilometer east of K4.5) and military camps/depots were set up in the general area. In the late 1970s, the general boom in informal housing found the vacant lands south of the original settlement to be extremely attractive as the cheapest land in Greater Cairo for someone with limited equity who wished to begin the owner-builder process. In 1984–85, parcels could be found for as little as LE4–6 per square metre. And the disadvantages of a remote location became less burdensome as various forms of both public and private collective transport into central Cairo became increasingly available along the Suez Road.

By 1985 informal development had expanded considerably. One area of squatting east of K 4.5 on the Suez Road was removed by the military, but in general, the informal extension process was ignored by authorities. Consequently, no power or water services were provided to the area.

The expansion process was extremely land hungry (walled land claims were large in area and only slowly subdivided), and vacant parcels were held for what was a very profitable speculative business. In the late 1980s, land claims reached south to what was planned as Medinet Nasser's east–west arterial to the ring road, and roughly at this time Ezbet el Haggana came into direct conflict with the eastward expanding housing developments of the Medinet Nasser Company. Eventually an understood limit demarcating the informal from the formal areas was established.

THE ARRAY OF TENURE POSSIBILITIES ON PRIVATE AGRICULTURAL LAND

As mentioned above, the majority of informal urban development has occurred and continues to occur on privately owned agriculture land on the fringes of cities and towns. The history of this land is important. A national cadastre of agricultural land was undertaken in the early decades of the 20th century which mapped and registered all agricultural parcels, most of which were smallholdings. To these were added registered parcels resulting from the break-up of large farm estates following the land reforms of the revolutionary government in the 1950s. As urban expansion accelerated in the 1950s and 1960s, the subdivision of private agricultural strips and extensions by owner-builders became increasingly popular. From a tenure point of view, three factors pushed this kind of urban development into increasing informality and illegality:

- contravention of planning and building laws
- contravention of laws protecting agricultural land
- ignoring property registration laws.

Thus, although millions of property owners in informal urban areas on agricultural land 'own' their properties and can exchange them, they are hopelessly far from satisfying even some of the prerequisites of formality and titled ownership. The following paragraphs briefly describe the array of tenure possibilities, starting with the most secure (although basic security from removal is normally good in these areas once a building is built).

Registered freehold tenure

In spite of the many contraventions that owners face, in rare cases it is possible to register informal building parcels on agricultural land and gain recognized title. This can occur only when the chain of transfer/inheritance (*tasalsul naql el milkiya* and *aalan el wirasa*) from the last time the parcel was registered (usually decades ago) can be established and documented, and documented proof of paying real estate taxes can be produced. In addition, the property itself must be properly identified, no mean feat when survey maps do not exist, or date from the early decades of the 20th century. If these obstacles can be surmounted, the effort still requires dogged perseverance, legal assistance, years of patience and usually influence/bribes. For the small minority of properties where the process is feasible, the result is hardly worth the time and money required, unless new construction is desired (see below).

Court-sanctioned registration of ownership

A new owner who wishes to register his property in the public registry but finds the above procedures impossible, may resort to the courts and file a lawsuit called *dawa saha wa nafaz*, a procedure that can be almost as Herculean, especially if more than a couple of informal transactions have taken place concerning the land. However, if the plaintiff eventually wins, the judge's ruling creates a document, which can be registered at the public registry as a substitute for the chain of proofs otherwise required.

Informal ownership with building permit and/or permit from the Ministry of Agriculture

Following the harsh military decree of 1996, construction without a building permit exposes the developer to stiff fines and imprisonment and makes obtaining such a permit worthwhile. Even though the law on construction requires proof of registered ownership as part of the application for a building licence, it is understood that in rare cases, and after considerable manipulation of the system, a developer may actually obtain such a permit, especially if the site is located along a main street and is considered to be inside city or town boundaries (*huduud el tanzim* or *el hayz el amrani*). Furthermore, both inside and outside these boundaries, someone wishing to build on agricultural land faces another military decree of 1996, which proscribes any construction on agricultural land. To circumvent this, another set of elaborate and costly manipulations of the system must be undertaken to have the land declared unfit for agricultural purposes (*ard boor*) by the concerned agricultural authorities.

Informal private ownership

The owners of the vast majority of urban parcels on agricultural land, both vacant and built up, enjoy a somewhat murky but nonetheless solidly recognized ownership. Their individual plots are usually the result of multiple mutations of the land over decades (sale of larger agricultural parcels to smaller ones, inheritance parcellation, incremental subdivision for building, resell of vacant plots, sale of built apartment units, etc.), and in each of these transactions simple written contracts of sale with two witnesses (*aurfi* contracts) are the only paper records, if that. These cannot be registered, and in any event registration would incur the significant land transfer tax (normally 2.5 per cent of the market value plus 1 per cent more as a registration fee). Yet the community at large and, most importantly, neighbouring owners, know of and recognize such transactions. Disputes are rare (although there are professional gangs who prey on absentee landlords). Should those involved in a transaction desire further paper legitimacy, recourse can be made to the courts by raising a *dawa saha wa towqia*. In these situations, the court confirms in a ruling that the two parties formally agree to the conditions of the transactions, but does not judge on the validity of the seller's ownership of the property itself.

Infrastructure provision adds only marginally to the perceived legitimacy of the informal parcel on agricultural land, since such provision will normally occur only long after the particular neighbourhood has become heavily populated.

Box 5.3 El Mounira el Gedida – a massive informal settlement on private agricultural land

Figure 5.3: A street in El Mounira.
Credit: David Sims

The area of El Mounira was originally intensively cultivated agricultural land made up of small, privately owned land holdings, located on the fringe of Greater Cairo in Embaba, part of Giza Governorate. Starting in the late 1960s, farmers began to sell off strips of land for subdivision into small building plots (average size 80 m²). Although the land had been registered as freehold and cadastred in the 1920s, it was rare that owners bothered to re-register land exchanges, inheritance and mutations, relying instead on simple written sales contracts and oral understandings. Thus the land tenure became more and more 'extra-legal'. Adding to the illegality was the fact that subdivision and building code laws were totally ignored, as were laws prohibiting construction on agricultural land. Yet in popular areas such as El Mounira the government tended to turn a blind eye.

The area, due to its inner-fringe location and good access to the rest of Cairo, exploded in construction and population in the 1970s and 1980s, reaching its physical limits and densifying rapidly. By 1992, its population had reached at least 300 000 living in three- to five-storey zero-lot apartment blocks on lanes rarely more than 3 m wide. (Gross residential densities reached 1850 persons per hectare according to the Census of 1996.) Social facilities were almost non-existent, vehicular access was nearly impossible, and there were no water or sewerage networks.

In the early 1990s, Egypt was threatened by a rise in Islamic fundamentalism. Although mostly centered in Upper Egypt, popular areas of Cairo also harboured Islamic groups whose cells plotted violent opposition to the state but also solidified their popular base by providing needed community services. Embaba, of which El Mounira formed the largest part, became fertile ground for these groups and became known as a main hotbed of fundamentalism, a no-go area with a law unto itself. The government, after ignoring the settlement for decades, suddenly woke up. In 1992, security forces laid siege to the area and arrested thousands of suspects. At the same time it launched a crash programme to provide utilities networks, access roads, etc. A community development association was even formed. Thus El Mounira's physical condition improved considerably, and the community gained a certain recognition, although it took a perceived threat to state power to stimulate these improvements. And the question of illegality of properties remains, with no schemes for regularization on the horizon.

Informal ownership of village land

Lands and buildings within village boundaries were never part of the original cadastre of agricultural land and for the most part remain purely in customary ownership (*il taabaa*). Owners may undertake to have their property ownership sanctioned and titled, following application procedures similar to those described above for *tamlik* of state desert land. Due to the high costs and hassles of such procedures, few owners bother, unless justified by the market values of such property (usually in villages that have been engulfed by urban expansion).

Waqf lands and reform lands

In these rather uncommon cases, government authorities administer the agricultural lands, and each has particular regulations concerning the recognition of informal settlers. In both cases, the payment of ground rent (sometimes called *hekr*) is usually sufficient for relatively secure tenure.

ASSESSMENT OF THE DEGREE OF SECURITY OF VARIOUS URBAN TENURE POSSIBILITIES

The following discussion assesses the main tenure and ownership recognition systems described above according to five separate criteria:

- protection against arbitrary eviction/demolition
- encouragement of investment and house improvement
- provision of infrastructure and public services
- application of market values to property
- provision of credit.

As each criterion is assessed, the relevance and impact on poor and disadvantaged families is given prominence.

Right to remain (protection against arbitrary eviction)

In strictly legal terms, only registered freehold land (and land which has been 'regularized' through the courts, as discussed above) enjoys full protection against arbitrary taking by the state. However, in practice, the right of tenants and owners in informal areas to remain is consistently high throughout the range of tenure possibilities, and in this the poor are not particularly disadvantaged.

In state-owned areas (mostly desert), the right of the state to take and dispose of squatter land without compensation is recognized in laws and contract, no matter how much intermediate tenure/recognition status the squatter may have acquired. However, in reality this right is almost never exercised. Informal housing on agricultural land may also be legally removed on payment of nominal compensation (based exclusively on the agricultural value of the land). However, in practice such taking is rare, and in the few cases where it has taken place, the government usually compensates building owners as well, irrespective of the tenure status.[6]

Ironically, registered freehold ownership does not protect owners entirely from arbitrary taking. The laws of compulsory purchase specify that compensation for properties taken for public purposes should be based on market values. However, the state calculates such compensation using an amortization formula based on the property or agricultural land taxes that apply, meaning that the actual compensation is many times less than current market rates. In addition, payments may easily be delayed for years, and owners who wish to contest compensation can expect court cases that will drag on long after the property has been taken.

From time to time, the state comes up with schemes to clear informal areas for redevelopment. But, since even squatters must be rehoused, these plans almost never see the light of day for the simple reason that the massive funds required for rehousing do not exist. More generally, the government, always strapped for funds, avoids if at all possible schemes that require compensating residents, either with alternative housing or cash payments.

Having said this, a couple of minor cases exist where the threat of eviction is somewhat real: just squatted areas and settlements on public rights-of-way. Yet even here, the threat of public disturbances and unrest makes local authorities reluctant to undertake clearances.

Security to invest

Based on the physical evidence, almost all urban tenure situations have given a very high degree of security to invest in buildings and to extend/improve them. In most informal settlements, the size and quality of investment one sees would not be possible if the builders, most of whom are individuals and extended families, were not reasonably sure that the results of their considerable sacrifices (in terms of time, money and sweat equity) would remain, and that they could occupy and/or sell the final product. Having said that, there are particular factors and minor variations which should be noted:

- The risk of demolition of investment in informal areas is highest at the time of construction, since afterwards, especially after occupation, the costs, hassles and political opposition associated with demolition becomes too burdensome on local authorities. There are a number of common precautions and manoeuvres that investors can take to minimize the risk, but these can be costly and require connections in government, especially after the 1996 decrees (see below).
- Investments are considerably more at risk in newer settlements on desert land and on the expanding fringes of these settlements, where government demolition campaigns are more likely to occur, especially if the encroachments are on land that the government (or powerful private interests) considers to have a high value. Thus in these kinds of areas scattered single-storey basic masonry buildings and enclosure walls are the norm, with rebuilding and more substantial investments coming later once the area has consolidated. In fact, most informal desert settlements began this way, with the original squatters making rational choices about the degree of investment versus the risk of loss, set against probable future gains (including future land values). In contrast, in newer informal settlements on private agricultural land, initial construction tends to be of the substantial reinforced concrete frame variety, although usually vertical expansion follows a wait-and-see period to confirm that the demolition risk is minimal.
- In 1996, the prime minister issued a decree making building without a licence punishable under military law, and courts have been placed under strict supervision to ensure that they enforce the law and associated punishments (penalties include a maximum of six months imprisonment and fines up to LE10 000). Since obtaining a licence is nearly impossible in most informal tenure situations, or at the least

is complicated, time-consuming and expensive, the 1996 decree brought construction in many informal areas both on desert and agricultural land to a near standstill. Recently, however, illegal construction has begun to increase again, especially in rural fringe and village areas and where local government control is lax or particularly susceptible to bribery. In general, the main effect of the decree has been to further escalate the costs of construction.

How do the poor fare under this system? In the past, poorer families with at least some modest capital could find relatively affordable small parcels of land in informal areas (the cheapest were found in desert squatted areas and more remote/rural settlements on agricultural land) and could begin the process of incremental, progressive construction under roughly the same degree of risk as their more wealthy neighbours. However, it should be clear that these days such poorer investors are becoming excluded, simply due to the increasing costs associated with circumventing the more recent controls on illegal construction. For the same reason, poorer families are finding it harder and harder to find affordable rental accommodation in buildings coming up in informal areas, since the investors are passing on these higher 'circumvention' costs of construction in the form of higher rents.

Right to infrastructure and public services

The provision of basic infrastructure (piped water, sewerage systems, metered electricity, paved roads, telephones, etc.) and public services (schools, health facilities, youth centres, solid waste collection, etc.) to residential areas has only the most tenuous link to the type or degree of formality of tenure. Comparisons of service levels across different parts of Egyptian cities show that it is the age of a settlement and its sheer size, in terms of population, that are the main determining factors. This said, it is true that the best services are found in formal upper-class neighbourhoods where some of the residents have inordinate influence in government. But these areas are preciously few, and in general they are older, mature areas. (In fact, newer smart neighbourhoods and 'formal' public housing estates frequently suffer from service deficiencies that can be as severe as those in informal areas.)

Why this situation exists requires a slight digression. Without exception, the funding for urban services comes from central government allocations or, in some cases, from foreign donors. There is little cost recovery and no mechanisms to finance improvements from local tax and non-tax revenues. The result is that urban infrastructure and services are always deficient and poorly maintained. There is a constant call on scarce government funds and, in the scramble, political reality, especially pressures generated on local politicians and officials, becomes the determining factor. No matter what its type of tenure, once an informal area achieves a sizeable population it begins to acquire a certain voice. The government, after the rise of fundamentalist extremism in the early 1990s in some informal areas, has begun to listen quite attentively. Of course, it helps if an area has an influential native son well placed in the realms of state power, but many of these politicians hail from, or have their power base in, older informal areas.

How do the poor fare vis-à-vis service provision? As mentioned above, 'ghettos' of the poor are rare, and so as long as poor families live in established informal or popular (*shaabi*) areas, they are not inordinately discriminated against. However, a poor property owner may find it more difficult to obtain utilities connections due to the 'informal' fees that need to be paid, especially if he or she must fabricate the necessary papers proving occupation. And it should be added that poorer families struggle more to obtain minimal education and health services due to the need to pay informal fees for such services, which are theoretically free or subsidized, but this has nothing to do with residential tenure per se.

Benefit from property values

Urban property markets in Egypt put a value on all land and buildings, no matter how informal or dubious the formal tenure situation, and market exchanges through simple sales contracts are easily accomplished. Even with formal properties, where sale or transfer of rights is proscribed by law (such as subsidized public housing units, special government land sales or fixed rental contracts), market transfers can take place through court-sanctioned powers of attorney (*towkilat*). Thus the question is, to what extent does the market *discount* property values to reflect different kinds of tenure informality? If there is a threat of demolition (rare, as discussed above, and not directly related to tenure), the market is quick to reflect this, and the discount is extremely steep. At the other extreme, the market usually puts a significant premium on freehold land ownership, especially if it is titled and registered (a rare situation in informal areas, and not all that common even in formal areas). All else being equal, a registered parcel in an informal area on agricultural land may command 50 per cent or more in value over a similar plot which is unregistered. And a titled plot will fetch twice as much or more as a similar plot under a simple hand claim in a desert squatter area.[7] Similarly, an informal property that is on the tax register will command somewhat more than a neighbouring property which is not.

Under the prevailing market system, poorer property owners are not particularly discriminated against, as they, as well as their richer neighbours, can easily sell their properties, no matter how informal the tenure situation. However, due to the high costs and hassles involved in registering their individual properties, they are less likely to gain the premiums the market may put on such formal titles.

Dis-benefit from property values

Several studies and academic articles point to the phenomenon of down-raiding or buy-outs of original inhabitants resulting from the titling (*tamlik*) and upgrading of squatter settlements in Egypt and the resulting jumps in land values (see Eiweida, 2000). This kind of criticism needs a closer look. In mature squatter communities, no matter how poor, the majority of holdings are locked out of the property market by the rights of tenants under the rent control laws. For the owners of such properties to sell and enjoy the full market price, he or she (or the prospective buyer) must pay the tenants to leave – a negotiated amount determined by similar payments in the area (usually a minimum of LE2000–5000 per room). Thus not only does the original owner enjoy a significant gain for selling his property, so too does the tenant for leaving. These are voluntary transactions, and it is not uncommon for people with attachments to their communities to forgo such market rewards even though they may represent windfall gains. To say that these original inhabitants are unable to manage such newfound wealth is more than a little patronizing.

In any event, most squatter areas, no matter how well they may be upgraded, will continue to be perceived by the market as lower-class *shaabi* communities, hardly attractive to the well-off and nouveau riche who have no lack of more prestigious locations to choose from in any Egyptian city. Thus the downward raiding, to the extent that it occurs, usually involves the slow metamorphosis to a slightly more prosperous lower-middle-class neighbourhood.

Access to credit

Tenure is not presently an issue when it comes to using a property to obtain credit, since no occupied residential property will be carried as collateral by banks, even if fully titled and registered. The reason is simple: eviction of inhabitants is prohibited by law in Egypt and, unlike most laws, this right of abode is strictly enforced.

This will change soon, when a draft mortgage law under preparation for some time is put before parliament for approval. This legislation will allow court-sanctioned repossession of residential units, even if occupied, should repayment of an outstanding loan (including mortgage) fall into arrears. Much hope is pinned on the law to dramatically expand effective housing demand through mortgages and thus resuscitate the depressed formal real estate market. The impact on general housing markets is likely to be much less significant, and on housing markets in informal areas practically nil. The main reason is that banks will consider only titled and registered properties with no encumbrances as collateral.[8] In addition, banks may fear unrest in attempting to repossess housing units located in unauthorized settlements. However, it will be interesting to see if the possibility of loans and mortgages stimulates individual efforts to title and register both existing and new properties, and whether the market will put an additional premium on these secure titles.

It should be added that there are other kinds of credit: small- and medium-scale enterprise loan schemes, buying vehicles and machinery on instalment, etc. Sometimes such credit is refused because the borrower is located in an informal area, and these kinds of credit are more accessible if one lives in a recognized area with a real address. However, the status of tenure is not itself an issue.

Security of tenure and gender

There are no legal statutes or informal practices in Egypt that directly restrict women's access to or control over property (other than property inheritance laws, derived from Islamic practice, which specify that female heirs receive half the shares of their brothers). However, it is common that informal properties are 'owned' in the name of the male head of family, and there are frequent cases of family disputes where brothers try to exclude their sisters from their rightful shares of inheritance. Also, in informal areas, many women do not have identity cards, which puts them at a disadvantage in property dealings.

CONCLUSIONS

The main conclusion of this assessment should come as no surprise: regardless of the kind of intermediate or informal tenure, de facto security correlates most strongly with the age of an informal settlement and its size. It is age and size that bring with them many of the informal recognition mechanisms and opportunities to move up the ladder of real security. Mature, more sizeable settlements are more likely to gain basic urban infra-structure and public facilities, and owners are more able to find market or close-to-market values for their properties. Thus the concept of 'critical mass' of urban informality is of paramount importance in Egypt.

However, the assessment made here shows that forms of intermediate recognition (especially *hekr* rent and real estate taxes) can play a role and help the situation of the poor, especially squatters on desert land. In par-ticular, the application of the property tax regime to informal areas seems to supply the best form of legitimacy (especially in desert squatted settle-ments, but also on informal settlements on agricultural land). Not only does it 'prove' existence in a physical and jurisprudence sense, it is now the prerequisite for utilities connections and, in desert areas, it is the first requirement in the long process of granting freehold title.

The property tax system as applied to informal areas has problems, most of which have to do with weak record keeping, lack of maps, feeble survey capabilities, the general apathy of public employees and the susceptibility to abuse. However, it generates revenue for the state, and this can be a tremendous advantage at the level of policy discussions about informal settlements and their future. It also begs the question: can you have taxation without representation?

In Egypt, one has a situation where an ineffective government has, in practice, abrogated its role as manager and regulator of urban development (except in high-profile focus areas, most of which are in the new desert settlements). Yet it still carries with it all the increasingly unrealistic legal and regulatory baggage which forces a myriad of accommodation procedures by individuals in order to accommodate or circumvent the system. Government actions – or more properly inactions – in effect recognize this.

What was the past is not the future. Urban informality in Egypt and the informal tenure security underlying it has, especially in the period 1970–85, greatly benefited the urban poor, both in producing a massive amount of housing which offered a range of choices affordable to most if not all, and in allowing poor people with at least some equity to participate in the process and enjoy its rewards. It is sobering to think what would urban Egypt be today without this. But there is a feeling that the opportunities the poor could seize on in the past are becoming fewer (and more expensive), with the supply of affordable housing units drying up while demand increases inexorably.[9] As a result, the housing problems for the urban poor and those with moderate incomes are becoming much more severe, with no alternative solutions on the horizon.

POLICY CONSIDERATIONS

It should be apparent that the introduction of innovative forms of urban tenure is not the 'silver bullet' that is key to solving urban Egypt's considerable and growing housing problems. Solutions lie in many areas, and it could be said that the imperative is to create conditions which build on and encourage the dynamic of informal housing practised by the mass of Egyptians, a phenomenon which until now the government has either ignored or tried, totally unsuccessfully, to proscribe. This means, for example, less stringent planning and building regulations, more community responsibility, effective mechanisms for financing services and infrastructure, and more responsive local government. In addition, the government needs to direct new informal housing development on to state desert land. And as part of this effort, new forms of 'starter' tenure could be devised which would encourage affordable settlement and investment but at the same time discourage vacant land holding and speculation.

CHAPTER SIX

Are services more important than titles in Bogotá?

Nora Aristizabal and Andrés Ortíz Gomez

INTRODUCTION

Looking at land tenancy on a broad spectrum, there are two extremes in Colombian cities. On one hand, there is the formal type of land tenure, and on the other the illegal one. The formal one is the traditional way, in which you buy land or a house and receive a deed that proves you are the owner. At the other extreme is possession without any title. This is the typical situation of the illegal squatters. However, intermediate tenure systems also exist, whereby even without titles, people have a property right that allows them to improve their unit and urban environment. Bogotá has been trying to overcome the limitations of low-income dwellings by providing investment and services, complemented by various intermediate tenure systems that have enabled people of low-income to improve their living conditions and security.

This chapter summarizes existing forms of land tenure, their characteristics, positive and negative aspects, and their impacts on poor households. It examines innovative approaches to providing secure tenure for residents of existing illegal settlements who obtain de facto security prior to the provision of freehold titles. Due to Colombian laws, these illegal settlements have access to services and public investment. The chapter also examines an alternative to the process of illegal settlements with the participation of communal groups, which facilitate the production of low-income housing developments through the use of intermediate tenure forms. The chapter explores ways in which the advantages of intermediate types of tenure can contribute to policies that allow the formal sector to produce cheaper units competitively and enable it to offer what the informal sector is presently providing. If intermediate forms of land tenure improve the quality of life of so many people in the world, why should a way not be found to institutionalize these procedures? Proposals for this are included in the final section.

BOGOTÁ, AN INFORMAL CITY

Bogotá's housing deficit is predominantly in the low-income stratum. By 1998, 6000 of the 30 000 hectares of the total urban area began as *piratas* or 'pirate' developments. There are 1433 urban settlements of illegal origin, the oldest of which were registered in the 1960s. These settlements corres-pond to 23 per cent of the urban area and 38 per cent of the population. Figure 6.1 shows how the these settlements have spread.

Bogotá will need 360 000 new housing units between 2000 and 2010. Additionally, 55 000 units should be replaced and 87 000 should be upgraded to reduce the number of families per unit from 1.48 to 1.37, in order to improve the quality of life. Overall, the city will need 500 000 add-itional housing units over the next ten years, an average of 50 000 a year.

Most low-income housing in Bogotá has been developed by the informal sector in an unplanned manner. More than 45 per cent of Bogotá's housing neighbourhoods developed between 1993 and 1996 were 'pirate urbaniza-tions'. Nowadays, 87 per cent of people who have their dwellings in those projects have obtained a legal and secure tenure status. Nevertheless, this process has taken more than 20 years in many cases. As a result, in 1996, there were more than 173 neighbourhoods in Bogotá that had not solved the legal tenure problem.

In the 1960s, many low-income neighbourhoods were developed on public sites that were invaded by communities, most of which were pro-moted by leftist leaders. This form of occupation was then substituted by illegal subdivisions of land, when many landowners realized that this could be good business without high risks. The pirate developers are normally landowners and typically have the hidden support of a local

Figure 6.1 A general view of Bogotá and its piratas or 'pirate' settlements. Credit: Nora Aristizabal and Andrés Ortíz Gomez.

Table 6.1   Bogotá's growth by uses, 1993–96

Use	Hectares	Percentage	Annual growth (hectares)
Formal housing	551.00	39.8	137.75
Informal housing	452.20	32.7	117.96
Industry	72.50	5.2	18.91
Institutions	87.50	6.3	22.82
Commerce	17.20	1.2	4.48
Metropolitan services	202.50	14.6	52.82
Total	1382.90	100.0	360.75

politician. They commonly own a large plot on the outskirts of the city, outside the urban area. These plots are near the low-income sectors and do not have public services, roads, etc. Moreover, they are often located in dangerous areas with a high risk of landslides or flooding, or may even be in areas that have been reserved by the city planners for future metropolitan infrastructure.

Generally, the land is sold informally by the real owner to a figurehead, to avoid legal problems and prosecution. In many cases, the figurehead is over 60 years old, because under Colombian legislation, senior citizens cannot be prosecuted. With a figurehead, the real landowner can say that his land was 'stolen' by someone who made the illegal development. The figurehead always disappears when the business has been finished.

The pirate developers subdivide the land into small plots, of between 36 and 72 m², in very long blocks, which complicates community consolidation. They do not reserve land for public areas, such as parks, infrastructure, schools and main roads, and they do not take into account Bogotá's planning regulations. Only narrow pedestrian ways about 3 or 4 metres wide are built for local roads. Densities of more than 100 dwellings per hectare are reached.

Pirate developers sell plots to the community with 'creative' payment systems. They do not take into account the buyer's economic stability. Instead, they implement threat groups, which collect the money and guarantee that everybody will pay. According to the law, buyers could stop paying the pirate at any time, because what they were sold was an illegal settlement. However, they pay because they are accomplices who know exactly the type of game they are playing, or because they are afraid of losing their invested capital.

Plots are then given to the families and people start constructing dwellings. Every weekend, a small quantity of plots is occupied. Neighbourhoods grow slowly, like an oil overflow, without making any noise. The authorities are not alerted to the creation of a new pirate urbanization. Nevertheless, authorities often know that an illegal neighbourhood is emerging, but they turn a blind eye because 'the simple fact was that self-help housing represents a means by which the poor could be accommodated at little cost to the state' (Gilbert, 1998). However, in spite of the lower cost in the short term, the cost for the municipality in the long term is much higher, according to the budgets of the service companies

The pirate developers are experts at doing their job. They often give communities a manual which explains how to exert pressure on local authorities and politicians in the search for public services, social facilities and legal titles. Moreover, it is very common to find the pirates working with local councillors, who promise infrastructure in exchange for votes.

ILLEGAL URBAN DEVELOPMENT

Once the illegal developer has disappeared and communities have begun to build houses on their plots, the struggle to upgrade the neighbourhood and obtain legal status begins. Several intermediate tenure systems appear as time passes.

Initially, communities build fragile water and electricity systems, which are connected illegally to the nearest public services network or are taken from contaminated springs. Since 1991, the new Colombian Constitution states that public services such as water supply, electricity, drainage and sewerage are a fundamental right, whether people have legal titles or not. Therefore Bogotá's utility companies have tried to serve these neighbourhoods. Rather than cutting the illegal supply and creating a social and political problem, they try to come to an agreement with the neighbourhoods. For example, the water company makes temporary agreements that consist of a fixed payment for 50 cubic metres per month, per house, until the company can build the infrastructure and install meters.

The most complicated problem for these communities is the lack of sewerage. When people start asking local authorities about this service, they realize that there is a contradictory law that forbids the city to make investments in areas that have not obtained the legal urban status from planning authorities. As Diana M. Beltran, manager of Bogotá's Public Space Defence Office, said, 'The city cannot invest in private areas because this is a crime in Colombia'. Therefore, if a neighbourhood is illegal, the tenure of roads and public areas has not been transferred to the city and continues to be private. However, the population does not need formal titles to be allowed to invest. Under Bogotá's legal framework it is enough that a plot, a road, a park, a reserve, etc., is defined as public land in the approved urban plan.

Urban legalization is fundamental not only to defining plots, public areas or roads, where it is possible to locate open spaces, parks, etc., but also to acquiring an intermediate tenure right. It represents the incorporation of the neighbourhood into the formal urban area. This urban legalization includes a definition of priorities, risks, infrastructure needs and, generally, all other work that must be undertaken by the local authorities, utility companies and the community to upgrade a neighbourhood and comply with city standards.

To achieve urban legalization, it is necessary to submit an urban plan with areas, topography and plot subdivision to Bogotá's planning office. Since 1996, Colombian law requires the urban legalization of any neighbourhood illegally developed prior to that year. Bogotá's planning department has been undertaking an ambitious programme in this direction. More than 320 neighbourhoods have been legalized since 1998, according to the information provided by the city planning office, and there are 173 in the process of approval. Before this law, the urban legalization of a neighbourhood took more than ten years. Unfortunately, after the law was passed, more than 34 hectares have been illegally developed and it will be necessary to wait for a new 'zoning amnesty' law.

The planning offices try to find the pirate developers so that they can clearly define the plot boundaries and the original title. They then request from them the land needed for public spaces and the relocation of people who live in risky areas. Although this request is not always granted, it is essential to facilitate the process of efficient land subdivision. Usually the definition of plot boundaries happens at the same time as the assessment of property taxes. Bogotá's authorities are very interested in the assignment of urban nomenclature, because at this point people begin paying property taxes. Normally, the community is also interested in paying this tax because, although they have no titles, they think it is a way to legitimize their property and acquire tenure security.

The struggle continues with the Bogotá Water Company. A community must get its neighbourhood included in the company's annual investment budget before the legal sewerage and drainage infrastructure construction can begin. However, many communities are not interested in legalizing this service, as meters and monthly bills follow (see Figure 6.2).

In time, neighbourhoods become consolidated. Finally, after several years, they develop all the necessary infrastructure and roads, but there are many dwellers who still do not have legal titles. It is at this moment that people realize the importance of a title. An official title is crucial if they want to borrow money from the banks or get government subsidies to improve their houses. Also, this step means making the transition from the informal sector to the formal one. In real terms, that represents an important added value in the housing market.

The first thing a community must do to begin the process of having titles issued is to find the original title and landowner of the undivided plot. The plot must then be divided into private sites and public areas, and after that it must be sold legally. The original owner should sign a new document listing all the residents and public area cessions. In addition, the original owner must pay the taxes corresponding to the sale. However, at this stage it is very common for the figurehead to have disappeared and for the pirate developer not to sign any papers because he argues that he has never divided and sold plots and he has never received money from dwellers. In

Figure 6.2   An informal house with water meter, Bogotá. Credit: Nora Aristizabal and Andrés Ortíz Gomez

spite of having been swindled, sometimes the new tenants prefer to make a new agreement with the landowner and pay more money to get the signed title, rather than lose all the money they have already invested. The other possibility is to go to court and begin a legal process of ownership. This method is longer and expensive, because communities must pay lawyers.

However, it is important to note that, in the Colombian context, people sell their houses informally as many times as they want without worrying about the title (see Box 6.1). They merely sign a new piece of paper or endorse the original one. Despite the fact that these papers are not legal and are not registered, poor people do not worry about it because they do not think their houses are at risk, or that they could be evicted.

Box 6.1   Salazar family: 1923–2001

Several intermediate forms of tenure have been used by four generations. The plot has been responsible for breaking away from misery, upgrading, starting a decent life and progressing. This case reflects the situation in relation to security, services, intermediate transactions and titles.

In 1923, the head of the Salazar family bought a piece of land on the outskirts of the city without a deed and started to construct a home. There were no services, streets or social facilities, and no transportation system. To get home, people had to walk for 60 minutes along a very rough, rustic pedestrian path.

The upgrading process was very slow. By 1961, a primitive access road had been built and it was a major step towards development. Twenty years later, the road was partially paved. Only ten years ago, a standard road was finally built. Originally, there were no utilities at all; they took water from a nearby creek and built trench 'latrines' for sewerage. In 1977, the community built an illegal communal water supply system, which they used until 1987, when a legal water supply was finally installed by the city. They have had electric power for the past 20 years and telephones since 1987. However, public transportation arrived only in 1994. Today, they have a recreational park that was built in 1998 (see Figure 6.3) and the neighbourhood has had a supermarket and a church since 1999. They are still working to obtain health facilities and schools.

Deeds were acquired after an ownership process in the 1980s. The head of the family died in 1988 and the plot has been subdivided into seven units, where five units were a division of the original plot and two of the new units were built on top of the original one. The original house lasted 75 years, but in 1997 it was demolished and two new units were built. A home-based enterprise was also built 15 years ago. The revenue from this business has allowed the family to buy three new plots in the same neighbourhood. What started out as a simple piece of land, without the security of any title, became the financial security that allowed the families to progress, even if the deeds and services were a long time coming.

This case has had different types of tenure. Initially there was no freehold, but after the legal process one general deed was obtained. Future rights have been transferred from different members of the family, and several private agreements have also been signed. However, the new plots acquired have deeds because the newer generations are aware of their potential credit, mortgages and subsidies.

The original buyers were a couple, the man died very young and the 'matron' lived 87 years. They had ten children, of whom seven survived to adulthood, 17 grandchildren and 25 great grandchildren. Through the history of four generations of a family, the socioeconomic profile has evolved. The first generation was very poor. However, today some of the grandchildren are professionals. They feel that they have improved thanks to the undeveloped piece of land bought by their great grandparents many years ago. Nowadays, as professionals, the new young generation thinks that titles are important as a means to improve. However, not all of the properties subdivided from the original plot have deeds, even though they have changed from person to person in the same family.

Figure 6.3   Park City upgrades. Credit: Nora Aristizabal and Andrés Ortíz Gomez.

WHAT INTERMEDIATE LAND TENURE FORMS EXIST IN BOGOTÁ?

Squatter settlements have had harmful social and environmental effects on the city. However, there are economic benefits for the poorest people that affect their living conditions positively, because of existing intermediate tenure forms. These intermediate tenure forms have been fundamental in giving housing options to millions of people who, in the formal market, have had no alternative but to live in a crowded, rented room. They have also reduced the social pressure on the Colombian government. These intermediate forms should be analysed as possible options in other countries. The following are the main forms of intermediate land tenure found in Bogotá:

- Tenancy by private agreement document and physical possession: this is a very common type of possession, especially in the initial stage of the illegal developments. However, sometimes this type of tenure lasts for 20 years or more before a formal title is achieved.

    In view of the fact that the plot subdivision is absolutely illegal, the only document the buyer receives to support the transaction is a promise of purchase and sale of rights. It is made on a regular piece of paper and is normally handwritten. In this informal document the number and location of the specific plot are defined. The figurehead generally signs this document, but it is never registered. When a plot is located in an area that could be legally developed, pirate sellers annex a certificate of land use issued by the planning department. This is done to demonstrate urban legality to the buyer, although the document is only an informative paper and not an approval.

Physical possession of the plot is the basis of this intermediate tenancy as it leads to the right of tenure, and consequently to the real ownership. This type of intermediate land tenure is individual, and can be transferred to someone else by selling, donating or inheriting it. When people want to sell their units a new private paper appears. These cases of exchange of tenancy produce as many papers as do the transfers of rights. The process of buying and selling goes on for even 20 or 30 years in the illegal framework.

- Declaration of possession: this type of intermediate tenure starts without any paper. In this case, a person goes direct to the notary and says that he or she has been living on a particular plot for more than five years. Colombian law states that, for low-income dwellings, the sole act of living in the unit for five years implies a right of tenure through the legal process of *pertenencia*. This is a way of acquiring a property when the real owner is not claiming ownership rights and there is a second party trying to become the real owner by possession. The property rights will go only to the occupants of the units, not to illegal developers.
- Transactions to buy and sell rights for future use: this is a very creative intermediate tenure form in which someone who is going to inherit a unit, or is going to have the right of tenure in the future, sells this right in advance to someone else.
- Urban legalization: this is not a procedure just to obtain deeds; nevertheless it has been the most powerful and commonly used form of intermediate tenure in Bogotá. Even though it started 25 years ago as a simple procedure, since 1996 it has become a strong collective intermediate tenure form in all settlements of illegal origin. This is innovative, because nowadays the legalization process is a way for families to secure the responsibilities of the developers and some of their rights without deeds, just with the de facto security supported by Colombian laws. Contrary to the Peruvian case, where the deeds are the main target, in Bogotá, de facto security, urban upgrading and services provision are the priorities and are considered more important than titles. Freehold is a later consideration. The intermediate tenure change leads to massive and faster urban transformation. The families, through a local representative, have to provide a plan, where public and private land is divided according to regulations. Bogotá's regulations allow the community to formally take on the role of the developer, and by doing so, gives them an intermediate right of tenure, which allows public investment and promotes self-upgrading.

There is another alternative to illegal settlements, which is known as 'intermediate tenancy through a communal group'. Colombian legislation allows group intermediation for self-construction projects, land trusts or similar. In this case, the owner of the plot has his deed and celebrates an agreement with a communal group, which starts collecting money from potential buyers to develop the project. This group then starts working towards the development of a low-income programme, such as utilities feasibility, urban permits and financial assistance. When they have all the requirements, they start the physical development of the plot by self-construction. This is a community land trust with three parties: the real owner of the land; the institution that will have the intermediate land tenure; and the low-income families, who will be the future landowners. Eventually, the titles are transferred from the owner to the institution and then to the buyers. There are different types of documents in these transactions. Some are between the landowner and the non-profit institution, and the others are between the non-profit institution and the buyers.

There are two types of communal groups. On the one hand, there are the non-profit organizations that have a social mission to provide housing for the poorest. On the other hand, there are illegal developers who use this legal figure as a façade. However, at some point the pirate group abandons the people and the settlement. What is innovative is that even if the developments are formal and comply with urban planning, they have only intermediate tenure forms, and freehold titles are not an initial requirement, thereby facilitating low-income housing production. Unfortunately, these alternatives cover only a small percentage of the housing deficit.

ADVANTAGES AND DISADVANTAGES OF INTERMEDIATE LAND TENURE FORMS

The main objective is to find out how the intermediate land tenure forms may contribute to diminishing urban poverty and increasing people's security. Three groups of intermediate land tenure are reviewed below. The purpose of this comparison is to look for advantages and disadvantages not only in the illegal settlements, but also in the formal developments.

The illegal development land tenure forms can be placed in two main groups: the type that transfers rights done by individuals, and the ones where community groups assume responsibilities for the urban legalization. From the point of view of title security, these types of land tenure offer only partial security. They are not secure in the sense that, in the long run, legality depends on a period of physical possession and especially on the success of a process of ownership (*pertenencia*). They are secure in the sense that there are laws in Colombia protecting them. Because the laws include the possession and the transference of possession as legal instruments, and many families have these types of possession, the majority of people are not really at risk of eviction.

While measuring the effects of this type of tenure on the urban market, it was found that its impact on the supply and demand of low-income units is positive because it contributes real options for the housing deficit of the urban poor and offers cheaper land for low-income housing. This is due to the fact that, while formal developers have great expenses, the pirate developers seek only profits and leave the economic burden of upgrading to the municipality. One of the most important advantages of the illegal developments is the time frame. Due to their illegal status they do not fulfil any of the requirements of legal urban developments and therefore they can have faster delivery to the families.

If the pirate urbanization phenomenon is analysed, these types of land tenure are encouraging illegal developments and are against formal and legal urbanization. An alternative against clandestine settlements has yet to be found. One thing that must be taken into account is that today, after a massive legalization programme developed by the city, there are still thousands of families located in reserved or risky areas waiting for a relocation payment. Urban settlements resulting from these types of urbanization do not contribute to an appropriate urban plan. The costs of upgrading facilities and services infrastructure for these types of developments are 2.7 times higher than in the planned settlements (see Figure 6.4).

People living in these settlements are exposed to substandard environments, affected by pollution, water contamination, noise, and undersized pedestrian and vehicle grids. Moreover, the illegal settlements have been affecting natural reserves and generating environmental risks. The diagnosis of public space is also dramatic. Bogotá has only 2.87 m^2 of open public space per inhabitant, which is very low in relation to international standards. The areas with the worst levels are those of illegal origin.

The housing for the poorest families should not only offer a place to live, but also a means of leaving poverty behind. The usual housing units resulting from the informal types of land tenure offer potential economic growth for the families because they usually have good-sized plots that offer the possibility of having home-based enterprises and progressive units. This is, perhaps, the aspect of informal dwellings that people like most.

Finally, the access to formal credit for the families living on illegal premises is impossible, because of the lack of a formal title. Moreover, most of the heads of these families work in the informal employment market. Therefore, neither the dwelling they 'own' nor the types of job they have are sufficient guarantee for financial support. Additionally, the illegal nature of the dwellings makes it impossible for these families to be eligible for government subsidies.

In evaluating the security of tenure offered by the institutions that hold intermediate tenure, it was found that they offer a great advantage, because the institutions have the capacity to protect a family's savings while they acquire real ownership. Moreover, these institutions are formal enterprises working for the poorest families, fighting against clandestine developments, providing cheaper, formal ways to have access to housing, while improving the people's quality of life. However, the solutions offered are not enough in comparison to the deficit.

Figure 6.4   Illegal water pipes. Credit: Nora Aristizabal and Andrés Ortíz Gomez.

Because these institutions are non-profit organizations, the housing units offered are more closely related to the users' needs in terms of plot size and construction standards, and less to economic feasibility. An adequate environment is guaranteed from the beginning, and even though the urban infrastructure and facilities might be built in stages, they comply with the minimum standards required by the municipalities. These developments are planned in co-ordination with the city's urban plans. A recent diagnosis carried out by the city planning office found that most of the problems of the different city structural systems are caused by the lack of planning of the periphery, where the illegal dwellings are located. The people with access to these types of tenure also have access to individual subsidy and credit. The promoter institutions (see Box 6.2) help the families to obtain the housing subsidy from the government. Some of these institutions help the families to get a better job or provide instruction for home-based enterprises. Nevertheless, although they have far better standards than the illegal settlements, they are not as well planned as most private developments and they have an even lower coverage than the private sector.

Box 6.2   'Corporación Minuto de Dios', money and land trust organization

Corporación Minuto de Dios is a private non-profit institution created in Bogotá in 1958 to develop self-construction low-income housing projects and community life. The mission of the corporation is focused on the urban poor, looking to promote individual and communal integral development, as well as social equality, tolerance and peace. The corporation also works on pro-grammes of employment, industry, health, culture, recreation, services and religion.

All the corporation's programmes are under the principle of 'Construccion de Comunidades', creating communities in order to reinforce Colombia's social structure. The housing programmes are oriented towards communal participa-tion, looking for self-structured organized groups and self-supported commu-nities. Since its creation, the Corporacion Minuto de Dios has built more than 30 000 low-income units. Currently they have 535 low-income houses under construction, 1951 units on an upgrading programme and 3575 on the prelim-inary phases prior to the construction.

The Corporacion Minuto de Dios has a division called Contigo ('With You'), which promotes change in finance areas. The objective of this division is the promotion of home-based enterprises ('micro-empresas') and assistance in titles, and housing acquisition. They also help families to obtain credits.

CONCLUSIONS AND POLICY RECOMMENDATIONS

Why are the clandestine settlements supplying most of the demand for low-income housing? Is it because there are no punishments for the devel-opers? Is it because they are the cheapest? Is it because of the lengthy legal processes? Is it because the city authorities are incapable of controlling these settlements? Is it because society does not care? All of these may be partly true. The point is that illegal settlements are the only option for the poorest today. Joint efforts have to be made to reduce prices of legal planned options. Additional efforts have to be carried out to produce really appropriate units that are competitive with the outcome of the pirate developments.

Projects developed by the non-profit groups are the slowest in Bogotá; public sector projects are the second most time-consuming, while private developments have better time frames in relation to the others. However, the fastest is definitely the illegal developer. The proposed policies in rela-tion to time are that the municipality allows the formal intermediate types of land tenure as legitimate ways of tenure for new planned projects. This way, the permits and urbanization licences will be obtained faster than today. Additionally, the municipalities should have faster mechanisms for low-income projects. The challenge is to complete these in at least the same time as those achieved by the illegal developers. Introducing self-permits with insurance policies and subsequent control could be useful.

There is a huge difference between misery and welfare. Respect for human dignity and projection towards growth starts by drawing a line for the standards of human environment. The right of tenure security is the basic point on that line where people seek the essentials for survival. How-ever, physical and social upgrades start to offer sustainability from that point on. If the right of tenure is the threshold for investment, intermediate tenure forms on planned projects that allow people to reach that point faster have to be used and institutionalized to surpass the poverty line.

Many poor people are able to obtain land, housing and services in the informal sector at prices and at times that meet their needs. However, formal ways of providing land with full titles are expensive and unaffordable because of the high premium that titles and urban regulations demand. By enabling people to obtain land cheaply and then work towards full titles over time, the system seems to have practical benefits. However, the system must be improved and formalized to effectively plan and build alternatives that make consolidation easier to achieve than it is at present.

Introducing innovative intermediate land tenure systems to apply in new settlements would have a great impact on security of tenure. Security in terms of ownership would improve, local investment and upgrading would be faster, and progressive units with good-sized plots would be offered. There would also be a significant reduction in the distortion of the urban land markets.

Many of the heads of urban poor families in Colombia are single mothers. The security offered by innovative and affordable formal intermediate tenure forms are essential for those who have to face bringing up their children alone. In addition, the possibility of starting a home-based enterprise, which these types of tenure usually offer, would guarantee much better quality time for the children and therefore a better society.

Solving the right of tenure is crucial, but it is not the only solution. Special regulations have to be implemented to find solutions that compete with the clandestine dwellings, and preventive actions are required to avoid the proliferation of new illegal dwellings. By creating innovative policies, the illegal developers would be discouraged. Intermediate land tenure forms for formal projects are indispensable for the existing poor, and no effort should be spared in granting them an adequate quality of life, minimum standards and innovative managerial approaches. Most of these ideas are innovative and therefore difficult to implement. Successful pilot projects are needed to prove results. For these to acquire credibility, their benefits should be widely disseminated so that the poorest families trust these alternatives and choose them over illegal settlements.

CHAPTER SEVEN

Current changes and trends: Benin, Burkina Faso and Senegal

*Alain Durand-Lasserve, in collaboration with Alain Bagré,
Moussa Gueye and José Tonato*

INTRODUCTION

In most developing cities, one of the objectives of the conventional approaches to tenure that were implemented in the 1980s and 1990s was the integration of informal land and housing delivery systems into the sphere of formal activities through the registration of land rights and tenure legalisation programmes. However, while this gives beneficiaries sound security of tenure, it is an expensive and time-consuming process, especially in contexts such as sub-Saharan African countries, where a dual legal system still prevails, the processing capacity of the administrations involved is limited, land-related information is out of date or incomplete and centralized land registration procedures are overcomplicated (Fourie, 2000). Frequent corruption in administrations responsible for land management and allocation and the low level of literacy among the populations concerned further aggravate the situation.

Clearly, in sub-Saharan Francophone African cities, the search for innovative tenure forms for the urban poor takes place in a context where conventional approaches have proved unable to respond to needs (Groupement de Recherche Interurba, 1995; Payne 1997). Conventional measures have failed, so far, to protect the poor in informal settlements against eviction, to upgrade tenure in existing informal settlements or provide basic urban services, and to provide serviced land for the urban poor (UNCHS, 1999c; Fernandes and Varley, 1998). As such, it is increasingly acknowledged that conventional approaches must be drastically reassessed and redefined (ISTED, 1998; Shelter Forum, 1999).

This chapter focuses on tenure policies for the urban poor in sub-Saharan Francophone African countries. We shall refer to these countries as 'countries in the subregion'. The current situation and trends in the subregion regarding urban tenure policies will be reviewed on the basis of recent empirical studies. Particular attention will be given to the analysis of the situation in Benin, Burkina Faso and Senegal. In these three countries, recent innovations regarding tenure for the urban poor, as well as potential for change, are clearly linked with the decentralization process, the emergence of municipalities with effective land management responsibilities and the pressure exerted by populations concerned (Annales de la Recherche Urbaine, 1995).

THE COLONIAL LEGACY: LEGAL AND REGULATORY FRAMEWORK AFFECTING TENURE IN THE SUBREGION

During the colonial period, a land management and allocation system was introduced to adapt land management to the needs of the colonial state and the capitalist mode of production. This emphasized access to individual ownership (freehold). A series of decrees stated that 'vacant and unclaimed land' should be appropriated and registered in the name of the state. Thereafter, any allocation or transfer of the property must be registered to the Land Department and advertised. This was the first step towards the realization of 'real rights', where land is the exclusive property of the state and any transfer of occupancy rights has to be authorized by the government. The notion of 'vacant and unclaimed land' is intentionally ambiguous, especially in contexts where customary/collective tenure predominates and the process resulted in large tracts of native land being incorporated into the state domain.

To limit the social impact of this constraining legal and regulatory framework, simplified procedures and formal recognition of customary rights were subsequently introduced in some countries of the subregion. This opened the door to further upgrading/conversion of customary rights into real rights and while this procedure achieved limited results, it gave customary owners a reasonable level of tenure security.

Following independence, the centralized land management procedures in most countries of the subregion remained largely intact. Unregistered land, including large tracts of customary land, was nationalized – in the name of social justice, equitable access to land and prevention of speculation (Mabogunje, 1992). However, registration of tenure rights was not systematically carried out and, to a large extent, land management procedures became a tool for registering land in the name of the state for the benefit of government officials and other groups who are clients of the state so that they, rather than the poor, became the main beneficiaries of the system (UMP, 1995).

For the majority of the urban population without access to freehold or any other real rights, access to land took place through precarious and revocable administrative permits to occupy, or housing permits. Within this context, customary tenure practices are either treated as illegal or tolerated, depending on the country (Durand-Lasserve, 1995). However, in most countries informal arrangements were set up to compensate customary owners in cases where their land was used for housing developments or as public land. This gave rise to arbitrary and clientelist land management practices.

The situation outlined above has resulted in a juxtaposition of land 'rights', based on different legitimacies and traditions (Tribillon, 1995 and 1993).

Four main, and often conflicting, land rights can be identified. The first is the right as stated by land laws and codes. Because little is known of its content and implementation procedures, its social impact is very limited. The second set of rights consists of those enacted or decreed by the state administration for its own convenience, in the name of the 'national interest'. State administrations take advantage of the nebulous characteristics of the laws and codes, and of their enforcing capacity to impose their own interpretation and decisions. The third right refers to customary laws and practices that play a key role in the rapidly developing urban fringe areas. It is tolerated as long as it does not jeopardize vested interests of other urban stakeholders, particularly government officials. Its legitimacy is unequally acknowledged between the countries and can be arbitrarily nullified by any administrative decisions. The fourth right is that of popular-informal practices. It combines customary inherited land management – as reinterpreted by urban populations – and informal transactions. For example, a land sale can take place if a deed has been signed before three witnesses by a person claiming a right to the land. This is the right most people refer to.

Land for housing the poor in Francophone Western Africa is provided through several delivery systems. Commercial formal land delivery, where registered land is developed and sold by professional developers, concerns a very small percentage of land sales and is targeted towards middle- and high-income groups (UNCHS, 1993). State- or government-controlled land delivery involves the sale of serviced or unserviced plots of land at a below-market price by public authorities to its client social groups. Beneficiaries are usually provided with a temporary permit to occupy, or a housing permit, which can be (in principle) upgraded to a permanent permit and later to a freehold. However, the procedure is so long and complicated that this rarely happens. This amounts to 10–40 per cent of total land transactions. Popular, informal or customary land delivery involves the sale of unserviced plots without titles and no legal guarantees by intermediaries or so-called 'customary owners'.

The supply of land for the urban poor is still dominated by customary interests (Benton, 1994). The term 'customary' covers a fairly wide range of situations and practices (Rochegude, 1998). Although most of the supply of peri-urban customary land is now exhausted, this has not put an end to customary practices nor, more importantly, to customary claims. In all sub-Saharan African countries, the customary system shows an astonishing resistance to any attempts at reform by the state, to radical reforms or to market pressure. Indeed, the system is able to integrate perfectly into the market in contexts where the demand structure, institutional framework and financing systems prevent the emergence of private formal operators (UNCHS, 1999c).

Unlike many developing cities in Asia, Latin America and the Arab countries, squatting – mainly on public land – is not a common form of access to land for the urban poor, who rather rely on rental housing in informal settlements and backyard shacks (Durand-Lasserve and Clerc, 1996).

However, demand over the past decade has made it increasingly difficult for the poor to gain access to urban land, as most land suitable for housing on the urban fringes has been already subdivided and sold. One result is the emergence of squatter settlements in areas not claimed by customary owners (marshy land, generally public land, etc.). The inhabitants of these settlements enjoy no security of tenure but are rarely threatened by eviction as the land has no market value.

EMBRACING CUSTOMARY AND INFORMAL PRACTICES: TOWARDS INNOVATIVE APPROACHES TO TENURE FOR THE URBAN POOR

Clearly, centrally based land management policies have not achieved their objectives and the result has been to consolidate the power of administrative officials, while diminishing that of the state (Platteau, 1996). Public policies specifically regarding the provision of land for housing for lower-income groups are similarly ineffective. While customary ownership has not been formally recognized by most governments in the subregion, any public land development taking place on such land has usually involved negotiations with the customary community concerned. Today this system is in crisis because of the gradual dissolution of customary communities and the weakness of central government (Rakodi, 1994). A reinterpretation of such practices can be observed, however, in countries and cities where customary communities in the subregion are granted some form of legitimacy. This shift can be interpreted in two different ways: for some observers it reflects the withdrawal of the state; for others, it is the first step towards a new land policy, whose aim is to integrate the diverse land markets.

The prevailing dual land delivery system is now being challenged in the face of pressure from market forces and international finance institutions. However, few states in the subregion have agreed to liberalize their land markets, apart from Mali and, to a lesser extent, the Côte d'Ivoire. Most other countries have postponed land market privatization measures (Mauritania), reluctantly adopted such measures but managed not to implement them (Senegal, Guinea) or created land development agencies with financial autonomy, but which still operate under the control of government administrations (Burkina Faso). As long as land management is the exclusive responsibility of central government administrations with a state monopoly on land and centralized land allocation and registration procedures, the potential for innovation is limited. However, in all countries of the subregion, and in particular Benin, Burkina Faso and Senegal, the state monopoly on land is gradually being dismantled. This has opened the door for innovative approaches to tenure for the urban poor, which are now beginning to emerge.

These initiatives are influenced by the decentralization process (which is generating new forms of co-operation and participation between local authorities, informal developers and the populations of irregular settlements), the emergence of municipalities with effective land management responsibilities, the pressure exerted by populations concerned and increased recognition of social practices, including informal practices (UNCHS, 1995). With the exception of Senegal, these innovations do not take the form of radical reforms, but rather must be seen as a longstanding political process where technical, administrative, regulatory and legal measures are taken under pressure from the civil society, in a context characterized by democratization trends and decentralization measures (African NGOs' Habitat II Caucus, 1996).

Access to urban land in Benin is characterized by the existence of a very dynamic informal land delivery system that is tolerated, and to some extent partly controlled by the state (Oloude, 1999). In a context of rapid urbanization, where the public sector has proved unable to provide low-cost land for housing, and where the formal private sector is unable to meet the demand from higher-income groups,[1] the customary sector is the only provider of land for housing in all urban and suburban areas. During the past two decades it has adapted to the pressures of urbanization and the increasing demand for urban land from low- and middle-income groups (Hernandez and Tribillon, 1994),[2] and informal or 'customary' practices regarding the provision of land for housing have been successfully integrated into formal procedures.

However, although customary rights were never formally abolished, the terms of their recognition allow for different interpretations and leave the door open to arbitrary administrative decisions. For example, security of tenure is not guaranteed in settlements that have developed on customary land until the area has been redeveloped. Other problems associated with customary land rights include the fact that customary rights are attached to a lineage, owned collectively by a group. A court can nullify the sale of such land if one member of the group believes that his interests, or the lineage interests, have not been taken into account. In the absence of land records or registration, identification of actual customary right holders is difficult, thus leading to land disputes. And finally, if transfer occurs, there is frequently confusion about the nature of the transfer: is it a gift (as stated in the customary tradition) or a sale (Tonato, 2000)? In the meantime, the state monopoly on land is being increasingly questioned and criticized, and various responses are being contemplated in order to respond to the needs of the low-medium- and low-income groups (Tribillion, 1992). These include decentralizing land management at municipal level, improving and simplifying registration procedures, replacing the 'housing permit' with a simpler and more flexible allocation system, and improving transparency in the land allocation process.

Burkina Faso is the only country of the subregion that attempted to implement a radical approach to tenure for the urban poor (between 1984 and 1991), in a context where they were encountering increasing problems in gaining access to urban land.[3] As in other countries of the subregion, the land tenure situation in Burkina Faso has to balance the customary system (which does not allow individual land ownership) and the state-controlled system (which provides real rights). The evolution of land legislation in Burkina Faso is marked by one overriding concern: the harmonization of relations between colonial and customary-traditional law (Bagré, 1999).

After independence, recognition of customary rights was confirmed. However, this subsequently rendered the approval and implementation of planning measures impossible and generated a chaotic urban web characterized by the unorganized juxtaposition of land development projects. In Ouagadougou between 1960 and 1984, all land development schemes initiated by the public authorities were jeopardized by customary interests. Despite several attempts to reform and improve existing planning procedures, overcome legal dualism and facilitate access to land for housing, the situation spiralled out of control in the mid-1980s under the pressure of demand for urban land. Scarcity of land (due to inadequate provision of land for housing by the public sector, and of the rising cost of land) resulted in a highly speculative informal market of 'housing permits', issued on customary land. This created increased tenure insecurity for a growing number of urban households and led to the expansion of informal developments on suburban customary land. In 1984, informal settlements on customary land represented about 71 per cent of the Ouagadougou urban area, with 65 per cent of the urban population living in these settlements.

In 1984, the new political regime very quickly declared its intention 'to eradicate the irregular squatter settlements', 'to fight against land speculation and the high cost of renting' and 'to put in place a housing policy which would be to the advantage of the workers' by giving 'each household their own plot'. A new department was established to deal with land development and housing problems, focusing particularly on the irregular settlements in Ouagadougou. In addition, several other measures were implemented, including drastic land reform in Burkina Faso relating to 'agrarian and land reorganisation'. In addition, the National Domain was created. Declaring the land to be 'the exclusive property of the state', this consisted of all land within the national boundaries and that acquired by the state. All land titles that had previously been issued to individuals were henceforth annulled.

These measures, backed by strong political will, led to the large-scale tenure and physical upgrading of the 'irregular' settlements. In all the towns of Burkina Faso, 125 000 plots for housing were created and allocated between 1984 and 1990, against payment of a symbolic use fee fixed at 300 CFA francs (US$0.5) per square metre in Ouagadougou and Bobodioulasso.

However, despite several attempts to improve land-related information, the lack of land records and registration resulted in the development of a parallel land market in new land developments and in areas where tenure had been regularized. This, combined with illicit practices among government officials, generated intensive land speculation. In addition, a lack of resources meant that basic urban services could not be provided in new and regularized settlements.

Although it did not achieve its objectives, tenure upgrading and mass allocation of plots to households living in informal settlements between 1984 and 1990 had a significant impact on the demand for urban land for housing and on land prices. The traditional alliance between political power and customary owners was weakened, thus providing new openings for innovative forms of land management (Bagré, 2001; Guiebo et al., 1994).

The ambitious and radical urban land management policy carried out between 1984 and 1991 emphasized three main orientations during the 1990s: the reintroduction of the notion of private land ownership; the tentative creation of a private land and housing development sector; and decentralization. The latter is seen by most experts, as well as by local elected bodies, as a key precondition for the implementation of innovative approaches to tenure. At the moment, however, the main obstacle remains central government inertia and its opposition to any reform that could result in a loss of its land management prerogatives.

In Senegal, colonial land management did not formally abolish customary rights but introduced the land registration regime. Shortly after independence, new land legislation was adopted that had major consequences for tenure in urban areas. The National Domain Law is peculiar to Senegal. The National Domain includes all the lands that do not form part of the public and private domain of the state, and all the land not registered by 17 July 1964. Accordingly, all customary lands are incorporated in the National Domain (Ndoye, 2000). In this context, customary land has a legal status compatible with the 'modern' land law.

The land of the National Domain is held by the state for development purposes. In urban areas, such land cannot be developed unless it is transferred to the private domain of the state or municipality, duly registered and then allocated to households. Allocation can take only the following forms: grant of superficy (surface area) right; long-term lease; or permit to occupy, which is precarious and revocable (Rochegude, 1998). Such permits do not formally guarantee security of tenure to beneficiary households. The allocation process is complicated, ground rent recovery is poor and the limited supply cannot cope with demand. The law does not recognize the existence of customary ownership, unless the land was registered before 1964.

This legal framework, designed to rationalize urban planning and land management, rather encourages the development of informal settlements. As a result, about 45 per cent of the population in the Dakar metropolitan region[4] is living in irregular settlements under the permit to occupy regime. However, it is worth noting that many households feel reasonably secure with such permits (Tribillon, 1995). Although living in an irregular situation, their settlements are not considered informal.[5]

Until the mid-1980s, provision of serviced plots and low-cost housing for the low- and low-medium-income groups in Senegal was the exclusive responsibility of government-controlled development companies. In order to free land for developing these projects, the Senegalese authorities relied mainly on evictions, thus worsening the housing backlog at metropolitan level. This policy proved to have severe limitations and drawbacks, with the target population usually not the poor but middle- and high-income groups. The majority of households, who did not have access to low-cost housing programmes, then applied for a plot of land allocated by the state.

The tenure regularization policy currently implemented in Senegal is the result of an in-depth study carried out at all government levels since the mid-1980s. It was actually implemented from the early 1990s onwards. There is a strong political will at government level to carry out a large-scale tenure regularization programme. A law on physical upgrading and the regularization of informal settlements was passed in the 1990s. Since 1997, any decentralization policy should offer an appropriate framework for the implementation of innovative tenure approaches. However, so far achievements have been rather limited in quantitative terms. However, they open the way for the large-scale implementation of an urban tenure regularization policy at national level.

NEW APPROACHES TO TENURE

In Benin, Burkina Faso and Senegal, new approaches to tenure can be interpreted as forming part of a new social and political deal. Recent years witnessed political will among governments to devise and implement sustainable urban land policies and new approaches to tenure for the urban poor (UNCHS, 1999b). Intervention by international aid agencies, lessons learnt from international experience and – more importantly – pressure from civil society, have accelerated the process. The subsequent changes and innovations have also been influenced by decentralization trends and new approaches to governance (empowerment of municipalities and mayors), as well as innovative forms of public–private partnerships involving informal actors (Payne, 1999), despite resistance on the part of central government officials in charge of land management.

With the exception of Senegal, where tenure upgrading and regularization of informal settlements has been implemented at national level since the early 1990s, ongoing changes are characterized by: a reinterpretation of the colonial legacy regarding land tenure; the formalization and integration of customary/informal procedures into a formal legal and regulatory framework; and improvement of existing land delivery systems based on the intervention of private land and housing developers. The third of these measures is targeted towards medium- and high-income groups and rarely reach the poorest segment of the income groups.

Benin: integration of customary practices in the sphere of modern law

Two types of formal land tenure predominate in Benin: freehold and housing permits. Freehold gives maximum security of tenure but, so far, very few freehold titles have been issued. Obtaining a land title is a long and expensive task, taking up to two years and costing between US$300 and US$600 for a 500m² plot on the periphery of Cotonou (Tonato, 2000). The housing permit system was instituted immediately after independence. It is allocated to households that settle on government land and to beneficiaries of plots in public land development schemes – but only on a temporary and revocable basis. In practice, it does give beneficiary households fairly good security of tenure. Although not formally permitted, it is transferable and until recently it could also be mortgaged (finance institutions are now reluctant to grant mortgage loans to permit holders because of the uncertainties regarding the legality of the land sale and the speculative aspects of the urban land market). Because of the cost incurred in the land titling process, which most urban households cannot afford, the housing permit is now considered by urban households as a quasi-freehold.

During the past decade, innovative approaches have combined customary land delivery channels with subsequent public intervention. The land delivery process can be divided into two stages (Tonato, 2000; Oloude, 1999). In the first, there is no intervention by the authorities: customary owners subdivide the land they own (or claim to own) into plots. Following a rapid survey, and according to a simple provisional layout, plots are sold to individuals. The land sale agreement is signed by the two parties, countersigned by four witnesses, and sometimes video-recorded. Although the sale agreement form is provided by the central administration and the sale is usually authenticated by administration officials, this practice is tolerated but not considered legal. At this stage, security of tenure is not yet guaranteed to occupants of the plot.

In the second stage, the public authorities intervene in the customary-initiated land development. When all or most of the plots have been sold, the government administration carries out a detailed survey (plot delineation, identification of 'presumed owners'), prepares a new layout plan and undertakes land readjustment for the whole scheme, in order to free land for services (see Figure 7.1). Each 'presumed owner' is then reallocated a plot, which is smaller in size (by about 30–40 per cent) and may be located in another part of the scheme. Beneficiaries are then granted a temporary 'housing permit'. This permit, which will be converted into a permanent permit after the house has been built, offers fairly good security of tenure. In principle, the permit can be converted into freehold title at a later stage.

Figure 7.1 Informal development on customary land on the fringe of Cotonou. The layout plan that accompanies the land readjustment scheme and tenure regularization imposes new building lines. Credit: José Tonato.

Burkina Faso: decentralization, democratization and innovative practices

In 1990, under pressure from international finance institutions, a review of land legislation in Burkina Faso was carried out. The land and tenure reform was reappraised, and in 1991, the Burkina Constitution was adopted. This liberated land markets, but measures taken during the agrarian and land reorganization between 1984 and 1989 that aimed to improve security of tenure in informal settlements were not repealed, thus confirming the right of beneficiaries not to be evicted. This had – and still has – a positive impact on the economic situation of people living in informal settlements. De facto security of tenure has encouraged housing improvement and investment in home-based economic activities (Bagré, 1999, 2001).

In 1991, the main provisions of the agrarian and land reorganization were reviewed, so that they could be adapted in accordance with the new political and economic situation. One important innovation was the legalisation of 'land allocation certificates'. These could then be used as a form of guarantee by borrowers. This represented a formal recognition of popular practices that already considered this certificate as a quasi-property title, as with the 'urban housing permit' (see Figure 7.2).

Popular demand for secure tenure forced the authorities to include a section headed 'Valorisation of the urban housing title' in the Third Urban Project, financed by the World Bank. This decision can be seen as a step towards the reintroduction of the land title that was abolished in 1984

Figure 7.2   A house in an informal settlement in the process of regularization. The number written above the door by the administration indicates the status of the occupants (informal owner of the house, resident or non-resident). Giving a number is the first step in the tenure-upgrading process, and the owner of the house will check that it remains clearly legible. Credit: Alain Bagré.

(Guiebo et al., 1994). The 1991 agrarian and land reorganization texts were once again taken up in 1996, to be adapted to the new political context and the market economy. According to a law of 1996, developed land belonging to the state could be sold by adjudication. Plots were therefore serviced and put up for sale by a public land development agency. In 1997, the state created the National Company for Urban Land (Société Nationale des Terrains Urbains, SONATUR) for the provision and sale of serviced land. These development projects, inspired by the site and services concept, take place on vacant land in suburban areas and do not concern existing informal settlements. This measure can be interpreted as recognition of the power of market forces in urban land markets and an attempt by the state to maintain its monopoly of the land market.

Despite this supply of public and private land for housing, a section of the population was still excluded from ownership and they continued to use the customary informal land delivery system. Although such practices did not conform to current legislation, the state was unable to oppose them. Reductions in forced evictions were more the result of popular pressure than a deliberate choice on the part of the state to ensure security of tenure (Bagré, 2001).

Senegal: large-scale provision of secure tenure

The Senegalese experience deserves particular attention for two main reasons. First, it is the first attempt in the subregion to implement a tenure regularization programme at national level. In this respect, it represents a major step in the recognition of the legitimacy of irregular settlements, despite resistance from a large fraction of central government administration officials. Second – and under pressure from these officials – the tenure regularization policy was exclusively based on the allocation of a title, the 'superficy right', which is a form of long-term lease (Rochegude, 1998).

Through a procedure known as the Superficy Right Grant (Concession de Droit Superficie), urban land of the National Domain can be leased (for residential purposes only) from the state for a period of up to 150 years. This long-term lease can be mortgaged, transferred and inherited. The ground rent of the plot is collected as a one-time charge when the plot is allocated. Lessees/beneficiaries are obliged to build on the plot within a period of three years, and according to norms and standards defined by the state, in order to avoid the costs incurred by a yearly recovery of the ground rent. If the lessee cannot do so, the lease contract will, in principle, be nullified and the plot reverts to the National Domain. In practice, this happens very rarely, even when the plot remains undeveloped (Gueye, 2000).

Box 7.1   The Dalifort settlement pilot project in Senegal

The regularization programme was initiated by the Senegal government, with the financial and technical support of the German Technical Cooperation Agency (GTZ), in 1986. It took place in a context of social crisis generated by large-scale evictions from informal settlements in Dakar in 1985. The initial objective was simply to improve the physical environment of irregular settlements. However, GTZ's experience in Latin America had already suggested that security of tenure – and consequently tenure regularization – was a key element in any settlement-upgrading project, as it was expected to encourage the populations concerned to participate in, and contribute to, the upgrading process.

The programme was initiated with a pilot project, which was to inform the implementation of a large-scale programme (Durand-Lasserve et al., 1993) (see Figures 7.3 and 7.4). In 1987, when the regularization project was decided, Dalifort was a small squatter settlement with a population of 7100, living on 520 plots, usually occupied by extended families. It is located in a marshy land, exposed to seasonal floods, in the northern fringe of Dakar. About half of the squatted land was privately owned (either land owned by or purchased from customary owners, or land owned by French citizens but not yet transferred to the state). The rest of the land was owned by the state. In the eyes of the public authorities, occupants were considered to be owners only of the dwelling units and squatters on the land, although most of them were able to provide a 'paper' sale (sale agreement authenticated by witnesses). Ninety-five per cent of the dwelling units were wooden shacks. The area did not have access to basic urban services. Seventy-one per cent of the population were renting their dwelling unit, 26 per cent were owners or co-owners of their unit and 3 per cent did not pay any rent. Nearly half of the owners of the dwelling units were not living in Dalifort (Gueye, 2000).

The selection of the Dalifort settlement as a pilot project area was justified because the inhabitants had already taken a series of community-based initiatives, such as the setting up of standpipes, a community health centre and classrooms, all built with contributions from the households concerned. Following a preparatory survey carried out in 1986–87 by the DUA-GTZ project team, local NGOs and residents formed a community group.

The implementation phase started as soon as the state declared the scheme 'of public interest', thus protecting occupants against forced eviction, and when the community had agreed on a physical upgrading plan. In a later stage, the state registered all the privately owned land under its name. This was the prerequisite for issuing titles to eligible occupants.

Resident representatives, project teams and public authorities engaged in a series of decisions and agreed on a set of rules regarding priorities for access to basic services, tenure regularization and cost recovery mechanisms. In the meantime, financial mechanisms were set up to provide access to credit for the beneficiary households and a trust fund was set up in 1991. According to eligibility criteria decided by the project, 600 households were entitled to 'superficy rights'. Cost recovery was adopted as a principle, although it was admitted that this would not apply to the pilot project.

Physical upgrading and tenure regularization was carried out in parallel. Between 1989 and 1992, the project was extended to other settlements covering large areas of Dakar and Pikine: Thiaroye, Pikine irrégulier, Arafat, Medina Fass Mbao. In 1991, a national upgrading programme of spontaneous settlements was launched by presidential decree and extended to other settlements in Dakar. About 100 000 inhabitants were supposed to benefit from this new policy (Gueye, 2000).

The most recent official documents mention physical improvements and tenure regularization as long-term government strategies for improving the living environment in irregular settlements in Senegal. In practice, central government has a much more tolerant policy on security of tenure. One of the main achievements of the tenure-upgrading policy is the de facto recognition of most informal settlements, and a drastic decrease in the threat of eviction. Several new and influential urban stakeholders are expected to back this policy: NGOs (especially Enda-Tiers Monde) and grass-roots organizations, which are lobbying for security of tenure and provision of basic services in informal/irregular settlements; and customary communities (recent political changes in Senegal have resulted in a move to recognise customary leadership in urban and suburban villages in the Dakar metropolitan region).

Figure 7.3 House and environmental improvements under way in the Dalifort project, despite the lack of piped water. Credit: Moussa Gueye.

Figure 7.4 Piped water delivered to individual plots. Credit: Moussa Gueye.

IMPACT AND ANALYSIS OF THE NEW APPROACHES

In Benin, public intervention in customary informal land subdivision guarantees a reasonable level of security of tenure to occupants. This, in turn, has had an impact on the quality of the built environment. In affected settlements in the capital Cotonou, the quality of housing and services is much better – in terms of layout plan, the use of permanent building materials and land reserves for infrastructures and services, for example – than in tolerated informal settlements initiated by customary owners in other countries of the subregion. The de facto security of tenure also facilitates better access to credit (Tonato, 2000).

This unusual form of partnership opens the way for an innovative approach to tenure, adapted to the prevailing dual tenure system, provided that minor adjustments are made to the legal and regulatory framework. It has several advantages. First, the state does not impose administrative costs in the land allocation process, at least not in the initial stage, as purchasers negotiate directly with customary owners. As noted above, it also offers reasonably good security of tenure and, for customary owners, land readjustment and redevelopment by the public authorities remains one of the simplest ways of obtaining relative security of tenure.

In Burkina Faso, popular informal practices and land delivery systems remain the main channel for access to land. In this respect, the 1984–91 reforms did not reach their expected target, and the public sector proved unable to have a direct, sustainable impact on land allocation for the low-income population. However, these reforms have consolidated the feeling of security among households living in informal settlements – security of tenure no longer has to be associated with holding a land title, but with a simple certificate of plot allocation.

Populations living in informal settlements also use the system of witnesses and receipts for cash payments countersigned by the police, and this is accepted in the courts for resolving land conflicts. The divergence from former practice represents the emergence and de facto recognition on the part of the administration of different types of paper, certificate and official land title, and even the acceptance of the popular notion of ownership, which is not that of government administration. Despite the fact that conditions for issuing land titles have become more flexible since the 1996 law, few such requests are made.

A 1986 survey covering four areas of Ouagadougou (Becker, 1990), has shown that two years after tenure regularization, permanent building materials, rather than scrap materials, were usually being used for housing. Another survey carried out in February 2001 found that the majority of households have improved their houses using permanent building materials after being granted an administrative permit. Although it is officially a provisional permit, it provides sound de facto security of tenure. The residents of most settlements regularized between 1984 and 1985 now have individual access to drinking water and electricity, roads have been opened (although they are not yet surfaced) and sewerage and drainage has improved dramatically. The construction of health centres and schools has also improved the living conditions of people. Although the innovation process is slow, trends indicate a steady improvement of the tenure situation of the urban poor.

The Burkina Faso situation results from several contradictory trends: formal practices versus informal land development practices; market forces and privatization versus government attempts to keep control of land management; and central government control of land versus local land management and allocation. Particularly in Ouagadougou, the innovative approaches to tenure must be seen more as the result of new social practices than as a deliberate action of the state. These can be observed at four main levels: (i) the improvement of the tenure situation of all households who benefited from land allocation after 1984; (ii) the revival and de facto recognition of popular informal practices and land delivery systems; (iii) the struggle of the municipalities to exert land management responsibilities; and (iv) the emergence of civil society organizations opposed to forced evictions and demanding more transparent land management procedures (Mathieu et al., 2000).

In Senegal, the physical improvement and the tenure regularization programme has had a positive impact on the few settlements that benefited from the programme, as well as in other informal settlements that are likely to be regularized in the forthcoming years. The Dalifort pilot has proved that it is possible to pass from an irregular situation to land regularity in a formal context. This is important for the low-income urban dwellers in terms of their rights to the city. For the first time in the history of urban projects in Senegal, the poor were seen and treated as citizens, and drawn in to the decision-making process regarding the upgrading and regularization of their settlement.

The security of tenure provided by the programme has had an impact on the economic situation of the poor households and on the improvement of their living environment. In the Dalifort settlements in 1978, 97 per cent of dwelling units were made of wood or scrap/recovered materials, but by 2000, about 40 per cent of constructions were permanent structures, ranging from permanent homes with a corrugated iron roof to two-storey buildings. While some beneficiaries do not have the means to make improvements to their home, they have nevertheless added extra rooms on their secured plot, which they intend to rent. They justify this by saying that they need this income to afford the price of the plot (Gueye, 2000). And in some rare cases, beneficiaries have been able to obtain a mortgage loan for improving their house.

It must be stressed that in Dalifort itself there are many owners who have not met their financial liabilities (cost of the 'superficy right'), but who have made considerable improvements to their homes, simply because they know that the threat of eviction is no longer hanging over them. Similar phenomena can be observed in settlements where the project is being negotiated with the population, or participatory planning is at least beginning, even though this may be before land regularization procedures are fully in place.

The lease system provides a high level of security of tenure and must be seen as a very significant improvement when compared with the conventional permit to occupy. The tenure-upgrading policy implemented in Senegal shows that security of tenure can be effectively granted to households living in informal settlements, and that the people's perception of the central government commitment and political will to embark on large-scale regularization policy is understood as a protection against forced evictions. From this perspective, the success of the DUA/GTZ project should not be measured only according to the number of 'superficy rights' delivered. It has provided de facto security of tenure for most households living in informal settlements that were eligible for tenure regularization. This situation made possible the large-scale intervention by NGOs and community-based associations to improve service infrastructures within the settlements concerned .

In the case of tenure regularization in Dakar and other urban areas in Senegal, preference was given to the 'superficy right' system rather than to freehold. Justification for this preference was that a long-term lease would make expropriation procedures easier and would reduce speculation. The unofficial reason is the reluctance of government officials in charge of land allocation and management to lose control of the land allocation system. It is arguable, however, that the granting of freehold would have been much simpler. The 'superficy right' system is cumbersome because it requires the intervention of two central government administrations, which, since independence, have maintained their monopoly of state-owned land management and allocation: the Department of State Lands and the Cadastral Department. This centralized procedure has limited the effects of the regularization programme.

OBSTACLES TO INCREASE EFFECTIVENESS OF THE INNOVATIONS IN TENURE

In Benin, Burkino Faso and Senegal, the main obstacles associated with the innovations are closely related to the difficulties encountered in the ongoing decentralization process: the weakness of conventional centralized land registration procedures; the cost incurred by the implementation of innovative approaches; and the impact of market pressure on regularized settlements (UNCHS, 1999b).

Centralized procedures hindering innovative approaches to tenure

In Benin, decentralization measures have had a limited impact on public land management and allocation. Although local authorities are part of the process, their role remains consultative. Decisions are made by central government bodies or by their local branches, and land allocation procedures are submitted to a strict control of central government. The decentralized Land Development Commissions set up in 1996 are restricted to administrative tasks, and they still operate under the authority of the central government representatives (préfets and sous-préfets). Overlapping responsibilities between local authorities and local branches of central government administrations, as well as persistent distrust between central government and local authorities, results in a confusing and sometimes contradictory set of administrative, regulatory and legal measures (Comby, 1998). This hinders the formal implementation of innovative tenure reform (Imothep-Planurba, 1997).

In Burkina Faso, the 1995 law on decentralization was expected to open a new perspective for the implementation of innovative tenure policies. It allowed for local authorities to have their own land, sold to them by the central government. Local authorities were also given a large array of responsibilities regarding urban planning, land management and development. However, municipalities still do not have land of their own. Except in cases where a freehold title or an administrative permit has been issued, the land still belongs to the central state or to state-controlled land development agencies. Central government is still reluctant to transfer its land management responsibilities to municipalities.

In some cases, tension between central government and local authorities has reached breaking point, with local authorities increasingly involved in the provision and allocation of urban land. At the same time, customary 'owners' are still providing land for housing to households that do not have access to formal land delivery channels. However, since the decentralization measures were adopted in 1998 and the new mayors demanded to take over tenure regularization and land development operations, community-based 'residents' associations' and 'crisis committees' have begun to emerge, sometimes supported by NGOs,[6] which denounce evictions and make demands for transparency in land management (Bagré, 2001). These demands and the accompanying demonstrations have occasionally forced the local authorities to account publicly for their actions. This new trend is an unforeseen and unintentional consequence of decentralization, and in future we can expect popular demands to influence official policies in favour of more recognition of informal settlements.

In Senegal, land management is not an area of competence that has been transferred to local authorities (Ndoye, 2000). The central state is still hesitating in this regard, believing that this responsibility is too important to be moved. However, since decentralization came into force (in January 1997), local mayors have begun allocating land. There have even been some cases of land 'sales' by locally elected representatives. One key question remains: is it reasonable not to transfer, to the local communities in particular, a minimum of land management skills, since the local administration has only limited powers of control and sanction? There may well be locally elected representatives who are allocating land to potential electors, their friends and relatives, but there are also many who are keen to make their local government economically viable. By delaying the transfer of responsibility to the local authorities, central administration is hindering the dynamics of local development, which would certainly have encouraged the local authorities to take their share of responsibility.

In the Dakar region, at least, this would be the best way of developing an approach to land development in the traditional villages and in many regular settlements like Grand-Dakar, Ben Tally and parts of Pikine, where most owners still hold temporary permit to occupy. Proposals for reforms to the policies on decentralization suggest a transfer of land management responsibilities to the local authorities. Such a transfer could have an impact on local authority income. It is, perhaps, too early to evaluate the contents of these reforms, especially as the changeover government intends to make its own contribution.

Weakness of centralized land registration procedures

In Benin, the establishment of an urban land register is the first step towards innovative public intervention in informal settlements. However, it has some limitations. First, the identification of 'presumed owners' can be difficult in a context where customary land sales are not recorded in a single 'land book', and where diverging interpretations of customary rights and practices give rise to a series of land-related disputes. Second, without updated land information and land record systems, public authorities cannot keep the speculative process under control (the same person can buy as many plots as he/she wants and can afford). In this context, land readjustment procedures are not transparent and leave the door open to corruption and clientelism.

Despite several attempts made during the past two decades to set up land information systems, cadastres or comprehensive land registers, neither Burkina Faso nor Senegal has an updated land registration system. Records kept at settlement level do not have any administrative or legal value for government administrations. More surprisingly, in a context where public land allocation remains the main formal land allocation channel, they still do not have a proper record of actual state-owned land. Identification of right-holders is a time-consuming process that considerably limits tenure upgrading and regularization attempts (Durand-Lasserve, 1993).

Economic liberalization, speculation on urban land and market eviction

In the 1990s, the adoption of market-oriented policies under the pressure of international finance institutions (World Bank, 1991, 1993), have generated new forms of exclusion. Market pressures – and market eviction – are tending to increase in settlements that have benefited from tenure upgrading and/or regularization. In all three countries, the lack of land records and registration resulted in the development of a parallel land market in new land developments. In areas were tenure had been regularized, exacerbated by the illicit practices of government officials, intensive land speculation was generated. In addition, lack of public resources prevented the provision of urban services to new and regularized settlements. Rigid cost recovery policies regarding urban services further aggravate the situation (Environment and Urbanization, 1993).

On the urban fringe of the main cities in Benin (Cotonou, Porto-Novo and Parakou), intensive speculation on plots for housing during the past two decades has induced a rapid increase in the price of land. Land that remains accessible to people of low income is now located far away from the city boundaries. The poorest segment of the population (about 10 per cent of urban households) has now no choice but to settle in remote areas on unserviced plots, or in squatter settlements in areas not suitable for urbanization (areas subject to floods). In addition, the cost of the land subdivision–readjustment procedure is relatively high and beyond the reach of the poorest segment of the urban population. Beneficiary households have to pay for the cost of development studies (about US$14), resurveying and plotting (US$75), construction of road and basic infrastructures (US$7–28), delivery of the housing permit (US$210) and, if required by the beneficiary, the freehold title (at least US$420) (Tonato, 2000).

In Burkina Faso, there is a tight relationship between the liberalization of land markets (after 1991 and 1996–97) and the development of informal land delivery systems still under the control of customary owners. Most benefits of the 1984–91 policy intended to benefit the poor have been jeopardized by the new market-oriented policy implemented in the 1990s. One of the problems is the cost of the 'use taxes', which beneficiaries had to pay when they were granted the plot of land. Many have not yet completed the payment of these, which might oblige some families to leave the settlements and live elsewhere.

In Senegal, about 15 per cent of the plots owned by 20 per cent of the Dalifort population have been sold on. Improvements to the living environment have led to a rise in rents (from US$5–20 per month for a room). The settlement attracts new tenants who are looking for an area with a little more social standing. The owners realized that after regularization, their plot, which had been purchased for a modest price, had tripled or quadrupled in value, and they therefore decided to take advantage of this and sell. Money from these sales was used to purchase a house in an informal settlement area further out of Dalifort, and/or to invest in some form of commercial activity (Gueye, 2000).

As in other countries of the subregion, most national experts are considering this phenomenon to be a major drawback. In our opinion, however, this is not the case. Measures to control or contain the so-called 'speculation' by the poor – as suggested by those experts – would probably create more problems than they would solve, and severely hinder any further tenure upgrading programmes.

CONCLUSIONS: MAKING INNOVATIVE APPROACHES MORE EFFECTIVE

The experiences of Benin, Burkina Faso and Senegal suggest that a number of steps need to be taken to implement innovative approaches to tenure for the urban poor. Some are purely technical measures and could be implemented and enforced in the short term. Others require more time, skill and resources. They can be summarized as follows.

Public intervention in informal land subdivision could be rapidly improved, especially regarding:

- the reassessment of the role of the state regarding land management and allocation
- the clarification of the respective roles of central government planning institutions, administrations in charge of land management and local authorities
- a reassessment of the prevailing legal and regulatory framework (McAuslan, 1998)
- the comprehensive inventory of government-owned land (private domain of the state).

Structural accompanying measures should aim to:

- develop simplified land information systems to monitor land transfers, improve public land management and keep land speculation under control
- set up financial mechanisms to facilitate the access of the poor to urban land
- transfer land management responsibilities to municipalities
- improve the financial and human resources of local authorities and their technical skill through capacity building (Afri-cities, 2000).

These steps can be simply achieved through technical adjustments of the legal and regulatory framework. However, lessons from sub-Saharan Francophone African countries, and especially the experience of Benin, Burkina Faso and Senegal, suggest that technical measures must be combined with political will and structural reforms (UNCHS, 1999b).

A first set of measures concerns land rights. Until recently, priority was given to tenure regularization which was seen as a prerequisite for physical upgrading and servicing, emphasis being put on the provision of real rights. Vested interests in land and resistance from central government officials are such that the proposed tenure-oriented approach was difficult to implement. Experience suggests that this approach could be reversed, with priority being given to physical upgrading and servicing (Durand-Lasserve, 2000). Formal tenure regularization could come later, based on an incremental tenure-upgrading process, when households need it and can afford it. For the time being, security of tenure could be guaranteed by a non-eviction commitment on the part of the public authorities (UNCHS, 1999a).

Another set of measures should aim to redefine the centralized top-down approach regarding tenure reform, through the integration of prevailing social practices among communities concerned and the recognition of the legitimacy of informal approaches to tenure, unless public authorities can provide sound alternative solutions. This requires the recognition and promotion of community participation (UNCHS, 1996, 1997).

Tenure security, housing investment and environmental improvement: the cases of Delhi and Ahmedabad, India

Amitabh Kundu

INTRODUCTION

Slum improvement in Indian cities involves massive investment in land and basic amenities. The rapid changes in the system of governance in recent years have brought in several new actors willing to undertake such investments. A large number of slum households have exhibited the capacity and willingness to contribute in terms of their labour and capital resources for improvements in their living environment. Communities as well as NGOs have come forward to share with public agencies the responsibility for resource mobilization, design and implementation of the projects, recovery of loans, etc. Interestingly, a few of the large industrial houses have also shown interest in the improvement of basic amenities and the micro-environment in slums, as these determine the health situation in the cities, which in turn is linked to their business interests.

Understandably, investment in the micro-environment by any of the actors is forthcoming only when there is a reasonable level of certainty that the slum residents are not likely to be evicted in the near future, so that the benefits of the investment can be reaped by the community. In other words, some kind of formal or informal assurance given with regard to security of tenure is necessary for the flow of investment to materialize on the ground.

The experience of giving land ownership to the urban poor in India, however, is that it leads to large-scale transfers and displacement of the original population through functioning of the market. In view of this, the authorities in many of the cities are at present resorting to giving or permitting intermediate forms of tenure such as occupation licences, limited leases, co-operatives, informal assurances of non-eviction, etc. These do not give ownership rights to individuals, particularly the right to sell the land, but generate enough confidence in them to invest in housing and the local environment.

Bearing this in mind, the present chapter analyses the existing tenure systems and their implications for slum and overall city improvement, with special reference to the metropolises of Delhi and Ahmedabad. The second section presents the broad demographic and socioeconomic characteristics of the cities, focusing on the growth of slums, their spatial distribution and public policies. The next section discusses various types of arrangements evolved over the years in the slum areas responsible for perceived tenure security. The profile of the slums selected in the two cities for primary surveys is presented in the fourth section. The fifth section examines the effect of perceived tenure security on investment in housing, basic amenities, quality of life, etc., in the slum colonies. The discussion in these sections has generally been organized into two sub-sections, relating to the two selected cities. The final section summarizes the conclusions and puts forward a policy perspective for future development.

DEVELOPMENT DYNAMICS AND GROWTH OF SLUMS

Delhi scenario

Population in the Delhi urban agglomeration has grown by about 4 per cent per annum in every decade since 1931. The growth, however, has been highly disparate within the agglomeration. The localities in New Delhi and Cantonment that, in general, had low population densities, experienced sluggish demographic growth.[1] The Municipal Corporation of Delhi (MCD), which already had pressure on land and its limited amenities, however, grew much faster, leading to deterioration in the micro-environment. The same is true for a large number of neighbouring rural settlements, where population growth was phenomenal.

The public resentment at the dislocation of slums led to changes in policy. The public agencies allowed slums to grow by their passivity and sometimes even provided certain basic amenities. This resulted in the number of slum households increasing from fewer than 40 000 in 1981 to over 250 000 by the late 1990s.

The MCD adopted a multi-pronged strategy to tackle the problem. It organized in-situ upgrading of the slum clusters through the provision of modified layouts and basic amenities. Each family could obtain a loan of Rs7500[2] from Delhi Co-operative Housing Finance Corporation (DCHFC), recoverable in equal instalments over a period of 15 years. MCD also provided basic amenities in the slum clusters without necessarily improving the dwelling units or interfering with the physical layout of the area. The beneficiaries covered were to be organized into multipurpose co-operative societies through NGOs and CBOs. It is, however, important to note that in-situ upgrading was a very small component in the strategy. The major thrust was the relocation of squatter families to alternative sites. Each household was provided with a plot of 25 m² on a leasehold basis (18 m² as a built-up area including toilet and 7 m² as an undivided share in open courtyards), as a cluster-town-house planning concept. Land titles were given mostly in the name of the couple (with the names of all the family members), which made the selling of property by an errant husband to meet his alcoholic or other needs, relatively difficult. Slum residents, however, were not evicted on a large scale as no political party was prepared to face mass protests and lose its vote bank. Also, the public agencies concerned did not possess the land or finance required to cover large sections of the population. Given this macro-perspective, it is important to see how people made formal and informal arrangements to remain in the central city and what factors gave them perceived tenure security, encouraging them to make investments in housing and basic amenities.

The Ahmedabad scenario

The demographic growth in Ahmedabad since Independence is, unlike Delhi, far from spectacular, the city being one of the slowest-growing metropolises in the country. This can be attributed to the collapse of its textile industry in the post-Independence period, which was disastrous for the local economy.

The story of Ahmedabad, in the state of Gujarat, could have been as tragic as those of many capitals in African and Latin American countries, which have been plunged into crisis by increasing globalization. This has eroded the economic base of traditional industries. However, the long historical linkages of the city/state economy with the national and international system and the entrepreneurial skills of the local community averted an impending disaster. Ahmedabad managed to stay in the upcoming industrial belt of Western India, which has been described as the 'golden corridor', and attracted industrial units in and around it.

Unlike Delhi, there has not been a high growth in employment within the municipal limits of Ahmedabad city. A large proportion of urban migrants seeking employment have been absorbed in the towns falling within the agglomeration but located outside the corporation boundary. Consequently, the threat of eviction has not been as imminent as in Delhi.

Understandably, there was no specific policy or programme for the physical upgrading or resettlement of the slum dwellers in Ahmedabad until the 1970s. The sudden flood in 1973 marooned about 2500 families living on the banks of the Sabarmati, putting the arduous responsibility of rehabilitating them on the civic authorities. To meet the challenge, the Integrated Urban Development Project (IUDP) was launched, which led to the creation of the first resettlement colony in the city. For a period of about a year and a half the flood victims were accommodated in transit camps with community-based water taps and toilets. Subsequently, houses were built under the IUDP on a plot 29 m^2 (292 ft^2), each given on a freehold basis. Services such as tap water and electricity were provided to each house. Importantly, the beneficiary families were involved in the project at every stage, from planning to implementation.

The second project for the development of slums was launched in 1984 under the sponsorship of the World Bank. The project explicitly recognized the importance of providing security of tenure to the slum dwellers. According to this scheme, slums were to be acquired under the town planning scheme[3] and the tenurial rights were to be given to the house-holds after charging them the costs of development. The slum dwellers registered under the 1976 slum census were eligible for the allotment of plots and improvement loans from commercial banks. Some money was to be collected as betterment tax for providing improved roads, drainage, street lighting and other facilities. The scheme ran into difficulties because of obstacles in land acquisition, as about 70 per cent of the slum population in the city were occupying private land. As a result, only 17 slums covering about 4000 families could be taken up for upgrading, and those too with enormous delays. The scheme was implemented during 1990–93, with a reduced outlay of Rs40 million against the expected figure of Rs460 million.

An innovative participatory approach to urban development in Ahmedabad, which has been hailed as a major achievement, was launched in the early 1990s. This neighbourhood and slum improvement scheme is based on a partnership between the municipality, NGOs, CBOs and the private corporate sector.

The major problem faced by the Slum Networking Project (SNP) and other slum improvement projects in the country was that households did not have legal tenure to their plot. This was the major disincentive for indi-viduals investing in housing and for the banks sanctioning loans in the city of Indore, where the project was first tried out. To overcome this difficulty, AMC has given an assurance to the slum dwellers that they will not be evicted in the next ten years. In many cases, the ownership right of the slum area lies with a private individual or is shared between the municipality and a private agency. In some others it cannot be clearly ascertained. In such situations, the AMC and the private agency have again assured the slum dwellers that they will not be evicted, and this has proved adequate in motivating them to join the project. The project has not been taken up on government lands reserved for developmental purposes, or on private lands under dispute or litigation.

There are suggestions to increase the contribution from slum house-holds to 50 per cent of the cost of physical development and the period of tenure to 20 years. These have been taken seriously in the AMC and are incorporated in the draft of the of state's slum policy. In general, NGOs and CBOs have not opposed the idea as they recognize that without this the SNP is unlikely to be continued. Large sections of slum households in dif-ferent parts of the city have shown a willingness to participate in the pro-ject, even with enhanced contributions, as they believe this to be the only way they can secure assurance from AMC against eviction.

It has been noted above that, unlike many other urban centres in the country, much of the land in Ahmedabad occupied by slums belongs to the private sector. This is in sharp contrast to the situation in Delhi. This lack of ownership rights vested in local authorities or the state government is expected to pose difficulties in giving titles or formal occupancy rights to slum dwellers. This is possibly the reason for the limited scale of the project. Of the thousand slum colonies in the city, the SNP has been taken up in only about 24.

THE EXISTING TENURE SYSTEMS IN DELHI AND AHMEDABAD

The tenure systems prevailing in the slums of Delhi and Ahmedabad have evolved over the past several decades. They have been modified from time to time in response to governmental orders, ordinances, policies and programmes that have been largely ad hoc in nature and rarely uniform in terms of coverage. As a consequence, a large variety of systems exist on the ground, indicating differential levels of tenure security. These may be presented as follows.

Formal title to land (patta)

As mentioned above, many of the households squatting in the city of Delhi before 1960 were evicted and resettled. By the mid-1970s, about 3500 households were given plots of 80 m² with 99-year leases. An equal number of tenements were also constructed and allotted to them on a leasehold basis. Unfortunately, there has been large-scale resale of property by the resettlers as the plot sizes were large and attracted higher-income households. Most of these resettlement areas have now been occupied by high- and middle-income households and are well integrated with the colonies in the neighbourhood.

Unlike in Delhi, formal land titles were given to households in Ahmedabad until the mid-1980s. Most of the beneficiaries were the victims of floods, resettled near Vasna, but there were a few who got land titles through the in situ upgrading project of the World Bank as late as the early 1990s.

Licences to households permitting residential use of land based on monthly payment of rent and subsequent bestowal of leasehold rights

The squatters coming to Delhi after 1960 were evicted and relocated on the periphery of the city between 1962 and 1977, with plots of 21 m² and shared services. They were permitted to construct temporary huts on designated plots. Initially, these were thought of as temporary camping sites and each household was charged a token rent. The resettlement of the slum population was undertaken on a massive scale during the 1975–77 National Emergency period. However, due to considerable public resentment, the government decided to increase the plot size to 26 m² and provided a higher level of services. Furthermore, it considered giving leasehold rights, on payment of a part of the cost. Unfortunately, a large majority of the households did not come forward to pay the fees for conversion of their plot from rental to leasehold property.[4] The system of providing leasehold titles was stopped in 1992, following a High Court order urging the government to provide only licences for the use of land which, it was hoped, would restrict the transfer of property.

In 1998, just before the state level elections, the state government once again offered leasehold rights to people in the resettlement colonies on payment of a one-off fee of Rs5000. Those who had purchased without formal authority from original allottees were required to deposit Rs13 500. This scheme also evoked a lukewarm response from the residents, and just a few came forward to take advantage of the scheme. This indicates that only a small segment of the resettled households have leasehold rights to their property. Most of them are still covered under the licensing system, although only a few pay the monthly fees. In the case of Ahmedabad, however, licences are not being provided by the Municipal Corporation.

Licences to co-operative societies in slum colonies taken up for in situ development

In Delhi, the emphasis appeared to shift from resettlement to in situ upgrading after the late 1980s. However, only a few colonies, such as Ekta Vihar, Prayog Vihar and Shanti Vihar, were taken up for development by the Slum Wing of MCD on an experimental basis. Households were given the right to use the land through licences issued to their co-operatives and each received a plot of 12.5 m² on payment of a nominal licence fee. The scheme was not replicated on a large scale in the city due to the unwillingness of land-owning agencies to transfer their land, and a lack of political will. However, another 5000 households in different areas of the city benefited from in situ development projects, with many reaping the benefit of licensing arrangements.

The households in slum pockets covered under the SNP project in Ahmedabad are receiving similar benefits. They have obtained the right to the residential use of land through the licence issued to the Association of Residents by AMC for a period of ten years. No individual has any document whatsoever indicating his or her ownership, even for a limited period. However, the registration of the households with the associations that have the certificate has given quite a high level of tenure security among the people.

Leasehold titles through co-operative societies in resettlement colonies

The households arriving in Delhi before 1990 have been given plots of 25 m² (18 m² for the plinth area with toilets and 7 m² as an undivided share in an open courtyard) on a leasehold basis in the new colonies set up in recent years. The MCD, however, chose to allot the plots to the co-operative societies, which in turn gave the land lease to individual families.

No formal tenure, but perceived security existed due to the provision of electricity, water supply, sewerage, etc.

Several slum colonies have been formally covered under governmental programmes providing certain amenities, or have informal access to these through personal or political connections. The launching of a governmental programme or the extension of water supply, sewerage, electricity, etc., is often seen as the initiation of a process of regularization of the colony, or at least the recognition of the possibility of its becoming regularized in the near future.

Individual photo identity cards, ration cards, formal or informal document of ownership of the dwelling unit

The perceived sense of security among a section of slum households is due to their possession of documents that may or may not have legal validity. It is possible to categorize the people on the basis of such documents and their perceived security in the following ways:

- *Photo identity cards issued to individuals based on official surveys establishing residence in the city on or before a cut-off date.* There are a large number of households in Delhi that possess identity cards as a result of their being listed in certain comprehensive surveys, conducted by state or local governments with the objective of covering them under a slum development programme. The most important among these is the survey conducted by the Food and Civil Supplies Department in 1990 for the issue of ration cards at the initiative of the then Prime Minister V.P. Singh. Nine hundred and twenty nine settlements and 260 000 households were provided with identity cards and metallic plates,[5] making these people feel better placed in relation to others. This can also be attributed to the policy declarations made or endorsed by government functionaries from time to time to adhere to the cut-off date in 1990 for identifying the beneficiaries of future programmes of resettlement or slum improvement. It is stipulated in several of the government documents that people with these cards (often referred to as V.P. Singh Cards) would be entitled to certain plot sizes on relocation. Indeed, in the few cases of resettlement that took place during the 1990s, the plot size was linked with the possession of this card or other documents establishing the date of their arrival. A similar comprehensive survey was undertaken by AMC in Ahmedabad in 1976 to identify the slum dwellers under the World Bank Scheme. Unfortunately, no card or certificate was issued to the households and hence this is presently not perceived as an important factor in security of tenancy.
- *Ration cards, voter's identity card or other documents establishing the residence of the household in the city on or before a certain date.* The legal system in the country gives importance to the duration of

residence at a place in deciding about eviction, provision of alternate sites, etc. As a consequence, households with ration cards, voter's identity cards, etc., feel relatively secure compared to more recent arrivals. Understandably, the level of the security perceived by the household depends on the duration of their stay.

▪ *Stamp paper receipts from the so-called owner of the plot or the prior occupant with signatures of local leaders, or legal personnel such as notaries.* Many of the households have 'purchased' land or their dwelling units from the previous resident, or middlemen, by getting the signature of the latter on stamp papers, with some local leaders standing as witnesses. These papers confirm the 'transfer of the structure of a house' in following payment by the present to the previous occupant. Most of these papers have no legal validity, but enjoy a degree of respectability among the community. They are even recognized at the local level in settling disputes.

It is evident that possession of documents as discussed above does not ensure security of tenure at the present location, but at best provides some kind of assurance of an alternative plot. The households may still make investment in the existing plot as they hope to carry the materials used in house construction with them.

Connections with the local leaders, councillors and functionaries of political parties

Many people in the slums have linkages with important personalities in the locality or the local governments and often act as conduits to the vote bank. As a consequence, they succeed in having access to amenities provided by public agencies. This gives them a feeling of security against eviction. Another important factor in obtaining perceived security would be the exact location of the colony or the individual house within the colony. Understandably, if the slums are located on land that is likely to be taken up for certain planned activities such as road construction, commercial complexes, etc., households will feel less secure. Similarly, within the colony, people residing in houses that are encroaching on roads, or overlooking a railway track or formal housing colony, feel more threatened by eviction. Thus perception of security is determined by factors specific to the area and the dwelling unit.

In order to obtain both an overall and an in-depth view of the impact of de jure or perceived security of tenure on the quality of housing and basic amenities at household and settlement levels, scanning surveys were undertaken with households in a limited number of settlements in both cities. In addition, qualitative information was gathered through discussions with government officials, voluntary organizations, slum and community leaders, etc. in the areas. The slums were selected from both the core as well as the periphery of the city, making it possible to incorporate the locational factors in operation. Proximity to commercial, industrial and residential areas also has a bearing on the level of perceived security and investments made by public and private agencies, including the slum households in improving the micro-environment. These, too, have been kept in view in selecting the colonies.

PROFILE OF SLUMS IN DELHI

Jawahar Camp in Kirti Nagar (JCK)

This is a colony notified by the Municipal Corporation as a slum (in short, a notified slum), located on the eastern side of Delhi, stretching up to the nearby railway track. It is located largely on public land, 15 per cent of which belongs to public works department (PWD) of Delhi government and 75 per cent to the railways (central government). The ownership of the remaining 10 per cent of the land is unknown. According to information gathered from the old residents, the settlement came into existence in 1978 and there were about 2000 households in 1994. Presently, the colony has nearly 2500 households, including tenants. Home owners account for about 55 per cent of the population, while the remainder are tenants paying between Rs200 and Rs250 a month. About 30 per cent of the dwellings accommodate more than one household. Summary statistics of the level of basic amenities for this and other selected slum colonies in Delhi is shown in Table 8.1.

Laxminagar Camp (LNC)

This cluster of settlements is located on public land on the bank of the River Yamuna and came into existence in 1977. About 45 per cent of the land belongs to the PWD of Delhi government, 40 per cent to Delhi Development Authority (DDA) and the remaining 15 per cent to the PWD of the central government. The original settlers are reported to have 'rented in' plots from a contractor who had leased the land from DDA for cultivation. In 1995, about 66 families were evicted from here and relocated at Papan Kalan so that a road could be constructed. However, 30 per cent returned to this colony. There was large-scale encroachment in the colony in the late 1990s. Presently, it has about 4000 hutments accommodating 6000 households.

Sonia Gandhi Camp at Smalkha (SCS)

This colony is located on the south-west side of the international airport and dates back to 1975, when a cement factory was established. Subsequently, the land was purchased by Sanjay Gandhi, son of the then prime minister. After his death, the villagers claimed the land, but it was formally taken over by the DDA through court orders. However, encroachment

Table 8.1   Availability of basic amenities and services in the sample slums of Delhi

Colony	No. of taps		Hand pumps		Toilet (no. of seats)				Per cent of households with electricity connection		Total no. households
	Legal	Illegal	Working	Non-working	MCD	Individual	Sulabh	Mobile	Legal	Illegal	
JCK	65	130	1	5	–	–	10	12	–	100	2500
LNC	150	250	33	–	–	550	54	56	60	40	6000
SCS	–	–	7	8	–	–	24	–	–	100	1500
ICH	3	5	1	–	–	–	–	10	–	100	470
ICS	–	25	1	8	20	400	–	–	–	100	650
SCT	27	150	–	50	–	–	60	–	–	100	6500
ACS	–	–	–	–	–	–	–	–	–	100	900
NRC											

Note: the quantitative data on amenities, presented in the table, together with the qualitative assessment regarding tenure security discussed below, were gathered through field surveys during Sept–Dec 2000. The information on NRC in Narela has not been included as the colony is in the process of development. People are still moving in and facilities in many areas are still to be provided. Also, these are not given for the colonies in Ahmedabad, as the amenities have been/are being provided to all households under the SNP.

continued in the colony in the 1990s. In March, 2000, the local government, with the help of police and local henchmen, demolished about 500 huts to widen a road, despite many of the residents possessing ration and identity cards. The slum dwellers, however, believe that the officials were in connivance with upper caste 'thakurs' of Smalkha village and were paid bribes to carry out the demolition work. Importantly, none of the households was relocated, but about 80 per cent of them rebuilt their huts soon after the demolition. At present, the colony accommodates about 1500 households in 1200 hutments.

Indira Camp behind Safdarjung Hospital (ICH)

This colony sprang up in 1977, inside the boundary of Safdarjung Hospital. After its demolition by the police in 1986, it was relocated outside the boundary of the hospital. The colony presently stands on public land that belongs partly to the Land and Development Office of the Delhi government and partly to New Delhi Municipal Committee. The number of huts has increased slowly, and by the late 1990s stood at 450, accommodating some 470 households. About 90 per cent of the households live in houses they own, while the remainder are tenants.

Indira Camp in Srinivashpuri (ICS)

This is a notified slum with three parts. It had about 300 huts in 1990, and this has recently increased to 650. Part one is the largest part, accommodating about 450 households. The other two parts have 100 households each. About 70 per cent of the land is owned by MCD and the remaining by Central PWD. Almost all households own their houses, although the ownership has changed in about 20 per cent of cases since 1990. Importantly, the price has increased tremendously during the past decade from Rs4000 in 1990 to over Rs40 000 in 1997–98.

V.P. Singh Camp in Tughlakabad (SCT)

This is a notified slum, which emerged in 1980. It is located on public land, one third of which belongs to the DDA and two thirds to Indian Railways. The number of huts has increased significantly from about 1350 to 6000 during the past decade. About half the residents have come here from other parts of the city. In 1999, the railways authorities wanted a portion of the land to set up their container depot, which led to the eviction of a large number of households. There were 539 among them with V.P. Singh Cards who were entitled to alternative plots. Of this 539, only 240 paid their Rs7,000 share of the relocation cost. The rest are reported to have sold their entitlements to property dealers[6] for an amount ranging from Rs16000 to Rs20 000. However, the demolition and relocation process has been stalled partially as a number of huts do not have identity cards and consequently cannot be relocated to the alternative site. Currently, about 6500 households are living in the colony. About 70 per cent of the households own their huts, while the rest are tenants.

Azad Camp in Sarita Vihar (ACS)

This is a notified slum, located on the Delhi–Mathura Road, near Apollo Hospital. The colony came into existence about 1980, but did not grow much initially due to a lack of developmental activity in the area. There were only 40 dwelling units in 1990. However, the number increased significantly during the 1990s, reaching about 800 in 1999. Much of the land belongs to the DDA and only 20 per cent is under the ownership of Indian Railways. About 80 per cent of the households live in their own houses.

A survey conducted by DDA before constructing a flyover in June 1999 identified over 224 hutments for demolition. Unfortunately, there was no plans for relocating the evicted households despite their holding V.P. Singh Cards. The owners of the demolished huts (only 69 huts were ultimately demolished) were told unofficially by the officers to rebuild their structures on DDA land on the northern side of the colony. Taking advantage of the uncertain situation, 180 huts have been built in addition to the 69 demolished huts, with a plot size of 9 m². The elected *pradhans*[7] of the colony are selling plots to the outsiders for about Rs5000. Apparently, the *pradhans* share the profits from this 'business' with the local police.

Narela Resettlement Colony (NRC)

This colony is located in the western part of Delhi and comes under the Narela administrative division. It is the largest of the resettlement colonies in Delhi. It has six sectors in which 1869 households have been allotted plots with leases of 99 years, as is the case in the formal housing societies in Delhi. The first group of households resettled here were those evicted from the slum at Andrews Ganj in outer Delhi in 1998. Subsequently, the people evicted from the slum colony at Chankyapuri in central Delhi during the same year were also relocated here. The most recent group to be resttled here are those evicted from Rajiv colony, located behind Nehru stadium, in 2000.

People here are facing serious problems of unemployment, as there is no industrial unit in or around the colony. They are, therefore, required to commute to far-off colonies, mostly to the original places where they still have contacts.

PROFILE OF SLUMS IN AHMEDABAD

Three slum colonies have been selected from among those covered under the SNP. These are Sanjaynagar, Sinheshwarinagar and Pravinnagar-Guptanagar (PGN phase I). In the first two colonies, the work has already been completed, while in the third it is ongoing. The first two colonies are relatively small in terms of their area as well as population: Sanjaynagar (SJN) has about 180 huts with a population of 1000, while Sinheshwarinagar (SHN) has 42 units with 225 people. The third slum, PGN, is a much larger settlement, comprising 1070 huts with a population of 6500. The reason for selecting PGN is that it is on the verge of completion. It should therefore be possible to examine the impact of short-term security of tenure on the investment in housing and slum improvement.

In the case of SJN, land belonged to the AMC and it was easy to give assurances against eviction and bring it under the SNP project. The same is true for SHN. The third colony is under private ownership. It is important that despite a large number of claimants to the ownership of the land, the corporation, through a negotiation process, has been able to give assurances against eviction for ten years and launch the project.

Sanjaynagar (SJN)

SJN is situated on a triangular plot of two hectares. A group of 17 households of the *pattani* community are reported to have first settled on this plot, belonging to Nutan Mills, in 1971. In 1976, the AMC acquired it and earmarked it for constructing a civic centre. Following legal advice, the *pattanis* increased their strength to 66 by bringing in more families and then approached the court, which directed the AMC to rehabilitate the slum dwellers. As AMC did not have the financial resources for rehabilitation, the residents of SJN stayed and a large number of new families moved in. The number of households had increased to 190 by 1997. It was selected as a 'pilot case' under the SNP at the initiative of Arvind Mills, the private sector partner in the project.

Sinheshwarinagar (SHN)

This slum is located in the north zone of the city and comes under the municipal ward of Naroda Road. This colony developed as a result of demolition of the Omnagar slum by the Corporation. At the time of launching the project there were about 42 households belonging to the *pattani* community.

Pravinnagar-Guptanagar Phase I (PGN)

In contrast to the other two slums, this colony is located on private land belonging to a number of self-claimed owners. The land originally belonged to the village *panchayat* and was classified as wasteland. With the expansion of the city, the village was brought under the jurisdiction of the AMC, resulting in large increases in land value. Subsequently, a number of people tried to grab the land by obtaining control through political connections or legal manoeuvres. There are seven localities in this colony, all developing at different times, and each having a different claimant of land ownership. Many households are still paying rents as self-proclaimed owners of the plot. The majority of the settlers possess some kind of stamp papers, signed by so-called owners, local leaders, notaries, etc., which may not stand up in court.

The level and quality of the basic amenities in SJN and SHN before the launch of the SNP, with licences for the use of land, were very low. Comparatively, the residents of PGN were in a better situation. More than three quarters of the households had access to a water supply and electricity connection.[8] However, unlike Delhi (Table 8.1), households here had obtained electricity connections illegally from neighbours and not from outside power lines and hence were paying the bills.

IMPACT OF TENURE SECURITY ON HOUSING AND BASIC AMENITIES

The case of Delhi

The impact of tenure security in Delhi is very different from that of Ahmedabad, since the slum households in Delhi, apart from those in resettlement colonies,[9] have no titles to their plots. Many, however, have a strong *perceived* sense of security, depending on their location, access to basic services, coverage under different governmental programmes, etc. In Ahmedabad, on the other hand, a number of slums have been taken up under the SNP and the residents have been given a formal assurance against eviction.

Perceived security among the slum dwellers promotes group feeling and facilitates community activities. It motivates CBOs, NGOs and even private agencies to launch capital projects for improving amenities such as roads, brick pavements, sewerage lines, garbage disposal and street lighting systems, etc., and to maintain them. For example, in the slum colonies of Srinivaspuri, where the perceived security is high, a large number of NGOs and CBOs have launched projects to improve the quality of the micro-environment. These have made arrangements for laying the pipelines and getting tap water by collecting money from the inhabitants, rather than waiting for the authorities to provide them. Almost all the pathways within the colonies have been paved, thanks to community-based activities.

The analysis of the statistical data gathered through the field survey allows identification of certain factors that have an impact on perceived security of the households and consequently their levels of investment. These are discussed below.

Location of slum: prime area and neighbourhood conflict

The location of a slum is the most important factor for determining the sense of security. The case of ICH in Delhi may be cited in this context. Here, the inhabitants feel threatened because of the plans for expansion of the circular ring road which passes through the colony. Police come to the locality every now and then, increasing their level of insecurity. The conflict with the Dabur corporate office in the neighbourhood is also an important factor in perceived insecurity. The slum dwellers believe that 'this company frequently terrorizes the people through government officials and police, by bribing them'. In the past, the courts have given stay orders on many of the developmental works, following suits filed from the slum.

A similar situation exists in SCS, as noted above. Here, a large percentage of the people feel the threat of eviction due to their constant conflict with the *thakur* community in the nearby village. ACS is yet another slum where the feeling of threat is high. The fear has increased in recent months because of the demolition of 69 huts on the highway for the construction of a flyover. There is, however, no neighbourhood conflict in this colony. Still another example of high insecurity would be Part III of Srinivaspuri Camp (ICS). People here feel vulnerable because the colony has encroached on the road connecting the circular ring road and the nearby DDA flats. Unlike phases I and II of this colony, all the houses in this phase are of *katcha* construction.

Public and private land

The perceived threat and its impact on investment in housing depends very much on the nature (public or private) of the land-owning agency. People occupying private land feel relatively secure compared to those on public land. This can be largely attributed to the legal process of slum eviction, which for a private agency is highly cumbersome. Also, the land-owning agency has to bear about 70 per cent of the costs of relocation, which comes to about Rs30 000 per household. There are several cases where the slum dwellers have successfully resisted private initiatives for eviction but are helpless before public agencies. The slum colony at Smalkha presents an interesting case as, despite ongoing conflicts with the neighbouring villagers and evictions in the recent past, a section of the people feel secure. This is because of the nature and lack of clarity regarding the land-owning agency. The high security level here manifests itself in the conversion of a number of *katcha* structures to *pucca* and *semi-pucca* houses.

Possession of personal cards

The most important document, which gives a tremendous sense of security to households, is the V.P. Singh identity card and token number. Examples of this can be seen in JCK (Kirtinagar), SCS (Smalkha) and ICS (Srinivaspuri).

The percentages of households having V.P. Singh Cards here are 50, 40 and 50 respectively, which are higher than other colonies surveyed. Importantly, the percentages of *pucca* houses here are also high compared to similar slum colonies, the figures being 70, 40 and 40 respectively.

Possession of ration cards, identity cards or registration of house owners on the voters' list are below the V.P. Singh Card in terms of creating a sense of security. The slum population in Delhi recognizes the importance of the former and makes an effort to procure these documents through legal or illegal means. Only those who have come to Delhi recently – since 1998, for example – have been unable to secure them, but their number is very low due to the restrictive policies adopted by the city government. However, the possession of such documents by the majority in all the colonies makes it difficult to assess the impact of this factor.

Availability of basic services

One important factor influencing the perception of slum dwellers is the inclusion of households under government programmes or their coverage by public agencies. Access to basic services, particularly obtaining electricity connection from the Delhi Vidyut (Electricity) Board, is a factor that boosts the sense of security. This has an immediate effect on the structure of the houses in the colony. One can cite the examples of the SCS and ICH. These two colonies have low levels of basic amenities compared with those available in the other colonies, confirming the residents' suspicions that they can be evicted at any time. The neighbours who are constantly making efforts to evict them also ensure that no government facility is extended to them.

The case of Ahmedabad

The most significant point about the three localities surveyed in Ahmedabad is that there has not been much buying and selling of plots leading to displacement of the original habitants. Since the AMC did not give licences to individuals, the risk of land changing hands was minimal. It is impressive that over 95 per cent of the original residents are still residing there, even four years after the SNP was launched. Importantly, the announcements that tenure is to be provided have attracted households from outside the locality. In the case of localities in Ahmedabad, however, the increase has been marginal – between 2 and 5 per cent – possibly because they are in a congested locality and there is not much land available for expanding the settlement. Also, these were taken up in the initial phase of the project and the assurances given by the AMC against eviction were not widely known or taken seriously. Furthermore, investigations in the field and discussions with the residents reveal that community networks built by setting up committees at the locality and street levels ensured that such transfers did not become the order of the day.

A large-scale subdivision of plots and an increase in the number of dwelling units are observed in many cities where the 'licence to use the land' has been given to slum dwellers. This occurs because adults other than the head of a household claim additional plots, taking advantage of the tenure security. Indeed, this phenomenon can be noted to a small extent in all areas covered by the Ahmedabad survey through the increase in the number of households. One may further notice an increase in the percentage of the small households – having fewer than five members – from about 30 to 45 per cent over a span of five years in Sanjaynagar (SJN) and Sinheshwarinagar (SHN) where the project has been completed.

It may be noted that despite years of residence, over 85 per cent of the households in the non-SNP colonies in Ahmedabad have not built *pucca* structures. Conversely, in all three colonies under the SNP, the percentage of *pucca* houses is over 90 per cent. This unmistakably reflects the impact of perceived tenure security on investment in housing. Within three years of the launch of the SNP around 80 per cent of the houses in Pravinnagar-Guptanagar have been upgraded, leading to conversion of *katcha* units to *pucca* houses. In the other two colonies the percentage is much higher – about 95 per cent. Therefore only a small percentage of people have not upgraded their houses. About 5 per cent of the households have added a room, resulting in an increase in their plot size from about 20m^2 to 60m^2. A similar number of houses have been converted into shops and commercial establishments.

On average, households have spent about Rs20 000 in SJN, Rs28 000 in SHN and Rs120 000 in PGN on house improvements. The households spending more than Rs10 000 account for over 50 per cent in SJN and 80 per cent in the remaining two colonies. The investment levels in PGN are higher as a number of the residents are either working for AMC or engaged in businesses with reasonable income levels. In the other two colonies, large sections are engaged in hawking and trading and hence have a small surplus income to invest in housing.

Improvements in the dwelling units in the SNP areas have been possible largely due to the availability of loans provided by the SEWA Bank. This is a major factor. In several other projects, people have been unable to upgrade their houses for the simple reason that they do not have enough funds. The possibility of securing loans from the financial institutions has been low and consequently they have been forced to borrow from moneylenders. This has put households in serious debt traps and resulted in their being dispossessed of land. Securing loans is not a problem under the SNP as the provision of credit through community networking is fundamental to the project. One would argue, therefore, that tenure security, backed by community networking, has created a different environment in Ahmedabad (Dutta and Batley, 1999).

The conversion of temporary houses into permanent structures, coupled with land tenure security, has also led to higher rental values. The rents of the single-room houses have increased by about six times in SJN and SHN, and by about three times in PGN. To a limited extent this has led to higher-income households replacing the poor tenants, but many of the old tenants do not mind paying higher rents because of the improved micro-environment and surety of residence, at least for a certain period.

The impact of this licensing provision is also manifest in the tremendous increases in property values. The increase varies across colonies, depending on their commercial importance and proximity to business areas. The value of a house has increased four times from Rs10 000 to Rs40 000 in SJN and SHN. PGN, being nearer to the city centre, enjoys higher commercial importance. The property values here were higher, between Rs30 000 and Rs50 000, depending on the condition and location of the house, even before the launch of the SNP. These are now valued at Rs70 000–80 000.

It has been noted in the case of Delhi that with perceived tenure security, CBOs have emerged and made investments in improving amenities. The scenario in the case of Ahmedabad is similar. Here, the SNP project has offered assurance against eviction for a period of time and envisages the provision of many of these amenities under its physical improvement component. Each household, for example, has toilet, water and sewerage connections. At the local level, road development and sewerage line connections to the main system falls within the purview of the programme. In accordance with official requirements, Rs6000 is spent per household for physical improvements, the amount to be shared equally by the individual beneficiary, AMC and a private agency involved in the project. Understandably, none of them would have come forward to commit their resources had there been no tenure security.

Maintenance of the amenities is also linked with tenure security. In the SNP slums of Ahmedabad, the result has been improved maintenance. Rs100 per household has been collected and retained at the community level. It is expected that the interest accruing from this money will meet the cost of maintenance, at least partially. The discussions with local NGOs, slum leaders, etc., reveal that the assurance from the AMC has been extremely important in building awareness and group feeling. This is a major factor behind the households paying all their dues.

This feeling of tenure security arising from the assurance given by the AMC has had a major impact on the SNP colonies. Discussions with the 16 heads of the households in each of the three slum colonies reveal that there has been considerable improvement in the physical conditions and access to basic services since the mid-1990s. The impact is visible in terms of improved pavements, roads, etc. All the households have been provided with tap water connections and water is supplied for two hours daily in the morning, giving per capita water consumption figures of 120 litres per day. Most of the households consider this sufficient. Toilets have also been provided to the households at a cost of Rs5700 each and have been connected to the city's main sewerage lines. The facility for storm water drainage has also been provided. These have improved the environmental conditions in the colonies, and prevented a number of diseases. Further, AMC has provided one dustbin for every 16 households in the colonies for the collection of garbage, which has improved the solid waste management and micro-environment in the colonies. Efforts are also under way to improve their educational, health and skill status through community mobilization (Acharya and Parikh, 2001).

The overall improvement in the environment of the colonies, along with the safe drinking water, hygienic improvements and better housing facilities, have enhanced the health status of the residents. The incidence of illness has declined from about 25 to 15 per cent (Joshi, 2001). Moreover, with the help of CBOs, the programme has succeeded in creating health awareness, particularly for the children, as is evident from the increase in the number of immunized children which has risen from 30 to 45 per cent.

The original plan of the SNP was to provide street lighting only and not individual connections. But the CBOs responsible for the mobilization of people realized that providing electricity to the households would substantially improve quality of life. For this, each household was required to make a payment of Rs3320 to Ahmedabad Electricity Corporation (AEC). Luckily, the people residing in SJN and SHN, most of whom belong to socially backward castes, had to pay only Rs670 because they could benefit from a scheme of Gujarat government and get a subsidy of Rs2650 each. In PGN, too, the people from backward castes took advantage of the scheme, but upper-caste households who were not entitled to this subsidy paid the total amount. The necessary amount was deposited with the AEC within a very short period. This is because the residents believed that besides the advantage of using electricity, getting a connection would reduce the risk of eviction. They consider electricity bills to be a proof of their residence, usable in a court of law. In other words, the electricity connection greatly enhanced the perceived security among the slum dwellers.

CONCLUSIONS AND POLICY RECOMMENDATIONS

Tenure security in India, formal or informal, has a significant bearing on investments in housing, basic amenities and the quality of the micro-environment. A large number of households in the selected cities have made such investments based on assurances given by municipal corporations against eviction, or perceived security without any formal communication. Over 80 per cent in the selected slum colonies have upgraded their houses, many obtaining individual taps, toilets and electricity connections, by mobilizing resources through borrowings and savings. The total expenditure varies between households, depending on their economic status; only 5 per cent have not upgraded their dwelling units due to a lack of financial resources. One can therefore argue that the poor are willing and able to invest their limited savings in housing and basic amenities when they get some kind of assurance, formal or informal, against eviction.

This sense of security is due to the fact that there has been no major relocation or eviction of slums in either of the cities for over two decades. It is only in the areas that are hazardous for human habitation (adjacent to rail tracks, etc.) or likely to be taken up for development in the immediate future (road expansion, construction of public utility, etc.) that residents feel vulnerable. However, squatters in conflict with the residents of neighbouring high-income colonies or industrial units share a sense of insecurity and consequently do not make investments in housing or amenities.

Perceived security among the slum households is dependent on a host of factors. Possession of identity cards that indicate their arrival in the city on or before a specified cut-off date (for example, V.P. Singh Cards in Delhi) is extremely important in this context. This is because many of the governmental programmes give importance to cut-off dates as an eligibility criterion. Consequently, areas that have a large percentage of people with such cards are viewed as more secure and encourage higher levels of investment. Similarly, being covered under a government programme, or getting access to amenities from a public organization contributes to perceived tenure security.

Many of the slum colonies have established links with influential political leaders through their local leaders. The residents thereby identify themselves with a political party and act as its vote bank. Frequent visits by the leaders, or the leaders bestowing privileges on the colonies personally or through governmental programmes, give signals to the residents as well as official machinery that these colonies are unlikely to be evicted. Slum dwellers consider the visits of dignitaries from national and international organizations as endorsements of their semi-legal status. All these factors increase perceived security and go a long way in motivating the households to make investments in improving their micro-environment.

Perceived tenure security in slum colonies, besides prompting individuals to make investments, also facilitates community organizations, NGOs and even private agencies to launch projects for improving basic amenities. They have invested considerable resources by constructing pavements, community toilets, sewerage and water lines. Even the management of the basic amenities becomes better when informal land security is provided at an individual or group level. With the granting of licences, even for a short period, people start treating their neighbours not as 'co-passengers in a night coach', but as a group sharing a common destiny. These community-based organizations – consisting mainly of women – are very effective in supervising the implementation of the project and also undertaking the responsibility of maintaining the existing facilities. They are helpful also in mobilizing resources to meet repair costs or maintenance work. Sometimes, the community meets its financial obligations collectively by putting in money on behalf of defaulting members. Furthermore, colonies that do not possess any formal tenure, only licences for residential use of land, do not, in general, attract massive inflows of population from outside the area.

At the time of executing developmental projects, officials have often demolished hutments in parts of slums, but permitted the evicted people to rebuild their units nearby, irrespective of their formal entitlements. This has been done mostly to avoid public unrest or court interventions. Such administrative decisions or informal permissions to rebuild the huts have been seen as official recognition of a colony, inviting investment in housing.

However, court orders issued during 2000 and since favouring the land owning agencies, together with large-scale evictions, have shattered the perceived security of slum dwellers. The city's administrators were going slow on evictions compared to other cities during the 1980s and early 1990s, since the massive evictions in 1977 had led to violent protests, firing by police and overthrowing of the government. However, they started again in Delhi in the late 1990s. Although data on the scale of such evictions are difficult to obtain, examples appear in the media almost daily and rallies by NGOs have been held to protest against them. The residents suddenly realized that their social and political connections, or a host of semi-legal documents, were not of much use in the event of intervention by a court. Despite staying in a slum for decades, having identity cards and even paying certain local taxes, many of the households were evicted. This has discouraged further investment in housing and amenities and slowed down migration of the poor in to the cities. The latest data from National Sample Survey (NSS) (1999–2000) and Population Census (2001) reveal that in-migration in urban areas has gone down dramatically and there has been a significant reduction in the level of poverty.

In the face of evidence that slum dwellers are capable of improving the micro-environment on their own, if only some kind of informal security is granted, the large-scale evictions in Delhi, Ahmedabad and several other cities raises an important policy question. Does the government, having withdrawn from the provision of infrastructure and amenities in the wake of programmes of structural adjustment, want the people to come forward and shoulder this responsibility? More importantly, do the poor have the right to retain their physical space in the fast globalizing cities in the country through their own initiatives?

Empirical data suggest that formal titles to land in the past have exposed the slums to market forces and pushed the poor to city peripheries or marginal lands. On the other hand, intermediate tenure or even informal assurance against eviction has led to growth of informal settlements in and around regular colonies. It has also made possible substantial investments in housing and amenities in these settlements. Interestingly, the Indian government wants the households, communities and NGOs to come forward and invest in housing and the local environment and fill the vacuum arising from the withdrawal of public agencies in the provision of infrastructure and amenities. This study, however, suggests that the environment created through judicial and administrative orders and large-scale evictions would get in the way of people making such investments or individual and community efforts making up for the withdrawal of the state. Consequently, the physical living conditions of the poor are likely to deteriorate and their in-migration into the cities is likely to slow down. This would tend to create cities wherein the poor would find it difficult to survive.

CHAPTER NINE

Legality and legitimacy of tenure in Turkey

Murat Balamir

LEGALITY AND LEGITIMACY

For the past five decades, land and housing tenure issues in Turkey have been largely determined by the legitimacy of realities, rather than the legal regulations concerning development, use and other activities of individuals on land. Rural populations began flooding into the primary cities in the late 1940s. The economic capacities and policy concerns in the country were far from meeting the immigrants' housing needs (Bademli, 1987; Keles and Kano, 1987; Payne, 1978/9). Scarcity of resources paralysed local and central governments providing land and infrastructures, and private investors could not procure the necessary capital to meet the costs of land and construction within the workings of the market system.

Under these constraints, the local attempts at self-settlement and self-accommodation were understandable and excusable. To begin with, the culture and practice of self-accommodation was not alien to urban newcomers. Islamic civil regulations (Seriat) and law (Mecelle, 1869), as practised during centuries of Seljuk and Ottoman rule, considered individual tenure on land in a relaxed context, especially when it came to nomadic traditions. It was based on local needs and local approval, rather than in deference to some absolute right. Absolute sovereignty in land (freehold) was, after all, that of the Divinity. The development and enjoyment of 'God's garden' was only ever temporary loitering for mortals. As long as there were no objections within the community, any structural needs could be directed by themselves immediately. If conflicts arose between individuals, the decision of the local judge (Kadi) would provide the final solution, which relied on convictions of legitimacy rather than the objective descriptions and rules of some universal law of land tenure.

As the transformation from 'subjectship' to 'citizenship' came to be maintained through the individuals' status within the Republic, so did many civil issues (land and property ownership included) previously dependent on local legitimacy alone come to require adjudication from some form of formal legal status and conditions. A new system of property rights was described in the Civil Code (based on Roman Law) and adopted in 1926. Freehold rights and a singular discretionary power over property were the fundamental private forms of tenure in Roman law, which served to complement the market system. 'Joint' and 'common' forms of tenure were considered only to be transitional forms of ownership. Leasehold rights, on the other hand, were not identified as a distinct form of tenure, but as a special easement on property, many forms of which were made available in the Civil Code. This is the basis on which all land-use planning activities, the Development Law and its attendant regulations are conducted, and all relations concerning real property are registered in the local cadastral and deeds offices. Total compliance with this ideal system has been a rare phenomenon, however, owing to the dramatic changes that have dominated urban growth in the country.

The historical legacy and the assumptions of the Republic's modern laws thus pointed in different directions. As authorities became incapable of guiding developments, immigrants followed their traditional instincts in settling and building, considering their actions as natural and socially legitimate responses for survival. New organizational models intended to reduce the costs of formal housing were also devised as logical solutions to the failure of markets and administrations. These economically justified, although unauthorized, arrangements were extensively adopted throughout the country within a decade and eventually gave rise to demands for the revision of existing laws. New laws were enacted specifically to assimilate these deviant forms of tenure into the legislative body proper (Uzel, 1987). The contemporary history of urban living in Turkey is thus a history of at least three major forms of innovative informal tenure arrangements which have been anonymously devised and widely practised since the early 1950s.

Processes of appropriation

Direct appropriation and spontaneous development of public (or private) land for instant occupation is the most common violation of the Civil Code and development regulations. The first step is to locate suitable land. This information is usually provided by acquaintances. The second step is the arrangement and immediate completion of construction work. An occupied dwelling complete with roof helps avoid outright eviction. Known as *gecekondu* ('built overnight') it provides the occupier with some security of tenure, even if a court decision has been made to evict. This is why *gecekondus* have become the initial objective of most immigrants, and more than half of the population of the three metropolitan cities in Turkey lived in *gecekondu* buildings at one point. Other steps taken to secure tenure are to produce evidence of being part of the urban system, such as regular payment of property taxes, invoices of network services, etc., which provides effective proof of de facto use and enjoyment of property and is credited to the owner should they apply for certificates of occupation and, eventually, freehold (Box 9.1).

Box 9.1   A case of appropriation

A low-level public functionary of the forestry management department for 24 years, SS was appointed to Ankara in 1996, when he was 45. On his arrival, he built a *gecekondu* close to his brother-in-law, who had been in Aksemsettin Mamak since 1988. *Gecekondu* builders throughout the last decade had preferred the area. He did not pay anyone for the land and does not know whether it belongs to a person or the state.

It took only a couple of days for him to construct four walls and a roof, hiring only a carpenter for a day. He paid for all the building materials, terracotta bricks alone costing TL6 million (US$75) per lorry load He was eligible for a short-term consumption credit TL20 million (US$250) from a bank referencing his work status. Once the foundations were laid, the municipal inspectors spotted him and demolished his work. 'If one is determined, however, one finds the right relations and persons, makes donations to get over such constraints and succeed in completing the *gecekondu*.'

He now lives in a two-room 75 m² *gecekondu*, with a garden of about 100 m² surrounded by poplar trees. SS is content with his home, even though he considers it 'a bit distant from the city'. He has not yet applied for a certificate or title, but will not refrain from making further investments while he is living there. He is confident that he will, at some stage, be eligible for the freehold.

With a net monthly income of US$200, the family does not own a car, but household items include a colour television, telephone, stereo system, computer, refrigerator, automatic washer, dishwasher and vacuum cleaner. His wife is temporarily abroad and their veterinary son is in military service. Their daughter is a university student in the physical education department.

There was no infrastructure when they moved in, but piped water became available the following year. Unauthorized use of electricity is extensive throughout the area, usually with further networking being made from an already unauthorized connection. Electricity becomes available soon after piped water is formally metered. SS has been duly paying all taxes since connections to networks have been made.

Even without titles, he believes that his *gecekondu*, in its current state, could sell for US$7000–8000. A similar one sold for US$5500 a couple of months previously. 'Living free is worth all that' and there is always the potential for a freehold on the land with at least a flat at the end of the process.

Payment of property taxes also enables the provision of collective infrastructure such as roads or public fountains, and public services such as public transport or primary health services. Extensions to metered power lines and connections to the telephone network also help generate a feeling of tenure security. The authorities are particularly conducive to rendering such services during election years. Recent cases of direct appropriation show unconditional access to land being obstructed by intermediaries. Ranging from community leaders to despots, they find land and organize the process as a business opportunity. Since occupation of

Figure 9.1   SS's *gecekondu* with his dustbin denoting municipal recognition, even though the settlement is still illegal. Credit: Aslı Kayıket and Saygın Can Oğuz

Figure 9.2   The garage shed has been taken down by the municipality inspection teams more than ten times! Credit: Aslı Kayıket and Saygın Can Oğuz

land is totally illegal, the judicial system cannot be relied on to protect residents in the case of conflicts. Instead, they use other means of establishing collective legitimacy, and disagreements between residents or intermediaries are resolved mostly by local arbitration. This is one of the basic reasons (besides the traditional means of social reliance and acquisition of information) why interactions in such areas serve to attract acquaintances, relatives and households from the same rural background into specific urban districts.

Processes of apportionment (shared ownership)

A second option for individuals who have the means for more substantial investments and tend to start their housing careers with relatively greater security of tenure, is to purchase a land-share. Shared ownership of large tracts of peripheral land serves to reduce the exorbitant costs of land in more central urban locations. The subdivision of such land is prohibited by planning regulations and the mandates of central authorities, both of which aim to avoid scattered development. According to the previous Development Law, the minimum allowable size of land subdivisions in such areas was 20 000 m². The relevant ministry relaxed this restriction to 5000 m² in 1972 (sometimes even less in special cases). The origins of shared ownership lie, therefore, in restrictions on the one hand, and the urgent needs of households for accommodation on the other.

Individuals co-operate in this process, buying land and physically subdividing it among themselves with the intention of building independently (Box 9.2). Alternatively, the original landowner, or an intermediary estate agent, may subdivide it and launch their own sales campaign. If individuals buy share titles of a large piece of cadastral land they are entitled legally to freehold rights, proportional to their shares, on every unit of land in its entirety, as stipulated by regulations on joint ownership in the civil code, and registry of title offices. The proportion of share titles is often expressed informally in terms of surface area. Identifying the location of this surface area takes place as a second step. This can give rise to serious disagreements among shareholders that cannot be resolved by the formal judiciary to the satisfaction of the individuals concerned. To overcome this problem, they draw up mutual private agreements (easements) to physically subdivide land into smaller sizes in order to start building independently.

Box 9.2   The tolerated success of apportionment (shared ownership)

MÇ's life story is similar to thousands of others, a dramatic transformation from a background of stable and stagnant rural life, into one with many risks, options and indefinite consequences in the city. Now at 66, he lives in Öveçler, south Ankara, with his wife and one of his three daughters. A bachelor when he first moved to Ankara in 1951 from Örenköy (a village about 200 km away), he lived as a *gecekondu* tenant for five years in Telsizler, an unauthorized district of the city, sharing a room with two fellow villagers. Having had his primary schooling back in the village, he initially worked wherever he found a job – in a bakery for a year, but mostly in the construction sector where he learned how to install electrical systems.

In 1956, he was drafted into military service and returned to the village in 1958 and married. The newlyweds settled in Ankara, Atifbey, as *gecekondu* tenants. MÇ continued his career in the construction sector, which enabled him to find a job as an electrician. One of the universities in the city recruited him through examinations in 1969. In 1959, he and a relative bought land, first in Solfasol, then Öveçler, where he now lives. Both times, they shared the land informally between them. The second time, he paid about US$1 per square metre for a 500 m² plot of private agricultural land outside the municipal boundaries. He was informed of the availability of this land through his countrymen; around 300 families had already settled in the area. MÇ worked with friends for about a week on the construction of two rooms and an entrance hall, built with pressed blocks. At the stage of laying foundations, municipal inspection teams intervened. He managed to complete the *gecekondu* and move in, living there for ten years. This was later replaced in two instalments with savings, by a two-storey, concrete building.

The couple have three daughters, the eldest of whom is married and lives elsewhere in Ankara. The second daughter is a lycee-graduate and is also married. The youngest daughter, who is working as an officer and has a university degree, lives with them. In 1991, MÇ retired from his job at the university. With his retirement pension he bought a flat in Ilker for his wife. For 13 years until 1990, he had had two cows and a chicken in the shed in his yard, selling milk to neighbours. At the moment, they seem to be well off with around US$700 net monthly income, including rental from his wife's flat and his daughter's salary; the other land in Solfasol is maturing for development, with his daughter's Skoda Favorit resting in his parking lot. In 1998, MÇ built a small house in the village. The family spends the summer months there, with no intention of settling. He is active in the Örenköy Citizens Association, whose membership is US$1 per month.

In the early years, there was no infrastructure in Öveçler, which had become overrun by *gecekondu* units. Water had to be carried from a communal tap and long walking distances to public transportation were common. Roads, piped water, energy lines and waste water systems were provided in 1965. After 1980, the telephone became available. The administration did not seek legal rights or titles for the provision of these services.

The Improvement Plan for the area, prepared according to Law 2981, has been in effect since last year, and as more and more shareholders come to agreements, construction begins on blocks of flats. MÇ has been paying municipal and property taxes regularly and has applied for the regulation of this property under the auspices of Law 2981. The plan for the district provides for a large green at the lower valley, which requires the public acquisition of an additional 28 per cent of the individual plots in addition to the usual 35 per cent in conventional procedures. The plan has compensated for this with extra floor area, increasing the permitted number of stories in blocks from four to five. The value of flats on the ground floor is around US$30 000, while those on the floors above could vary between US$45 000 and US$60 000. Land values have increased with the plan and regularization from $10–20 to US$250–500 per square metre. MÇ has criticized the plan for allowing individuals who have illegally appropriated public land identical rights to his as a lawful buyer of land from a private owner. The rearranged plots have up to 12 joint owners who, according to him, make it difficult to make free agreements, demanding a court decision as a solution.

MÇ's land of 240 m² was reduced to 130 m² during the process, considered to be equivalent to a flat. This equity is transferred to a plot, subject to its development in joint ownership with eight other owners. Even if others buy this right, it should still provide him comfortably with sufficient monies for a decent flat. Having begun with a total disregard for the existing legal system, after a gradual recognition of rights and building up of equity, this is the result of 50 years of determination, patience, entrepreneurship and confidence.

Figure 9.3   MÇ's *gecekondu* from the front entrance. Credit: Aslı Kayıket and Saygın Can Oğuz

One of the public responses frustrating this process has been the refusal to register shares in the title offices in the specific manner the shareholders have agreed on. Attestation of the private easements by the public notary is also often denied. The problem then is the mutual trust, kept on probation during the limited effective period of ten years according to the civil code for the legal status of private easements that have fragmented rights of ownership. At the end of this period, any of the shareholders can go to the courts and claim rights on all of the land. A High Court decision in 1975 challenged the civil code, confirming shareholders' disposal rights on specific locations of the jointly owned land. This removed some of the uncertainty in the process, even if it did not provide full tenure security. Even if a court decision for legal subdivision is made, the existing Urban Master Plan (UMP), or its regulations, may not allow its implementation. Despite all these obstacles, developments based on informal processes of land sharing today cover large areas in metropolitan cities. Since no records are kept, other than those of the local cadastral offices, formal data on shared ownership, or information concerning transactions, are not available. The cadastral records could also be deficient in many cases, due to the totally voluntary nature of shared ownership. Independent research has indicated that more than two million sales were made between 1978 and 1979, 800 000 of which were made by citizens abroad (*Hürriyet*, daily paper 1.9.1979). Buildings completed on shared land had already exceeded 100 000 units by November 1972. In the Istanbul metropolitan area alone, two million shared plots occupied around 34 000 ha of land. The average size of these plots is 170 m², varying between 100 and 250 m² (Karagözoglu, 1986).

In areas where there is high demand for housing and, therefore, every reason to construct multi-storey blocks at high densities, informal estate agents usually intervene, subdividing the land with self-prepared plans and acting as intermediaries to market the subdivided pieces. Contracted developers may then be involved in the construction of unauthorized blocks of flats and in the marketing of individual apartments. In many cases, the whole operation may be run by one agent/developer. In other cases, the landowner, acting as an entrepreneur, prepares an informal physical plan, and after coming to private agreements with shareholders, allows share titles (Box 9.3).

Box 9.3   The estate agent in shared ownership

In an interview held during a recent case of apportionment in Serpmeevler, Ankara East, an agent explains the functions fulfilled by his occupation. The area belonged to the local villagers of Üreyil, who used it mostly to cultivate wheat. Some of this land belonged to HB who, in the 1970s, was determined and able to buy more. Just before 1980, he subdivided his lands informally into pieces of 300 m², marking out the boundaries himself. He then began selling these pieces with titles in joint ownership. Construction activities in the area began in the mid-1980s. Since then, 'D. Emlak,' the estate agents in the area, claim that about 2.5 million square metres of land have been sold. Prices could vary between US$5 per m² in the earlier years, to US$20 per m² more recently.

Although the majority of transactions were made in terms of 'shared ownership', that is, voluntary and mutual agreements of purchase on private land, there may be individual or local cases among these where private and public land has also been appropriated and/or marketed.

There had been no infrastructure during the 1980s. By the 1990s, piped water and electricity had become available, although mostly used with illegal connections. In 1994, the Social Democrat municipality provided the waste-water system. Much 'contribution' was made by the agent himself in convincing the authorities to accelerate the pace of development. Preparations for the Rehabilitation Plan for the area commenced in 1986. This increased all land values, to US$80 per m² for sites close to the main road and US$40 per m² for the more distant.

Since private subdivisions are illegal, it is not possible to obtain building permits. Development in shared ownership is, therefore, a double breach of law. More precisely, there are numerous illegal steps that may be accounted for in the process. The preparation of a subdivision plan, agreements being drawn by shareholders, the implementation of the plan by physically subdividing it, its disposal by different individuals – all are illegal procedures. Any form of construction on shared land is also unauthorized. This could have serious consequences in the case of multi-storey blocks of flats, should things go wrong structurally, inflicting physical harm on individuals. It is the responsibility of engineers to fulfil a number of procedural conditions that are recorded. None of these is undertaken, however, and separate apartments are unofficially transferred to individuals solely on the basis of being a subshare of a shared land title. A flat owner may thus end up with a share title representing a minute fraction of the original total freehold.

Buildings on shared land may take many physical forms, with developments having different housing densities. Depending on investment capacities, perceptions of tenure security, features of location and the nature of demand in the area, developments may vary from simple *gecekondu* units to substantial single houses, multi-storey blocks of flats or, sometimes, development at even higher densities than allowed for in planned areas (as in the case of Demetevler, Ankara, Box 9.4). Building activities often start with a *gecekondu*, or a modest single house, with the intention of modifying it later with extensions. In most cases, redevelopment takes place with multi-unit blocks replacing earlier and simpler buildings, as tenure is consolidated and property prices increase with urban growth. Such areas may, therefore, witness different levels of exploitation and uneven rent levels. But, irrespective of how such an area is initially developed, the end result is that of flat ownership in blocks.

Box 9.4   Demetevler

Demetevler is the earliest and most intensively built up of unauthorized areas in Ankara. This is realized in terms of processes of apportionment. In 1940, an area of about 200 ha, located within the Atatürk Forest Farm at the north-west of the city, was transferred to private owners by a court decision. According to the 1957 plan of Ankara, the area remained outside municipal boundaries. The three original owners of the cadastral land had, in view of the growth of Ankara, subdivided the land into 19 pieces, no larger than 2 ha each, as stipulated by the Development Law. The neighbouring Yenimahalle Municipality had flourished since its beginnings in 1956, and had reached a population of 30 000 by 1962. Infrastructure was thereby available for the adjacent Demetevler area. Estate agents prepared subdivision plans for the area and the earliest high-rise blocks appeared by the end of 1960. By 1970, almost no vacant land remained. In 1980, the National Security Council banned the construction of blocks in the area. Legalization procedures were allowed with the introduction of Law 2981 (Box 9.5) in 1984.

By 1985, high-rise developments of between six and 15 storeys dominated, accommodating almost 5 per cent of Ankara's population, with the highest densities (1542 persons/ha) more than twice that of the densest formal residential quarters in the city. By the end of the 1990s, the total number of title holders was 12 885 (11 633 flats and 1252 plots). There were 453 blocks, 10 855 flats and 1716 commercial units, and 500 shareholders existed with less than 1 m^2 in terms of land area. Densities were also high due to wider land coverage, and there were 15- and 16-storey buildings as little as 2 m apart. On the other hand, land reserved for social facilities was at its lowest possible level, with 0.40 m^2 per person for educational facilities (instead of the standard of 6.5 m^2) and 0.01 m^2 per person for green areas (instead of 7.0 m^2), with no space left for health services.

Even though subdivision plans and construction work are both unauthorized, holding a legal deed for land makes individuals feel more secure than those living in *gecekondu* units built on appropriated land. However, when the number of people in this category becomes sufficiently large, they can lobby the local authority for the ratification of their plan and subdivisions. In this way, they can exploit the High Court decision (1975) to legitimize their actions, constituting a basis for intended constructional activities. Making life still easier for them is Law 2981 (1985), which provides avenues to freehold status in land and buildings. This law is applicable in cases of both appropriation and apportionment (Box 9.5). These procedures often lead to the ownership of one or more apartments in a block of flats, maintained by the revision of local plans providing for higher densities and facilitating renewal processes.

Box 9.5: Law 2981 concerning unauthorized buildings
(1984; revised 1986 and 1987)

The Law guides the owners of unauthorized buildings in their application for legal status, with titles designating each building as either 'allowable', 'allowable only if improved' or 'not allowed'. If requirements are fulfilled, the first two cases could be awarded with an immediate construction permit.

All unauthorized forms of building (inclusive of cases of appropriation or apportionment), those under construction at the date and all infringements of permission in authorized buildings are eligible for application. Owners, developers or those who use and enjoy the rights of property (or their legal representatives) are entitled to apply to the local authorities. They are obliged to facilitate the procedures of application, take all necessary steps to prepare local plans and carry out immediate evaluation of the status of individual applicants. In this, three procedures could be followed:

1   In the case of unauthorized buildings that stand on rightfully owned land, permits could be granted immediately if these buildings are in line with regulations. Alternatively, if these buildings require rehabilitation, permits are awarded after such work is completed.
2   In the case of unauthorized buildings standing on public land (treasury, waqf or local authority), no more than 400 m² of land is (compulsorily) sold to the owner of the building in 12 equal payments distributed over four years at the maximum.
3   For those buildings constructed on other people's land, a mutual application, in agreement with a landowner and an owner of unauthorized buildings, is possible. In this case, either a subdivision of land is made and registered, or co-existence is tolerated on the basis of shared ownership. If, on the other hand, the landowner would rather demand a transfer of tenure to the owner of the building, this could be maintained through the courts. They would first determine the land value and then make a decision for compulsory transfer. If the owner of the unauthorized building declines to abide by the court decision, a second decision for eviction is made.

The local authority could choose to acquire large areas occupied by *gecekondus* through compulsory purchase, impose a Rehabilitation Plan or reserve the public share of land and then recoup costs by selling it on a compulsory basis to *gecekondu* owners. In the Rehabilitation Plan, local authorities are more likely to exercise their prerogatives provided by the Development Law in the rearrangement of land, allocating individuals' property rights in terms of 'joint ownership' or 'flat ownership'. Up to 35 per cent of land could be allocated for public services, without compensation. In practice, a flat is equivalent to approximately 400 m² of land. In all circumstances, the approval of Rehabilitation Plans would take no more than one month.

If existing unauthorized buildings are considered 'allowable', they are immediately granted titles and permits so long as there are no border infringements. Otherwise, these problems would have to be settled either by agreement or a court decision. Owners of buildings to be 'improved' have to settle their border infringement problems and remove, or improve, the components required within six months. Otherwise, the local authority is entitled to carry out the operation itself. Title certificates are given to *gecekondus* on the proviso that no member of the household has another dwelling,

The law is not applicable to non-residential buildings, either those infringing water reservoir protection zones or motorway and railway safety zones, or those situated at riparian protection zones. *Gecekondus* inappropriately located in proximity to historical buildings would be removed with equivalent rights provided elsewhere. For those buildings under construction, the law is applicable only if they have already laid the foundations. Whatever the case, the law is applicable only once, for any building or property.

All fees and charges for the procedures are payable to local authorities in equal monthly instalments for up to 18 months. Reduced charges are applied to unauthorized buildings currently used for public services, or those in industrial or agricultural use. All pecuniary fines given to unauthorized buildings are annulled as of the date of law.

Now in its second and third generation, it is undeniable that the process of apportionment begun in the 1950s did, in general, facilitate the housing of the urban poor with relative improvements in their conditions, providing greater confidence in their progression in wealth and social status. This is maintained for many by a feeling of having a stake in the system. As an innovative contribution, shared ownership offers a greater number of options to people and, with most transfer taxes avoided, enables easier market transactions of land and property. The process of apportionment is not only a means of cheaper accommodation for households with modest incomes, but is also an institution, supported by the coalition of interests of households, landowners, realtors, contractor builders and intermediaries, in many cases even including local administrations.

Households participating in this process could either purchase or build themselves dwelling units with legal shared titles, and at cheaper prices. Access to cheaper housing is possible since land requirements can be minimized, labour and materials kept at tolerant standards, and all procedural costs avoided. Alternatively, more spacious dwellings become affordable when compared to what can be purchased in formal markets.

Landowners prefer to co-operate with an estate agent, as it is in their interest to make the most of their land by avoiding a 'public share'. With formal development procedures, a 'Public Rearrangement Share', corresponding to a minimum of 35 per cent of land, is subject to obligatory transfer from private to public ownership with the designation of public roads and facilities, etc., in a local development plan. This is, in essence, a compulsory acquisition procedure, without compensation. The plan's prerogative is to declare a higher rate, in the case of which compensation is paid, although this always falls short of market values. On the other hand, the agent's informal plan will usually have narrower roads, less space reserved for public services and be more tolerant in the spacing of buildings on individual plots (Meral, 1996). Landowners are also capable of avoiding property transfer taxes in the process, since procedures are off the record. During the earlier stages of shared ownership (in the 1950s and 1960s), landowners or estate agents often placed advertisements in the media to sell as many shares as possible and create vested interests to tackle legal obstructions.

Agents prepare the informal subdivision plans without necessarily complying with procedural requirements and planning standards. This maintains a minimal loss of land to roads, parking spaces, green areas, etc., maximizing the number of plots that can be marketed. Subdivision plans prepared in this manner are usually grid plans with small plots. It is the agent's responsibility to market and advertise the property. For the agent, business in shared land means no subdivision costs, no waste of time and money in bureaucratic procedures, and no taxes suffered in shared sales (except perhaps the costs of shared titles). The agent would benefit should any neighbouring public land adjacent to his be designated by a local development plan for public services such as hospitals and school sites. These lands could also be marketed as though owned, almost without liability to the seller. It is thus often possible and beneficial to sell areas reserved for roads, infrastructure, etc. Although it is an offence, it could prove beneficial, since with a sufficient number of individuals engaged in the operation, it is often possible to have the plan itself amended.

Developers operating under these circumstances have no technical restrictions and suffer no procedural costs. There are no professional fees, taxes, public supervision or fines to be paid. All procedural costs of formal development and construction are avoided. These circumstances can be further exploited by employing non-skilled, uninsured labourers and low-standard materials. Furthermore, the developers can receive advance payments from the prospective home owners in their marketing of apartments and can begin construction using minimal capital of their own. The number of storeys, the shape and size of the building, and other constructional decisions are entirely dependent on the marketing capacity of the developers, rather than being controlled by technical or administrative constraints.

For local public administrations, the process of apportionment and the existence of shared-ownership relations help the poor to house themselves, providing a solution to one of the most challenging of public obligations. In return, the relatively lower costs of public management of urban services in unauthorized districts under shared ownership helps local administrations retain an electorate group that is far easier to please and manipulate than residents in formal housing.

Processes of appurtenance

Multi-unit residential blocks in urban areas, both authorized and unauthorized, represent approximately 85–90 per cent of all residential investments in Turkey. They are constructed using a model of co-operation between the entrepreneur (contractor developer), the landowner and other households participating in the venture. The entrepreneur, with the consent of the landowner, obtains access to land and is thereby capable of receiving payments from prospective owners of flats (Balamir, 1992). Prior to development, the sharing of appertaining parts of a building is described by an easement drawn up for the purpose. This is a method of concentrating capital for substantial investments and a means of overcoming the costs of expensive urban land. The landowner would usually receive 25–50 per cent of the prospective building, depending on the value of the land. The owners of more central sites and building plots with higher densities (as granted by the local plans) are likely to achieve higher shares. The rest of the prospective apartments in the building block are the entrepreneur's, who recovers his profit and the cost of construction from the sale of these assets. The entrepreneur then markets his share, with the options of selling prior to or during construction, or after completion, depending on the level of demand and his estimates of capital requirements and market tendencies.

This kind of arrangement is normally carried out on freehold land with building permissions being obtained through formal procedures. However, the civil code can tolerate conditional tenures only temporarily, allowing such easements concerning the distinct use and disposal of 'independent parts' of buildings for up to ten years. Following this, any of the shareholders could go to court for the termination of joint ownership. The courts would usually then decide to end the existence of multiple freehold rights in the building, often consolidating ownership rights in a single title with the owner who has the largest share in the property.

The earliest cases of such arrangements date back to the early 1950s, when most were agreements between relatives or closely related individuals. Within two decades, development under this mode of agreement was adopted throughout the country. A large number of households engaged in this informal tenure system and made significant investments themselves in blocks of flats. There was sufficient political consensus, therefore, for the preparation of a law to secure this type of tenure arrangement. After decades of experiencing a socially legitimate, but illegal, state of tenure relations, and after substantial political lobbying, this insecurity was eventually removed with the enforcement of the Flat Ownership Law in 1966 (Box 9.6). This allowed freehold tenure in 'independent parts' of buildings, describing also the rights and obligations of shareholders in the management of buildings.

Box 9.6   Flat Ownership Law (1965; revised 1983)

This law provides a framework of operations for the landowner, developer and individuals to act in partnership in the construction and joint ownership of buildings as a method of sharing a multi-unit building and using it independently and privately, and also to regulate the collective running and maintenance. Flat ownership can be registered with the titles and cadastral offices 'in agreement' prior to development or, if the building is completed, as 'de facto' with reference to its project. The law describes the 'independently usable parts of buildings' and identifies each part in terms of a 'share', a ratio to unity representing the total value of the property. A 'management plan' is drawn and registered with the titles offices, identifying rules of conduct, obligations and rights of respective owners. On land and in 'common places' like stairways, lifts, shafts, etc., partners have rights proportional to their shares.

In the management of the building, a manager is elected among the owner-partners for the year. Every detail to describe the democratic running of the premises is clarified by the law: the procedures of meetings, methods of meeting

> expenses, penalties against unfulfilled obligations, disturbances to neighbours, etc. The use of flats in the building is strictly confined to categories of 'non-disturbing'. Management tasks are to be carried out in turn, encouraging participation in responsibilities. Many decisions can be taken by a majority of shares and partners. Most of the maintenance and running costs are also shared proportionately. However, those issues demanding substantial investments and involving changes affecting the whole building require unanimous agreement.

Although 'co-existence of independent ownership rights in buildings', in real and legal terms, exist in other countries, the process of appurtenance observed in the Turkish case is unique for a combination of factors:

- The process functions primarily in the 'formation' of stock, rather than in subdividing existing stock or marketing a previously produced set of buildings.
- It is the dominant form of housing provision and urban living throughout the country, adopted within two to three decades, and not comparable with any other available example.
- It is unique in its evolution within the legal context, in which a new law was made for its legitimization. In other countries, provisions already existed for such forms of ownership in various laws prior to its practice.
- The emergence and spread of this process in Turkey is purely a market phenomenon, whereas in many other countries, explicitly manipulative public policies (related to upgrading, renewal or the privatization of stock) are usually responsible for its practice.
- The process of appurtenance in Turkey generates new capital, rather than consuming existing investment resources or capital transferred from another sector of the economy. This source of investment is directly extracted from households' savings, which has relatively low opportunity costs. This is capital gleaned from consumption, to generate operational and effective capital in moderate sizes of construction investments. In the case of condominiums in other countries, it is the use of existing large-scale capital that is responsible for investments in the first place. Sharing of buildings in this case is only a secondary procedure.
- The landowner, entrepreneur-developer and the households make up the three distinct parties involved in the process. In other countries, developments of this nature reveal single or two-party operations.
- Urban populations are stratified into new classes of status and wealth, based on the roles of parties involved in this process. Since accessibility of housing stock as a new pool of social and material resource varies between these parties, urban society is differentiated by cleavages of tenure in a manner different from the conventional forms of tenancy (Balamir, 1996, 1992, 1982). Housing wealth in urban areas is thus determined directly by this unequal-share generating process.

■ Although real variations are generated in housing wealth and status between subsets of households, this has little impact on spatial disparity of the emerging 'housing classes'. Rather, a symbiotic coexistence in stock is the rule, blurring the perception of polarizations, and generating a mosaic of tenures. Tenants, owner-occupiers, rentier households and janitor households all huddle together in the same building as interdependent parties in the process of appurtenance. This outcome is dissimilar to the geographic structuring processes of many cities of the Western world.

■ Market forces that favoured the institution of flat-ownership are barely capable of reunifying the fragmented rights in any building, as it becomes necessary for any comprehensive physical change or redevelopment. It is thus an ultimate form of property relations, in the sense that a self-guided exit is not possible (Balamir, 1975). This implies an extensive and absolute urban paralysis.

The reasons for, and results of, the process of appurtenance are therefore specific to Turkey in terms of capital formation and investment behaviour, development procedures, sharing of economic values, social stratification based on this shared wealth and their distribution in space. The processes of appropriation and apportionment, in their gradual transformation into more secure forms of tenure and more substantial investments, inevitably lead to the state of affairs in physical and social terms, determined by the process of appurtenance.

These innovative and informal property relations, anonymously devised as forms of ownership, ultimately served to meet the urgent urban housing demand. They have been so successful in their function as frameworks to facilitate home ownership that housing production exceeded in the aggregate those of many comparable countries. It is particularly relevant to describe these processes in terms of tenure transformations, relating them to the underlying legal and economic forces, rather than housing 'provision processes', which relate them only to observable physical end products, the latter classified as *gecekondu* units, blocks of flats and mass housing complexes (Balamir, 1969, 1975, 1999).

The order of these processes, as roughly explained here, represents a gradation through processes of housing acquisition, from the lowest income to higher income, as well as a gradation in the complexity of organization and the scale of capital involved. An inverse order was followed, however, in official recognition and 'coming to terms with the real world' and in resolving the conflicts between law and conduct. The case of appurtenances involving the largest volume of investments was resolved first by the Flat Ownership Law (1965). The other forms of unauthorized urban property relations were to be decisively integrated within the formal system in 1985 with Law 2981, even though almost a dozen ineffective legal provisions had been made since the 1940s.

FORMS OF LEGITIMACY

Awareness of socially legitimate conduct is by no means achieved by direct acquisition of a simple piece of information, but through a total experience of a complex and overlapping set of reasons, social circumstances and justifications. As such, it may be possible to distinguish layers of legitimacy, just as degrees of illegality could be identified. If traditions, habits and collectively tolerated norms relating to the formation of the living environment are considered to constitute a cultural and historical legitimacy for unauthorized forms of tenure in Turkey, several other types of legitimacy can also be accounted for within the processes discussed. The desperate circumstances of migrants, a state between existence and non-existence with few options, brings forward the strongest of human values in the decision-making and evaluations of authorities and others concerning interventions.

The legitimacy of any struggle to survive is the common implicit understanding and the dominant attitude of administrations and society at large. The *gecekondu* settlers themselves are aware also of the need to prove themselves in merit and reputation. This feeling usually motivates them to participate in local activities and accumulate all forms of evidence concerning their willingness to co-operate with authorities, their presence in the area, and their regular payment of taxes, bills and invoices for infrastructural services, all of which imply the functioning of processes feeding into an acquired legitimacy for being there. So long as there is no systematic counter-decision, official challenge or action to the illegal state of any of the above processes, a mutual understanding is nurtured where some implicit or latent legitimacy prevails. Constituting large parts of the electorate body in the city, political legitimacy of the *gecekondu* population rewards them with social recognition and the provision of public services. Whatever the extent of illegality, current enjoyment of tenure rights has a social value in its use and exchange. This also reflects the likelihood of permission for development and receiving full freehold rights in future stages and an embedded potential legitimacy in the process. The combined effect of these possible forms of legitimacy is always more powerful than the will of administrations to enforce or implement some constraint in law.

TOLERANCE BREEDING INJUSTICE

Although official discourse has always discouraged people from having illegal status and tenure in their formation of *gecekondu* buildings and other unauthorized developments, the real policy of tenure in Turkey generally favoured the poor. There may be much to learn from this experience of various innovative tenure forms and their inclusion in the official system for other countries where, not only the urban poor, but all income groups are involved.

In general, administrations have been very tolerant, to the extent that they have frequently been accused of populism. Irrespective of how laws are encroached in efforts to minimize the costs of land and housing, the local and central authorities ignore most of the offences and often choose to legalize them. Decisions and actions to evict or demolish are politically unrewarding as the media and public at large support the victims. In practice, individuals are seldom prosecuted for this kind of offence and there are no mass evictions, unless unauthorized developments are in the way of a public project, protection zones of reservoirs, archaeological sites, etc.

About a dozen laws have been made since 1948 that, in various ways, condone informal tenure and development offences. These often demand that some unauthorized developments be either removed (providing cheap building materials, credit and public land for the owners) or improved. The alternative proposition was the prevention of *gecekondu* buildings through the provision of cheap public housing. These remained, however, as good intentions with limited implementation. The currently effective Law 2981 allows higher densities in local renewal plans for both *gecekondu* areas and other unauthorized developments (Box 9.5). This is not only a process of securing tenure, but also a benevolent provision of development rights resulting in the production of blocks of flats wherever justified by demand, often providing several dwellings to the original, illegal, occupiers of land.

Movement from illegal to legal forms of tenure, however incremental, is no simple act or operation but a social transformation involving not only the acquisition of new status, rights and privileges, but also new undertaking of commitments and obligations. As rights of ownership of property materialize, individuals realize that they are more and more entangled in the many constraints of civil and development laws. Second, individuals now find it essential that they resort to the legislative system proper, rather than the informal conflict resolution methods they conveniently exploited previously in their disagreements concerning property development and use. Third, individuals discover that the infrastructural systems and public services are no longer freely or benevolently provided; instead, they have to wait in queues and pay in real terms. Furthermore, the property they now own, more than a source for financial borrowings, is also an asset that could more be easily taken away against their economic mistakes in urban business decisions and deals in which they may not particularly be well experienced.

The question of injustice in gender relations is also generated within the processes described above, and how this affects the status of women has no simple answer. In general, the move from a rural background to the large urban context implies reductions in women's roles. Multiple productive tasks in the village, covering agricultural work, food processing, house management and child care, are drastically minimized, if only due to the loss of the first. Finding their productive energy, capacities, knowledge and skills redundant in the city, women become more dependent on men. To acquire a more productive status at home, many tend to look for part-time and informal occupation in the city, and usually find employment in house cleaning and maintenance, or baby-sitting. Unless this is maintained, a minority of women may be worse off than they were in the village and almost imprisoned at home. The second generation of women, however, are more able to remove the barriers, and even in the worst cases of male orthodoxy, women are much better educated and able to find greater options in the job market. The household surveyed in Box 9.2, for instance, had three daughters. The first was a graduate of the primary school (the minimum required schooling is now eight years), the second received a college degree and the third is a university graduate, employed by one of the universities in Ankara. Tenure security has positive effects on this process. The relative position of women has been further strengthened with the very recent changes in the Civil Law (2001) introducing the principle of identical sharings of property wealth in the family.

The successful evolution of various types of tenure and their adoption into the legal system has indirectly inflicted injustice on law-abiding households. There are also dramatic variations in the ways that opportunities are exploited by the various factions of the poor themselves; these remain as current social problems. Depending on where the demand for more intensive development begins, some households can acquire several apartments, others can only console themselves with the acquisition of a freehold status on property they originally appropriated some decades ago. Yet it is tenants in *gecekondus* who are the most severely punished by the transformation of these buildings into blocks of flats. The poorest of all, these tenants are evicted in the process and have to move to other *gecekondu* areas, mostly of lower quality but with higher rents as the market is narrowed. The uneven distribution of opportunities, wealth and options open to households in these processes can generate disappointment and despair. The provision of tenure security can also generate speculation, leading to avoidance of improvements, rather than encouraging savings and investments to improve the home environment. Distracted from purposeful investment intentions, the availability of credit can be of little significance and meaning to the individuals. It is therefore the differential nature of benefits arising in the processes that needs to be monitored.

The other detrimental consequence of the overall process is neglect in fulfilling the social objectives of local urban plans, where sacrifices are often made in technical standards of open spaces, provision of public services and infrastructure in order to maintain private demands, overriding public interest. However, the very same processes also imply considerable waste, deviations from existing development plans, and commitments of infrastructural and urban services investments. Costs are therefore duplicated. The double standard in physical and social terms is an arbitrary form of conduct and represents a twilight zone between legality and illegality, often punishing the law-abiding citizen.

A major problem with tolerance is, again, the provision of permits to unauthorized buildings, the construction standards of which are totally uncertain. Municipal construction and occupation permits imply a public guarantee of such buildings, which are totally inappropriate to an environment with high probabilities of earthquake hazards. In this manner, public commitment is made to compensate for an extremely vulnerable stock, constituting another indirect but considerable cost to law-abiding citizens.

The Turkish experience currently stands as a case where innovative forms of tenure have evolved (rather than having been deliberately devised and imposed) and extensively practised in a free market environment, earlier than those observed in many other countries. Furthermore, and despite the ignorance and negligence of policies (mostly identified here as tolerances), this experience has in general been successful in supporting and promoting the integration of the poor into the real urban fabric, both physically and socially. As such, this experience may prove relevant not only to the developing parts of the world, but also in the economically better-off contexts.

During the formative years of processes of appropriation and apportionment of stock, the provision of low-cost land and infrastructure, with a perspective to likely future transformations, would have made good policy. Community centres created to settle local disputes, generate job opportunities and provide a base for all types of urban information would have had immense value for a smooth and rapid integration of settlers into the economy and urban mode of life. The flat ownership system stands today as a precedent, a universally relevant and successful model of collaboration in the construction and management of property resources, and could contribute to the cases of privatization efforts as in 'Common-hold' arrangements in England or in countries of the former Soviet Union.

PART IV

ALTERNATIVES TO TITLES AND ILLEGALITY

CHAPTER TEN

Bolivia's land tenure experience

Fabian Farfan Espinoza

CONTEXT

Bolivia's economy underwent important structural adjustments during the 1980s due to high inflation, low living standards and high unemployment rates. The cities were not prepared for all the changes needed to cope with the accelerated movement from rural to urban areas. One of the main phenomena of this critical period was the 'reallocation process', during which the Bolivian National Mines were closed down. The miners were moved from their workplace to other regions, without a serious jobs replacement scheme. The majority of those who did not get governmental support, or did not agree with it, moved to the main cities. Miners became squatters, surrounding the cities looking for a piece of land on which to live, and informal settlements started to grow faster than ever.

The early 1990s saw a decline in agricultural activities, giving people even less incentive to remain in rural areas. With more and more people moving to the cities, small municipalities could no longer afford to run their own offices. During 1993 and 1995, national government prepared several laws to combat the critical situation that the whole country was now facing. Two key laws were No. 1551, the Community Participation Law (LPP, Ley de Participacion Popular, 04/20/1993) and No. 1654, the Administrative Decentralization's Law (LD, Ley de Descentralizacion Administrativa, 07/28/1995).

Initially, community groups had called the LPP law 'the damnation law', because of the changes it had to go through. But as they began to understand it, this law became an important tool for the development of the rural and urban areas and the participation of communities in the decision-making process within municipalities.

The LPP law divided the country's nine departments into 'municipalities zones', with both rural and urban areas, within their legal boundaries. This requires central government to transfer to the municipalities a percentage of tax revenues based on the number of citizens that belong to it. Local government uses that money, based on the population's needs and claims, to improve and develop the cities and raise the quality of people's lives. The law gives strong legal support to encourage people to participate in the decision-making process and also to control budgets. Small municipalities have been facing enormous changes, particularly since the law was passed.

Previously, most of them had economic support from neither central government nor their departments, whereas nowadays they have greater access to the participatory planning process to improve conditions in both rural and urban areas. Among other factors, this law is further increasing migration rates to the main urban areas because of important municipal investments in infrastructure and services.

Although Bolivia is one of the poorest countries in Latin America, with more than half of the population living below the poverty line, people have strong cultural and social values such as solidarity, self-help and community participation. People have joined together by family links, friendship, job or any kind of relationship, to develop *pasanaku*, well known around the world as ROSCA (Rotating Saving Credit Associations). ROSCA started as a response to the inability of poor people to access 'formal' bank credit. They represent an 'informal' means of helping people to earn money without bureaucratic procedures, high interest rates and wasted time.

Another informal initiative in Bolivia and some other Latin American countries is the *anticretico*, or *anticresis*, experience. Before discussing this innovatory tenure system, however, it is necessary to explain the difference between 'formality' and 'informality' in the Bolivian context. All activities develop within a certain framework of regulations and laws. Those recognized by the national, regional or local authorities are called 'formal' (i.e. plot or house purchased, access to a private bank loan, stable private or public job). In such cases *formality* is related to *legality*.

Conversely, activities that do not have any legal support are called 'informal'. Then *informality* can, in some cases, also be related to *illegality* (squatters, invasions, street vendors). But when it touches on practices such as *pasanaku, anticretico*, etc., it is neither illegal nor formal.

DIFFERENT TENURE APPROACHES

Land ownership is a major issue for Bolivians because of the cultural patterns, economic stability, secure tenure and capability to access a formal credit institution (private banks, co-operatives, etc.) given by using the land or house as collateral for a loan.

It is estimated that 60 per cent of the country's urban areas have some tenure problems. These range from mistakes in the cadastral registration and incomplete legal ownership papers to the lack of any legal property right (Ramirez and Bazoberry, 1997: 39). Bureaucratic procedures and rigid regulations force people to leave almost 40 per cent of the total plot area for open space, one of the main factors discouraging them from seeking legal land tenure. Streets and public open spaces account for 38–60 per cent of the total land area in new settlements, depending on location. Low-income groups are unable to follow this regulation because of high land costs.

For anybody seeking legal land tenure, there are formal steps to follow. Although, in some cases, the whole process of clearing tenure papers can take only a month, it can often take years, due to unclear property rights, unclear titling, and differences between the real plot size and the legal size requirements. There are two institutions that have to register and give the right to legal titling.

The first institution is the Architects Association (Colegio the Arquitectos de Bolivia, CAB), which has for many years registered all projects before they can be approved by the local government. Although this office does not give legal titles, all approval processes have to go through it in order to guarantee architects' design rights. Without a professional architect's signature and the Architects Association stamp, no further steps towards securing tenure can be made.

The second institution is the municipality, which gives the final approval. This process starts with the first review, held by a municipal lawyer who is responsible for checking legal property papers. Next, surveyors visit the plot and check that there is no mismatch between the real plot area and the legal plot area. This group of municipal employees also has to check for constructions that have been built outside legal procedures. If there is any irregularity in the site or the plot size, the process is stopped until the owner has made the correction. In a case where the real plot size is bigger than the size of the title plot, the municipality will sell the remaining area. This procedure can take from six months to several years.

During the late 1980s and early 1990s, there was a major initiative held by both institutions to encourage people to acquire legal land tenure using a process called the regularization of informal housing (Regularization de la Vivienda Clandestina). The whole period lasted little longer than two years, but during this time, architects and the municipality's staff became unable to meet the existing demand. The process had strong popular acceptance because people were able to get legal titles without having to conform to construction regulations. Therefore, we can say that there is a mismatch between people's cultural patterns and the current construction regulations (Farfan, 1999).

There are other tenure patterns in Bolivia in addition to ownership, rent and leasing, as shown in Table 10.1. The *anticretico* or *anticresis* contract type of tenure has two different names, the former as used by legal procedures means 'against a normal credit', and the latter, which is used most commonly, means 'against the crisis'. This is a traditional arrangement intended to improve the economic condition of those involved in the informal housing system. Nowadays, it is becoming 'legal' or 'formal' and is recognized by national laws because of its importance to Bolivian peoples' livelihoods. There is also a mixed system, an alternative solution to a normal rent contract or *anticretico* contract.

Table 10.1 also shows that the third most common tenure used in Bolivia is the *anticretico* but, in reality, this percentage is greater because the source refers only to contracts signed using legal procedures, which will be explained later. Informality increases again because of the bureaucratic procedures required to establish a legal or formal contract. In practice, it is

Table 10.1   Tenure categories in Bolivia

Description	1996 %	1997 %	1998 %	1999 %
Property	52.5	57.8	56.4	51.5
Rent	19.8	19.1	21.7	21.0
Anticresis contract	6.9	6.9	7.8	7.5
Mixed contract	0.3	0.1	0.1	0.0
Given for services	3.3	3.2	3.2	3.6
Given for partnership	17.1	12.9	10.7	15.9
Others	0.2	0.0	0.1	0.4

Source: National Statistic Institute (INE) (1999)

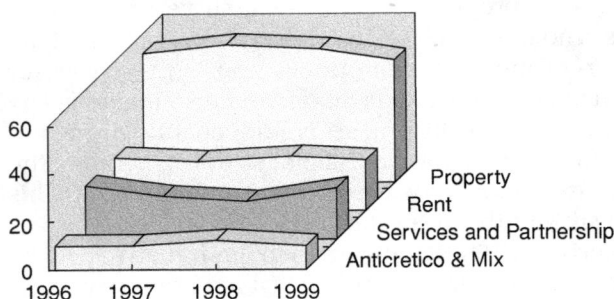

Figure 10.1   Main tenure categories in Bolivia

likely that *anticretico* system should be at least five points higher, due to the common 'informal' use of the system.

ANTICRETICO AS AN INNOVATIVE TENURE SYSTEM

Anticretico is a mechanism involving two parties, with the owner of the house on one side and the person who needs a shelter on the other. A legal contract is made between them in which the former receives an amount of money from the latter for the right to use the owner's property for an agreed period. This includes several responsibilities.

Property owner's responsibilities (supply side)

- The property has to be free from any legal problems. No mortgage can be taken out using the property.
- The property owner has to deliver the house in good condition (with well-functioning infrastructure, no services debts, etc.).
- The property owner has to sign a document of agreement. (This contract can be made for two years or more, but always includes a compulsory period and an optional period.)

- The property owner has to pay all the annual property taxes and is forbidden to use the property as collateral while the agreement is in force.
- At the end of the contract, the property owner returns the money in full in order to get back the right to use the property.
- Although the economic situation has been improving since the structural adjustment programmes began in the 1990s, all contracts are made in US dollars as the official currency for the agreement in order to maintain their monetary value and reduce the impact of economic inflation.

Property user's responsibilities (demand side)

- The property's user has to give an agreed amount of money in order to use the property.
- The property's user has to sign the same document of agreement as the property's owner. (This can be made for two years or more, but there is always a compulsory period and an optional period.)
- The property's user has to pay for any running expenses, such as electricity, water supply, sewerage, etc.
- At the end of the period, the property's user must return the house to the owner in the same condition that it was found in.
- The property has to be used in ways as stipulated in the contract.
- There is no right to rent or give the house to anyone who is not part of the agreement.

The *anticretico* system also encourages users to maintain their houses through special contractual clauses that entitle them to purchase the property after the contract period has expired. This usually happens when the agreement has been in force for longer periods of four to eight years, or if the owner is unable to return the original sum when the deadline arrives. Any house improvements have to be agreed by both parties within a specific budget, and must also be returned at the end of the contract.

The advantages and disadvantages of the *anticretico* system are detailed in Tables 10.2 and 10.3. There is efficient use made of existing housing stock because, as shown in Table 10.1, more than half the population are in property ownership, with some of them owning more than one asset. High levels of migration to other countries also increase the availability of existing houses.[1] The *anticretico* contract does not require any communication between owner and user during either the compulsory period or the optional period (if applicable). This can be seen as both an advantage (no social and living interference) and a disadvantage (lack of property use control – property damage). Houses in the historic centre are commonly used in this system because they can easily host more than three families, an important fact.

Table 10.2   Advantages of the *anticretico* system

Property's owner	Property's user
Obtains an amount of money without interest rates to pay	He/she is able to live in a house without a monthly payment
This money can be used for commercial activities, the construction new houses, etc. If the property's user is a trustful person he or she will maintain the property as necessary	The money given to the other party becomes the basis for property purchase. All the maintenance and housing improvement's investment will be returned at the end of the contract period
The money becomes collateral in case of property damage	The legal framework places the house as collateral to secure the property's user's money

The system has widespread social acceptance[2]

Table 10.3   Disadvantages of the *anticretico* system

Property's owner	Property's user
A bad investment can result in the loss of the property due to the lack of cash flow	Has to live in the house for at least one year; withdrawal of money is not allowed during this time
Lack of cash at the end of the contract period will incur additional fees	The money invested does not earn any interest and it can lose its value after the contract time has elapsed
The shelter cannot be used for activities other than the one stipulated in the contract, in order to avoid property damages	The property's owner can use the house as collateral for a mortgage. In case of bankruptcy, the bank has the first right to the house

After long use of the system, the government has made a legal framework to increase security for both parties. But taxation fees have had to rise which discourages people to go through the legal procedures

The system does not have strong support from the formal sector of the economy

Due to the *anticretico* contract, there is no communication between the owner and the user during the compulsory period and the optional one if applicable. This can be seen as an advantage (no social and living interference) and also a disadvantage (lack of property use control – property damage)

Box 10.1 Case study of Cecilio and Margarita

Using the *anticretico* system was the preferred alternative for a retired couple, using one of the two assets belonging to them. Cecilio (the property's owner) signed a contract with Margarita (the property's user) under the following conditions:

- Contract amount of US$18 000.
- Made for a two-year period; the first year compulsory, the second optional.
- The contract had to be signed using legal procedures.
- Taxation fees to be shared between both parties.[3]
- Property's user (MG) must deliver the house at the end of the contract in the same condition that she found it.
- Property's user has the option to purchase the asset if both parties can make an agreement at the end of the stipulated period (*anticretico con opcion a compra*).

Both parties followed the contract as described. At the end of the period, Margarita decided that she wanted to purchase the house as the facilities and commodities (shops, school, workplace) she found in the area were better, particularly important to her as a single mother with two children. In the meantime, Cecilio and his wife had decided to sell it because they also had better facilities in their other assets and it was too much for them go through the maintenance of two dwellings.

Cecilio and Margarita hired an architect to assess the value of the house. After all the information had been provided for them, they fixed a price for the asset and the *anticretico* money was put down as a guarantee, while Margarita arranged a mortgage from a private bank. After a couple of months, they signed the final purchase document for the house.

Nowadays, Margarita and Cecilio's families have a friendly and close relationship.

Conclusions

1 This case study shows that, if both parties follow the written agreements and legal procedures, the conclusion of the contract can benefit both parties.
2 In order to secure the property user's investment, the house's title was used as collateral and the property's owner couldn't use the asset to get an extra bank mortgage.
3 Although the contract had legal support, the social values of both parties were important in order to follow all the agreements.
4 High taxation fees work against the system. The property's user ought to pay the tax fees, but internal agreements can be arranged to facilitate the procedure. In this case, the expenses were shared between both parties.

THREATS TO THE SYSTEM

Although in the early years this system was very flexible, well known, commonly used, enjoyed high social acceptance and was created to help poor people to access a secure shelter without bureaucratic procedures and expensive fees, market and legal forces have caused the tenure system to lose its essential features. The major threats to the system are as follows:

- The legal framework gives important protection to both parties from fraud, but the procedure has a high tax fee.
- There are bureaucratic steps to follow that take a long time to complete.
- There is no clear legal framework, therefore the contracts that accompany the regulations make an enormous difference in tax payments and lawyers' fees.
- Real estate private companies (Empresas de Bienes Raises) are contract intermediaries which, again, increase the price of the contract and involve other factors in the process.
- There is a lack of support from formal credit institutions.
- Insurance companies do not help the system to develop or encourage people to get into the system because of better, more secure facilities.
- The property's user risks losing money if the contract is biased, or if the property owner behaves badly.

Box 10.2   Oscar and Julia

Julia is a hairdresser with two children attending primary and secondary school. Julia's husband decided to go to Argentina to find a job and improve the family's income. However, after a couple of years they never heard any more from him. Julia's business helped her to save some money to shift from a rental contract to the *anticretico* system. She is unable to access a governmental housing subsidy because she doesn't belong to the subsidy target group. Then Julia signed a contract with Oscar (the property's owner) for a small apartment with two rooms, a kitchen and bathroom, under the following conditions:

- Contract amount of US$10 000.
- Made for a two-year period; the first compulsory, the second optional.
- The contract had to be signed under private contract.
- No taxation fees to be paid as the contract was illegal.
- Property's user (Julia Flores) had to deliver the house at the end of the contract in the same condition that it was given.
- Water and electricity fees had to be shared with the other families living in the same house.

Julia had a very high-risk contract, without legal support. She had tried to avoid the high taxation fee, as the property's owner had not wanted to share the cost. After two years living there, she decided to prolong the contract for another period under the same terms.

During the third contract year, Oscar decided to take a long trip abroad, without any explanation to Julia. Months later, she was notified by a private bank to leave the house because of a credit debt left by the former owner. Julia hired a lawyer to try to recover her investment from the owner since the bank has the first right over the property because the mortgage is bigger than the value of the house.

Processing the claim took more than three years, during which time Julia had been going backwards and forwards, from office to office and court to court. She was able to recover just US$3000 from the owner's relatives with which she had to pay lawyer's fees. In the end, Julia lost her investment and had to move to another place on a rent contract to start the cycle all over again.

Conclusions

5 This case study showed that when neither party followed the written agreements and legal procedures, by the end of the contract, both had lost their investment.
6 The property's owner proved untrustworthy, taking advantage of the other party to get more money through the property use right.
7 Although the contract had no legal support, social values had been important to the property's user and she trusted in the house owner's behaviour.
8 High taxation fees work against this form of tenure. The property's user is responsible for paying the tax fee. In this case, they tried to avoid the payment because they couldn't reach an agreement and the property's user couldn't afford it.

The mixed system of tenure is also being used in Bolivia. The characteristics of this alternative are intended to help people who can't afford to pay the amount of money required in a normal contract. Instead they have an agreement with the property's owner, paying half of the *anticretico* value and paying the other half off as a normal rental fee. This kind of contract also has advantages and disadvantages, as shown in Table 10.4.

Table 10.4: Advantages and disadvantages of the mixed tenure system

Advantages	Disadvantages
No total sum of money to use as a contract for a secure shelter	No legal framework supports the mixed system
A higher proportion of low-income groups can reach the mixed system	The house owner takes a high risk on the monthly payment
Much research in developing countries shows that poor people have a strong commitment to paying off their debts	The statistics do not represent the real number of people using this system due to its 'informal' nature

Due to the rent fee, there are monthly communications between the owner and the user. This can be both an advantage (checking the housing condition and housing use) and a disadvantage (interfering with the property owner's control)

THE LEGAL FRAMEWORK

The increasing number of people using this system has made the central government establish a legal framework that can provide security to both parties involved. This legal framework, mentioned in the civil code (*codigo civil*), stipulates forms of contract and taxation fees. There is also a new strategy from a private bank encouraging people to save money to take out a loan for an *anticretico* contract with more flexible mortgage facilities.

With an *anticretico* contract, the following procedures have to be followed by the both parties:

- All persons who sign a shelter *anticretico* contract (owner and shelter seeker) have to register with the Contributors Unique Registration (RUC, Registro Unico de Contribuyentes).
- Taxation fees have to be paid at the end of every quarter.
- The contract amount is divided into 12 (number of months) with 10 per cent of that sum calculated as a supposed monthly fee. (Three supposed monthly fees have to be paid *at least* once every quarter.)
- If the contract is signed using foreign currency (US dollars), the amount of money has to be changed to the national currency (Bolivianos), based on the exchange rate on the day of payment.
- Every payment is to be made in the national currency (Bolivianos).
- The payment includes tax at a rate of 13 per cent.
- Forms 84 and 71 are to be used in declaring payments.[4]

Example:

If an anticretico *contract were to be using US$10 000, the calculation would be made as follows:*

US$10 000 (Contract amount)	÷	12 (No. of months)	=	US$833.33
US$833.33	*	10% (fixed factor)	=	US$83.33 (supposed monthly fee)
US$83.33	*	3 (a quarter)	=	US$249.99 (quarterly payment before taxes)
US$249.99	*	13% (taxes)	=	US$282.49 (quarterly payment after taxes)

After a quick analysis of these figures, we can see that the property's user will pay US$282.49 every quarter, or US$94.16 every month. If we compare this US$94.16 with a normal rental fee of US$250 (for the same house), we can see that the amount of money spent on taxation fees is quite high, approaching 40 per cent of a normal fee. If we go further and look at payments after taxes at the end of the contract (normally two years) the property's user has to pay US$2259.84, which represents 22.6 per cent of their money invested, plus the inflation rate and currency depreciation. This situation makes people remain under informal contracts.

CONCLUSIONS

Land tenure is a major problem in Bolivia due to cultural patterns, economic instability and social needs. As a result, all Bolivian families have a great commitment to finding secure shelter.

Shelter provided by the 'formal sector' (governments, private institutions, etc.), only benefits a small number of families with the terms and conditions often working against people in low-income groups, who represent more than half of the Bolivian population.

Although formal housing supply is important, informal alternatives have increased to fill the gap. Bolivian history shows that families use innovative tools like the *anticretico* and the mixed systems to improve their living conditions and their economy. These initiatives encourage people to save money and to invest it in a secure shelter. After some years of saving, they will then be able to purchase a house. This purchased shelter may be the one they are living in under an *anticretico* contract or an alternative. They are also able to take out private sector loans using the money saved as collateral.

It is also important to implement *anticretico* as a community-centred or co-operative approach, because of the importance of social values, which help prevent exploitation of the process. Based on this scheme, private finance institutions (banks, co-operatives), micro-finance institutions, national funds and NGOs could promote this initiative by providing loans with lower interest rates and flexible regulation.

The *anticretico* contract makes efficient use of existing housing stock and, as shown in Table 10.1, more than half of the population are in property ownership. The major groups belonging to this category are middle- and high-income, and in many cases one family owns more than one property, which is why there are houses available for this system. Another reason is the high rates of migration to other countries; those people prefer to have an *anticretico* contract instead of a rental contract because of the distance and because it provides capital that they can invest in their new living environment.

Anticretico contracts can easily improve living conditions, as most houses are in urban areas where infrastructure is provided with the house. It is not common to give a shelter to a large number people (except students' rooms), to control overcrowding.

The government still does not provide enough support for these kinds of contract to enable them to improve the environment. Although legalizing and creating a legal framework protecting both parties involved in case of conflict is an important initial step, regulations should facilitate and encourage people to enter this system. But recent experience shows that bureaucratic procedures and high legalisation fees are working against the customer's economy.

Finally, this system has proved to be a very important tool in improving living conditions, reducing poverty and developing low-income group economies. The experience also shows that this mechanism is used by all Bolivian people and has widespread social acceptance.

CHAPTER ELEVEN

The Certificate of Rights story in Botswana

Saad S. Yahya

INTRODUCTION

By African and even world standards Botswana is not a poor country, in terms of both land area and natural resources. The population of 1.7 million enjoys a per capita income of US$3000 compared to Africa's average of US$1000. The wealth comes from diamonds, nickel, coal, soda ash, tourism and beef exports. The abundant land resources are reflected in the layout of towns and villages, while the national policy dictates that every household is entitled to at least two plots, one for residence and the other for sustenance, including women-headed households. Although the towns are fairly small (the largest, Gaborone, which is also the capital city, only has 220 000 people), the level of urbanization is fairly high at 50 per cent.

LAND TENURE CATEGORIES

There are three types of land in Botswana: freehold, state land and tribal land. Within the above broad categories, individuals can hold a variety of interests depending on whether the land is urban or rural.

Freehold land

This consists largely of grants made during the colonial era. Some freehold was granted to citizens after independence 'to encourage them to participate in the development of the new capital Gaborone' (Mathuba, 1993). Covering about 6 per cent of the total land area, freehold is found mainly in designated blocks along the eastern and southern boundaries of the country and in the Ghanzi block in the west. In Gaborone, several freehold owners have subdivided their farms for sale to the public for up-market residential development.

State land

This constitutes about 23 per cent of the total land area. In urban centres, individuals are allocated state land for residential, commercial and industrial purposes and such land is administered under the state Land Act (Cap

32:01). Grants of state land are made by the President, while the land is administered by the Ministry of Lands Housing and Environment through the Director of Lands working in collaboration with the Department of Town and Regional Planning and the Department of Survey and Mapping. Citizens receive first priority when allocating land, and allocations can be in the form of either Fixed Period State Grant (FPSG) or a Certificate of Rights (COR), which is the subject of this chapter.

Customary (tribal) land

The third land category, which constitutes the bulk (71 per cent) of the total land area, is where most people live. The land is owned by the community through land boards, which hold it 'in trust for the benefit and advantage of citizens of Botswana and for the purpose of promoting the economic and social development of all peoples of Botswana' (Section 10 (1), Government of Botswana, 1993, Tribal Land Act Chapter 32:02, as amended by the Tribal Land (Amendment) Act 1993). Customary tenure is common in peri-urban settlements. Individual landholders within the customary system enjoy exclusive rights to their holdings and plots, which are transferable and can be fenced off to exclude other people. Mathuba (1993) summarizes the main characteristics of customary land as follows:

- Land holders have security of tenure.
- Land rights are inheritable.
- Eligible people have easy access to land, which is distributed free of charge.
- Customary land rights can be enjoyed in perpetuity.
- Land is not supposed to be a commodity.

Since 1970, the administration of tribal land has been the responsibility of the land boards, of which there are 12, assisted by 37 subordinate land boards. The composition and functions of the land boards are set out in the legislation. For example, one of their principal functions is to allocate land for a variety of purposes using the instruments prescribed by legislation.

OWNERSHIP OPTIONS IN URBAN AREAS

Land in towns can be acquired in one of the following ways.

- The Fixed Period State Grant (FPSG) is a ground lease in all but name. It is a grant of 99 years under the State Land Act and carries the normal development and restrictive covenants. The current practice is to collect the land servicing cost or market price (whichever the Director of Lands has to charge according to the prevailing policy) within four years. While this has the short-term advantage to government in that costs can be immediately recovered and funds recycled, it imposes an undue financial burden on the grantee and weakens his capacity to develop. The developer may prefer to pay only a proportion of the price initially and the rest as an annual ground rent, which is common practice elsewhere. The disadvantage of extending the repayment period is the additional administrative and rent collection costs. Mortgageability should not be affected since it is a government grant.

■ Certificate of Rights: this was developed in the 1970s to cater for the needs of the urban poor as an alternative to squatting. Thus, the majority of Self Help Housing Agency (SHHA) plots are held under COR. The holder has the right to use and develop the land, but ultimate ownership belongs to the state. In theory, the COR is mortgageable, but most financial institutions will not accept it as collateral. The reason is that lenders are wary of the possibility of revocation and the council's right to enforce collection of the service levy. Even the Deeds Registry will not register a charge/bond against a COR. However, a COR can be converted to an FPSG on payment of survey and registration fees and some owners are choosing this option. At the same time, there is a freeze on the issue of new CORs in new low-income housing areas and FPSGs are issued instead, which is not necessarily a progressive step since the COR suits poor and low-income self-builders who do not qualify for credit from formal institutions. The conditions for converting COR to FPSG are:
  - on-site water connection
  - survey of the plot
  - payment of conversion fee
  - registration of the plot.

■ Squatting: sensitive as this matter may be, it is a reality that must be confronted. There are a few squatters in Jwaneng (one of the most prosperous towns in Botswana), Ghanzi in the Kalahari desert near the western border with Namibia, and Francistown, the second largest town. The squatters have de facto rights, which, in time, will need to be recognized either through upgrading or resettlement. The squatters in Ghanzi and other desert towns present a peculiar problem in that they are seasonal squatters who have to leave their settlements in search of pasture and game.

■ Freehold: there are very few urban freeholds. A number of private developers in Gaborone have been subdividing and servicing residential plots on their freehold farms for sale, mainly to the rich. No new freehold grants have been made by the government in recent times.

In peri-urban areas outside municipalities, one can obtain land for housing development through one of the following customary channels.

■ Certificate of Customary Land Grant: this is an allocation by the land board for traditional uses, i.e. residential, ploughing and grazing. Such a grant may be cancelled if the land has not been developed for five years without sufficient excuse, or if it has not been used or developed for the purpose of the grant.

- Lease: land boards may grant leases in common law for residential purposes. The minister's approval is needed for grants to non-citizens. Leases are registrable in the Deeds Registry and may be mortgaged. Lease applications are initially dealt with by subordinate land boards, which pass their recommendations to main land boards for decision and signing of the document as lessor, the term being 99 years for residential and 50 years for commercial and industrial leases.

The above property rights present a wide range of possibilities for accessing land to suit a variety of individual circumstances. Gradations of formality as well as conversion possibilities are built into the system, which has evolved over a period of three decades, not fortuitously, but rather through a conscious land reform programme. Further refinements and improvements will be required in future to respond to pressures imposed by demographic changes, urban poverty and declining stocks of uncommitted state and tribal land.

Thus, although the COR lies midway between tribal rights and a state grant, and is fully marketable and developable, people see the State grant as ultimately desirable and feel frustrated by the various barriers preventing them from attaining that goal (see Box 11.1). The following analysis attempts to show that the COR is a viable alternative to full title on the one hand, and illegal settlement on the other.

Box 11.1   Popular perceptions of land issues related to the Certificate of Rights

In a series of group discussions held in various towns in 1997, the following observations were made by participants regarding plots held under the COR:

- Self-help plots are being sold off by beneficiaries
- Plot sizes are too small to comfortably establish a business
- Finance is not accessible due to collateral requirements and the high cost of borrowing
- There is unauthorized private economic activity in self-help housing areas
- Plots on old self-help housing areas are not surveyed
- Private surveyors are expensive and not available when needed
- People are not paying the service levy
- New serviced plots (under state grant) are unaffordable
- Authorities do not allow thatch in towns

These observations are generally still valid.

THE ORIGIN OF THE CERTIFICATE OF RIGHTS

Self Help Housing Agency (SHHA)

The COR was created in the early 1970s as an inexpensive and simple tenure model for the implementation of the SHHA programme. Owing to its success, it was endorsed by the 1983 Presidential Commission (Government of Botswana, 1983). This programme was introduced in 1974, to facilitate the provision of affordable housing to first-time, low-income urban house owners. The first area where the COR was applied was Old Nabedi, the oldest slum in Gaborone. It replaced the temporary occupation permit, which had been used until then to formalize settlement by new immigrants from rural areas. To date, the programme has benefited low-income urban households in Gaborone and six other towns. In fact, the majority of poor people in urban areas live in SHHA neighbourhoods.

Under the programme, which was administered by city and town councils, the government serviced residential plots measuring 375 m², including roads, drains and potable water. Sewerage and electricity were introduced in later schemes. Prospective beneficiaries who had incomes of between 1800 pula (P) and P10 000[1] per annum applied for the plots. Applications were considered on a first come, first served basis and qualified applicants were provided with security of tenure initially through the COR and, commencing in the mid-1990s, the FPSG. An accompanying building material loan was made available at subsidized rates of interest on request, to cover part of the building costs.

During the Accelerated Land Servicing Programme (1991–98), a total of 6365 SHHA plots were serviced in the urban centres, to supplement those COR plots already allocated.

The SHHA programme has witnessed substantial physical improvements since the implementation of the Accelerated Land Servicing Programme. Before the latter programme, SHHA plots were provided with only basic infrastructure, including earth roads, drains, public water standpipes and a substructure of pit latrines. Beneficiaries were also provided with security of tenure through a COR, while the building material loan limit was P1200. All the above have changed to the higher standards noted earlier.

The SHHA is by far the most successful low-income shelter programme (in terms of number of beneficiaries) introduced by the government. Largely based on the COR, it has provided housing for about two thirds of all urban households and has effectively averted the incidence of squatter development in the urban centres. Before the Accelerated Land Servicing Programme, there were about 26 700 COR plot beneficiaries, 5834 of whom have had access to building materials loans. Available data from the Ministry of Lands, Housing and Environment indicate that only 1892 plot owners have since converted to the FPSG. The high retention rate (93 per cent) indicates that the COR has some inherent advantages which owners are unwilling to forgo, in spite of the apparent allure of a more 'permanent' fixed-period alternative.

Presidential Commission on Land Tenure

The 1982 document on the National Policy on Housing (Government of Botswana, 1982) put in motion a process that resulted in a fundamental review of the national land policy by the Presidential Commission on Land Tenure, which was appointed in May 1983. The Commission sought to integrate land policy with economic and social development (Government of Botswana, 1985: para 1.03):

> *A land tenure change is just one change among many which may be necessary to create or provide new economic opportunities. A land tenure change alone which runs ahead of other developments can be dangerous as it can be socially disruptive and create landlessness before other economic opportunities are available.*

Following a cautious approach, the Commission recommended and government approved that the FPSG and COR remain the standard tenure in urban areas. This subsequently formed the backbone of the land distribution programme and the president later appointed a commission to look into land problems in peri-urban areas. The resulting report recommended changes on a wide range of matters relating to tribal land administration, including planning, allocation, development and transfers. It also proposed the strengthening of land boards. These efforts culminated in the Tribal Land (Amendment) Act 1993. This was only one of a series of steps taken to give effect to the reform process. As a result, the land tenure picture is much clearer and the respective functions of the land boards, town/district councils and Department of Lands are (more or less) clearly defined. What is even more important is that the 1983 Commission on Land Tenure gave credence to the COR as one of the two basic types of state grant in urban areas. But to implement this policy effectively, it was necessary to devise a land distribution programme that would cater for the needs of the rapidly expanding urban population.

HOW THE CERTIFICATE OF RIGHTS WORKS

After nearly three decades of existence, the COR works well and forms a permanent feature of the urban development scene in Botswana, despite recent moves to suspend new allocations for reasons that will be discussed later. The government sees it as an interim stage, which can enable the poor to gain a foothold in the property market before moving on to a higher title with acceptable credentials in the credit market. In the following paragraphs, we shall examine the various characteristics of the COR and how they affect the daily lives of poor people.

Grant conditions and perceived security

The COR is a grant in perpetuity, which entitles the owner to use the land for the approved purpose without let or hindrance. The conditions of the grant are spelt out in the grant deed (a simple two-page document), which is given to the allottee by the municipal or town council. One of the conditions is that the grantee should pay a monthly service charge 'in consideration of the rights granted to the occupier for the services to be provided by the council to the plot in respect of which this certificate is granted. . .'. This means that for as long as the service charge is paid regularly, the owner can feel secure. If he should wish to convert his COR to a FPSG (equivalent to a 99-year lease) he needs to satisfy the following conditions:

- Commission a cadastral survey, costing about P1000.
- Arrange a water connection, which costs about P600, equivalent to a month's minimum wage.
- Register his new title at the Deeds Registry in the Attorney General's office; there is no registration fee if the value of the plot is below P20 000.

The first step in the conversion process is for the owner to apply to his local council. The Attorney General's office then does the registration after the survey diagrams have been lodged with the Director of Surveys. This is a fairly simple process procedurally (one hears complaints about the shortage of surveyors, but this is not a serious issue for now), but for many households the cost is prohibitive. And in any case, there are no inherent advantages in the FPSG unless one wishes to mortgage the property. According to the Principal Housing Officer, 'the benefit is more psychological than anything else'.

Affordability

A basic attribute of the COR is that plots with minimum services should be allocated free of charge, apart from the monthly service levy of P12. A building loan on subsidized interest rates helps the owner start to develop the plot. The loan amount varies according to the applicant's income. When the programmes started, the maximum loan amount was P3600, which has since risen to the current (2001) maximum of P20 000, repayable in 15 years. Repayment must not exceed 25 per cent of monthly income. The 1997 Housing Policy Review document states, 'Roughly speaking, a well constructed house of modest standard costs approximately P900 per m^2 (1997) if contractor built at economy specifications. . . A completed unit of 50 m^2 would cost P45 000.' Therefore, the materials loan could make a significant contribution towards building a modest house on a self-help basis.

Thus the contribution of free land, basic services and a materials loan makes development of a COR plot an easier proposition than it would otherwise be. However, from the point of view of the tenants, rents are too high.

Access to services

The original COR plots were provided with basic services, including roads, storm-water drainage and potable water. Indeed, a large proportion of the plots still use pit latrines, although many areas now have public sewers and nearly all plots have individual water connections on plot. Electric power lines were also a later addition. By the year 2000, the process of upgrading the infrastructure was almost complete.

Since the network is already provided, it is easy for a household to make a water connection, although the cost (P580–600) is quite high. Gaborone City Council has tried to force each house to connect to the water mains by closing all the public standpipes. But this well-meaning policy did not succeed because politicians intervened and demanded to know where the people would get water and 'why should citizens go thirsty?'

Since COR holders occupy plots in central urban locations, they enjoy other services one would expect to find in such situations, such as telephone connections, taxis and public transport (Gaborone and other large towns have no buses, but taxis are the most common form of transport).

The municipal authorities also provide schools, health centres, police posts and public open spaces. Low-income owners visited in Gaborone were all well endowed with such facilities. The municipal ward office accommodates the housing officer and his staff, whose job is to monitor the general maintenance and cleanliness of community infrastructure, as well as collecting the monthly service charge. Indeed the ward office normally has a full team of professionals and technicians, including a housing officer, social worker and maintenance officer.

Participation by women

Where CORs were first allocated in the early 1970s, women's participation in the programme was not viewed as an issue. There was no conscious discrimination, but some allocation criteria, such as evidence of regular employment, had a discriminating effect. The 1999 Housing Policy Review document acknowledges the difficulties experienced by women in getting institutional and employee housing, credit, training in the construction sector and even in renting private sector accommodation if they have children.

All the same, statistics show that female-headed households do better when it comes to managing and dealing with family housing problems. In the early 1990s, house ownership was higher, both nationally and in urban areas, among female-headed households (Table 11.1). There were also more female landlords than male in urban areas, which is a credit to the COR scheme. Indeed women used to get more COR plots than men, but some of them subsequently chose to transfer ownership to spouses, not necessarily with a happy ending.

Table 11.1 House ownership among poor women 1993–94 (per cent)

		Own	Rent	Pay SHHA levy
National	Poor MHH	68	26	13
	Poor FHH	82	12	10
	Very poor MHH	91	5	5
	Very poor FHH	92	3	6
Urban	Poor MHH	39	57	34
	Poor FHH	46	42	41
	Very poor MHH	63	32	54
	Very poor FHH	66	21	56

MHH, male-headed household; FHH, female-headed household
Source: Government of Botswana (1997)

The Department of Housing is anxious to see that plot allocations are gender neutral. The law has recently been changed to enable married women to register title in the Deeds Registry in their own name without their husband's consent. Financial institutions are, however, not so understanding, and they still tend to discourage married women from borrowing without their husband's approval. Field surveys revealed several elderly ladies who had owned a COR since programme inception and had brought up many children and grandchildren on the plot (see Box 11.2).

Box 11.2 Age and experience matter

One of the older residents of the Gaborone West neighbourhood is Mrs Ntenegi. She has lived there since 1987, and although the plot is officially owned by her husband (now retired), she considers it her own, and she hopes that his children and grandchildren will inherit it one day. She likes the place because everything is there, she has had no problem with the council or the government, and – most important – she gets a good income from letting out five rooms. She collects P700 a month from the tenants, who are mostly local lads and girls, all single.

Mrs Ntenegi would not even think of upgrading to an FPSG because she is building a new house (three bedrooms, sitting room, kitchen, bathroom and toilets) behind the original one on the same plot and she would rather deal with the council than the central government. Council requirements for developing COR plots are less stringent, for example when it comes to water and electricity connections, sewerage and development density. She started building the new house in 1991 and it is still unfinished, because she has to rely on her own savings.

'The toilets are no good,' she says. 'The pit latrines get flooded when it rains heavily.' She wishes something would be done about them. Flush toilets would

make her new house so much more attractive and valuable. When does she hope to complete construction? 'When God wills.' The old house had taken only three months to build.
Source: Field observation

Institutional change

While the introduction of the COR gave municipalities the responsibility for managing large housing areas within their territory, they also assumed a heavy political and administrative burden. Complaints about poor cost recovery are frequent. Residents are not happy with pit latrines and the council has to mediate between the divergent interests of landlords and tenants. The ward offices are a great asset, since they enable council officials to deal with problems on the ground as they arise. Residents on their part have formed ward committees to look after their interests. Committee officials (e.g. chairman and secretary) are elected by the general membership.

Access to credit

Although the COR was originally designed to enable holders to access credit from the Botswana Building Society and other financial institutions, this has not happened. This is because of the fear entertained by the institutions that the COR is a temporary ownership right which can be revoked at any time by the government and that the level of services is below the acceptable minimum. But in any case, the building materials loan scheme has obviated the need for owners to resort to commercial mortgage funds.

Those owners who have already built a house and wish to raise funds to extend the property or start a business have the choice of upgrading their title to the FPSG, which is mortgageable. So access to credit is not a problem for most households, since a range of options exists. Although strictly speaking, the municipal council has the power to revoke the grant under certain circumstances, this seldom happens. Conditions under which a COR can be revoked are:

- non-payment of the service charge
- failure to repay the materials loan
- failure to develop within a reasonable period.

For practical and political reasons these conditions are difficult to enforce.

Transfers

There is no restriction on transfers of COR plots provided the new purchaser is approved by the council, which has to ensure that the plots do not find their way into the hands of rich people or foreigners. Even so, some plots (there are no precise data on the quantity) are bought by middle- and high-income purchasers. The majority of the original purchasers (or their heirs) are still there, although not all are resident. Field surveys found a small proportion (about 20 per cent) of houses occupied exclusively by tenants. Landlord–tenant relationships are discussed below.

Workplaces

Residents of COR areas are allowed to operate small businesses. Common businesses are 'tuck shops' (small grocery), laundries, furniture workshops and so on. Strict supervision by ward office staff means that the shops and workshops are always neat and well maintained. Unauthorized kiosks and other structures are rare.

Box 11.3 Two brothers and an only son

Here is how the lives of three young men have been greatly influenced by family investment in a COR plot.

House X in Extension 14 has chairs, tables, wardrobes and cabinets lying in the yard. It is a furniture workshop operated by two brothers. With the help of eight employees they make all sorts of wooden furniture and sell it in Gaborone and Jwaneng (a diamond mining town). It was their father who started the business, but he now has a full-time job with the Disaster Relief Department and does not spend so much time working with them. He is also Secretary to the Village Development Committee. Asked whether they pay rent to their father, they said no.

Across town in Broadhurst is a young man called Moses. He relates his story thus: 'The property was owned by my father, who passed away in 1978. I supervise everything, but unfortunately I have not had the chance to go and change the title to my name. Mother is trying to do that for me. You see, I am an only son, and was still at school when we moved here in 1977. We were relocated from another spot where the government wanted to acquire the land for development. So we did not apply, and the plot was given free. We feel secure here, and there is no question of selling. We will only move from here to go back to the village one day.

'I have to find the money for the change of name. In the meantime I pay the service charge in advance, and the council does not give me any problem. They have promised us proper sewers, and when they do that I can develop properly, maybe demolish the existing house and build a new one. We have water, but I want electricity and a sewerage connection. All the same, the pit latrine is OK for now. We get flooding in the rainy season because neighbours have blocked the drainage channels. That is the one thing I do not like about this place.

'Tenants? No, not for me. I live with my mother, and the house only has four rooms, a very nice house though a bit small.' Moses's father had taken a P100 loan in 1977 for roofing sheets, but no loan has been taken since. The current value of the property should be over five hundred times the initial materials loan.

Disputes

An owner can appeal to the minister of housing against the council's decision to revoke, and the Housing Department operates a committee to advise the minister. Inheritance disputes are normally resolved by the council. A small proportion (about 2 per cent) of plots have not been developed. This is always a source of friction with the Department of Housing and the municipality.

One clause of the grant deed specifically states that ownership rights can be passed on to heirs upon the grantee's death. Indeed, many of the original owners have since passed away and their sons and daughters are now looking after their properties, as exemplified by the case of Moses Hiri of the Broadhurst neighbourhood in Gaborone.

The council also has to deal with other day-to-day conflicts with property owners:

- Illegal structures: 'People just build extensions because they want to rent them out. Every plot has an illegal structure.' Demolition is almost impossible because of the political implications.
- Service levy arrears: landlords come to town at the end of the month to collect rents and go back to the villages without bothering to pay the service charge. Of course they do not tell the tenants anything.
- Materials loan: since the loan is paid in cash, some borrowers pay the deposit, collect the money and disappear.

Interviews were conducted with ten heads of household (eight owners and two tenants) with a view to identifying their main concerns and perceptions regarding the COR as a tenure form. The results are summarized in the following paragraphs.

House owners

Most house owners have lived there for a long time, since the 1970s, with only a small proportion having ten years of residence or less. Some are second generation owners who inherited from their parents. All owners feel secure ('This is my property, nobody can evict me'; 'I have no problem with the council or the government'). However 'upgrading' or conversion to an FPSG is not seen as a priority; in any case it has its drawbacks, for apart from being expensive, the state grant constrains you if you want to build a larger house because the rules require wider way-leaves for the sewerage truck.

When the CORs were first allocated, the recipients built fairly quickly, typically within a year. Later allottees and second buyers took longer. Only a minority of allottees took advantage of the building materials loan scheme. One woman completed her three-bedroom house in 1995 and while she occupies it herself, she thinks she could easily get P500 per month if she let it. She thought the COR was a good arrangement for a lot of people who cannot afford better. She did not want to rent out any rooms because of the noise made by tenants, people coming in and out, and wear and tear to the house. Most houses are not so upmarket, since tenants rent accommodation by the room, each taking one or two rooms. Rents vary from P100 to P150 a month per room depending on building condition (for example a ceiling in the room makes all the difference) and availability of services. The average rent is therefore about a quarter of the minimum wage. The quality of the house tends to be better if the landlord lives on site.

What are the advantages and disadvantages of owning a COR plot? The owners appreciate the proximity to the town centre, the peace and quiet, and the availability of essential services (Table 11.2). It is not merely the existing services that are important, but also those promised by the authorities. The prospect of having streetlights or sewerage seems to have enhanced residents' perceptions of neighbourhood worth and hence property values. On the disadvantages side, environmental concerns weigh heavy, such as pit latrines, garbage collection and (for some locations) nearness to industrial areas.

Table 11.2   Advantages and disadvantages of owning a COR plot as seen by plot owners

Advantages	Disadvantages
Near town	
Near taxi stop	Pit latrines
Near shopping mall	Pollution and noise from industrial area
Near schools	Poor access from main road
There are no problems here; no trouble from the council	Flooding in rainy season
I like it here	
Roads and power supply will improve soon	
I own the place – it is mine	
Everything is here	
No shabeens (bars in private houses)	
Value of property appreciates, unlike cars: 'My house is now worth P150 000'	
Plot can be developed	
Quiet area	
Street lights	
'I sleep nicely, no problem'	

Tenants' perceptions of well-being are different from those of landlords. Some of them resent the fact that landlords collect money at the end of the month and then do not pay electricity bills or service levies, especially landlords who live in rural areas. One woman tenant in Gaborone's Extension 4D said

> *I have stayed here five years, and I do not feel that secure. The landlady used to complain about the water bills. She accumulated big arrears and then blamed the tenants. Now we have arranged to pay our bills direct.*

Like everywhere else, tenants on COR plots feel exposed to landlords' whims and market pressures, although they appreciate the secure environment and quality of urban services available.

During the 1970s and 1980s, the COR and SHHA programme were synonymous, since the COR was the sole tenure instrument given to allottees of self-build plots. Since its inception, the programme has undergone many improvements, e.g. infrastructure upgrading, which is an ongoing process; introduction of the FPSG; and computerization of land records. It is a vital part of the national urban scene, having resulted in 27 000 houses and over a billion pula (US$200 million) in investment. Its contribution to softening the effects of poverty and preventing the emergence of unplanned settlements on a large scale is immense. COR and the related housing programme also contributed to social harmony in a society with strong aversions towards controversy and conflict.

Why the COR was successful

Other factors that have contributed to the success of the COR include:

- a simple deed as evidence of ownership
- ownership in perpetuity
- low initial cost (i.e. free land)
- basic services on plot, plus social facilities (schools, clinics, open spaces and so on) essential for family life in a well-planned environment
- affordable service levy
- option to upgrade services and one's property, plus the promise of better things to come
- transferability through sale and inheritance.

Support services rendered by the municipal authorities through ward offices have helped to maintain a measure of harmony and stability in the neighbourhoods. However, well-trained professionals are needed not only to collect revenues and monitor environmental quality, but also to work with local committees and other community institutions.

The mixing of various income categories in the same area, although unorthodox, has removed the glaring disparities in environmental quality and social standing which are common in other African countries. Houses on COR stand side by side with medium-income apartments. It has also tended to flatten the land value curve, so that you do not find the sharp peaks and valleys associated with upmarket and poor neighbourhoods.

Changing circumstances

Efforts to protect property rights and streamline the state land administration machinery unfortunately took their toll on the COR. The various laws protecting property rights have been strengthened, while the Deeds Registry has been working smoothly and both lenders and borrowers are adequately protected. This is an achievement that forms a good foundation for developing the property market. But in the process of strengthening the relevant institutions, it was found by the authorities that the self-build programme was largely a stopgap measure and a more lasting solution had to be found. Hence the move to phase out the 'certificate' and introduce the 'grant'. In any case, why should a prosperous country such as Botswana mess around with unserviced plots on tenuous title when it could provide most of its urban population with fully serviced land accompanied by state-guaranteed security? Botswana wanted to distinguish itself from other African countries that were struggling with squatters and a chaotic land tenure situation. Other factors that contributed to the COR falling from favour include:

- the association of COR with self-help and inferior housing
- problems of obtaining mortgages from finance houses that were not happy with the municipal powers of revocation and repossession
- 'fronting' by poor people who were in fact agents of speculators, non-citizens and rich nationals
- improved capacity of the government to install services, making it important to recoup servicing costs as quickly as possible
- the emergence of new national priorities, new problems, new realities
- a lack of defenders and advocates among professionals; for example, private sector lawyers and surveyors did not benefit in any way from the continued existence of the COR.

Thus by the mid-1990s, the forces working against the COR were much stronger than those in favour and by that time the government had already suspended the issuance of CORs. The emphasis had shifted to the full implementation of the Land Servicing Programme. The effect of the phase-out is to marginalize those who cannot meet the new affordability criteria and also force those already holding CORs to aspire towards a 'better' option, which they cannot afford since conversion costs are quite high. Data from our field survey indicate that owners see no urgency to convert.

POLICY IMPLICATIONS

The COR served the country well as a way of forestalling illegal settlement. As a result, nearly 100 000 people were housed under that tenure type, and in spite of conversions to state grants (estimated at 7.5 per cent of the original 27 143 plots) by some house owners, there are still many plots in

Botswana's towns that enjoy the security offered by CORs. It is an adaptable and poor-friendly type of tenure that ought to remain in the statute books so as to retain the range of choices now available. If conversion were made easier and less expensive it would be an extra incentive for owners to remain under COR, since there would be little pressure to change to a 'higher' tier.

The seemingly insurmountable problem of making the COR acceptable to credit institutions also needs to be tackled. Experience from other countries, such as Kenya and Tanzania, indicates that it is possible to safeguard the interests of secured creditors without undermining the right of the municipality to enforce the collection of service charges and property taxes. Apart from legal innovations, it is also necessary to find ways of counteracting the severe shortage of key professionals such as land surveyors, physical planners and conveyancers.

The decision to 'freeze' the COR is, on balance, a wise one under the circumstances, since there is always the possibility that economic circumstances may change and its merits will once again be appreciated. The COR and the tribal lease are the two instruments that could rescue Botswana's urban poor in times of adversity. In fact, in the year 2000, the authorities were reviving the use of CORs to relieve the pressures in emerging squatter settlements in towns such as Ghanzi in the west and Katsane in the north. A small number of certificates are issued as special cases on an ad hoc basis when plots have to be allocated on the basis of the old standards. Fortunately, the government has realized that although circumstances have changed over the past three decades, the COR is one of the best avenues for fast-track resettlement in stressful urban situations, being capable of giving poor people tenure security with basic services at minimum cost. Thus, while conventional tenure approaches will be dominant for the foreseeable future, it is likely that the COR will not completely disappear. It will also remain as a model for other countries that are not as rich or as well organized as Botswana to emulate.

CHAPTER TWELVE

Combining tenure policies, urban planning and city management in Brazil

Edesio Fernandes

THE CONTEXT OF TENURE POLICIES

This chapter is divided into two parts, followed by a general conclusion. The first part presents the context in which tenure policies in urban areas have been formulated in Brazil. Following a discussion of the legal-political conditions for their implementation, the innovative tenure policies adopted in Porto Alegre and Recife are introduced. The second part provides an analysis of four case studies in those two cities.[1]

It has been widely recognized that the process of intensive urbanization in Brazil is characterized by social exclusion and spatial segregation. While 82 per cent of the population are estimated to live in urban, especially metropolitan, areas, the vast majority of these people are living in very precarious material, social and environmental conditions – often illegally. Indeed, the lack of affordable and adequate housing options has brought about a proliferation of irregular and illegal forms of land use and development. This is the result of a combination of three factors:

- the absence of a comprehensive housing policy at all levels of government and the legal-political restrictions on state action to control urban development
- the highly concentrated, privatized land structure formed over five centuries
- the unfavourable dynamics of the speculative urban land market, which has produced a large number of vacant serviced areas in the main cities.[2]

Over the decades of intensive urbanization since the 1930s, most people have gained access to urban land through the acquisition of plots in the widespread 'irregular' and 'clandestine' *loteamentos* and the formation of thousands of *favelas*. While the former are illegal land subdivisions developed mostly by informal private companies in peripheral areas, the latter result from the invasion of both public and private land, originally in more central areas. Housing for low-income groups has largely been the result of precarious self-construction in both *loteamentos* and *favelas*. The production of affordable, technically adequate and serviced housing for the lower-income groups by state agencies has been insufficient at all levels and in some large cities, such as Sao Paulo and Rio de Janeiro, unregulated rental practices have provided housing opportunities to a large number of urban poor. This is particularly in *corticos*, the dilapidated private houses usually situated in central areas, where thousands of families live in precarious and hazardous conditions.[3]

Full, formal security of tenure is virtually non-existent to the people who live in the irregular/illegal settlements, although the legal, political, social and economic consequences of this fact have varied according to the different situations. For a long time, people living in peripheral *loteamentos* have experienced restricted access to public services, formal credit and finance, and other socio-legal limitations because of their illegal situation. However, as a rule, *favela* dwellers have been the most vulnerable groups. Experiencing the same legal and socioeconomic difficulties, they have also been more directly exposed to forced eviction. This powerful combination of legal discrimination, political vulnerability, economic incapacitation, social exclusion and spatial segregation has turned these tens of millions of urban poor into second-class citizens. Although this process has affected all low-income social groups, researchers have particularly stressed the impact it has had on women and children.

The historical context

Having started in the 1930s, the intensive urbanization process in Brazil reached its peak in the 1960s and 1970s. Political redemocratization and economic restructuring since the 1980s have gradually brought changes in the pattern of urban management, including the increasing recognition by some municipalities – given the absence of a national policy – of the need to confront the process of social exclusion and spatial segregation. As a result, important tenure policies have been formulated in some cities within the context of regularization programmes aimed at upgrading and legalizing *favelas* and irregular/clandestine *loteamentos*.

To some extent, breaking with the tradition of political centralization, municipal government was significantly strengthened in legal, political, administrative and financial terms by the 1988 federal Constitution. The conditions for the promotion of socially oriented, democratic urban management by the local state were improved by this Constitution, which explicitly recognized the principle of the 'social function of property and of the city'. Among other important developments, it also recognized a special right of urban *usucapiao*, a form of adverse possession for those occupying private areas up to 250 m². This encouraged the formulation of municipal policies aimed at legalizing and improving tenure conditions in informal settlements.[4] Within this context, a fundamental change in the orientation of tenure policies has become evident in many cities. After decades of evicting the communities living in illegal settlements, or denying them services, credit and rights, the local state has increasingly come to tolerate them. Eventually – albeit in an incipient way – it has proposed improvements in conditions of tenure through the legal and technical regularization of such areas. This started with the PRO-FAVELA programme imple-mented in Belo Horizonte in 1983, but since the late 1980s/early 1990s, land tenure regularization has been attempted in a number of cities, espe-cially by those municipalities explicitly committed to promoting demo-cratic urban management as well as democratizing access to urban land and housing. Municipal government has become the main agent in this process. The long-term inaction of the federal government on the matter has been reduced even further, to the provision of occasional financial transfers to federated-state and municipal programmes, as well as the creation of some legal-financial mechanisms.[5]

Generally speaking, the tenure policies implemented within the context of the *favela* regularization have been more consistent, systematic and suc-cessful than those proposing the regularization of irregular/illegal *lotea-mentos*. This is probably due to the greater level of socio-political mobilization in *favelas* over the decades, because *favela* dwellers have always experienced a more precarious legal status. As such, they are more vulnerable to eviction than the residents of illegal *loteamentos* who originally purchased land titles from whoever presented themselves as the legitimate owners.

Despite the increase in urban poverty exacerbated by economic global-ization, the country's concentrated (urban and rural) land structure and its elitist capital and income distribution system has remained largely unchal-lenged. Over the past two decades, increasing numbers of people have had to resort to informal means of access to urban land and housing. In the main cities, even the acquisition of plots in illegal *loteamentos* has become unaffordable for growing numbers of people. *Favelas* have been formed in urban areas on a daily basis, and now include peripheral areas. Even the action of the most progressive local administrations, such as those in the hands of the Workers' Party (*Partido dos Trabalhadores*) has been hindered by the extent of the accumulated housing deficit and other urban, social and environmental problems. Local state action has also been negatively affected by the impact of Brazil's long-standing financial and monetary crisis. Another significant problem has been the lack of a proper legal-institutional sphere in the country's constitutional order to address the metropolitan dimension of most urban, social and environmental problems. The scope for municipal action is clearly restricted.

Legal-political conditions for the formulation of tenure policies

Historically, Brazil's legal system has recognized the co-existence of differ-ent land tenure systems. During the colonial period (1500–1822), the Por-tuguese legislation – based to some extent on the notion of the social function of property – included several forms of leasehold rights. Many of these rights have survived the political changes in the country and were eventually incorporated in the 1916 Civil Code and subsequent land-related legislation. In theory, there are several forms of real rights in Brazil, of which freehold rights are just one. Others would include *enfiteuse, servidoes, uso, habitacao* and, more recently, *concessao de direito real de uso.* Freehold rights can be recognized as individual or collective (condominium) rights. Nominally, all such rights provide security of tenure and protection against eviction. However, the reality is that since the colonial period, the notion of full individual freehold rights has been dominant and the other forms of real rights have been much less significant. Indeed, most of the few existing tenure systems based on real rights other than freehold rights are obsolete remnants of Brazil's colonial past, often relating to land belonging to the Church or the state.[6]

In this context, one of the main problems affecting urban management is that the socially oriented tenure policies provided for in the Constitution (and which imply broad scope for state action) still lack support in the basic provisions of the overall legal system. In fact, the assumptions of progressive tenure policies, such as those supporting tenure regularization programmes, are at odds with the prevailing individualistic legal definition of property rights as laid down in the 1916 Civil Code, which is still in force.[7] There has been general confusion between housing rights and property rights, and an ill-thought, immediate association between security of tenure and the recognition of individual property rights. Most people and organizations (governmental and non-governmental) promoting security of tenure through regularization policies are under the impression that only through the recognition of full freehold individual titles will security of tenure be achieved.

In some cases, this association between individual ownership and security of tenure has been politically motivated. This is particularly the case when the adoption of tenure policies has been defended by groups (such as those linked to the progressive branch of the Catholic Church) that view the recognition of individual property titles as a means of promoting long overdue land reform. Moreover, the powerful ideological and cultural implications of the notion of full individual ownership should not be underestimated. In part due to the country's unstable economic production and lack of a social security system, land ownership has played a central role in Brazil's history. To most people in *favelas* and elsewhere, security of tenure equals individual ownership. A recent survey among the members of the *Movimento dos Sem-Terra* ('Landless Movement') in the countryside of Brazil – deemed by many to be subversive, dangerous agents who have violently questioned the country's land structure – indicated that 75 per cent of them wanted to be given full freehold individual titles.

Invasions, irregular land subdivisions and all other forms of precarious occupation, as well as the widespread practice of illegal construction, are a reflection of the land markets (formal and informal) and the overall political system. They are also the result of the nature of the legal system, particularly the land laws, property rights laws and registration laws, which are deeply elitist and exclusionary. The adoption of legal instruments which do not reflect the socioeconomic realities determining access to urban land

and housing, and the lack of proper regulation, have played a perverse role in aggravating, if not in determining, the process of social exclusion and spatial segregation.

Since the pioneering tenure policy of Belo Horizonte was formulated in the early 1980s, most tenure regularization programmes have followed the same formula of regularization by local government based on the recognition of individual freehold rights. This has proved to be one of the factors determining their failure.[8] On the whole, many tenure regularization policies have been relatively successful regarding the upgrading works and service provision. However, they have largely failed to promote land legalization, especially in those *favelas* occupying private land, given the high financial costs and legal and technical difficulties involved.

Innovative experiences of tenure regularization

The legal-political formula supporting the tenure policies of Belo Horizonte has been reproduced in several cities, such as Salvador, where the same problems have been identified. This situation has become even more difficult given the conservative legal provisions in force regarding the definition of individual property rights, which have long favoured economic exchange values and the interests of landowners and economic groups to the detriment of the principle of the social function of property. Given this conservative legal culture, in many municipalities the action of judicial power has also significantly reduced the scope for state intervention in the domain of individual property rights. It fails to recognize the social right to housing and favours the interests of the original landowners even in situations where the land occupation has been consolidated for a long time.

Expressing their particular socio-political and historical circumstances, other municipalities have attempted to formulate innovative tenure policies to support regularization programmes based on different legal-political notions and instruments. Learning from the accumulated experience over the past 15 years in Belo Horizonte and elsewhere, Porto Alegre and Recife have formulated policies that take into account the difficulties involved in the legalization of invaded public and private land through the provision of individual property titles. They have also taken into consideration situations in which legalized plots had been immediately sold by the original occupiers who then moved on to invade other peripheral areas, thus starting the whole process all over again. As a result, the policies currently being implemented in Porto Alegre and Recife are based on the assumption that individual property rights do not necessarily achieve the main goal of most tenure regularization programmes – the integration of illegal areas and communities into the broader urban structure and society. They are based on the principle that tenure regularization policies must be reconciled with the need to improve the conditions of socio-political citizenship.

Policy makers in those cities have also begun to view the phenomenon of urban illegality from a different perspective. As such, they see the state's social obligations in terms of providing adequate and affordable housing rights, and not necessarily providing property rights. Among other things, this has resulted in a different treatment of invaded public and private land, including a move away from the traditional provision of individual freehold titles in public areas. The new policies formulated in Porto Alegre and Recife are founded on a recognition that social housing rights do not automatically entail the privatization of public land, particularly in the Brazilian urban context where the amount of existing public land is negligible.

In both Porto Alegre and Recife, tenure policies have favoured the recourse to the legal institute of *usucapiao* as the principal means of upgrading tenure and the legalization of settlements in private areas. They are based on two notions. First, that whenever possible, the original landowners should not benefit through financial compensation from public funds. Second, that neither the state nor the market have met the housing needs of those people occupying vacant/under-utilized land and that such land has failed to fulfil its social function. They have also supported the legal notion that time creates rights, as much as it abolishes them, and that the occupiers of private land should be accorded their own property rights – rather than as beneficiaries of property rights created by the state through expropriation (and subsequent sale or transfer). This means that the role of the local government in private areas should, wherever possible, be limited to facilitating or mediating the confrontation between the occupiers and the original landowner for the judicial recognition of the occupiers' freehold rights.

To a lesser extent, the new tenure policies have also considered the economic implications of regularization programmes on the land market and on the financial capacity of the residents in informal settlements. The tenure rights recognized are meant to promote legal security of tenure, minimize distortions on the land market, facilitate the social and spatial integration of the areas and communities, and to guarantee the permanence of the original occupiers on the land once it has been upgraded and regularized. These policies also have a gender dimension; regardless of their legal marital status, women are given a priority treatment once the recognition of titles is promoted. As a rule, tenure titles have been issued in the names of both partners.

As mentioned above, the Brazilian legal system allows for a gamut of alternative legal-political options apart from individual freehold ownership. This ranges from diverse forms of leasehold to still largely unexplored forms of collective ownership, allowing for varying degrees of state control. The most 'innovative' approach to tenure rights in urban areas in Brazil, as applied in both Porto Alegre and Recife, concerns the utilization of the legal-political instrument entitled 'Concession of the Real Right to Use' as the means of recognizing security of tenure. This has been done within the context of broader municipal programmes aimed at the legalization and upgrading of *favelas*.

THE CONCESSION OF THE REAL RIGHT TO USE (CRRU)

CRRU is one of the real rights recognized by Brazil's legal system. This means that it is a material right over the land, which can be opposed against claims from other parties, and not a mere civil obligation to be resolved through the payment of compensation. It is not a simple administrative permit or a precarious certificate of authorization and, as such, cannot easily be revoked.[9] It is a form of leasehold – a real right over someone else's property. As there is no such thing as 'a continuum' or 'degrees' of rights in the Brazilian legal system, the CRRU is a real right in itself, with its own peculiar characteristics, and it does not lead to full ownership. The CRRU provides legal security of tenure to the beneficiaries and can be registered at the registry office, thus pre-empting eviction.

The CRRU has been used to legalize settlements in public land. The public, usually municipal, authorities have conceded the right to use the land through a specific leasing contract, but have retained ownership of the land. This makes it possible for them to legally control, to some extent at least, its occupation, use and transfer. In principle, the CRRU admits the transfer of the right to the beneficiaries' legal heirs, as well as allowing the original beneficiaries to sell and rent out to third parties and use the property as collateral. It can be used to generate individual rights or in a collective manner, creating a form of condominium. It has been applied in different ways by the various municipalities. Some have not allowed the *inter vivos* transfer of the titles by the original beneficiaries; others have allowed it subject to previous authorization by the tenure regularization agency, by the local residents' association, or by both. The time limit set for the allocation of the CRRU has also been treated differently in the different municipalities, and most known contracts have varied from five to 50 years. Different treatments have also been given to the questions of whether the beneficiaries should pay for the rights, how much they should pay, and how the payment should be made. In principle, the registration of the CRRU title renders the beneficiaries liable for local property tax, but local legislation can exempt them temporarily or permanently, and the experiences have varied.

CASE STUDIES: PORTO ALEGRE AND RECIFE

This section analyses the tenure policies employed in Porto Alegre and Recife, cities where the CRRU has been used for some years now within the context of municipal regularization programmes. It describes, briefly, the practical application of the CRRU, when and why it was introduced, and how it has been applied. Drawing on existing data and literature, and inter-views with local residents, community leaders, academics and other important stakeholders in governmental agencies and NGOs, some of the strengths and weaknesses of both experiences of tenure regularization are discussed. For comparative purposes, in each city reference is also made to cases where the tenure policy was not based on the CRRU. The analysis is based on the following research questions:

- To what extent have the tenure policies promoted effective or perceived security of tenure?
- To what extent have they achieved the intended promotion of socio-spatial integration?
- To what extent have they enabled improved access to credit and services for residents as well as improving their willingness to invest in their houses?
- To what extent have they incorporated a gender dimension?
- To what extent have they been effective as instruments of poverty eradication?

THE EXPERIENCE OF PORTO ALEGRE

The municipal administration of Porto Alegre, one of Brazil's largest cities, has been in the hands of the Workers' Party (PT) for three full consecutive terms. A fourth term started in January 2001. Under the motto 'Courage to Change', the PT has confronted many long-standing problems experienced by the low-income population. Among other measures, the government has adopted a policy of 'priorities inversion', in which the issue of security of tenure is fundamental. The city's 'Popular Administration' has been sys-tematically committed to promoting urban reform and 'the right to the city', especially by democratizing the access to urban land and housing. Together with a very progressive urban planning apparatus, Porto Alegre has pioneered the ground-breaking political experience of participatory budgeting, with the local associations effectively participating in the defin-ition and distribution of an increasingly large part of the city's investment budget.[10]

Since 1990, Porto Alegre has adopted innovative tenure policies within the scope of programmes aiming to regularize the local *favelas*. From the start, such programmes have been combined with urban planning regula-tions. Since 1995, following the path opened by Belo Horizonte's PRO-FAVELA programme, the areas to be regularized in Porto Alegre have been classified as AEIS (Special Areas of Social Interest) by the municipal zoning scheme, as well as subjected to specific regulations by the prevailing plan-ning laws. Such provisions include, for example, restrictions on the size of plots and constructions and specifications in terms of land use. These planning regulations aim to keep the residential and social character of the

AEIS and therefore to keep the affected communities on the land. They prevent land subdividers from buying the upgraded and legalized plots in order to integrate them into the official land market aimed at the middle- and upper-classes, for example merging them and erecting larger and taller buildings. Having created a specific institutional apparatus to manage the tenure regularization programme, Porto Alegre has also opened an important institutional avenue to guarantee the participation of the AEIS residents in the participatory budgeting process in different forms in area- and theme-based forums.

According to several people working for technical agencies and NGOs involved in the original formulation of the tenure regularization programme in the late 1980s and early 1990s, a choice was then made, and approved by law in 1991, to favour the utilization of the CRRU in settlements in public land instead of the transfer of full freehold titles. The basis of this decision was to provide social housing rights and security of tenure without giving up public land, and to minimize the likelihood of the beneficiaries being 'forced' out under pressure from the land market. Although more studies are still necessary to assess the extent to which the policy has interfered in the land market, on the whole land prices in AEIS with CRRU seem to be lower than in less restricted areas with full titles.[11]

Porto Alegre is one of the few municipalities where there has been a systematic, and increasingly successful, municipal programme aimed at promoting the upgrading and legalization of irregular/clandestine *loteamentos*. Several measures have been taken to legalize the occupation in such areas through the recognition of the freehold titles the residents had purchased in good faith – but which were legally flawed transactions.[12] It is in the regularization of the *favelas*, however, that the most innovative tenure policies have been employed. Although *favelas* on private land have been increasingly upgraded regardless of their legal status, thus creating the perception of secure tenure, the official policy concerning their legalization is to support the affected communities in their claim for the judicial recognition of *usucapiao* rights whenever possible. However, they have not been fully successful as there is still a resistance on the part of the local judiciary to the notion that the constitutional institute of special urban *usucapiao* is applicable without previous regulation by federal legislation. Although this is the dominant view held by the conservative legal sectors nationwide, the special urban *usucapiao* has already been successfully applied in other municipalities in Recife's metropolitan area, such as Jaboatao dos Guararapes, where it has been supported by judicial decisions and registered by the local registry office.[13]

Two areas were studied in Porto Alegre, namely Vila Planetario, where the CRRU has been employed, and Vila Vargas, where the older, pre-PT tenure policy is based on the recognition of individual freehold rights.

Vila Planetario

Vila Planetario is a *favela* formed in the 1950s on public land located in the city centre, and where the CRRU has been implemented since the early 1990s (see Figure 12.1). It has become emblematic of Porto Alegre's tenure regularization programme, and in demonstrating that security of tenure can be realized through the CRRU. Given the continuous strong mobilization of the original occupiers (most of whom are paper scavengers), and despite the area's attractiveness in market terms (because of its central location) and the upgrading work and service provision by the municipality over the years, the legalization of the occupation has had no impact on the land market. The CRRU contracts were signed in 1993, with 90 families being granted individual titles. Most people who are currently living in the area have been there for a long time, and have not felt the need or been under any pressure to sell. Between 1993 and 2000 only one family left the area.

Although the restrictive local legislation only allows for the CRRU titles – valid for 30 years – to be transferred *causa mortis* (on the event of death) by the beneficiaries to their heirs, there is currently a proposal supporting the possibility of *inter vivos* (while alive) transfer. This will be subject to planning legislation and previous approval by the public authorities. A process of community participation should help to guarantee that the new occupiers fit within the socioeconomic profile of the area as a whole. Local women have been especially active in the mobilization and regularization process, with gender sensitivity embraced both in law and in practice. Most titles have been issued under the names of both partners regardless of their official marital status. In one case, after the CRRU title had been given to an unmarried couple, a celebrated judicial decision reverted it to the woman's

Figure 12.1 Vila Planetario, Porto Alegre: CRRU title. Credit: Edesio Fernandes.

name after she separated from her partner on the grounds of domestic violence.

Vila Planetario is an exceptional case in that the tenure regularization programme has been supported by significant public investment in housing. Since the initial housing programme was implemented, residents have continuously maintained and improved their houses using their own means and resources. According to the residents interviewed, access to informal and, in some cases, formal credit has been increasingly recognized, especially for the acquisition of building materials. There is also a good record of payment of the taxes due to the local administration.

The Jardim Planetario ('Planetarium Garden'), as the area was renamed by some people following regularization, is provided with postal services, electricity, residential water provision, rain and sewage drainage, street paving, organic rubbish collection and selected rubbish collection. The area is close to schools, health centres, hospitals, squares, parks and all sorts of commercial activities. The regularized residential estate has gradually integrated itself with the neighbouring areas, and its road system has been increasingly used by the residents in the neighbourhood, who now feel safe. As a result of the upgrading works, the area already has the appearance of an ordinary working-class neighbourhood. The community's participation in the participatory budgeting process has resulted in several achievements, such as the recent construction of the local crèche, which is run by the community, and the opening of a small public square with trees and benches. If the signs of socio-spatial integration are clear, the interviews with the politically aware residents and community leaders have also pointed to the existence of improved conditions of socio-political citizenship.

However, there are still some legal obstacles to full legal recognition of the tenure policy. In Porto Alegre, there has been legal resistance to the registration of the CRRU on the part of registry offices, preventing the recognition of full security of tenure. According to the Brazilian legal system, only the registration of the title constitutes ownership. Such resistance is based on a conservative legal interpretation supporting the idea that the CRRU – created by federal legislation in 1967 – cannot be applied by municipal policies before that legal instrument is further regulated by federal legislation. However, in other municipalities, such as Recife, the CRRU has been used for a long time without major legal resistance. In any case, this legal controversy should be resolved in the near future, with the imminent approval of the national urban development law by the National Congress, making it possible for municipal legislation to regulate the matter.

Another problem concerns the fact that granting tenure rights to individual occupiers depends on the legalization of the *favela* as a whole. In legal terms, a *favela* is viewed as a form of *loteamento* and has, therefore, to adhere to the provisions of the existing federal legislation. Until the law was changed in 1999, the legalization of the subdivision required that at least 35 per cent of the area should remain as public land for the installation of public equipment, collective facilities, and green and open spaces. However, this has proved to be a difficult task in regularization programmes as the informal areas have been densely occupied for a long time. As such, special and expensive arrangements (for example, expropriation of neighbouring areas) have been necessary to comply with that legal requirement. As a result, the municipal planning department responsible for approving land use and subdivision has opposed the legalization of the individual Vila Planetario plots (as proposed by the municipal department in charge of the tenure regularization programme) before the whole area is legalized. This institutional conflict has been harmful. Indeed, when interviewed, a local judge, clearly sympathetic to the recognition of tenure rights for the residents, expressed the view that his job reinterpreting the legislation in a more progressive manner would be made easier – especially given the hostile overall legal culture – if the municipal agencies involved could find a way of working in unison.[14] However, this particular problem seems now to have been resolved due to the recent change in the federal legislation relating to *loteamentos*. By allowing the municipalities to dispense with the requirement for 35 per cent of public areas by municipal legislation, this should facilitate the approval of the legalization of the informal settlements – and therefore of the individual plots.

Interviews with local residents, community leaders, public officials and other involved parties have indicated that, despite the wealth of educational materials distributed by governmental agencies and NGOs, and even though the residents may not have a full understanding of the nature, technicalities and implications of the CRRU, there is nonetheless a widely held, strong perception of security of tenure. This perceived security of tenure is despite the fact that, with the prevailing legal obstacles to the registration of the titles, technically the CRRU beneficiaries still do not have full legal security of tenure, nor can they legally offer their properties as collateral.

Vila Vargas

Another AEIS, Vila Vargas, is a *favela* formed in a private area located relatively more distant from the city centre. In keeping with the dominant approach at the time, in the mid-1980s the local authorities proposed to legalize the area by transferring full individual freehold titles to the occupiers. At the time of writing, this still had not happened. The original proposal was to expropriate the area and sell the plots to 310 families, some of whom have long finished paying the monthly instalments determined by the local authority. After experiencing several problems, the area was eventually acquired by the local administration. However, the community leaders interviewed resent the fact that the administration, now under the political leadership of the PT, has not made any special efforts to give continuity to the previous administration's tenure policy and is not prepared to commit itself to the legal, political, financial and technical costs associated with that policy. According to the technical staff interviewed, it seems that part of the problem concerns the legal difficulty, explained above, of approving the overall *loteamento*. As a result, neither the area nor the individual occupation has been legalized. In legal terms, the residents, having no titles, still have no real rights and no proper security of tenure. It is expected that this situation will be resolved in the near future.

The occupation of the area has been consolidated for a long time but no public investment in housing has been made. The original houses, and all improvements to them, have been the result of self-construction and informal collective endeavour (*mutirao*). As has also happened in the case of Vila Planetario, access to both informal and, to a lesser extent, formal credit has reportedly been increasingly realized. Despite their less consistent mobilization (compared to Vila Planetario), the local community has increasingly taken part in the participatory budgeting process, and there has been a continuous undertaking of several upgrading works and service provision by the municipal administration. The gender dimension in the mobilization and in the tenure regularization process is less evident than in Vila Planetario, and the record of local tax payment seems to be poorer. On the whole, however, signs of socio-spatial integration and improved conditions of socio-political citizenship are visible, albeit in a less consistent way than in Vila Planetario.

Nevertheless, as in Vila Planetario, there has not been a major change in the original group of occupiers of Vila Vargas over the years. Moreover, regardless of the remaining legal obstacles to the recognition of security of tenure, there is a widespread perception of security of tenure. Although neighbouring areas have recently been invaded, it seems that Vila Vargas is of little interest to the official land market, and informal internal prices do not seem to have risen in any exceptional way either.

THE EXPERIENCE OF RECIFE

One of Brazil's oldest cities, Recife is also one of the most complex cities in terms of its tenure policies. It combines several difficult factors: a volatile, traditionally populist context of local politics, which has an intense and contradictory relationship with a history of strong social mobilisation; a wide variety of processes of land occupation supported by, and generating, diverse, complicated and obscure legal regimes; and an enormous extent of urban poverty and illegality, aggravated by the faltering local investment in urban infrastructure. Recife has some of the most consolidated and professional NGOs and social movements in action in Brazil.

Unlike Porto Alegre, until 2000 Recife had no coherent programme aimed at regularizing *loteamentos*. The programme of tenure regularization in Recife's *favelas* – also combining upgrading and legalization measures – was formulated in the early 1980s, soon after that of Belo Horizonte, and it was also largely due to the significant action of the Catholic Church.

However, very different decisions were then made in Recife with regard to the legal-political instruments to be adopted to legalize tenure in the local *favelas*.[15] Regarding the public areas, the CRRU was deliberately chosen by the local administration, in what was a pioneering decision, for the political reasons described above. It should be stressed that most of the informal settlements are on public land. Regarding the *favelas* in private areas, a decision was taken to support the communities in their claim for the recognition of *usucapiao* rights, again mainly for political reasons. Following Belo Horizonte's paradigmatic model, all the areas in Recife to be regularized have been classified as ZEIS (Special Zones of Social Interest) in the local zoning scheme, and specific urban planning regulations apply.

The local political context in Recife over the past two decades has been more contradictory than that of Porto Alegre. While most of the tenure policies, regularization programmes and the broader urban laws were approved in the more progressive and participatory political climate of the late 1980s and early 1990s, later political changes have indicated less governmental commitment to enforcing those policies, laws and programmes. However, a very significant institutional apparatus was created in the late 1980s to enforce the AEIS legislation. This 'PREZEIS' involved the participation of several community leaders as well as representatives of public, religious and non-governmental agencies, and made it almost impossible for the government to change the basic rules of the game, something that certain conservative sectors would certainly desire.[16] Ironically, in Recife, some of the most significant, socially orientated and ground-breaking judicial decisions on the matter of tenure legalization have been passed. Nevertheless, significant changes are expected soon, as the Workers' Party won the 2000 election and took office in January 2001. Recife has not adopted the participatory budgeting process yet, but this is likely to happen soon, as is the renovation of the institutional structure supporting tenure regularization programmes. Judging from the experience of Porto Alegre, this should affect the outcomes of tenure policy in that in widening the scope for popular participation, a more consistent commitment should be given to public investment in informal settlements.

Coronel Fabriciano

Coronel Fabriciano (Figure 12.2) is a former *favela* on public land close to the city centre, recognized as an AEIS as a result of the strong political mobilization of the original occupiers. The CRRU has been successfully used and, in a pioneering way, registered at the local registry office. The case of Coronel Fabriciano is even more innovative, because in a ground-breaking legal-political formulation, the CRRU has been applied in a collective manner – the title applies to the whole area and the occupiers have condominium shares.

Given the fact that the tenure legalization programme has been successfully registered, unlike in Vila Planetario in Porto Alegre, the legal tenure is

Figure 12.2 Coronel Fabriciano, Recife: CRRU title. Credit: Edesio Fernandes.

secure in Coronel Fabriciano. The local legislation allows for the CRRU titles – valid for 50 years – to be transferred *causa mortis* by the beneficiaries to their heirs, as well as recognizing the possibility of *inter vivos* transfer, subject to both respect for the planning legislation and previous approval by the public authorities. Again, a process of community participation is expected to help ensure that the new occupiers fit within the same socioeconomic profile of the area as a whole, and property titles have been issued in the names of both partners, regardless of their official marital status. As has happened in Vila Planetario, there has been some initial public investment in housing, and since the programme was initially implemented, residents have continuously improved their houses using their own means and resources. Interviews also revealed that access to informal and, in some cases, formal credit has been increasingly recognized, especially for the acquisition of building materials.

Recife's AEIS have been upgraded and legalized to different extents: for example, 52 per cent have had at least partial draining and street paving implemented, 35 per cent have had sewage systems implemented and 35 per cent have been partly legalized. Only Coronel Fabriciano can be considered to be fully legalized. Most public services have been provided for some time now and some collective equipment has been implemented, although the area would benefit from more systematic public investment. In any case, as a result of the upgrading works the area has gradually gained the appearance of an ordinary working-class neighbourhood, physically integrated with the neighbouring areas and official road system. There are some other significant signs of social and spatial integration, although less visibly than in Porto Alegre. However, regardless of the participation of community leaders in the PREZEIS participatory management, the conditions for the tenure regularization programme to promote socio-political citizenship need to be improved. There is a poor record of payment of the local taxes due, which appears to be largely due to the local administration's inefficiency in imposing and collecting them.

Many of the residents have lived in the area for a long time, but, unlike in Vila Planetario, in Coronel Fabriciano there has been some internal mobility since the area was firstly regularized. This appears to have been influenced by personal reasons or problems related to widespread urban violence. However, the overall socioeconomic profile of the area has been maintained, as internal land and property prices have been kept at low rates. Some of the transfers of rights have been promoted informally, without the previous approval of both the residents' association and the public agency, due to the regularization agency's lack of institutional capacity. Also in Coronel Fabriciano, despite the area's central location, its potential attractiveness in market terms, the undertaking of several upgrading works and increasing services provision by the municipal authorities over the years, the tenure policy seems to have had next to no impact on the external land market.

Interviews with local residents, community leaders, public officials and other involved parties have indicated that there is not a full understanding of the nature, technicalities and implications of the CRRU, especially among the local residents less involved with the activities of the residents' association.[17] This does not seem to worry them, possibly because they have reacted – with success – when they have felt threatened. For example, when the original CRRU contracts were proposed with only a five-year validity, the community leaders managed to force the local authorities to turn them into the current 50-year contracts. Ironically, although there is a general perception of security of tenure, and despite the area's unique legal status and corresponding legal security of tenure, a combination of external problems seems to have affected the perception of security of tenure held by some of the more worldly wise community leaders. Their fears have resulted from the decreasing internal social mobilization; less commitment of the public authorities over the years; unstable broader local political context at the time of the research; and particularly the expected pressure resulting from major public investment in neighbouring areas to expand the underground system. Afraid that the new developments will threaten their permanence on the land, community leaders are now trying to mobilize the local residents to pay the local tax. Perhaps because they still remember the time when they were vulnerable to all sorts of external pressures, they believe that if they have registered titles *and* pay their taxes, they will be guaranteed protection against the economic pressure from land developers.

Brasilia Teimosa

Brasilia Teimosa ('Stubborn Brasilia') is a ZEIS corresponding to a *favela* in a public area owned by the federal government, where, in the late 1980s, the community resisted the proposed legalization through CRRU and demanded the attribution of full individual freehold titles instead. This conflict resulted in the state government taking over the tenure regularization programme following political negotiations with the federal government, but the promised titles have not been granted. In the absence of titles and registration, residents have no legal security of tenure. It is a symbolic settlement because, as its name suggests, it was built in the late 1950s at the same time as Brazil's new capital. Its 'stubbornness' has to do with the fact that the community has survived countless attempts at forced removal over the years, largely due to the fact that the settlement is in a most attractive central location, overlooking both Recife's harbour and its beautiful urban beach, Boa Viagem. The area has had an important history of social mobilization, although it seems to be currently more divided than in the past. Although the area is formally recognized as a ZEIS, the participation of its leaders in the management of PREZEIS seems to be more complicated and less active than is the case in Coronel Fabriciano.

All housing is the result of self-construction, as there has been no housing programme implemented in the area, and householders regularly make housing improvements. Access to informal, and to some extent formal credit has been increasingly realized. In fact, the area already has a densely consolidated occupation, and there are widespread commercial and building activities, including several multi-storey residential and commercial buildings. Recently introduced commercial activities have included English language and computer classes. As a result, the area has gained the appearance of a middle-class neighbourhood. In fact, the area is very popular among Recife's middle classes for its seafood restaurants with their live music.

Brasilia Teimosa has gradually been upgraded by both official and informal processes and, although it would benefit from more systematic public investment, for an informal settlement it is very well serviced and physically integrated with the neighbouring areas and official road system. However, if there are clear signs of spatial integration, there are also indications that the conditions of social integration have been less consistent. Although the interviewed residents seem to share a basic perception of security of tenure, meaning that they do not believe they are likely to be evicted by the government, the fact is that there seems to exist a high social mobility in Brasilia Teimosa. Increasingly, people are leaving the area as a result of relatively alluring offers, and also because pressure from the internal and external land markets has resulted in high property and rental costs. Although there are no precise figures, some of the people interviewed have mentioned that the offers accepted by traditional residents, although appealing at first, have not been sufficient to enable them to relocate to another formal and central area. Given the lack of legal security of tenure and the more precarious protection of the area by the PREZEIS apparatus, land speculation seems to be very intense. So much so that, despite the illegality of the occupation, a booming construction industry and an escalating gentrification process are clearly taking place with the reported arrival of low middle-class professionals. Internal land, property and rental prices are on the increase. There is no clear gender dimension in the political process and the conditions of socio-political citizenship are not evident.

MAIN LESSONS FROM THE CASE STUDIES

The cases of Porto Alegre and Recife indicate that it is critical that the recognition of urban and tenure rights takes place within the broader, integrated and multi-sectoral scope of city and land use planning, and not as an isolated policy. This will prevent distortions in the land market and minimize the risk of eviction of the traditional occupiers. There must be a proper integration between the tenure policies and laws supporting regulation programmes and the overall urban legislation. Moreover, both experiences show that it is important to reconcile the objectives of providing housing options, recognizing security of tenure and promoting socio-spatial integration. Housing rights are not, and should not be, restricted to individual property rights. As will be discussed below, the legal institute of the CRRU, when employed within the broader context mentioned above, is an efficient instrument to help achieve this goal.

The incorporation of the informal areas to be regularized into the broader municipal zoning scheme and existing land use legislation has been instrumental in safeguarding the original populations. Even in those areas where there has been significant internal mobility, the community's original socioeconomic profile has been largely retained. Such developments seem to be directly related to the articulation of the regularization programmes with urban planning strategies and laws. Indeed, the creation of special zones for the informal settlements in the local zoning scheme seems to give the areas and their residents a form of social and legal identity vis-à-vis the broader urban society and the land market. The case of Porto Alegre shows that, regardless of the restricted legal tenure situation, the actual permanence of much of the original population in the areas and the minimal impact of the tenure programme on the land market cannot be explained only in terms of location. These factors have to be primarily attributed to the fact that both areas have been incorporated as AEIS within the scope of the broader zoning scheme and corresponding planning legislation. This legal recognition has played a fundamental role in minimizing the pressure from land developers and other interested parties, in that, by affecting the possibilities for land use and development, it impacts on land and property prices.

Moreover, in both cities, the legal-political mechanisms supporting socially oriented urban management strategies have had a fundamental role in giving the residents a political arena in which to defend their rights and put their claims forward. A fundamental factor has been the continuous commitment of Porto Alegre's municipal administration to the tenure regularization programmes since the late 1980s, by creating a specific institutional apparatus to manage them. In particular, the incorporation of the special zones into the city's participatory budgeting process has been of utmost importance in creating a socially oriented political culture of urban management.

The case of Recife also highlights the importance of combining tenure policies and regularization programmes with the urban legislation as the condition not only to guarantee security of tenure, but also the permanence of the population – which is the ultimate objective of tenure and regularization policies. However, Recife's experience shows that the creation of ZEIS alone is not sufficient to provide protection to the areas against the land market. There is a fundamental relation – although not always a positive one – between tenure, regularization and urban planning policies, and the broader politico-institutional context of urban management. The volatile political context in Recife has resulted in a less systematic commitment by the local administration to the tenure regularization programmes and a more fragmented participation of the residents in the programme's management apparatus.

In this context, location seems to be a central factor in determining the level and nature of the process of social mobility in the areas. Both Coronel Fabriciano and Brasilia Teimosa are centrally located and integrated into the city's urban structure, although coastal Brasilia Teimosa certainly appeals more to the land market aimed at the middle classes, and Coronel Fabriciano has its attractions too. In Coronel Fabriciano, given the combination of ZEIS/planning regulations/legal security of tenure through CRRU and the residents' political participation in the PREZEIS management process, the relative internal mobility has respected the socioeconomic profile of the original group of occupiers. In Brasilia Teimosa, the combination of a nominal ZEIS classification/lack of planning regulations/lack of titles and the residents' fragmented political participation has not provided efficient protection against the dynamics of the internal and external land markets. High social mobility and gentrification have been brought about by increasing land, property and rental prices. Brasilia Teimosa is the exception that proves the rule.

This seems to be a potentially winning combination: a technically adequate tenure regularization programme based on consistent legal-political framework; the combining of a tenure regularization programme with broader urban planning legislation; together with progressive politico-institutional mechanisms enabling the effective participation of the affected communities in the city's urban management process. Once the remaining legal obstacles are removed, Porto Alegre's experience of land tenure regularization through utilization of the CRRU should become even more successful, in that it will provide housing rights, recognize security of tenure and help to promote socio-spatial integration.

It remains to be assessed whether or not tenure regularization programmes have a major impact on urban poverty. The upgrading of the areas, the introduction of services and the recognition of some forms of rights have unquestionably improved the basic daily living conditions of the affected communities in many ways. Women have particularly benefited from better service provision and, as a result, in some cases have been able to spend more time in income-generating activities. However, if they are to have a more significant impact on the growing urban and social poverty, tenure regularization policies have to be both part of a broader set of public policies aimed at promoting urban reform, and supported by policies specifically aimed at generating job opportunities and income. Although both Porto Alegre and Recife have recently launched some socioeconomic policies aimed at meeting these goals, it is a task largely beyond the scope of the local state. It requires, instead, more systematic intergovernmental relations and exchange as well as the formation of public–private partnerships.

Are property titles necessary?

In both Porto Alegre and Recife, upgrading works and service provision have not depended directly on the completion of the tenure policies and land legalization process. Tenure policies and regularization programmes have been implemented in areas already consolidated, in social, political and urban terms, where it has been increasingly accepted that the residents are entitled to service provision, public equipment and collective facilities. Housing has been largely the result of self-construction, and improvements have been made regularly. Naturally, there are better conditions where there has been public investment in housing (e.g. Vila Planetario and, to a lesser extent, Coronel Fabriciano). Access to informal and, to some extent, formal credit, particularly in obtaining building materials, has also been possible regardless of the areas' legal status. On the whole, socio-spatial integration has improved as a result of regularization policies, even in the absence of tenure titles. As a result, even where the tenure legalization process has not been completed, there is a generalized perception of security of tenure. This means that residents feel safe against the threat of eviction by the government and have some access to credit and services. In fact, in those areas where there has been consistent social mobilization and ongoing regularization programmes, there seems to exist less interest in obtaining land titles than was the case in the 1980s. However, many of the people interviewed mentioned that having titles would be good to protect the rights of their families and especially their heirs.

As indicated by the cases of Recife, and especially Porto Alegre, another set of political, social and institutional circumstances may, even without the context of full formal legalization, create a solid perception of tenure security. This perception has been strengthened by the fact that the residents' rights to remain in upgraded settlements have been increasingly recognized by other actors and by general public opinion, effectively encouraging the residents to invest in their dwellings and in the overall urban economy.

This poses the question as to whether titling is necessary. I would argue that, however generalized it may be, the perception of security can be – and often is – false. Having a title becomes important when a conflict arises, be it a legal confrontation between the occupiers and the original private landowner, a domestic or a family conflict; or because of other external economic factors, such as major public works which may make the occupied areas more attractive to the formal land market – as is the case in Brasilia Teimosa. This seems to indicate that the terms of the socio-political pact supported by the combination of urban legislation and political-institutional mechanisms – generating the perception of security of tenure – are essentially precarious and can be changed to the detriment of the residents' interests.

Moreover, it should be stressed that, being restricted to consolidated situations, tenure policies have not been applied to the vast majority of informal settlements in Brazilian cities. Invasions have taken place on a daily basis. More recent informal settlements do not usually qualify for tenure legalization, and the growing communities living in such precarious areas lack security of tenure. They have frequently been evicted by both the government and private landowners. Given the constant changes in the local political contexts, in many cities where the tenure policies and regularization programmes are not consolidated, such as Sao Paulo, several cases of removals by the public authorities have been reported. In other cities, such as Belo Horizonte, tenure legalization programmes have been increasingly opposed on environmental grounds, especially given the fact that many informal settlements are located in environmentally sensitive areas. In other cities, such as Rio de Janeiro, tenure legalization programmes have been directly affected by the impact of drug trafficking. In many cities, external factors have intensified the pressure from the (informal and formal) land market.

It is in this context that the utilization of the CRRU can promote more effective conditions of security of tenure for the urban poor. Besides providing legal security of tenure, the CRRU can provide both the local state with improved tools to handle its legal-political responsibilities and the affected communities with better chances to remain in the regularized areas. It has a direct impact on land prices, it allows for some degree of state control of the transfer of the titles, and it ensures that the state's obligation to promote social housing policies and recognize housing rights materializes. The CRRU also ensures that public investment is not immediately capitalized upon by the economic interests of land subdividers and commercial developers. Once the remaining legal obstacles are removed, tenure policies utilizing the CRRU should become even more successful, in that they will provide housing rights, recognize security of tenure and promote socio-spatial integration in a combined manner.

CONCLUSIONS

Tenure policies supporting regularization programmes have a remedial nature. At the risk of bringing about unintended and even perverse results, they should be formulated within a broader set of public policies based on direct state intervention and significant public investment in urban areas, particularly in housing and infrastructure. This includes large-scale rehabilitation projects, social housing and urban renewal programmes, and the residential occupation of vacant/under-utilized serviced land and buildings in central areas. Tenure policies and regularization programmes should also be reconciled with comprehensive and preventive policies aimed at transforming the nature and dynamics of urban development so that it can revert to the benefit of the whole community. In particular, it has become increasingly evident that an effective response to the growing housing problem in Brazil – and the only way to promote urban reform in the country – depends on the combination of the following factors:

- a wider democratization of the overall political decision-making process to address the fundamental question of land/wealth reform
- systematic, technical and financial co-operation between all governmental levels
- the formation of public–private partnerships within a clearly defined legal-institutional, socially orientated framework.

That said, it is imperative to recognize that the upgrading of informal settlements is fundamental to redressing the unequal spatial distribution of public services and equipment and collective facilities. It is also necessary to address the grave urban, social and environmental problems resulting from the process of informal land development, thus helping to promote the spatial integration of those areas and communities within the broader urban structure. Moreover, the recognition of some form of tenure rights to the enormous population already living in illegal and precarious conditions is of utmost importance. Legalization of the informal settlements is critical so that the urban poor can become proper citizens, in socioeconomic as well as legal-political terms.

Although urban illegality in Brazil is not at all restricted to the less privileged social groups, given the serious consequences of a lack of tenure security to the urban poor, several arguments have been used to justify the need for public policies to implement tenure policies for those groups. These range from ethical, humanitarian and religious to socio-political and, more recently, economic reasons. However, the consideration of legal arguments has been less clearly articulated. As a result, there have frequently been mismatches between policies, goals and strategies, and the legal-political instruments adopted, resulting in all sorts of distortions and even in the failure of most tenure legalization programmes. In particular, the nature of the right to be recognized to the occupiers of informal settlements or, in other words, the nature of the role of the state in the process of land development. This implies that the definition of the social and financial obligations for the tenure regularization policies has rarely been made explicit. Again, tenure legalization is not an isolated measure and needs to be conceived within the broader scope of urban and legal management and reform. Moreover, within the context of Brazil's legal system, tenure legalization can take fundamentally differing forms, and the choice of the legal-political formula to be adopted deserves careful examination. The legal solution adopted in a particular case will work properly only if it is the result of a democratic and transparent decision-making process that effectively incorporates the affected communities.

On the evidence of the existing literature, data and the case studies discussed above, formal tenure legalization does not, per se, guarantee socio-spatial integration, especially when it is promoted through the attribution of individual freehold titles. Much as one can understand the appeal of the notion that illegal settlements and activities constitute valuable 'dead capital', the evidence of this review suggests that, in the Brazilian experience, formal legalization, especially through the recognition of full freehold rights, such as proposed by the paradigmatic experience of Belo Horizonte, does not necessarily entail security of tenure. It is fundamental to guarantee that the promotion of individual security of tenure is compatible with the state's responsibility for the provision of housing rights to the urban poor and the socio-spatial integration of the affected communities.

POLICY RECOMMENDATIONS

A number of policy recommendations can be drawn from the Brazilian case studies. These include the following.

- Tenure policies cannot be formulated in isolation and need to be conceived within the broader context of a set of preventive public policies and direct investment in infrastructure, service provision and housing policies aimed at promoting urban reform.
- The objectives of guaranteeing individual security of tenure and protecting against eviction have to be reconciled with other social interests to fully justify the state intervention, especially to make the socio-spatial integration of the areas and communities possible; to guarantee the permanence of the original occupiers on the land once it has been upgraded and legalized; and to improve conditions of social citizenship.

- The recognition of housing rights and the guarantee of security of tenure cannot be reduced to the recognition of individual property rights.
- The choice of legal instrument(s) to be used to promote land legalization and security of tenure has to take into account, and has to express, the local political context and the broader objectives of regularization programmes.
- Land legalization and tenure programmes have to be articulated with urban planning schemes and laws to improve the conditions of socio-spatial integration and to minimize distortions in the land market. The creation of special residential zones for social housing, with specific urban regulations, within the zoning scheme deserves consideration.
- Tenure programmes have to be supported by a clearly defined legal-institutional apparatus within an effective and participatory management process at all stages.
- It is fundamental that policy makers promote better popular awareness about the general objectives of tenure regularization programmes as well as about the specific nature and implications of the legal instrument used to promote legalization and security of tenure.
- Tenure programmes depend on continuous state action and systematic and renewed public investment; the effective participation of the communities in the city's budgeting process is a privileged way to guarantee all the above objectives.
- Tenure programmes have to be supported by legal-institutional measures and public policies aimed at widening the conditions of access to formal credit and finance for the residents.
- The gender dimensions of the process of urban development need to be taken into consideration by the time of the formulation of tenure programmes to redress historical and cultural inequalities.
- Tenure regularization programmes can have a more direct impact on urban poverty only if they are part of a broader set of public policies aimed at promoting urban reform and are supported by socioeconomic policies specifically aimed at generating job opportunities and income, which process requires systematic inter-governmental relations, public–private partnerships and renewed social mobilization.

CHAPTER THIRTEEN

Community Land Trusts and other tenure innovations in Kenya

Saad S. Yahya

OVERVIEW OF LAND TENURE IN KENYA

Land ownership has been a major issue in Kenya for a long time. The struggle for independence was centred on getting land back from the white settlers. Even in post-colonial times, land issues have been a dominant factor
in the historical progression of the country's economic, social and environmental spheres. Kenya is primarily an agricultural economy and land is the
principal source of livelihood for the majority of its 31 million population.
It is an indirect source of all material wealth and is valued because its
possession confers security and livelihood, prestige and power.

The current land tenure system is a combination of English land laws
and African customary laws. The co-existence of the formal written and
informal (customary) systems can cause confusion. The system seemingly
evolved out of the initial superimposition of a settler economy over a territory in which various land laws and tenure systems already existed, and
the subsequent need to transform a former colony into a modern state
where land and other resources are controlled by nationals. There are three
types of land tenure in operation in Kenya, as outlined below.

Private land

This refers to individual/private tenure where land is owned exclusively by
individuals or companies. It is either freehold, where the holder has
absolute ownership, or leasehold for a term of years subject to the payment
of a land rent and certain conditions on development and usage. The bulk
of land in this category was located in the white settler areas and
townships, i.e. the former native reserves (now trust lands), which were
adjudicated and registered for Africans.

The conventional method of converting land under customary tenure to
modern tenure has three stages. These are:

- adjudication of individual or group rights under customary tenure
  under the Land Adjudication Act
- consolidation, where each individual or group has rights and is
  allocated a single consolidated piece of land equivalent to several
  units under the Land Consolidation Act

■ registration and entry of rights in the Record of Existing Rights or Adjudication Register in the Land Registry and the issuance of a certificate of ownership.

Thus land assembled by land-buying companies (discussed later in this chapter) for its members would be considered private land.

Customary land

Land under customary tenure is held communally. It is also known as trust land. Under customary tenure, absolute rights over land were vested in the family group, while individuals enjoyed the right of occupancy only for subsistence purposes. This type of tenure exists in areas that have not yet been transferred (or 'alienated') through registration. It is administered under the Trust Land Act 1965, which deals with all trust land.

Although customary tenure is slowly thinning out, it is still the most widespread tenure system in the country, especially in the arid and semi-arid lands. This land is held under trusteeship by various county councils for its residents. The communal nature of this type of tenure is also said to discourage individual investment in land and its proper management, although there is not sufficient evidence to support the argument.

Public land

Public tenure refers to land that is owned by the state for its own purposes or that which is unutilized or unalienated and is supposed to be reserved for public purposes until privatized. It is administered under the Government Lands Act (GLA) 1965. The phenomenon of government land originated from the Crown Land Ordinance of 1902, which declared all 'waste and unoccupied land' in the protectorate as 'Crown Land'. The categories of government land include forests, water bodies, national parks, alienated government land and unalienated government land. The Government Lands Act empowers the president to make grants or dispositions of any estate, interests and rights in or over unalienated government land.

Recently, there has been a rapid loss of public utility land as a result of allocation through presidential grants. This arbitrary allocation of public land is commonly referred to as the land-grabbing phenomenon. The Commissioner of Lands deals with disposal of government land, which is then registered under the Registration of Titles Act or the Registered Land Act. Table 13.1 summarizes the main characteristics of the three types of tenure.

Land and poverty

The written law does not differentiate between men and women. However, women are generally poorer than men. For traditional reasons they are

Table 13.1 Basic categories of land in Kenya

Land category	Ownership	Type	User	Government legislation
Government land	Government on behalf of the public	– Utilized – Unutilized – Unalienated – Reserved	Government use General public use	Government Land Act Cap 280 Administered by the Commissioner of Lands
Trust land (Communal)	Trusteeship under county councils (customary laws and rights)	– Utilized – Unutilized	Local residents, various uses, e.g. agriculture, pastoral, self, etc.	Trust Lands Act Cap 288 Constitution of Kenya
Private land	Private individuals	Freehold and leasehold tenure	Registered Individuals and organizations, various uses	Registered Land Act Cap 300

Source: Republic of Kenya, 1999

content to have the family land registered in the name of their husband, son or brother, even if they contributed to the purchase price or inherited the property. Ownership by women is, however, more prevalent in urban areas, where slum landladies and female entrepreneurs are a common phenomenon.

The close relationship between control of land rights, political power and ethnic dominance has climaxed, especially during the closing decade of the last century, in the eruption of intense hostilities between pastoralist and farmer, landlord and tenant, developer and conservationist, munici-pality and citizen. These events have been widely reported in the media and documented by researchers (Githongo, 1997; Malombe, 1997). A com-mission of enquiry was appointed by President Moi to investigate the cause of these conflicts but its report has never been published. The one lesson we should learn from those events is that land rights can be extinguished as easily as they can be created. Security of tenure is predicated on stability, respect for justice and human rights, and a working judicial system. Opiata (1999) writes, 'Indeed the main driving force (in Kenya) behind the earnest quest for, and acquisition of title deeds, has more to do with the power it confers upon the holder than security.'

Urban poverty

Poverty is defined by the two million urban poor not merely in terms of low income but also in terms of exclusion from access to land, housing, financial and social services. The underlying cause is adverse economic trends, which have resulted in reduced investment in formal sector economic activities. The effects of reduced economic growth have been exacerbated, at least in the short term, by economic reforms, which have led to falling real wages, increased prices and loss of public sector jobs.

The urban unplanned settlements pose a special challenge. The residents are virtually excluded from urban life and economy, apart from providing cheap labour and swelling the voters' registers. They have to suffer exploitation by slum landlords, evictions and violence. Living conditions are vividly depicted in numerous recent surveys of urban poverty and slum housing. Research undertaken in Nairobi and seven other towns showed that one adult in three has had an encounter with enforcement agents (Yahya and Agevi, 1997). Half of those interviewed have experienced eviction or demolition. At the instigation of the human rights lobby, Nairobi City Council has agreed to a moratorium on evictions. This is part of the wider efforts of the Nairobi Informal Settlements Coordinating Committee, which has been fighting for security of tenure and has prepared a strategy paper for the management of Nairobi's slums. But again the basic issue boils down to the poor's entitlement to land rights. Ongoing work on innovative approaches to tenure will hopefully help to widen the range of available policy options.

Three of these options are examined in some detail below: community land trusts, temporary occupation licences and share certificates in land-buying companies. These unconventional approaches provide alternatives to the process of illegal settlement.

COMMUNITY LAND TRUSTS

Community Land Trusts (CLTs) are a new land management model first adopted in Kenya in the early 1990s, whose main thrust is to make land tenure sustainable and to minimize the negative effects of the land market on poor people. They give local communities long-term control over the use and future allocation of land and their habitat and thus become a powerful tool for community development. The Ministry of Local Government, through its Small Towns Development Project, attempted to bring together the various stakeholders to address the complex question of urban settlements within the smaller towns in Kenya. Working in conjunction with the German Technical Co-operation Agency (GTZ), Voi Municipal Council, the Commissioner of Lands, NGO staff and the people in the settlements, the Ministry has attempted a novel programme of promoting an alternative land tenure model within Tanzania-Bondeni Village, a settlement accommodating poor households in the small town of Voi, some 350 km south-east of Nairobi.

The Tanzania-Bondeni settlement is located in the southern part of the old township area of the Voi Municipal Council in Taita Taveta District. The town had a population of 15 000 people in 1989, of whom 4730 were living in Tanzania-Bondeni. The residents have lived for many years in temporary and semi-permanent structures, since the council did not allow them to put up permanent ones and the land did not belong to them.

A baseline survey was carried out in 1989. Tanzania-Bondeni is a typical informal settlement with all the problems that are found in such settlements (Aiemwa, 1991). The people were in constant fear of eviction and demolition of their structures by the authorities. The condition of the houses reflected this fear – of 530 structures in the settlement, about 62 per cent were built of temporary materials and fewer than 1 per cent were constructed with permanent floors. Most houses were dilapidated, overcrowded and lacked adequate facilities (see Figure 13.1).

The settlement had large households, with an average of seven persons for structure owners' households and even larger for tenants, and a high ratio of female head of households – 41 per cent of the structure owners' households. However, the squatters in the settlement had been very stable, with about 77.1 per cent of the owners and 49 per cent of the tenants having lived there for over 30 years.

Development of CLT in Kenya

The CLT concept was developed in the US but has its origin in traditional African and Islamic land tenure systems. It is an attempt to marry the two conceptually different systems in order to suit the present reality. The first documented attempt at linking the two was made in the US in the late 1960s. In the search for a suitable tenure arrangement, the Ministry of Local Government Small Towns Project (see Box 13.1) picked up the idea from a workshop that was sponsored by Ford Foundation in 1990 to introduce CLT in Kenya and show how it could be adapted to the local situation.

Box 13.1   Small Towns Development Project (STDP)

STDP is funded by the German Technical Co-operation Agency (GTZ) and implemented in collaboration with the Ministry of Local Government (MLG). The project aims to:

1   build management capacities of local authorities in order to make them more independent in service provision
2   help the MLG to become a reliable advisory institution for local councils
3   disseminate successful management strategies throughout the country.

Local Authority Development Programmes are one of the outputs of the project. STDP selects some of the projects in the programmes for implementation through their funding.

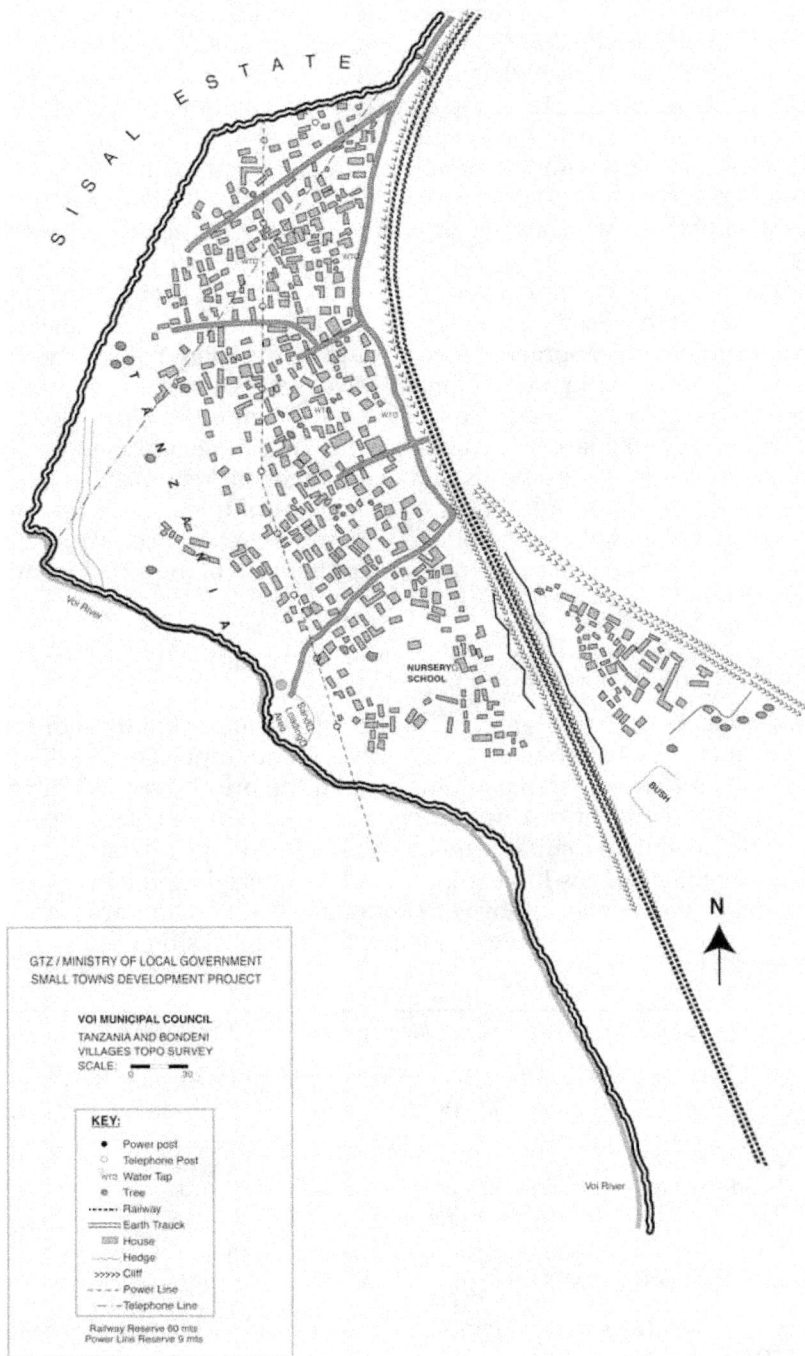

Figure 13.1   Bondeni settlement–topo survey carried out in 1991.

Based on the results of the socioeconomic survey, priority number one for the structure owners was the security of tenure (title deeds), followed by improvement of housing and water supply, while the tenants prioritized improved housing followed by improved water supply and electricity. Also, 46 per cent of owners had indicated that they were willing to provide labour, 27.2 per cent could pay cash and 26.8 per cent could provide material or other inputs.

After sufficient consultation, the CLT model was preferred to individual titles as the tenure system suitable for them (see Box 13.2), mainly because it provided a sustainable security of tenure. The basic concept of CLT is that the land belongs to the community, with individual members owning the development and improvements that they have undertaken in their plots. This discourages absentee landlords. If a member wants to move out of the settlement, he or she can only sell the development on the plot, but the land is not included in the sale price.

Box 13.2 The process of selecting a CLT

The STDP in collaboration with the Ministry of Local Government and the Voi Municipal Council initiated the formation of the Residents' Committee. The committee was made up of the area councillor, the chief, and elected representatives from owners, tenants, women and youth. Many training workshops on communication, self-reliance, leadership and upgrading in general were held. The different types of land tenure were also discussed. The Residents Committee, together with the Voi Municipal Council and STDP, held public meetings, after which the community overwhelmingly selected single title because they had been living together as one community without discrimination since the beginning of the settlement.

Kenyan law only recognizes individual titles and not more than a few individuals may be registered as owners even when a whole village or large family are joint owners (Jaffer). Second, the Lands Department is traditionally used to issuing titles with standard conditions, and attempts at fashioning creative leases with innovative conditions of tenure security would face bureaucratic blocks. Third, the law was severely limited to specific ownership patterns, which were not universally applicable. The Registered Land Act only recognizes individual ownership and is applicable only in certain parts of the country. The CLT model therefore had to be articulated in a manner that would allow for the establishment of a legally recognized communal ownership system, which, although registered under one of the individual title ownership systems, was also linked to a separate law for the registration of associations. This was to ensure that the fundamental basis of a CLT, i.e. collective ownership of land with specific conditions as to user rights for its members, is fully recognized in law.

Guidelines to disseminate the CLT concept were prepared and translated in Kiswahili. A certain minimum requirement for success had to be included in legal provisions and social guarantees addressing the following concerns:

- control of speculation in land transactions
- restrictions on disposal of the property without prior consent and approval of the community
- retention within the community of all subsidies of a public nature
- mechanisms for the maintenance of affordability of housing for the poor
- participation, control and empowerment of the community in the process of social organization.

The project explored a number of possibilities within the existing laws, with the assistance of a legal team. This resulted in five separate legal documents, i.e. the Constitution and Rules of the Society, the Trust Deed, the head lease, the approved development plan (see Figure 13.2) and the subleases. They were prepared and registered in such a way that they were interlinked and reinforced each other (Box 13.3).

Box 13.3   Linking the five legal documents

- The community was first organized into a legally recognized entity with its own constitution and rules consistent with the concept of CLT. The registration of the community was then formalized under the Societies Act.
- The Society prepared a Trust Deed to guide the Board of Trustees on how to manage the society's resources in accordance with the CLT concept. The trustees were then appointed and registered as Tanzania-Bondeni Community Land Trust.
- To reinforce the Trust Deed, conditions consistent with CLT were negotiated with the Commissioner of Lands to be included in the head lease.
- Since the land was to be allocated under one title, the approved development plan showing the boundaries of each plot, roads and public purpose plots had to be prepared and registered in the Documentation Registry.
- Finally, the subleases from the trustees to each qualified member of the society were prepared for providing the security of tenure, regulating the utilization of land and for binding the lessee to the principles of the CLT.

Three committees were established to co-ordinate the implementation of the project at the national, local authority and community level: The Project Promotion Committee, an inter-ministerial committee, was responsible for developing policies and co-ordinating implementation, while the Technical Task Force chaired by the town clerk provided technical input. There was also a Residents' Committee/ Management Committee

Diverted Seasonal
Stream

Lagoon

Nairobi - Mombasa
Railwayline

Voi River

Future Primary School

Plots Reserved for
Future septic tanks

Nursery
School

Riparian Zone For
Urban Agriculture

Future Community
And Health Centre

GTZ / MINISTRY OF LOCAL GOVERNMENT
SMALL TOWNS DEVELOPMENT PROJECT

VOI MUNICIPAL COUNCIL
TANZANIA AND BONDENI
VILLAGES TOPO SURVEY
SCALE:

N

Water Reticulation
System

KEY:

- ● Power post
- ○ Telephone Post
- ⊕ Tree
- ------ Railway
- ===== Earth Trauck
- ▼ ▼ ▼ Mashy Area
- >>>>> Cliff
- - - - Power Line
- — · — Telephone Line
- ▭ Plan

Railway Reserve 60 mts
Power Line Reserve 9 mts

Voi River

Nairobi - Mombasa
Railwayline

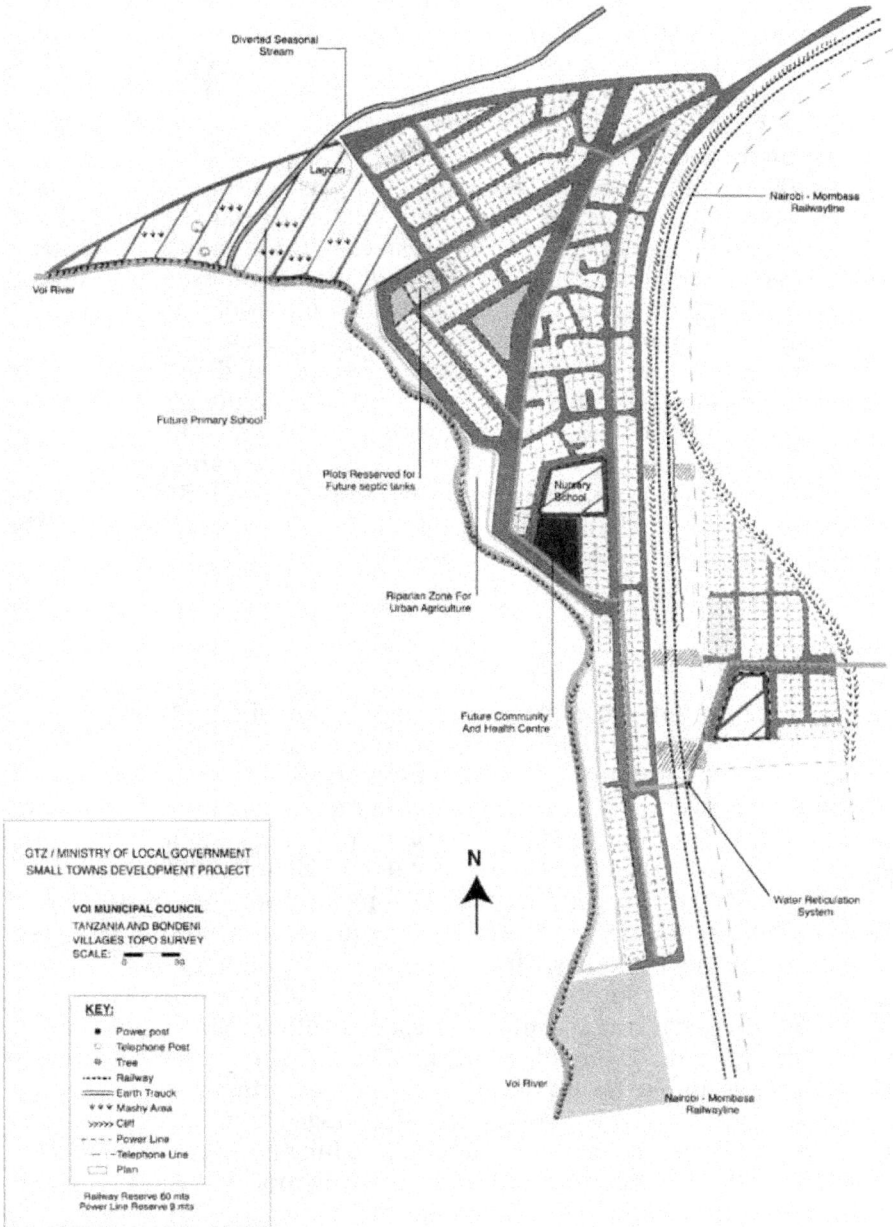

Figure 13.2   Approved development plan of Bondeni.

consisting of elected members, representing owners, women, youth, tenants, the area councillor, chief and municipal council representative.

Partnerships were formed with Kenya Wildlife Services, National Co-operative Housing Union (NACHU), the National Water Conservation and Pipeline Corporation, University of Nairobi, Barclays Bank Voi Branch, Kenya Railways Corporation and Voi Sisal Estates Ltd. These organizations helped the community with the design and implementation of some components, including roads, provision of credit, training, facilitating the acquisition of land and the collection of money.

The CLT is administered by the registered trustees, the highest policy-making body responsible for all matters related to transactions in, and management of, land. There are nine trustees in three categories of membership (lessees/tenants/friends). The Management Committee/Residents' Committee of the society is responsible for the day-to-day activities of the CLT, including preparation of budgets and managing the assets.

Budgets and audited accounts have to be approved by the Board of Trustees and members of the society during the annual general meetings. Accounting and financial management guidelines have been prepared to assist the CLT to protect their funds and to facilitate transparency and accountability. Another system required the members to deposit their contribution directly into a specific bank account. The same arrangements will be made for the collection of infrastructure development fund.

Strategies to ensure sustainability of the CLT project

The CLT has adopted reasonable annual lease fees, enabling the trustees and the municipality to meet their recurrent expenditures. To ensure that land remains with the community, the CLT retains first right to purchase housing and other improvements located upon its land. A 'resale formula' has been adopted for determining the purchase price for houses and improvements to ensure just compensation. Lessees can use their subleases for loans.

To ensure that the target group is not forced or bought out because of high building standards, the head lease has included conditions that recognize the existing buildings. The owners are, however, required to gradually conform to local authority building by-laws. Infrastructural standards can be determined by the community, based on affordability. Local artisans were trained in development control to make them conversant with council bylaws, public health bylaws and CLT requirements.

Preferential access is given to the less advantaged members, followed by long-term residents who are either tenant or adult and eligible members of the families of lessees. Both tenants and family members must be members of the society before they are eligible for plot allocation. The elderly, and low-income and female-headed households are given preferential access. Absentee lessees are not allowed, unless extenuating circumstances are demonstrated, and even then for a maximum of only two years.

Training of communities, committees and artisans on various aspects of the CLT has been one of the key strategies. Community workshops on legal documents and other matters, and regular public meetings ensure that members know their obligations. This has created awareness on how the community can improve themselves and their surroundings. The local authority is now confident to manage a similar process in neighbouring squatter areas.

Legal documentation can be adapted with some modification to suit other communities. Two video documentaries (one in Kiswahili for local communities and the other in English for policy makers) have been prepared to capture the experience and community participation in the formation and implementation of the CLT.

Impact of the project

Considerable changes have taken place in Tanzania-Bondeni since mid-1992. Although the layout plan resulted in half of the structures being moved, the affected householders were resettled within the project area. A total of US$23 750 has been collected for a cadastral survey and US$150 is collected every month as membership fees, which are used to pay salaries for an administrator and other administrative costs.

All roads were opened and some selected for laterite surfacing. Water pipes were laid and connected to a reliable water supply. In addition, a drain causing flooding during the rainy season was diverted. With the assistance of University of Nairobi researchers, a model house was built using stabilized soil blocks and sisal-reinforced roofing tiles and is now being used as offices for the Residents' Committee.

Many of the new houses coming up in the project area are using soil blocks produced by donated equipment. The training of artisans and youth in the production of building material and improved sanitation has enhanced their standards of building. A total of 565 houses have either been rehabilitated or newly constructed, of which 88 are permanent. All houses have corrugated iron-sheet roofing and their own sanitation facilities (septic tanks or pit latrines). This construction activity has increased employment and supplemented other income-generating activities. The community built a nursery school using its own funds, and is now planning to build a primary school.

The CLT has enabled the community to marshal resources from various sources. Four housing co-operative societies have been formed in the settlement to assist in the rehabilitation of houses under the Housing Rehabilitation Programme of NACHU. These co-operatives have encouraged their members to save as part of the condition of acquiring loans. NACHU has provided housing rehabilitation loans amounting to US$43 125 to 29 members of the CLT. The loans ranged from US$125 to US$1062.50. So far there has been no default on the repayment of these loans. Construction of houses has also been financed through individual savings, loans from employers for those in formal employment and through self-help groups formed by some members.

The most innovative self-help group within the CLT for construction of houses was Mjengo Self-Help Group, formed in June 1996. Its 52 members aimed at building permanent houses for those members who did not have sufficient funds (see Figures 13.3 and 13.4). It was agreed that whenever possible all the construction inputs would be bought from within the membership. Through the process, the group provides employment for 17 of their members, who earn between US$30 and US$60 per month.

The layout plan provides for residential areas and residential/business area with an average plot size of about 9 × 15 m, a market area and other plots for public use, including schools, a health centre, a community centre and open spaces. All roads providing accessibility to each plot have been opened and the surfacing of about 5 km of selected roads was completed at the end of 2000. Seasonal drainage has been diverted and necessary flood control measures, including building retention walls, have been undertaken. The area is now more accessible for the regular collection of solid waste by the municipality and for public transport.

Structure owners and tenants have formed one strong community and the numerous training events throughout the process have transformed the community into a self-confident 'Settlement Society'. Committee members and their leaders have undergone various training courses and have been exposed to other upgrading projects in Kenya through exchange

Figure 13.3   Houses on CLT before. Credit: STD/MOLG, Kenya

Figure 13.4   Houses on CLT after. Credit: STD/MOLG, Kenya.

visits. As a result, the leaders are now responsible for co-ordinating the development of the settlement area.

The project is being sustained largely through funds raised from the community. Once the project is fully developed, the CLT will contribute US$2375 per annum to the council as rates (property tax). Moreover, the implementation of the project has been providing some residents and local artisans with income-earning opportunities through the use of labour-intensive techniques. Other income-generating activities have been initiated, including sand harvesting.

The effects of community mobilization have gone beyond the project area. The main aspects of the CLT process, which are being adopted in many communities, are summarized in Box 13.4.

The payment of membership fees continues to be a problem and the management of CLT has had to come up with ways of ensuring payment. These measures include withholding benefits from a member until all outstanding payments have been completed, i.e. withholding survey certificates, barring members from participation in elections and withholding approval of building plans by the council. Another obstacle has been the opposition by the youth to allocation of plots to tenants. Several meetings were held with the youth before this issue was finally resolved.

Box 13.4   The essential steps in replicating CLT in informal settlements

- Formation of settlement committees with initial registration as self-help groups.
- Opening bank accounts for membership fees, and survey and development of their settlements.
- Preparing the list of owners, structure numbers, tenants and sizes of their households.
- Carrying out a topographical survey to pick all the structures in the settlement for planning purposes.
- Planning of the area with participation from the community
- Applying to the Commissioner of Lands through the Local Authority and District Plot Allocation Committee.
- Upgrading of group to a society and registration under the Societies Act. The society then appoints trustees and registers them under the Trustee (Perpetual) Succession Act.
- After the approval of the development plan, cadastral survey and showing of beacons, opening of the roads, reticulation of water supply and improvement of other infrastructure development.
- Finally, the owners develop their houses using their own funds.

Outcomes

The Voi experiment is the first of its kind in Kenya. The government is now being encouraged to reconsider its land tenure policy in the light of the CLT experience in Voi and to expand creative thinking based on an African perspective of land tenure that benefits the community rather than just the individual.

There is a need to demystify jargon and write the laws and related documents in a style and format that can be readily understood and absorbed by the majority, so that the message can be spread further. The Voi experience has shown that the people can grasp the new CLT concept very quickly, internalize it and put their faith in it. However, it took much longer to convince those in power. Hence the teaching and attitudinal change activities should be aimed more at the bureaucrats than the people. Other observations with policy implications include:

- People willingly accept long-term restrictions on the sale of their land, thus removing it from the market in order to guarantee long-term security. They usually sell because of speculators' pressures or incapacity to develop the land. There should be a package of support to help the poor retain possession.
- A clear prior understanding of local traditions and custom, particularly with regard to women's participation, is important. Proactive measures, e.g. keeping 'reserved' seats for women on committees, can lead to increased involvement at grassroots decision-making level.

- The need for alternative policies and attempts at redressing the issue of urban shelter for the poor is urgent. Official policy neglect ensures an increasing alienation of state-controlled land (presumed to be held in trust for the people) and its transfer to the rich and the politically connected.
- The experiences in Voi show that communities are willing to meet the cost involved in securing tenure once they have understood the procedures. CLT members can borrow money for housing construction and repay the loans even for those members without regular employment. Furthermore, the communities can enforce development control within their settlement areas in collaboration with the local authority.
- The Voi CLT shows that achievement of equity is possible if the negative effects of the market economy are curtailed and the community's cohesion is maintained.

An arrangement that has the support of a defined and fairly homogeneous community, a receptive and sympathetic local authority, and a committed group of shelter professionals and financial backers is best poised for success. That conjunction of positive forces outlined above was present in Voi in 1991 when the CLT experiment was first mooted. Fortunately it still exists.

OTHER TENURE INNOVATIONS

In addition to a freehold or a long-term lease and squatters' rights, there is a range of interests in land that can be described as quasi-titles ('quatits'). This is not because they offer inferior security to the holder but because they are not recognized as bestowing 'ownership' in the traditional sense of the word. They are also not negotiable in the formal debt market. Two such interests are the temporary occupation licence and the share certificate.

Temporary occupation licences (TOLs)

The granting of licences for temporary occupation of land is governed by Government Lands Act (chapter 280 of the Laws of Kenya) in part V under sections 40, 41 and 42. These sections give the Commissioner of Lands power to administer TOLs on unalienated government land.

The Nairobi City Council, on the other hand, acts under delegated powers in administering TOLs on lands within the council's jurisdiction. These include reservations, wayleaves and public utility land that is not being utilized. The same principle is applied in other municipalities. But not everybody has the wherewithal to go to the town hall to look for a site to develop. So the really poor have to approach the local chiefs (the lowest rank in the regional administration hierarchy), who have claimed for themselves the power to dictate where squatters should build, and to dispense illegal licences. In addition to the power, normally exerted with much pomp and ceremony, chiefs also benefit from the money they extort from the allotees in the form of unofficial allocation fees. Some chiefs grant only annual permits, which means that the owner of the structure must pay for a new permit every year or risk demolition and eviction.

The issuance of TOLs by the Nairobi City Council (NCC) is a procedure that is not guided by any clear policy framework. The procedure was passed by a council resolution in 1985, which empowers the town clerk, with the chief valuer as the council's agent, to allocate land for temporary occupation to enable small business and micro-enterprise activities to locate near their markets. Invariably, therefore, TOLs are issued in residential neighbourhoods for activities that complement the residential function.

Before an application can be approved for allocation it must be circulated to various relevant departments for comment and must be recommended by the local administration (i.e. district officer) and the councillor for the area. On approval, the applicant is issued with a TOL governed by terms and conditions. The procedure is relatively simple and applicants do not need to hire professional surveyors, engineers or architects to assist with documentation. Among the conditions are the stipulations that the allocation is temporary; that only temporary materials will be used for building; that the building will be used for the agreed purpose; and that the licence may be terminated by one month's notice on either side. The licensee is allowed to fence his plot in with temporary materials. The implication is that the site will be required for public purposes at some future date, and the council does not wish to commit itself to a long-term grant, which will entail compensation on revocation. In practice, however, licensees seldom vacate their plots, taking the risk of investing in substantial structures, temporary or otherwise.

Activities that are favoured by NCC for TOL approvals include:

- grocery kiosks and tea rooms
- small businesses and micro-enterprises such as builder's yard, hardware stores, garages and furniture workshops
- churches and other religious installations built of temporary materials, e.g. timber or under canvas
- informal schools.

The following areas are excluded from TOL allocations:

- land under power lines
- areas under easements and wayleaves
- riparian land and wayleaves
- areas subject to planning approvals
- private land.

Decisions on whether or not to approve a particular application are made by the town clerk and city valuer, who have the responsibility of reconciling planning and safety requirements with market demand for development sites and the city's cash requirements.

So how big is the TOL business at City Hall? The number of applications has been growing steadily, rising from 278 in 1986 to nearly 2000 in the year 2000. On average, less than half of all applications received annually are approved (Table 13.2). This is understandable, considering the combination of technical, financial and political criteria guiding allocation.

The central government also grants TOLs, either on its own behalf or through the Kenya Railways Corporation, which manages large tracts of land in those districts served by rail. Indeed the Government Lands Act has special provisions (Part VI) for the creation of TOLs (see Box 13.5).

Table 13.2   Summary of TOL applications approved by NCC 1986–2000

Period	No. of applications	No. of allocations	% Allocations
1986–90	1160	328	28.0
1991–95	1760	750	42.6
1996–2000	5696	2265	39.8

Source: Nairobi City Valuer's Department

Box 13.5   TOLs in the Government Lands Act

Part VI – Licences for temporary occupation of land (S40–41).

(1)   Licences to occupy unalienated government land for temporary purposes may be granted by the Commissioner.

(2)   Unless it is expressly provided otherwise, a licence under this section shall continue for one year and thenceforward until the expiration of any three months' notice to quit, provided that the notice to quit may be served upon the licensee at any time after the expiration of nine months from the date of the licence.

(3)   The rent payable under a licence under this section, the period and the agreements and conditions of the licence shall be such as may be prescribed by rules under this Act or as may be determined by the Commissioner.

(4)   The benefit of a licence under this section may, with the consent of the Commissioner, be transferred by the licensee, and the transfer and the consent thereto shall be endorsed on the licence.

(5)   The occupant of any Government land under a licence under section 40 may remove any hut or other building erected by him during his occupation of the land at any time before the licence expires.

Development of TOL plots

Since licences are given on a yearly basis, holders need to develop their plots as soon as possible in order to ensure renewal. In a survey of 17 TOL plots undertaken in Nairobi's low-income neighbourhoods the following trends were discovered:

- Plots are just big enough for a small business and maybe a room or two to sleep in. The majority of plots (77 per cent) were between 250 m^2 and 500 m^2 and the rest below 250 m^2.
- The monthly rent collected by the council, for most tenants, is 1200 Kenyan shillings (Ksh) (US$15) per month. A few people pay less. This rent level is equivalent to a third of the average monthly income in unplanned settlements, and therefore quite affordable.
- All the licensees have developed their plots. While production sheds, workshops and kiosks are common (see Box 13.6), houses that can accommodate a number of domestic and business activities are also found.
- Electricity and water are widely available (connection rates stand at 88 and 65 per cent respectively), but sanitation is more problematic. Only one of the 17 properties was connected to a sewer; the rest depended on pit latrines or no such facility at all. Electricity facilitates business and enhances the home environment.
- TOLs make an important contribution to generating employment in poor neighbourhoods. Of the plots surveyed, 53 per cent had six persons or more working on the premises.

Box 13.6   Sweetened baobab seeds

Mama Abdul used to be a teacher. She gave up her job and put all her savings into a kiosk selling general provisions, soft drinks and snacks specifically packaged for schoolchildren. Her kiosk is on Nairobi City Council land across the road from a large primary school. She obtained a TOL for the land (about 200 m^2). Her teenage daughter helps her sell a variety of snacks and confectionery items, such as baobab seeds soaked in syrup, cassava crisps, fruit-flavoured ice cubes and tamarind juice (Figure 13.5).

After deducting costs, Mama Abdul makes enough money to cover her household expenses. But she and her daughter have to work long hours preparing each day's supplies.

Two years ago Mama Abdul won an award from a soft drinks multinational for operating a model kiosk. Her achievements as a businesswoman were aired on television throughout Africa, and she was given a TV set as a prize. So she built a concrete deck around her kiosk so that her teenage customers can watch football matches and other sports programmes.

Figure 13.5 The TOL is ideal for kiosks and other small businesses. Credit: Saad Yahya and Associates

- A majority (88 per cent) of the licensees planned to make additional improvements to their properties, e.g. building more rooms or additional sheds.
- Initial development and subsequent improvements are self-financed, with very little dependence on formal credit; only 18 per cent of the respondents reported having resorted to credit.

The value of planned improvements ranged from Ksh5000 to Ksh100 000 (US$ 63–1250). Such investments enhance security, although all the respondents reported that they felt secure anyway:

No eviction threats have been issued by the city council against us. From time to time the local administration (i.e. central government officials) disturb us but since we have a TOL they cannot evict us (a group of self-employed women operating a garage).

Before getting the TOL my building was demolished twice. Now even the City Council 'askaris' (police) cannot touch me (a businessman who spent Ksh20 000 (US$250) to build a general provision kiosk with a residential wing).

Initially the council allocated me a site on Langata Road, but I was relocated to the present site when construction work on widening the road started. I was given a month's notice, which shows some concern on the council's part and that they are willing to respect the TOL (a garage owner who had built a temporary structure of timber and corrugated iron with water and electricity connections).

The results of the field survey are summarized in Table 13.3. Although the TOL is supposed to be a special interim arrangement, the very fact that hundreds of licences are issued annually in Nairobi, let alone the other towns, is testimony to its importance in the national distribution of land development opportunities.

Table 13.3   Analysis of TOL survey in Nairobi

Particulars	Attributes	No.	%
Plot size	250 m²–500 m²	13	76
	Less than 250 m²	4	24
Permitted use	Garage	7	41
	Kiosk	1	6
	Small-scale industries	4	24
	Other	5	29
Rent	Over Ksh1200 per month	0	0
	Ksh1200 per month	11	65
	Ksh1000 per month	6	35
Improvements (existing)	Kiosk	1	6
	Workshop	8	46
	House	3	18
	Fence (only)	2	12
	Other	3	18
Services	Electricity	15	88
	Water	11	65
	Sewer	1	6
	Pit latrine	8	47
	No latrine	2	12
No. of persons employed	Over 20	1	6
	15–20	2	12
	11–15	1	6
	6–10	5	29
	1–5	5	29
	None	3	18
Planned improvements	Sheds	4	23
	More rooms	2	12
	Secure fence	3	18
	Permanent structures	1	6
	Other	5	29
	None	2	12
Use of credit	Yes	3	18
	No	14	82

Shares in land-buying companies

At the time of independence, the government was under great pressure to settle the millions of landless Kenyans. Settlement schemes only nibbled at the problem of landlessness and although by mid-1978 a total of 5 million hectares had been bought to settle the landless through the schemes, the number of landless people was soaring (Kiarie, 1990). The government therefore encouraged people and institutions to pool their resources to purchase land. These institutions took the form of land-buying companies and co-operatives (LBCs and co-ops). The co-operatives were registered under the Co-operatives Act and the LBCs under the Companies Act, although their operations were similar.

Notwithstanding their names, these companies and co-operatives are a mode of gaining access to land, not a form of communal or co-operative ownership. There are now many LBCs, although they are plagued with lots of managerial and financial problems and have often fallen into disfavour with the government because of abuse by politicians.

LBCs began to emerge in 1964 and were organized in such a way that their aim was to acquire the land and then subdivide it to members according to the number of shares each held. However, as Kiarie (1990) found in her study, some of these companies had other objectives, including: to uplift the living standards of members through investments and activities such as coffee farming, purchase of residential and commercial properties, and marketing company produce collectively.

The study, which focused on rural LBCs, also revealed that many members were ignorant about the objectives. All they were keen on was to own land. Membership in LBCs is acquired in various ways, such as by subscribing to the memorandum and joining the company immediately upon its incorporation, or by allotment. This occurs when a member acquires the shares from an existing member by way of sale or gift. The other way is by transmission, i.e. an involuntary transfer as a result of death or bankruptcy.

In certain instances, individuals buy land on their own by negotiating with the owner and later join forces to form a company for the purpose of protecting their interests, thereby relying on 'strength in numbers' (Gitau, 1998). This becomes an advantage when land or housing is developing informally, or when pooling of resources is necessary in order to acquire services and infrastructure. The block title deed may be used as collateral in banks to acquire loans. The first documented references to urban LBCs are to be found in David Etherton's landmark study of Mathare Valley (Etherton, 1971). He found 22 companies controlling 7628 rooms. Of the 33 563 people who lived in company housing, only 7 per cent were members, the rest were dependants or tenants.

LBCs often play a significant role in the initial stages of settlement. They identify land to be bought, negotiate the price, and scrutinize accessibility and other characteristics. The land bought is often at the periphery of urban areas and is relatively cheap because it has no services. Most of the land is subdivided illegally due to the prohibitive planning standards, although NCC has created mechanisms for fast approvals and affordable standards, as will be discussed later. In practice, the members own the land they settle on, but the subdivisions and developments may be illegal because they are outside the formal zoning plan. The members are therefore interested in the practicalities of the tenure and not in the details of the law. Box 13.7 lists some of the reasons why LBCs are so popular.

Box 13.7   Ten reasons why land-buying companies are popular

- It is simple and inexpensive to form and register a limited liability company. It can cost as little as Ksh10 000 (about US$125).
- A company can be an effective rallying point for mobilizing and organizing people with a common development goal; members can decide to sell shares only to like-minded persons.
- Company legislation encourages democratic governance with annual general meetings, election of officers and audited accounts.
- All members own company assets: surplus land and other assets can be sold and the proceeds invested in services and other improvements, or allocated to members in the form of bonus shares.
- Government supervision and interference are minimal, while assistance from government can be sought.
- Members can borrow in the market either collectively or individually.
- Through the company, members can establish their own rules and standards for guiding and executing development.
- Members can develop at their own pace, sell and otherwise deal in their property as they wish, subject to company rules and national legislative restrictions, e.g. planning restrictions.
- The share certificate provides adequate security for most purposes
- The share certificate can be upgraded into full title once certain requirements have been fulfilled.

The number of shares held determines the plot size one gets once the land is bought. Some companies are dissolved or become dormant soon after purchase, leaving the members to develop their plots individually. Many companies were known to buy land and hold it for several years before subdividing it to the shareholders. In other instances, companies subdivide the land and distribute it to members without issuance of title deeds. Where the plots are formally distributed, the shareholders are allowed to deal with them as they deem fit. In instances where titles are still held by the company, the shareholders use the land as 'tenants at will' and may be ordered to quit as directed by the company if they have not completed paying the purchase price.

Depending on the materials and building methods used, a three-room house can cost anything from Ksh400 000 to Ksh800 000 (US$5000–10 000)

Municipal support and encouragement can help to reduce costs by allowing traditional materials (mud and wattle, thatch, timber, coral rag, etc) and new technologies. Such approaches are allowed by the 1995 amendments to the Kenyan building code (Government of Kenya, 1995).

LBCs have been associated with various problems. Many of the problem-ridden companies have been placed under probe committees appointed by the government. Common problems include:

- leadership squabbles
- illegal recruitment of members and over-recruitment of shareholders
- political interference
- financial mismanagement
- double allocation of plots
- misappropriation of company funds
- long delays in buying and apportioning land to shareholders.

The LBCs operating in urban areas also have the problem related to land conversion and subdivision of large farm holdings. As a result, the subdivisions are often illegal and do not conform to the established regulations, acting as a hindrance to the provision of secure tenure. Where the land is illegally subdivided and allocated, the shareholders may not get title deeds and cannot therefore use their land as collateral for bank loans.

Political interference is also a common problem. This comes in various forms, such as the requirement of permits for members to hold their meetings as stipulated in the security laws, enabling the state to keep the companies under surveillance. Politicians also use the members to gain political support and votes from the shareholders in return for political protection. It is probably inevitable that the cut-and-thrust of Kenyan political life should feature in LBC operations, since some companies are huge (witness the mammoth 20 000-plot Embakasi Ranching Company described in Box 13.8) and command a lot of power apart from influencing the destiny of thousands of families. In spite of all these problems and difficulties, LBCs are a popular vehicle for land acquisition in highland towns.

Companies in certain locations in Nairobi have benefited from the alternative development control approaches adopted by the city. A presidential decree directed and mandated the NCC to provide technical advice and approve the subdivision proposals submitted by LBCs scattered in Nairobi's outskirts. Through this enabling environment, by 1993 over 30 000 plots were regularized in less than 15 months, whereas this would have taken over five years using the standard approval methods. These zones are in the eastern outer suburbs of Nairobi, mainly on semi-arid savannah lands, which were European-owned sisal farms in pre-independence days. The subdivisions listed in Table 13.4 are in these zones. For example, in 1991 a total of 8910 plots were created this way in that part of the city, with a potential for housing nearly 100 000 people. The ownership of each plot was evidenced by a share certificate issued by the company.

Box 13.8 Embakasi Ranching Company

This is one of the largest companies operating in Nairobi, and anything but a ranch. Owing to its size (20 000 plots) it has been in the process of recruiting members, selling shares and allocating plots for well over a decade, depending exclusively on its own administrative machinery and professional consultants. Here is the experience of three members, Joyce, Kiseli and Samson.

Joyce used her savings from a secretarial job, together with help from her father, to purchase two Embakasi shares in 1995 for Ksh120 000 (US$1500). She bought the shares in the resale market. She was then given two additional bonus shares, so she now has four quarter-acre plots, amounting to an acre. The plots have water supply, road access and electricity, and although her neighbours are building (mainly houses in stone and iron sheets, with some shops along the main road), she prefers to wait. Property values are rising fast. By early 2001, each quarter acre plot would fetch Ksh100 000 (US$1250) in the market. This trend is likely to continue since the area is adequately served by public transport, schools and private clinics. Crime is a problem, but it is no worse than in other similar neighbourhoods. In fact, the security situation is relatively good. The one thing that worries her is that the subdivision is next to a sewage farm, and to make matters worse the NCC plans to establish a new refuse disposal site also adjacent to the neighbourhood. However, there is a lot of resistance from the residents.

The company management co-ordinates the provision of infrastructure. There is an office on-site where the directors meet twice a week: to allocate plots and discuss problems with members. One long-standing problem is surveying of plots: although there is an in-house surveyor, one can wait several weeks to be shown one's plot, and a fee (up to Ksh30 000, i.e. US$400) has to be paid for the service. Nobody knows these problems better than Kiseli.

Kiseli and his friend Samson work as 'beacon men'; their job is to assist the surveyor place the concrete corner markers on the plots. They make the beacons and sell them to allottees. That way they make enough to live on. In fact, Kiseli is developing his plot, which he inherited from his late grandmother. He is building only a single room in corrugated iron sheets, which he will occupy with his wife and three children. He will spend Ksh90 000 (US$1125) on the construction. He can now sell his plot for Ksh200 000 (US$2500) if he wants, since it is well situated, but new plots (30 m × 30 m) in remote locations are being allocated for Ksh60 000 (US$750) each. He plans to have an electricity connection on his plot as well as water from the company borehole, for which the charges are Ksh200 (US$2.50) per month. The access to his plot is now rather poor.

Other workplaces on the estate include shops, garages and small workshops.

One of the innovative development approaches adopted by the NCC is blanket approvals. This process involves relaxing subdivision standards. It includes permitting plot accesses at a minimum width of 6 m and not insisting on provision of all infrastructural services and facilities to the council's adoptive standards. The blanket approval procedure unconditionally

Table 13.4 NCC subdivision approvals for land-buying companies (November 1990–June 1994)

Owners*	LR	Location	Area (ha)	No. of subplots	Date approved
Grogan Mabati Group Co. Ltd	336/28	Off Outer-ring Road Ruaraka	4.11	137	16/11/90
	6845/11	Embakasi	17.84	76	16/11/90
Ruaraka Properties Co. Ltd	336/32	Ruraraka Road Ruaraka	4.40	92	16/11/90
	4345/6	Kamiti Road	7893.00	1507	16/11/90
Ruaraka Development Co. Ltd	336/31	Ruaraka Road Baba Dogo	4.67	151	16/12/90
	6821	Kangundo Road Njiru	18.29	327	6/12/90
	10904/R 10904/2 10903, 7209,5874, 45–48	Komarock Road (Embakasi)	5600.00	20 000	6/12/90
	8469/7&8	Kangundo Road Kasarani	52.69	1403	15/3/91
	336/27	Off Baba Dogo Road (Ruaraka)	4.65	190	17/5/91
	6845/126	Komarock Road (Njiru Estate)	6.82	206	14/6/91
	6823	Koma Rock Road (Njiru Estate)	13.64	420	14/6/91
	8469/110	Off Thika Road (Kasarani)	28.28	790	14/6/91
	8469/11	Off Thika Road (Kasarani)	28.28	790	14/6/91
Mutirithia Wa Andu Co. Ltd	7659/6	Off Kasarani Road Njiru	8.50	341	13/9/91
	8469/5&6	Kasarani Road (Njiru)	42.75	757	13/9/91
	8479	Kasarani/Njiru	74.46	2081	13/9/91
	8569/5&6 (14847 New)	Off Kamiti Road Kasarani	70.04	1932	15/11/91
	8480/1	Kasarani Road (Njiru)	1547.25	2030	15/5/92
Ngundu Farmers Coop Society	11593	Off Komarock Road (Dandora)	1528.40	760	15/5/92
Mwihike Farmers Co. Ltd	8469/ 13,12,14	Kasarani Road (Njiru)	43.12	958	15/5/92
	82/733	Embakasi	5.59	252	16/6/94

*Where no name is indicated an individual lodged the application.

relieves the LBCs and co-operatives of their responsibility to build comprehensive services networks. However, the individual plot owner is required to have connected the plot with water prior to submitting building plans. The Commissioner of Lands also has to give final approval on these subdivisions before provision of the infrastructure, which makes it possible to acquire titles sooner, thus raising the credibility and value of the share certificate.

The blanket approvals have proved successful and provided an ideal policy implementation approach and appropriate tools to deal with securing land for poor people. The policy guidelines were laid down bearing in mind that high-density development without supportive high-standard infrastructure will be unstoppable and urban land supply in virgin areas will continue to be dominated by LBCs and co-operative societies and their informal operating systems.

In his submission to the city's Town Planning Committee, the director of city planning and architecture presented a long and well-argued policy paper requesting the adoption of the blanket approval procedure on the grounds that 'It is apparent . . . that urban land development planning has not been able to shape developments resulting from land conversion and subdivisions organized by LBCs and co-operative societies due to the fact that planning is armed with inappropriate tools and policy implementation approaches '(NCC Town Planning Committee minutes of 18 July 1997). What he meant was that planning as practised at City Hall was not supporting popular efforts to create new land tenure solutions.

Another Kenyan town where LBCs are active is Nakuru. By co-operating with the municipal authorities and caring NGOs such as Intermediate Technology Development Group, World Wildlife Fund and the Architectural Association of Kenya, the municipal council helps members enhance their tenure security and the value of their properties in a variety of ways, such as:

- zoning company-settled areas as special areas for the purpose of applying a simplified building code
- managing fast building permit approvals for company members
- training company members and artisans in the use of inexpensive building technologies and materials
- organizing design clinics where members get advice on house extensions, conversions, plot subdivision, sanitation and building a shop or workshop on the plot
- organizing neighbourhood groups for improving drainage, refuse collection, disposal and recycling.

In fact, one could view LBC operations as a form of decentralization in that the companies take on many of the functions and responsibilities that would otherwise be borne by the local government.

Outcomes

To conclude, one must ask the question, how novel are share certificates and occupation licences as ideas and methods? They are actually old instruments amenable to new applications. They can respond to new demands by making land available to the poor on terms they can comfortably meet.

Although LBC subdivisions are planned to form self-contained neighbourhoods with all the essential community facilities, they nonetheless tend to be far from workplaces. TOLs on the other hand, being business- and service-oriented are often in strategic locations, e.g. on a business thoroughfare or between factories in the industrial area. However, they both offer a suitable environment for living and working, the two basic requirements of a poor family. Sympathetic attitudes among planners and other municipal officials, encourage savings through the use of standardized type plans and other devices (Yahya et al., 2001). We have seen, for instance, how Nairobi has installed special approval procedures for LBCs, which is one of the many steps on the road to land ownership using this route.

The upgrading potential of share certificates and TOLs (as sitting tenant the owner will always have first claim on any new titles being issued) makes them attractive to speculators. It also puts them on the fringes of the credit market, in that whereas a bank loan would be out of reach, an advance from a credit union (called SACCOs in Kenya, i.e. savings and credit co-operative, of which there is one in every sizeable government ministry or institution) is possible. There are also several government-sponsored micro-credit institutions willing to lend to enterprising businessmen and investors. But the amounts are small and interest rates high.

MEETING THE CHALLENGE

In the course of preparing the policy context and case studies, a wide range of property rights was observed, from freehold through share certificates to adverse possession. We can categorize available interests into four regimes.

- Customary entitlements, predating colonial transformations, which clearly distinguish between collective and individual rights. One could include here religious entitlements such as wakf endowments for mosques, schools, orphans and destitute families.
- Statutory rights conferred by acts of parliament and subsidiary legislation, that is freeholds and leaseholds in their various forms.
- Adaptations of statutory tenures such as letters of allotment and share certificates. These creative modifications enable legal instruments to be used in unforeseen and unorthodox ways.
- Incipient rights, i.e. property rights in formation, largely the result of governmental and court response to popular pressures.

It is possible for entitlements to move between categories in the course of time. For example, absolute statutory title (freehold) can be downgraded into a modified or adapted freehold through:

- transfer restrictions
- development restrictions
- servicing limits
- transaction costs
- zoning
- encumbrances
- threat of expropriation or forced sale
- planting squatters on the land.

Intermediate status can be arrived at either from above or below. Downgrading, curtailment and deliberate postponement are all ways of arriving at intermediate title. The share certificate is a good example of postponement. It is an interim document, which is marketable and can be used to raise capital from some lenders. New thinking is thus emerging and unconventional practices developing without being seen as innovations because they are home-grown, almost spontaneous and not deliberately designed by academics and consultants. The three innovations analysed in this paper have had a variety of impacts on the Kenyan urban scene. Table 13.5 summarizes the main characteristics of the three tenure types.

SUMMARY OF CASE STUDY FINDINGS AND CONCLUSIONS

The case studies have demonstrated the importance of history, culture and politics in shaping urban land tenure. Written laws are selective in their application, since to gain access to the statutory domain one has to know the right people. A symbiotic relationship exists between landowners, house owners, tenants and authorized squatters. This arrangement makes the work of municipal administrators easier. The case studies have also shown that the process of illegal settlement can be restrained by using approaches such as the ones examined above.

While Kenyans are waiting with bated breath for the outcome of the Land Law Review Commission and Constitutional Review Commission, the courts are continuing to adjudicate land cases and establish precedents, which sow the seeds of new land rights. Injunctions and restraint orders have saved thousands of squatters from eviction; so has the moratorium on demolitions and evictions announced by the government and NCC.

So what conditions offer a favourable climate for tenure innovations to emerge and prosper? What makes some innovations more popular and durable than others? What are the catalytic forces that trigger experimentation and adaptation of existing practices? On the basis of evidence available from the Kenyan experience one could probably hazard the following rules.

- History and culture can provide useful frameworks. Urban land administration can therefore borrow a lot from traditional agrarian communal values, in Africa at least.
- Social tension engendered by population growth, urbanization, polit-

ical changes and similar upheavals encourages the development of novel approaches to tenure. The propensity to innovate is greater when there is a catalyst or urgency that must be met.

- For a new approach to work, it must offer the prospects of tangible financial or other benefits to the participants. Capital appreciation of the property, rental income or the ability to run a business far outweighs any inconveniences caused by title restrictions.
- A clear and stable land law regime is therefore crucial, since it helps to strengthen the feeling of security. That security is enhanced by documentary evidence such as a licence or share certificate. The real estate submarket in which the poor operate is remarkably resilient to economic and political shocks. People invest in spite of swings in inflation, interest rates and similar indicators. This feature makes it easier to experiment and innovate.
- It is important to have in place a broad strategic and structure planning framework, managed, as is the case in Kenya, by the municipal authorities. This ensures access to bulk infrastructure and control of settlement expansion. Imaginative and concerned professionals are in a position to provide legitimacy and technical respectability to new tenure arrangements. They can provide the training, orientation, presentations to the authorities and international agencies, and operation manuals.
- Friendly sponsors help to strengthen the case and deepen the pool of resources. Donor agencies, private sector backers and committed NGOs all contribute towards success provided the basic concept is right and the local people retain ownership.
- The local authority has to be sympathetic and supportive by relaxing or modifying building and planning regulations, streamlining procedures, offering technical assistance, or just monitoring and co-ordinating the work of the private sector.
- Leadership does not always have to be 'efficient' in the strictly technical sense. More important is the ability to mobilize efforts and resources and to articulate the goals and wishes of their constituency. LBCs have worked reasonably well in spite of the leadership struggles and management lapses.

Finally, the availability of public land can help, but that is only one element since where the land is already densely populated, distribution to residents can be problematic. As the stocks of public land are rapidly diminishing, ensuring adequate living space for the poor will in future depend increasingly on our ability to design new ways of owning and sharing private property.

Table 13.5 Comparative analysis of innovative tenures

	Community Land Trust	Land-buying company	Temporary Occupation Licence
Description: what is new?	Land is owned by whole group and improvements by individual members; modification of traditional systems annual renewals	Company or co-operative society acquires large farm for subdivision to members; uses commercial vehicle	Revival of old instrument; enables allocation of public land for a short period and specific purpose
to meet social needs			
Location: – case study – other	Case study in Voi Other cases being implemented elsewhere	Case study focuses on Nairobi Vehicles widely spread in Kenya highlands region	Roadside and corner plots are popular Widespread practice in municipalities
Scale	Started in early 1990s; movement growing steadily	Several million urban residents settled in this way	About 600 plots allocated in Nairobi annually, probably twice as many nationally
Main participants	Slum dwellers, but new settlements on virgin land also possible	Poor people and lower middle class Newly urbanized people Trade union members, e.g. teachers, civil servants, etc.	Small businesses, NGOs and other operators in residential areas
Policy framework	Active promotion by Ministry of Local Government	Strict monitoring and reluctant facilitation by government; viewed as troublemakers	Strict scrutiny of applications to discourage permanent development
Legal context	Societies Act Trustees Act Registered Land Act	Companies Act Land legislation Planning and building legislation	Government Lands Act Local Government Act
Type of survey	Formal survey with markers preferable but not essential	Members prefer precise survey with beacons (markers) to avoid confusion	No survey needed, but only sketch plan of proposed development

Perceived security: – owners – tenants	Owners feel secure because of lease document plus association membership Tenants are also represented in association	Share certificate perceived as guarantee of security and passport to title Tenants have little protection	Owners feel they are protected by the city/municipal council Subletting not common
Effectiveness	Investment through self-build or construction contract Shared profits on resale Recognises rights of the poor and encourages participation Access to formal credit rather limited Women active in association	Members start building soon after allocation Value appreciation as settlement consolidates Enables poor people to pool strengths and resources Some banks recognize certificate Women can join in their own right	Although 'temporary', investment can be substantial and can include living accommodation Transfers possible with permission Enables traders and craftsmen to invest in business Rapid capital appreciation Simple and inexpensive allocation procedures
Ineffectiveness	Rather new and not widely known	Directors' powers open to abuse Excessive control by politicians Few women in leadership position	Over time temporary becomes durable
Constraints	Potential of creating ethnic or elitist enclaves Large amounts of documentation	Need for efficiency and transparency as required by company legislation	Limited amounts of available public land
Partnerships	Local authority assists in a variety of ways NGOs and private sector contribute expertise and resources	Easy to collaborate with other private sector operators	Small businesses can access micro-credits in the NGO and informal credit systems
Future potential	Can spread countrywide if procedures are streamlined and simplified	Good prospects of further growth	Not likely to see appreciable increase, being a special arrangement, but will continue to be a useful instrument

Source: Author

CHAPTER FOURTEEN

Going against the grain: alternatives to individual ownership in South Africa

Lauren Royston and Cecile Ambert

INTRODUCTION

Historically, alternatives to ownership, including leasehold, deeds of grant and permits to occupy, have been in operation in South Africa. However, these rights existed in a context of discrimination as black South Africans were prohibited from owning property until 1986, when full individual ownership was introduced for the first time. As a result, individual ownership rights are now viewed by many as a matter of political redress. Although principle and policy promote secure tenure and a range of tenure alternatives,[1] individual ownership currently dominates in housing implementation. Since 1994 most new housing delivery and settlement upgrading projects under the subsidy scheme have resulted in individual ownership rights being granted. The financial and legal vehicles for alternatives that do exist have had a limited impact on this trend. The most innovative alternative currently being implemented in an urban context is group ownership of co-operative housing, although its replicability and scale are limited.

This chapter explores what formal alternatives to individual ownership currently exist in South Africa. To put the tenure issue in context, it begins by arguing that the capital subsidy scheme is the single means by which security of tenure is attained in South Africa's current housing framework. It identifies that only one subsidy instrument – the institutional subsidy – caters for options other than individual ownership. Next, an examination of several legal vehicles for alternatives reveals that implementation success has been mixed. Having established that the only real scope for formal alternatives is under the social housing umbrella, funded by the institutional subsidy, the chapter then proceeds to analyse two institutional subsidy case studies from a tenure perspective. Both case studies are collective housing examples. They represent alternatives to the conventional approaches to providing secure, legal tenure. In the South African context, this amounts to an alternative to the formal, developer-driven housing delivery, overwhelmingly dominated by individual ownership. The selected cases are also alternatives to the process of illegal settlement and neither is an example of illegal self-built housing. One is new construction on a greenfield site and the other is a conversion of existing rental units.

HOW PEOPLE ACHIEVE SECURE TENURE IN SOUTH AFRICA'S CURRENT HOUSING FRAMEWORK

The granting of tenure security is a by-product of implementing the supply-driven housing framework through the capital subsidy scheme. Introduced with the housing policy in 1994 (Republic of South Africa, 1994), the subsidy programme is the single instrument for tenure upgrading in South Africa's current housing framework. It provides six funding options to eligible people in the income bracket of US$450 (i.e. ZAR3500)[2] per month and below, only one of which promotes alternatives to individual ownership. Project-linked subsidies are made available to provincially approved housing projects and provide for individual ownership. These subsidies enable home ownership for first time buyers. Since the scheme was introduced, 95 per cent of approved subsidies fall into the project-linked category (CSIR, 1999).

The Discount Benefit Scheme, a second subsidy option, allows long-term tenants of public rental stock to receive a discount on the historic cost of a property. In most cases, the houses are transferred to individual ownership, although an alternative form of tenure known as family title is also being granted (addressed in greater detail below). The individual subsidy gives individuals access to a housing subsidy to acquire ownership of, or upgrade, an existing property, or to purchase or build a new property. Consolidation subsidies are available to individuals who have received housing assistance under the previous government in the form of a serviced site. The Hostel Upgrading Programme provides assistance for the upgrading of publicly owned hostels.

Institutional subsidies are made available to housing institutions developing affordable housing stock and provide for alternative forms of tenure, including lease, instalment sale, rent-to-own, a form of condominium title and group ownership (Social Housing Foundation, 1998). The regulations provide that tenure rights granted through the institutional subsidy may not be converted until four years have elapsed. Just under 1 per cent of the subsidies allocated fall into this category (CSIR, 1999). Although it represents a limited share of the total subsidies allocated to date, the popularity of the institutional subsidy appears to be increasing. A factor in its favour is that it enables the allocation of the highest subsidy amount – US$2130 – to the institution instead of the graduated subsidy levels linked to household income. Evidence exists in some projects that the subsidies have also been made available up-front, rather than in the phased manner applicable in the main subsidy route. Finally, institutional subsidy projects have been successful in leveraging additional finances, including access to credit.

ARE THERE OPTIONS OTHER THAN INDIVIDUAL OWNERSHIP?

Although individual ownership dominates in implementation, legal and financial options for alternative tenure do exist. As the previous section demonstrated, the only financial vehicle for options other than individual ownership is the institutional subsidy. Several legal instruments have also been developed, although their implementation record is varied. The proposed Land Rights Bill, for example, intended to provide blanket protection and non-statutory, non-registered secure tenure to people living on land in former homeland and trust land areas, which is mainly registered as state land (Development Works, 1999). It intended to protect rights' holders against deprivation, give them decision-making power in respect of the land and the right to benefits accruing from the land. The Bill was, however, temporarily shelved in the course of 2000 following a change in political leadership at the Department of Land Affairs and apparent concern about the impact of the proposals on traditional leaders. Second, the Communal Property Associations (CPA) Act of 1996, which recognizes communal ownership, was drafted with the intention of enabling groups benefiting from the national land reform programme to hold, manage and possess land rights communally. CPAs have been implemented mainly in rural communities, although urban examples exist, such as the Victoria Mxenge settlement in Cape Town, developed by the Homeless People's Federation.

'Family title' is a third alternative to individual ownership. The need to register family, as opposed to individual, rights arose in the Gauteng Province from conflict emerging in families, especially in Soweto, during the process of identifying rights' holders in public rental accommodation. The transfer to occupants of houses held under leasehold arrangements commenced in 1993, with the introduction of the Discount Benefit Scheme, which enabled tenants to purchase rented units at historic cost, less a discount of US$1000 (Development Works, 1999). Since the transfer process began, competition – sometimes violent – between siblings and grandchildren over recognition as the individual rights' holder has emerged. Many township areas in which the transfer of houses is occurring are characterized by overcrowding, because of historical restrictions on the urbanization of black South Africans and the under-supply of housing, leading to a critical backlog. In the past, subletting or sharing household members were able to add their names to the record of leasehold rights. Since the inception of the transfer process, individual ownership has become a source of exclusion and conflict among people who were previously co-beneficiaries. Civic organizations and the provincial government became aware of the need to develop a legal response to this situation of conflict. The feasibility of holding rights as a trust or a company was debatable as the recurring administrative and financial requirements of the rights are high. Instead of introducing new titling mechanisms, regulations were developed to record family members as the rights' holders on a contractual basis. The regulatory provisions of the 'Family Title' mean that even if the rights are those of ownership, they are held by a family or jointly by spouses. This procedure may limit resale, but beneficiaries of the discount benefit scheme were willing to restrict their rights to dispose of the property in order to ensure continued family access to the tenure right.

Fourth, initial ownership, provided for in the Development Facilitation Act of 1995 (Republic of South Africa, 1995), was introduced to expedite the registration aspects of township establishment and speed up housing delivery (Development Works, 1999). The Act introduced a process of phased access to ownership rights in the course of township establishment. Preliminary planning, surveying and registration can take place prior to services being installed. The initial ownership rights comprise the right to occupy and use land, acquire full ownership of the land, encumber the right by means of a mortgage or personal servitude and sell the right. No land development applications using this section of the Act had been made at the time of writing. Problems with the land development procedures introduced by the Development Facilitation Act are partly responsible, as well as certain factors relating to initial ownership itself. Procedural problems are linked to the onerous up-front planning application requirements, the costs of which developers are required to bear on risk. In addition, it is perceived that incremental tenure raises the costs of regularization, amounting to a duplication of planning, surveying and registration procedures. Finally, provincial subsidy regulations generally specify that the final tranches of subsidy funds will be released only once registration of individual ownership rights has taken place, thereby making the initial ownership process unattractive to housing developers, who remain by and large the primary implementing agents of the housing subsidy.[3]

Various forms of alternative tenure exist under the social housing umbrella. Social housing is not new in South Africa, although the institutional subsidy, which facilitates its development, is an initiative of the democratic government. Long-standing social housing examples in South Africa include public rental housing, communal land holdings in rural and peri-urban communities, and informal rental (Social Housing Foundation, 1998). The experience of tenant-initiated buy-outs in the Johannesburg inner city in the early 1990s pioneered the development of the institutional subsidy to promote an institutional housing subsector (see Box 14. 1). Social housing institutions take a number of legal forms including not-for-profit organizations known as Section 21 companies, share block companies, public or private companies with shareholding and co-operatives (Social Housing Foundation, 1998). Tenure takes the form of lease, instalment sale, rent-to-buy, a form of condominium title and group ownership (Rust, 2000). These institutional forms were adopted and applied to the housing sector, as a legal framework specific to social housing does not exist in South Africa. Co-operatives are perceived as advantageous over other social housing institutions because they combine several characteristics. They are tax exempt, meaning, for example, that interest accrued on monthly charges is not taxable. In co-operatives, profit can be accrued by members, implying that a financial return can be obtained on the investment in housing. Membership is linked to residence, so resident participation in management is high.

Box 14.1   Pioneering the collective ownership model – the Seven Buildings Project

The Seven Buildings Project is located in the Johannesburg inner city. The project is composed of seven separate buildings, which are home to 2000 tenants in 446 flats. Increasing rentals led to severe overcrowding as people began to sublet their units in order to afford the high rental costs. Negotiations between the organized tenants and the owner were held and resulted in an agreement allowing tenants to pay subeconomic rents while investigating the possibility of raising funds to purchase the buildings. This resulted in the formation of the Seven Buildings Working Group, co-ordinated by a legal NGO. In March 1993, agreements to buy the buildings were signed. The unwillingness of the financial institutions to provide bonds in red-lined areas was bypassed by mobilizing the institutional housing subsidy and accessing a loan from the Inner City Housing Upgrade Trust (ICHUT). The tenants engaged with the Housing Department to secure subsidies to be allocated collectively to the Seven Buildings Company instead of being allocated individually to the occupants of the buildings.

The size of the project (2000 tenants) led to severe management difficulties and conflict over increases in monthly charges, as well as numerous crises of leadership. From 1998 onwards, payment boycotts were experienced, which led to liquidation of the company beginning in 2001. Despite these later difficulties, the project paved the way for collective ownership in urban South Africa.

Although co-operatives have a long history and an established record in several industrialized countries with stable housing, lending and economic environments, co-operative housing models are a recent phenomenon and an important alternative to conventional housing delivery in South Africa. Pioneered in the Johannesburg area by Cope Housing Association,[4] the co-operative route is also being applied and developed in other parts of the country. Co-operative housing has been spearheaded by the collective action of groups of tenants seeking to address unsatisfactory housing and the activities of a well-developed network of local and international NGOs. Actors in the social housing movement have long identified the absence of an enabling legal framework as restricting the development of housing co-operatives (Rust, 2000). Until recent negotiations with government made it possible to register housing co-operatives, most registered co-operatives were agricultural initiatives. Cope was able to register the Newtown Housing Co-operative as a result (see Box 14.2 for facts a glance about the Newtown Co-operative). Before this, 'co-operative-like' housing institutions were established with the legal status of not-for-profit companies or closed corporations. The Everest Court not-for-profit Section 21 company is an example. Everest Court is presently being registered as housing co-operative (see Box 14.3 for facts about Everest Court).

Box 14.2 Newtown: from vacant public land to membership-based co-operative

This is a vacant land development project. The population is young (most residents are 25 to 35 years old) and there is a majority of female-headed households. Monthly household income is a minimum of US$270 (to cover equity payment and monthly charges).

The site is owned by the Gauteng Province and is well located with good access to socioeconomic opportunities. A private sector housing developer – Grinaker Housing – was awarded rights to develop social housing on the Newtown site in 1997. Cope, promoting co-operative housing, initiated a partnership agreement with the developer. The remainder of the site was developed in partnership with Johannesburg Housing Company for rental.

The project received an institutional subsidy and external resources are mobilized by the housing developer and Cope from the Homeloan Guarantee Company and the Social Housing Independent Development Fund.

Institutional subsidy recipients are calculated at approximately 350. Equity payment of approximately US$340 is required. Total development costs were US$2.4 million. Construction and recruitment of beneficiaries began in 1999 with three-storey 'walk-ups' located in an enclosed compound. Average construction costs were US$5850 per unit.

Cope holds information sessions to inform prospective members about rights, obligations, and financial and institutional arrangements. Registration of housing co-operative happens in parallel. Cope and registered co-operatives enter into legal agreement for the performance of administrative and management functions. Resident satisfaction with quality is high.

Box 14.3 Everest Court: from evictions to tenant management

This is a refurbishment project consisting of a four-storey building in Hillbrow, Johannesburg inner city. The scheme was erected in 1952 and consists of 35 apartments – most one-room flats plus three residential rooms at the roof level. Most residents have been there over 10 years and earn between US$110 and US$240 per month. Ten out of 38 households are female headed. Residents launched a rent boycott in 1989 in protest against lack of building maintenance, safety and security problems, and rent increases. Tenants began depositing US$30 per household into a trust account and the landlord applied for a court order to evict, later attempting to sell. The tenants resisted eviction and negotiations began when tenants resisted the sale of the building to outsiders. A sale agreement was eventually reached and the Everest Court Investment Company was established in 1994. Tenants pay US$4700 deposit for the building towards an instalment sale, using monthly contributions into a trust account.

Members of the company appointed Cope to provide property management services and oversee refurbishment activities. A subsidy application was submitted to the Provincial Housing Board by Cope on behalf of tenants, and was approved. On Cope's advice, the private company converted to a 'not-for-profit' Section 21 company in order to link its shareholding with occupancy,

Cope initiated a second round of price negotiations with the landlord to make outright purchase of the building. An agreed purchase price of US$37 000 was paid, using part of the subsidy. Subsidy funds are also used for refurbishment, including structural works, upgrading of services and security measures. In 2000, Cope campaigned for the registration of Everest Court as a housing co-operative due to an exit repayment mechanism that enables members to benefit from monthly charges.

The company that owns Everest Court is responsible for acquiring, holding, developing and/or improving the building and the land on which it is situated. The Memorandum and Articles of Association stipulate the rights and obligations of the company's board of directors who manage the property and are responsible for the financial, legal and administrative aspects of the institution. Residence is linked to membership of the company. A use agreement sets out the rights and obligations of the company members. All members of the company have the right to occupy specified flats in the building and to participate in the management of the company by electing the board of directors. Members are not entitled to dividends on the profits made by the company, which bars them from acquiring returns from the sale of any of the company's assets. This differs from co-operative arrangements under which profits can be accrued by the members. Should the registered member pass away, his or her spouse will automatically become a member of the company, although membership cannot be transferred to a third party unilaterally. This means that the membership cannot be sold on the open market, that the purchaser has to be eligible in terms of the company's rules and regulations, and that the board oversees the sale of the membership.

In the Newtown project, the tenure form is also one of group ownership. The co-operative owns the housing stock and the members collectively own the co-operative institution. The property is registered in the name of the co-operative in the Deeds Registry. Residents in the development are all members of the co-operative. Membership is governed by rules and regulations set out in the use agreement, by which all members are bound. For example, the use agreement stipulates that membership may be transferred only at the discretion and on the authority of the board. The member may apply for permission to transfer the rights of occupancy and membership to children, parents or spouse. Under the statute that governs the co-operative, its members must also be members of the housing management co-operative, limiting the scope for an individual member to influence the selection of his or her successor. Members have exclusive use rights over the units in which they reside, although these rights may not infringe on the rights of other resident members or on the collective. For instance, although provisions are made in the statute to enable members to sublet their units, this is subject to the approval of the board, in order to avoid conditions of overcrowding that might put a strain on services. The use agreement also regulates obligations such as paying monthly charges, maintaining the collective parts of the development and good neighbourliness.

STRENGTHS AND WEAKNESSES OF THE CO-OPERATIVE HOUSING ALTERNATIVE

Security of tenure

In Everest Court, tenants have a history of arbitrary evictions and rent increases. They are in no doubt that, comparatively, they are considerably better off than they were before. Residents in both cases are confident that access cannot be terminated without due process being followed. Where it exists, dissatisfaction relates more to the housing stock than to tenure form. For example, many members in both projects reflected on the desire for larger housing units should household size increase, or should their financial situation improve.

In both cases, the use agreement stipulates criteria and procedures for the deprivation of rights. In the Newtown project, the agreement may be terminated by the member or by the co-operative, should the member breach any of its terms. Two months' written notice is required. The housing co-operative is governed by a board, which includes residents' representatives, thus enhancing the sense of security members have about decisions the board may take relating to eviction. In instances where individual and collective interests compete, the rules governing the running of the co-operative and the use agreement provide for the protection of individual rights and procedures for mediation and conflict management. This is particularly relevant in respect of deprivation procedures and of the disposal of the property owned by the co-operative. For example, a process of appeal is written into the co-operative's constitution and may come into effect when the board threatens to evict an individual. The agreement of all members is also a requirement in respect of the sale of part or the whole of the property owned by the co-operative.

In terms of the use agreement, members' inability to pay their monthly service charges, which cover the costs of maintenance, management, loan repayment and municipal service charges, may result in deprivation. Committee members in Newtown felt strongly that their rights are only nominally different from ownership and that, as such, little could threaten their tenure security, except for the monthly costs. One member in Everest Court and four in Newtown have opted to leave the project due to household financial difficulties.

Stakeholders explained that housing costs in similar housing types far exceeded those currently experienced in the co-operative. Rentals as high as US$200 per month have been reported for an inner-city bachelor flat. Residents who were previously renting privately owned apartments were often paying double the amount in rent that they are now contributing in the form of monthly charges. While many Newtown residents may have experienced lower housing costs in former black townships, they believe that higher costs are offset against lower transport contributions, due to their inner-city location. Previously, transport costs consisted of up to 20%

of household income. A one-bedroom flat in the Newtown project incurs monthly charges of approximately US$100 (depending on the exact square meterage of the unit), while the costs in a two-bedroom flat are approximately US$110 per month. In the rental project, adjacent to the Newtown Co-operative, one- and two-bedroom flats cost US$105 and US$130 respectively per month in rent.

The board members were conscious of the limitations of group ownership in respect of the collective vulnerability of the group to financial difficulties experienced by members. They expressed concern that, should individuals not abide by their payment responsibilities, then the group as a whole would suffer, as the company's cash flows would be affected. Three defaulters have been evicted from Everest Court. However, the collective ownership model is more flexible than private rental, as group management is linked to sympathy for the individual circumstances of members. For instance, in Everest Court, board members have engaged in a negotiation process, which resulted in agreement on paying the debt in instalments.

Resident control of property management is a central co-operative principle. Most stakeholders mentioned the resident management aspects of co-operative tenure as advantageous, arguing that it contributes to ensuring the long-term sustainability of the project because active involvement of resident members in management limits the dependence on external capacity. Resident management makes an important contribution to perceptions of tenure security as the residents themselves are involved in decisions about deprivation of rights, rather than an outside individual or body to whom they have little or no access. However, this factor is tempered by the option held by non-resident stakeholders with a financial stake in the co-operatives, such as Cope, the provincial Department of Housing and the Social Housing Institution Development Fund, to sit on the board. Even if they choose not to, these parties have significant management powers because of their financial involvement. The balance between resident management and the management functions of external stakeholders will change over time as their financial roles in the projects decrease.

The resident management function does come under pressure at times, particularly in relation to the financial aspects of the co-operative, including increasing the monthly charges. In addition, some informants, notably provincial government officials, cautioned that not all households find the prospect of resident management desirable because of the time commitment required. (Sello's story in Box 14.4 tells of an individual's experience of both the financial aspects and tenant management.) The resident management factor may explain why some eligible households chose the adjacent rental housing project in preference to the Newtown Co-operative.

Financial return from investment in housing

Residents of co-operatives are required to make an initial investment in housing in the form of an equity payment. They also contribute monthly

---

Box 14.4   Sello's story

Sello was one of the first occupants of the Newtown Co-operative. He was introduced to it by his sister, also residing in Newtown. Sello explained that the process of gaining access to the project is onerous, but that it teaches members to grasp the extent of responsibilities and duties they hold in respect of the co-operative. As the community liaison officer, he is aware of the overall running of the co-operative and the experience of the other members, who approach him with grievances and suggestions. He is concerned that, in spite of the thorough education process which prospective members undergo, numerous members are still unaware of the full implications of co-operative tenure. Sello also mentioned that, to date, four members have had to leave as they were unable to meet the monthly charges.

Prior to moving to the co-operative, Sello resided in Soweto, as a subtenant in a council-owned home. Although his housing costs were modest (US$35–70), his commuting costs were significant. As such, the amount he presently spends on housing costs as a member of the co-operative is offset by the savings he achieves in terms of transport costs. He explained that although he had never felt insecure in terms of his tenure arrangements in Soweto, he now realizes that if a relative of the household with whom he had been residing had been in need of accommodation, he would have had to make way. Sello explained that he envisages staying in the co-operative for as long as it fulfils his housing and tenure requirements: a place where one can come home at night and dream in peace and safety!

---

charges to cover the costs of management and maintenance. The majority of role players identified the single most significant trait of co-operative tenure compared with alternatives, especially rental, as the financial return residents stand to gain in the form of the exit repayment, an entitlement on leaving the co-operative. In both projects, it has been agreed that the exit repayment should be calculated as the amount of the original equity payment plus a percentage of the total monthly charges paid by the member during occupancy. An incoming member must make the exit repayment. The institutional subsidy does not disqualify social housing beneficiaries from accessing other subsidies on leaving the institution. The exit payment could therefore be used to improve the quality of the housing stock which departing members may access as part of another housing subsidy option. While the exit repayment is a clear advantage in the Newtown case, a loan is required to finance further improvements to Everest Court, as most residents do not have sufficient savings to finance such an endeavour. Given the poor material condition of the building, improvements are required if the exit repayment is to be meaningful. However, there are concerns that few residents can afford the additional financial obligations linked to the repayment of the loan.

Subletting is an acknowledged form of income generation and accommodation provision for the urban poor. In both co-operative cases, the use agreement specifies that a member may, while unable to occupy the unit, sublet it subject to board approval. Evidence exists of some members engaging in the practice of subletting a portion of their units as a means of generating additional income, although this appears to be without the approval of the board. The size of the units does, however, limit this possibility and service thresholds may be unable to accommodate increased density were this practice to increase in scale.

Home-based income-generating opportunities appear to be susceptible to regulation in the co-operative model. For example, an Everest Court member was evicted because he was running an illegal liquor outlet from the building. Although the use agreement does not contain regulations prohibiting home-based enterprises, the nuisance associated with this particular activity, including violent drunken brawls, was such that the residents collectively forced its closure. To this day, bringing liquor on to the property is strongly regulated.

The use agreement envisages the ability to make improvements to the property, albeit with some procedural restrictions such as the need to obtain permission from the board. It is intended that exit repayments will take into account increases in the value of the housing stock due to improvements. However, the Newtown project manager explained that residents are discouraged from making alterations to their units in order to keep exit repayments within reasonable limits, thereby ensuring continued affordability for incoming members.

Access to finances: the subsidy, external funding and formal credit

South Africa's subsidy programme has enabled both projects to obtain funds – for refurbishment (Everest Court) and land and housing development (Newtown) – via the institutional subsidy that caters specifically for social housing institutions. Most respondents identified the ability to leverage external funding as a benefit accruing from group ownership. Cope has played an important role in accessing funding from statutory housing finance agencies. As far as formal credit is concerned, collective responsibility for repayment is seen to alleviate the risk that lending institutions perceive low-income households to pose (see Box 14.5). The Newtown Co-operative committee members reported that residents would have been unable to access loan finance as individuals, but loan finance has been obtained for the institution. In Everest Court, there are concerns that members may not be able to afford the increase in monthly charges, if a loan were to be obtained.

Access to formal services

Formal service delivery to the poor does not occur outside the ambit of the subsidy scheme in South Africa, where it is pooled together with the delivery of tenure and 'top structure'. In other words, the housing subsidy

---

Box 14.5   Cindy's story

Before moving to the Newtown Co-operative, Cindy lived in her parents' home in Soweto. To cover board and lodging, she used to pay US$33 per month. She reflects fondly on the house but decided to move because she wanted more independence. At 28, she explained, it was about time she had her own place! When Cindy first heard about the project, she had doubts about living in the inner city. She mentioned, though, that when she saw the development, she decided that the co-operative is a desirable option. She is content with the size of her unit, as she feels that this is a norm for townhouses. She is aware that compared with other subsidy options, and tenure arrangements, the co-operative project has enabled the leveraging of loan finance . . . an exception in the South African context, where 'banks don't lend to the poor'!

---

enables access to services. Minimum service levels are prescribed in subsidy regulations. Tenure form therefore had little influence on access to services in either project. Instead, service delivery is a component of the capital investment programme for which the subsidies were used.

Simplified administration of rights

South Africa's registration system is highly centralized and costly. It would be unlikely to be able to accommodate any large-scale regularization of informal rights. Increasing concern is being voiced at the incidence of informal transfers in subsidy projects occurring after the first round of registration, and in some cases before this. In contrast, the provisions pertaining to the transfer and registration of rights in the co-operative system are flexible since they are administered by the support organization and/or the board and do not require the payment of transfer costs. A register of co-operative members is kept at the registered office of the housing co-operative. It is interesting to note that, although the local management of rights is an important benefit of the co-operative model, none of the role players and stakeholders interviewed in the course of the research identified it as an advantage as compared with other tenure forms.

Dependency on external support

As well as being instrumental in promoting the co-operative housing model, Cope Housing Association, as support organization, has played an important role in establishing the institutional arrangements, informing and educating prospective beneficiaries and co-operative management. With its links to the Norwegian co-operative housing model and institutions, Cope has added significant capacity to the projects. It is arguable that the projects may not have been viable without the roles that Cope performed. Cope expects that in the medium to long term its role will be limited to accounting and financial management activities. The residents' management structures will increasingly have to assume management responsibilities as Cope's role diminishes over time (see Box 14.6). The management capacity-building role that Cope performs is critical if the housing institutions are to become more self-sufficient.

Box 14.6   Lybon's story

Lybon was born in 1958 in Engcobo in the Eastern Cape, where his family resides on tribal land held in custody by the traditional leader. In 1979, Lybon found work with a construction company, where he worked for eight years. He was housed in a Soweto hostel by his employer, who debited US$2 per month from his salary to cover rental costs. In 1980, the company relocated its work-force to workers' compounds, where residents paid a monthly fee of less than US$1. In 1989, Lybon moved to Navarone Court (now Everest) to escape the intolerable hostel environment. He explained that the affordability of housing costs in the co-operative is a great benefit. He is also appreciative of the fact that the residents are able to control increases in monthly charges. He is concerned about the decreasing involvement of Cope in supporting the management of the co-operative, as he feels that some of the residents sitting on the board of directors may not act in the collective interest of all residents but use their position to pursue their own interests. Although Lybon is satisfied with his current situation, he hopes in the future to own a townhouse in an environment that is safe from crime, and is open and spacious.

CONCLUSIONS

The main strength of the co-operative model lies in the security of tenure arising from the protection derived from open rules and regulations about deprivation and from the role that residents play in management. Simple and localized administration of rights, access to credit and financial return from the exit repayment represent additional advantages of the co-operative housing route. On the other hand, dependency on external support presents serious challenges for scale and replicability, and the existence of the required capacity and commitment for resident management will differ from case to case. Finally, the opportunities for income generation through home-based enterprise or subletting are more limited compared with ownership.

Several key contextual factors have made the development of a housing subsector dedicated to co-operatives possible. The South African research thus demonstrates some legal, financial and institutional pre-conditions that were necessary for the implementation of an alternative tenure form in an environment dominated by individual ownership.

An enabling legal framework promotes security of tenure and a range of tenure options, primarily through the nationally binding principles for land development contained in the Development Facilitation Act of 1995. However, considerable effort was required to adapt commercial co-operative statutes to suit the housing framework, as a legal framework for social housing does not exist in South Africa. Although several legal instruments for alternative tenure have not been implemented, a supportive financial framework has made the single most important contribution to the successful implementation of social housing, including group ownership through the co-operative model. However, until co-operative housing has established a track record that demonstrates its financial viability to attract commercial lending support, the availability of the institutional subsidy is likely to remain a precondition for replicability. The institutional support mobilized to spearhead the sector has also contributed significantly to the emergence of the co-operative movement. Without the technical expertise and grant finance received for establishing institutional capacity, the extent of Cope's interventions would have been severely limited. Finally, the perception that the rights are closely aligned to individual ownership greatly enhances the acceptability of the co-operative model. In short, political acceptability of alternatives is required, especially in a context characterized by historical denial of access to ownership rights.

Both Everest Court and the Newtown Housing Co-operative are located in Johannesburg's inner city. Although the institutional housing sector was pioneered in the context of refurbishments, the development of several greenfield projects demonstrates that its application is broader. However, the application of the co-operative model to informal settlement regularizsation or to large, more peripheral developments remains untested in South Africa. The demand for individual ownership, the resident management role and the ongoing financial contributions required may contribute to making the co-operative model unsuitable in some circumstances. The availability of real, implementable alternatives to respond to such diversity of need is required.

Institutionally subsidized housing developments held under a range of tenure alternatives, of which co-operatives are one example, are innovative options in an environment dominated by individually owned, developer-driven housing. The institutional subsidy regulations stipulate that the institution must remain the owner of the property for a minimum of four years. It will be important to monitor the extent to which social housing institutions sell to individuals once the four-year period has expired. If individualization occurs on a large scale, then it will be appropriate to conclude that the institutional subsidy is more a facilitator of institutional housing delivery than a vehicle for alternative tenure arrangements. If, on the other hand, collective tenure is retained on a significant scale, a real and long-standing alternative to individual ownership will have been developed and sustained.

A level playing field: security of tenure and the urban poor in Bangkok, Thailand

Radhika Savant Mohit

SECURITY OF TENURE

By law, there are only two possibilities with regard to security of tenure in Bangkok: the legal or illegal occupation of land. However, in reality, there are a number of options between these two extremes for the urban poor. While the law recognizes only the legal forms of tenure, the authorities themselves accept and recognize a range of other tenure arrangements. Consequently, there is a wide range of indicators that the urban poor use to assess their security of tenure. Van der Linden (1977) wrote in his study on the *bastis* of Karachi that it is these perceptions of tenure, whether right or wrong, that are decisive in how secure the urban poor feel and in influencing their investment in their immediate and surrounding environment.

In Bangkok, different tenure arrangements, providing different levels of security, allow more than a million people to find access to land and housing. Van der Linden used the '16 annas of hope' as indicators to determine how much hope the *basti* dwellers of Karachi have that the land would some day be their own. Hope-giving indicators are social or political signals that allow low-income communities to believe they can stay on the land. The extent of signals present and their interpretation can allow for the perception that legal statutory tenure is a possibility, or that tenure is secure for a period of time. Perceptions with regard to security of tenure vary with different social, political and economic circumstances. They are also influenced by tradition, society and cultural values, and can vary with time. For example in Bangkok, when land prices of areas are low, there is much more security of tenure. However, as the city develops and land prices increase, there is a greater threat of eviction by the landowner. Similarly, when initial numbers of residents are low, landowners feel less insecure about regaining the property from these low-income communities and are therefore less inclined to threaten eviction if they have no immediate use for the land. On the other hand, larger numbers of residents would make eviction that much more difficult.

This chapter addresses two issues with regard to security of tenure for the urban poor in Bangkok:

- What are the signals that give low-income communities enough security to live on a piece of land to which they themselves accept they have no legal right?
- What are the priorities for security of tenure for low-income communities?

BANGKOK AS A CASE STUDY

As Thailand's primate city, Bangkok has experienced tremendous growth and related pressures on land. While there are many intermediate-sized cities in Thailand, in 1990 Bangkok was 50 times larger than the second largest city of Chiang Mai and constituted 57.6 per cent of the country's urban population. The city has for long been a target of in-migration and saw a twofold increase in population during the period 1960–97 (Table 15.1.)

Table 15.1 Registered numbers, change and density of BMA's population, 1960–97

| Year | Population | Population change | | Population density |
		Number	%	(persons/km²)
1960	2 168 657	–	–	1382
1970	3 516 829	1 348 172	62.17	2242
1980	5 153 902	1 637 073	46.55	3399
1990	5 546 937	393 035	7.63	3583
1996	5 584 963	38 026	0.69	3560
1997	5 604 772	19 809	0.35	3573

Source: Bangkok Metropolitan Administration, 1997 and 1998

What is significant is that the official population data in Table 15.1 do not account for a large number of residents who for various reasons do not have a house registration. These include many living in informal settlements and transient migrants.

DIFFERENCES IN STATISTICS

In an effort to obtain a clearer countrywide picture of urban poverty, community networks teamed up with the National Housing Administration (NHA) information unit, Urban Community Development Office (UCDO) and several NGOs around the country to conduct a survey, which covers poor communities in 310 cities of Thailand. Table 15.2 shows some of the dramatic differences in statistics that were discovered.

Bangkok saw tremendous economic growth prior to the 1997 economic crash. Land speculation and inefficient land policy and management by the

Table 15.2   Statistical differences between official and community surveys

City	Official survey	Community survey
Nakhon Sawan	19 slums	53 slums
	3500 houses	9950 houses
Ubon Ratchathani	6 slums	23 slums
	1432 houses	5450 houses
Khon Kaen	7 slums	23 slums
	1210 houses	5977 houses
Nakhon Ratchasima	17 slums	26 slums
	3215 houses	5309 houses
Ayuthaya	28 slums	53 slums
	1475 houses	6611 houses

Source: UCDO (2000)

government led to a spiralling of land prices and the cost of housing beyond the means of low-income families. Travel times in Bangkok are considerable, so location is a decisive consideration for the poor, who need to live near employment and other income-generating activities. Under the circumstances, low-income people were forced to settle for less-than-adequate housing, often with low levels of tenure security. However, quoting Angel, Benjamin and De Goede from 1977, 'everybody is housed in one way or the other, and there are no people sleeping on the streets'. The situation holds more or less true for Bangkok even today, unlike many other mega-cities in Asia.

INFORMAL SETTLEMENTS IN BANGKOK

The urban poor are a varied lot. There are differences in their income levels, household sizes, education levels, employment opportunities and length of stay in the city, therefore they have different housing needs. The most affordable housing for the urban poor are the informal settlements, although they have the least security of tenure.

Concentrating on the physical conditions, housing quality, infrastructure and building density, the UCDO (now renamed Community Organisation Development Institute, CODI), NHA and Bangkok Metropolitan Administration (BMA) have defined informal settlements or 'slums' in the context of Thailand as:

A group of buildings with a housing density of not less than 15 houses per rai (1600 m²), in an area characterised by overcrowded, deteriorated, unsanitary, flood and poor conditions of stuffy, moisture and non-hygienic accommodation, which might be harmful for health, security or the source of illegal action or immorality areas (Government Housing Bank, 1997).

The definition does not directly address the issue of legal or illegal occupation of land and makes no differentiation between squatters, land-rental
slums or the various other tenure arrangements existing within informal
settlements in Bangkok.

MAGNITUDE OF BANGKOK'S INFORMAL SETTLEMENTS

In his 1984 survey, Pornchokchai identified 1020 informal settlements in
Bangkok (i.e. the BMA and parts of two adjacent provinces, Nonthaburi and
Samut Prakan). 'By using a fairly accurate count of the number of households' and a 'generally accepted average of 5.5 persons per household', he
estimated the total population living in those settlements at 1.01 million
(Pornchokchai, 1985). NHA surveys in 1988 and 1990 indicated that there
were 1078 settlements with 1.06 million inhabitants and 981 settlements
with 946 839 inhabitants, respectively. The latest information available
found a total of 910 informal settlements, with 208 699 households and
1 167 082 persons in Bangkok (Government Housing Bank, 1997).

While a comparison between the years of 1985 and 1996 shows a decrease
in the number of informal settlements, it shows an increase in number of
households and population and a trend of increasing number of informal
settlements in the suburban areas (Table 15.3).

Table 15.3 Distribution of slum settlements in Bangkok in 1990 and 1993

Zone of development*	No. of slum settlements		Slum population	
	1990	1993	1990	1993
CBD zone	338	325	374 500	355 333
Urbanized zone	295	318	351 819	406 744
Suburban zone	315	580	220 520	494 193
Total	948	1223	946 839	1 256 270
Bangkok population			5 546 937	5 572 712
Share of 'slum' population to Bangkok population			17.07%	22.54%

*CBD zone covers an area of 5 km radius of the city centre; urbanized zone covers an area of 10 km
radius; suburban zone covers an area outside 10 km radius.
Source: Pacific Consultants International Suuri-Keikaku Co. Ltd (1997)

The decreasing number of informal settlements in the inner-city areas
shows that some communities have been evicted. The increasing number
of settlements in the fringe areas can be explained by the city's development and growth, where opportunities for the urban poor to be gainfully
employed in the fringe areas of the city have increased. The fringe settlements also account for new settlers, who now do not have the option to
move into the inner-city area simply due to lack of space, as well as those
who have been evicted from inner-city areas or moved for other reasons.

TYPES OF INFORMAL SETTLEMENTS

Bangkok's informal settlements are of two types: land-rental slums and squatter settlements (Yap, 1992).

Land-rental slums

The land-rental slums are the dominant type of informal settlements in Bangkok. Rather than occupying a plot of land illegally, the urban poor negotiate with landowners for permission to settle on their land. However, a variety of arrangements between renters and landowners can be observed in these settlements. Because Bangkok's development is mostly unplanned, there are many plots of land that are not worth developing until land prices are much higher or they are connected to main roads. Landowners allow low-income families to occupy such land on a temporary basis. The parties may or may not sign a contract document. Low-income families then occupy the land and build a (temporary) house. In the case of a signed contract document, the contract can usually be terminated with 30 days' notice. The occupants usually pay a nominal rent to the landowner. In some cases, a middleman rents a land parcel and, with or without the knowledge of the owner, subdivides it to rent it out to low-income households. Slum dwellers who rent from a landowner may further subdivide their house and rent it to another family. Some dwellers build single rooms for rent in a settlement.

Squatter settlements

Only a small percentage (16 per cent in 1992) of the informal settlements in Bangkok are pure squatter settlements. They are mainly found along canals and railway lines on land belonging to the Irrigation Department and the State Railways of Thailand. Besides 'pure' squatter settlements, there are many land-rental slums where rental agreements have lapsed and there is an indication that the landowner wished to recover the land plot.

The different types of tenure arrangement existing within land-rental slums should indicate the security of tenure perceived by those communities. For example, a community with a legal contract would have a higher level of security than one where there was a legal contract, but which on expiry has not been renewed by the landowner. While eviction may not be an imminent threat, there is an indication that the landowner might be looking to change the use of his land. However, levels of security that are perceived within communities may or may not always be directly related to the legal contractual arrangements or status of the slum (Table 15.4). Most slum communities in Bangkok have been in existence for several years.

Table 15.4 Legal status of slum settlements

Type of contract	BMA		Provinces*		BMR	
	Abs	%	Abs	%	Abs	%
Legal contracts	494	48	174	42	668	46
No contracts	220	21	87	21	307	21
Contracts expired	73	7	4	1	77	5
Some household within a single community with contract	5	0	4	1	9	1
No information	240	23	141	34	381	26
Total	1032	100	410	100	1442	100

Abs = absolute numbers; BMA: Bangkok Metropolitan Administration/Area; BMR: Bangkok Metropolitan Region
*Samut Prakhan, Nonthaburi, Pathumthani.
Source: Yap, (1992)

THE HOUSING DELIVERY SYSTEM IN BANGKOK

The different housing submarkets that develop in a particular city depend on a number of factors, such as economic growth, population growth, employment and income structures, land tenure rights, and the government's policy and attitudes towards informal settlements.

Public tenure

The rapid economic growth of Thailand in the late 1980s and early 1990s had two consequences on low-income communities and their housing conditions. Low-income groups saw an increase in real income and purchasing power. This allowed them to move to low-income formal housing provided by the government or private sector. However, the economic growth also led to spiralling of land prices, making it increasingly difficult for some sections of low-income groups to find affordable land and housing in the city centre.

The NHA established in 1973 absorbed the function of prior public agencies in providing low-cost housing to the inhabitants of Bangkok. In the period 1976–80, the NHA proposed to construct 120 000 housing units and began by initiating the construction plans for 36 868 units. In 1978, it realized its plan was overambitious and unaffordable. The NHA subsequently adopted a new plan (Accelerated Plan 1979–80), which was to construct 5600 walk-up apartments, developing sites and services schemes for 19 610 plots, and upgrading slums for 26 000 households. In 1980–81, this plan was abandoned due to limited subsidies received from the central government. A further reduction in subsidies resulted in the NHA trying to cross-subsidize low-income housing by constructing middle- and high-income housing. However, the NHA competes poorly with the housing offered by the private sector.

Land-sharing arrangements

With increasing property values in the city, slum communities that have previously shared some form of rental agreement with landowners find themselves threatened by eviction. While some communities accept some form of compensation and leave, NGOs have been successful in persuading a number of communities not to give up their land easily, but work towards an arrangement of land sharing. A land-sharing arrangement divides the given plot into two parts, one to be leased or sold to the slum community to rehouse its members under conditions acceptable to the community. The second part of the plot is made available for the landowner to develop free of any encumbrance. By accepting a land-sharing arrangement, the authorities and the landowner recognize the legitimacy of both the landowner and slum community.

Land sharing is based on the principles of densification, that is rehousing the community on a smaller plot of land; reconstruction of existing structures as a result of densification; participation by the community in decision-making and negotiations; and maximizing cross-subsidies to allow the land sharing to be successful. Land sharing as a solution to improve security of tenure has been used in a limited number of cases in Bangkok. Some comparative figures for these projects are provided in Tables 15.5 to 15.7.

Land sharing as a solution can be used in only certain very specific cases. It needs well-established communities who are willing to carry out lengthy negotiations. It also requires that some families, either with or without compensation, leave the plot before a land-sharing agreement is reached, to allow for densification. Very often it is the poorer families who leave. Land sharing also ignores the differences in income levels within a slum community. While some might find the compensation offered by the landowner an attractive short-term solution, some households leave after

Table 15.5 The slum community's land before and after land sharing

Land-sharing projects in Bangkok	Original slum area (hectares)	Area after land sharing (hectares)	% of land for slum community
Wat Ladbukaw	1.60	0.32	20
Klong Toey	n/a	n/a	n/a
Manangkasila	1.75	0.67	38
Rama IV	8.50	2.40	28
Sam Yod	0.95	0.65	68
Soi Sengki	1.10	0.60	55
Inthamar 10	0.30	0.10	65

Table 15.6   Number of households before and after land sharing

Land-sharing projects in Bangkok	Original number of households	Households remaining after land sharing	% of household remaining
Wat Ladbukaw	300	67	22
Klong Toey	1780	1080	61
Manangkasila	500	198	40
Rama IV	1000	850	85
Sam Yod	210	192	91
Soi Sengki	216	198	92
Inthamar 10	85	70	82

Table 15.7   Types of land tenure in land-sharing projects

Land-sharing projects in Bangkok	Tenure
Wat Ladbukaw	Freehold title to the land
Klong Toey	20-year lease period
Manangkasila	Year-to-year lease
Rama IV	20-year lease on the flats
Sam Yod	20-year lease on the flats
Soi Sengki	Freehold title to the land
Inthamar 10	Freehold title to the land

Source: Yap (1992)

the land-sharing agreement has been reached, as they are unable to make the necessary payments (see Box 15.1).

Resettlement

At times, landowners and slum communities can work out a compensation deal whereby, for an agreed sum of money or an alternative piece of land, slum community members can be persuaded to vacate the plot of land. The compensation allows slum community members either to buy land on the urban fringe or to move to an NHA-designated resettlement site. The NHA allows slum communities to buy a plot of land on an instalment basis over a period of 10 to 15 years. Water and electricity are installed free of charge by the BMA. Resettlement schemes have met with limited success because of the distance of the resettlement projects from the city and thereby the decreased income-generation opportunities.

At times, slum communities have themselves identified land tracts where they would like to resettle and have managed to negotiate deals with the landowner. Two famous cases in Bangkok are the resettlement of the slum community of Soi Sutiporn and that of Rachadapisek slum resettlement. The success of these, however, benefited from a number of other factors,

---

Box 15.1   The Rama IV land-sharing agreement

The Crown Property Bureau owned the land on which the slum community of Rama IV lived. In 1966, a fire demolished many of the houses in the settlement. Some of the households had a lease contract for occupying the land. The Crown Property Bureau asked the community to vacate the land and leased it to a developer, although some lease contracts were still to expire. When all contracts expired the landowner threatened eviction of the 700 families. The community organized itself and, with political support and support from NGOs, it created a well-publicized campaign. In 1981, the developer designated 2.4 ha to construct four eight-storey buildings to house the slum dwellers. The flats were to be made available on a 20-year lease. Demolition in the slum started in 1991.

The Rama IV land-sharing project's construction was completed early in 2000. The process of establishing claimants to the housing provided under this project, and the subsequent long period of construction, took its toll on the initial cohesiveness of the community. Some of the settlers who were eligible for housing had moved away by the time the project was completed and units allotted to them were ready. Some settlers accuse the committee that represented the residents of foul play, claiming that the committee and community leaders have obtained several units for themselves. The residents who live in the project are also divided in their commitment to the original agreement on payment of rent. Some refuse to pay the Crown Property Bureau their dues. Lack of action against non-payment by the Crown Property Bureau has led to bitterness among those who have regularly paid their dues. A number of units have been sublet by the original residents and many have returned to live in unauthorized settlements, supplementing their income with the rent received from their units in the Rama IV project.

---

such as access to free land, political involvement and community cohesion. Such factors are often intrinsic to a particular case and cannot always be replicated.

Private sector

From the 1980s, private developers in Bangkok moved into the provision of low-cost housing schemes. The late 1980s and early 1990s saw a proliferation of row house schemes and single-unit condos. While outright purchase of these may have remained out of reach of the lowest income group, the rental has been affordable to many. However, the architectural design of condominiums and the occasionally remote location has limited appeal to families and are more suitable to single individuals.

CASE STUDY: SAMAKEE PATTANA COMMUNITY LAND RENTAL, AN OPTION FOR THE URBAN POOR

The Samakee Pattana community is approximately 15 km from the city centre. This community has been squatting on a plot of approximately 6.4 ha for the past 12 years. At present there are 498 households residing in the area. In February 2001, the community worked out a land-rental tenure arrangement with the landowner with the help of the NHA and two NGOs. The case provides insight into security of tenure as a priority, the social dynamics that influence security of tenure and other indicators that may enhance or detract from perceptions of tenure security.

History of the community

In 1989, ten households moved to occupy the site, which belonged to the Clergy Hospital Foundation. Most of the families were occupied in waste recycling. The surrounding area had rice fields and there was only a clay path to approach the plot. Most households came directly from the provinces and were unaware of the need for documents to prove land tenure rights. However, as early as 1989 the resident families had already started reserving tracts of land and later residents had to buy the right to those reserved tracts. In 1989, the going price for a piece of land within the plot was US$80. Although no documents were exchanged, in the discussions with the original residents there is mention of paying the money to the 'right' person. This payment to the 'right person' gave the residents enough security to build on the tract of land, although in real terms they had no legal form of tenure.

In the period 1990–91, the Rattanakosin Insurance Company informed the residents, numbering approximately 30 households, that they had leased the site from the Clergy Hospital Foundation. Rattanakosin Insurance Company put up a number of boards stating that the land was under private ownership and the squatters would be removed. The 30 households were not greatly perturbed as, at the same time, certain staff of the company assured the residents they could stay. Whether this was done in lieu of money or some other form of compensation to the staff of the Rattanakosin Company is unclear.

By 1996, there were approximately 300 resident households. A number of the residents were those who had been evicted from other land plots. Nearly 30 per cent are believed to have moved from the Klong Toey community.[1] After leasing the land for five years from the Clergy Hospital Foundation and giving silent sanction to the community to reside on the land, the Rattanakosin Insurance Company threatened the community with eviction and served five of the community leaders with a court notice. None of the residents was sufficiently insecure under this threat of eviction to leave the community. This might also be attributed to the NGO involvement with the community starting late in 1995, which worked to increase awareness on land tenure issues. The community entered into discussions with the company and also the Clergy Hospital Foundation. The Clergy Hospital Foundation informed the residents that they should take up the matter directly with the company. Before the community and the Rattanakosin Insurance Company could enter into meaningful dialogue, the Rattanakosin Insurance Company declared bankruptcy in the 1997 Thai economic crisis. Rattanakosin gave up the lease for the land and the threat of eviction passed. In early 1999, with the help of the NGO and NHA, the community began negotiating directly with the landowner, the Clergy Hospital Foundation, a rental lease arrangement to occupy the plot legally.

The key stakeholders

The Samakee Pattana community, like all other low-income communities, is not an homogeneous one. Income levels vary from approximately US$90 to US$225[2] per month. Seventy per cent of the people are employed in the informal sector and even those employed in the formal sector are on a temporary or daily basis. The community can be divided into two main groups: those who rent houses and those who own houses, although the ownership has no legal basis. The initial settlers own houses within the community. Many of them reserved land tracts within the plot and have sold these to newcomers. The going price for a land plot in the year 2001 was US$700. Those who rent houses do so for a monthly rent of US$12–15.

The buying and selling of land tracts and/or houses reserved by community members persists, although all concerned parties know that the land actually belongs to the Clergy Hospital Foundation and the community members have no legal right to it. Many community members who have faced eviction before are also party to this process. No documents are exchanged, although there is keen awareness with regard to the importance of land title deeds. Once a land tract is bought, the new owner has to build up his house quickly to consolidate ownership. The ability to reserve land and sell it has some relationship to the clout an individual holds in the community. This may be by way of an individual's family size, income level, and connections to persons outside the community and/or leadership within the community. Time and again, reference to buying the land from the 'right' person was made.

A number of those community members who have been evicted from other slums have been allocated land in the NHA's relocation schemes. They have relinquished their right to a 'legal' plot for locational reasons or lack of funds to make the downpayment required by the NHA, although some of them have paid a higher amount of money for their house at Samakee Pattana.

The Clergy Hospital Foundation is a trust organization meant to provide health services to Buddhist monks. Thai people donate money and, at times, land to this organization for the purpose of 'merit making'. The Foundation manages approximately 416 ha of land donated by various persons. It rents land to many communities who lived or were associated with the different land plots prior to their being donated to the foundation. The trust has an advisory committee with 15 members. A subcommittee of five members from within these 15 was designated to negotiate the contract agreement with the community.

In late 1995, a Thai NGO – the Building Together Association – started work in the community. Building Together was established in 1981 with three focus areas: encouraging housing co-operatives among poor communities, providing legal aid to communities and supporting the development of appropriate low-cost building materials. Simultaneously, Building Together's sister concern, the Training Centre for the Urban Poor, started working in Samakee Pattana. More recently, the Slum Women's Network has also started work there. With the help of the NGOs, the community started savings activity in 1996. Today, the savings group is in the form of a housing co-operative with 390 households as members and approximately US$8890 in a savings account and US$4450 in shareholdings. The NGOs have played a major role in raising awareness about land tenure issues within the community. However, they are the first to admit they cannot in any way influence the buying and selling of land tracts among the community members. They also played a key role in the negotiations between the landowner and the community, especially on legal issues.

The NHA receives a subsidy of approximately US$270 per household if the community does not move, and US$1500 from the government if the community relocates, to provide infrastructure such as roads, walkways, water supply and electricity in low-income settlements. The NHA has participated in the negotiations between the Samakee Pattana community and the landowner and agreed to invest in infrastructure for the community, provided a sufficient lease period was obtained from the owner.

The contractual negotiations

The contractual negotiations between the Clergy Foundation Hospital and the Samakee Pattana community for lease of the 6.4 ha took over a year and a half to conclude (late 1999 to April 2001). Initially, the landowner wanted a US$22 000 deposit and US$0.17 per 4 m² as rent.[3] The community negotiated and an agreement was reached to pay a US$2200 deposit and a total rent of US$580 per month for the site.

The tenure period was the main cause of disagreement between the landowner, the Clergy Foundation and the community. The community sought a 15-year lease period with an automatic renewal if the community did not default on rent. This lease period was also supported by the NHA, which was hesitant to provide infrastructure to communities with shorter lease periods. The community was negotiating for a contract document to be drawn up which would include the NHA, the Building Together Association, the community and the landowner. This would make it difficult for the landowner to break the contract or amend it in a manner unfavourable to the community. The lease agreement was to be made in favour of Samakee Pattana's housing co-operative.

After a year of negotiations, the contract drafted by the landowner in late December 2000 offered a three-year lease with no clause for contract renewal, and the right to increase the rent. The contract also prohibited the community from any kind of construction activity without the permission of the landowner. The landowner also stipulated that the involvement of the NHA not be made public.

At this point, reflection by the key stakeholders was necessary. The Clergy Hospital Foundation is a semi-philanthropic organization and it would not be in its best interests to take an aggressive stand against a low-income community such as Samakee Pattana.

For the NHA, the successful resolution of the contractual arrangements would serve as a model and the surrounding publicity would help the NHA leverage additional government funding. Similarly for the NGOs involved, the publicity generated by its role as a key facilitator would enhance its credibility. The motivation for the community in seeing a successful resolution of the contract was that there would be increased security of tenure and access to basic infrastructure.

In April 2001, an agreement to rent the land plot to the Samakaee Pattana community for a period of 21 years was finalized. In a public meeting, the contract document between the housing co-operative of Samakee Pattana community and the Clergy Foundation was signed, with the NHA and Building Together NGO as supporters. The community members pay a rent of US$0.06 (Bt3) per 4 m^2 to the housing co-operative of which Bt1.5 is given to the owner and Bt1.5 is retained by the co-operative for management of the co-operative and the savings scheme. The Clergy Foundation receives a total of approximately US$530 per month for the 6.4 ha site. The contract is to be renewed every three years and although a rental increase is allowed, it cannot exceed 20 per cent. The Clergy Foundation obtains the rental amount from the housing co-operative of the Samakee Pattana community, which in turn will collect it from the people after decisions about the layout plan and infrastructure arrangements are made.

FACTORS INFLUENCING SECURITY OF TENURE

Tracing the development of the Samakee Pattana community and the contractual arrangements between the landowner and the community highlights that security of tenure is related to the various dynamics and power balances among the different stakeholders. Perceptions of security of tenure are further influenced by some subtle, qualitative factors and also by some substantial indicators.

The patron–client relationship

For five years before the the eviction notice was served in 1996, the Rattanakosin Insurance Company's only action against a fast-growing community squatting on its land was in the form of notices that they had leased the land. Some of the company's own staff assured the community that they could stay, although whether this was in lieu of some form of remuneration cannot be determined. Community leaders and others sold land tracts on the plot, assuring the newcomers of tenure, although this had no legal basis. Community leaders often served as moneylenders, which allowed them varying levels of control over individuals.

After a year's negotiations the draft contract offered by the landowner in December 2000 read as an anticlimax. However, the community leaders and the NGO working towards the resolution of negotiations remained unperturbed. On closer questioning, the research team was informed that of the five committee members working on behalf of the Clergy Hospital Foundation, the community and NGO had lobbied with four to gain support for the arrangements and conditions put forward by the community. For the fifth, who had strongly emphasized the legal issues in the whole process, it would now be a 'loss of face' to agree to the demands of the community. In early January 2001, the community and NGO planned to lobby with an individual within Thai society who was considered to be at a higher position, to request the single disagreeing member of the Clergy Foundation to agree to the demands of the community. It would only be correct and proper for that individual to then acquiesce.

Thailand's hierarchical society plays a crucial role with regard to perceptions of security. Class structures and positioning within the class structure are based on age, education, income levels and/or family backgrounds. Individuals of a higher class can either offer protection and/or dictates, the challenge or questioning of which would be considered highly inappropriate. The patronage system, which prevails directly or indirectly in most parts of Asia, connects the urban poor and the powers that be. It allows the urban poor to live and work in an informal setting with a minimum level of security in exchange for money and political support for those in power in the city.

The patron–client relationship might also provide insight into why many of the poor communities in Bangkok choose to negotiate some form of a rental arrangement, although not necessarily legal, rather than squat and simply occupy vacant land. Most of the land in Bangkok is in private ownership, and in the social hierarchy it would probably have been improper for low-status families like rural migrants to simply invade vacant land or confront urban land owners and government agencies on their rights to the land once they had occupied it for a number of years. This attitude is also reflected in the way evictions are handled by the slum dwellers. Many, although not all, evictions in Bangkok are silent evictions, i.e. when told to vacate the land the slum dwellers leave without much objection (see Box

15.2). Some communities received compensation from the landowner; however, open confrontations have been few in number.

Box 15.2   Evicted and settled...

Khun SS has lived with his family in the Samakee Pattana community since 1995 and works as a hired hand for housing repairs. He originally lived in Soi (street) Ramkhameng 42 in a suburb of Bangkok. He rented land from a middleman and was going to build his own house. There were about 20 other families residing at Soi Ramkhameng 42 at that time. One day this small community was told that the middleman to whom they paid for renting the land was only the caretaker. The original owner served the community with a legal notice and asked them to vacate the land within seven days. They were each paid approximately US$70 for moving. All families moved within the prescribed time period.

Khun SS's daughter-in-law's father told him of vacant land in what is now the Samakee Pattana community. He says he was wary of being evicted again, but was assured by his daughter-in-law's father that it was OK for him to build his house in the community. Although he did not pay for the land, he says many who came after him had to because by then residents had started reserving land tracts.

Location

The relationship between place of employment or access to income-generating opportunities and the area where the urban poor choose to live is well established. Many poor households with access to sites in the NHA's relocation projects choose to return to rental slums or squatter settlements in the city simply because of the distance of the relocation projects from the city centre. The average distances of relocation projects in Bangkok are 25 km from the city centre, which is 1.5 to 3 hours' travel time. (Bijl et al., 1992). Not only is access to employment limited, but so too is access to affordable education, entertainment and health facilities (see Box 15.3).

Physical quality of structures

Low-income settlements in Bangkok are characterized by extremely high population densities, they lack proper drainage systems and are susceptible to flooding. The houses are made of second-hand wooden planks or asbestos sheets and are usually built on stilts over stagnant water. Narrow, winding footpaths serve as pedestrian walkways. With no solid waste collection system, garbage piles up under the houses. Sanitation systems are rudimentary and are in the form of concrete rings used to build a cesspool under the toilet. In general, these conditions are far from what is acceptable as standard norms, being made of substandard materials and lacking sanitary facilities. However, in comparison to slum

> **Box 15.3** Title to land not always affordable
>
> 'I was evicted from the Rompoong Community which had occupied land belonging to the Railway Authority of Thailand. The land was to be leased to the Hope Well project in 1996. We were each given Bt16 000[4] for removing our things. NHA allocated us land at Chalongkroong but we had to pay Bt10 000 as a downpayment and Bt1500 per month for a 15 year period.'
>
> Khun NG, who is a gardener with Klongton Hospital, renounced his right to the land plot allocated by NHA because the monthly payments were too expensive. He came to live at Samakee Pattana in 1997 because it was quite close to where he worked and to his children's school. 'I bought the right of the land plot in Samakee Pattana from a man who was on the community's committee. I paid Bt30 000[5] for 30 wah^2 (120 m^2). Later I bought the adjacent plot on sale for Bt28 000. I had to build the house quickly to show my right to the land.'
>
> On being asked if he was scared of being evicted from Samakee Pattana when he paid for his land plots, Khun NG replied, 'No because when I paid the money, the person who sold me the land plot took me to meet a powerful man who was then member of parliament who backed what the owner had said.'

communities in some other countries the conditions would not be considered too bad.

The condition of houses in Samakee Pattana is no different from that described above. However, most residents find their housing structures to be adequate and do not feel the need to make major improvements to them. They would, if possible, prefer a concrete ground-level structure, but it does not seem to be a major concern. What is more of a concern is the expansion of the house to accommodate the extended family.

Access to services

The Samakee Pattana community has increasingly been able to gain access to basic services, although not always officially.

In 1996, the community obtained two temporary central water connections from the Metropolitan Water Authority (MWA). Each connection cost US$3600,[6] of which US$2000 served as guarantee money and US$1600 was for the installation. The community themselves have extended individual PVC pipes from these central connections, to the houses. Each house connection has a meter and a group of 20 meters forms a substation. Subcommittees formed by members of the community monitor these substations and are responsible for collecting the necessary monetary amount for consumption of water from the individual houses. In this manner, all households have individual water connections. However, the MWA charges a progressive rate, i.e. the larger the consumption of water the higher the rate. The MWA does not recognize the individual connections, but only the two mains and classifies them as industrial connections. This results in the community paying at a rate of

US$0.36[7] or Bt16 per cubic metre, which is twice the average household rate.

Access to electricity is by informal connection to surrounding private houses and businesses. They are charged at the discretion of the owners.

The community gained access to temporary housing registration in 1997 (election year), which allowed them to vote. This has enabled them to register their children in schools. Prior to this, individuals outside the community who had housing registration were paid to enrol the community children as their own. A day care centre for small children had been set up by one of the NGOs in the community. Access to credit is still largely in the form of loans from the moneylenders in the community, many of whom are community leaders.

Socioeconomic issues

Low-income communities are a mobile population. Many come and go with changes in their access to employment and other opportunities. The Samakee Pattana community highlighted a related issue. The working population, aged approximately 35–55 years, see a continuity in their stay within the community; but the younger generation, very often more educated than the older generation, see life in the community as temporary and are confident that they will be able to move out and upwards.

For a large number of woman-headed households there is a strong preference to rent rather than own houses. This is mainly because they do not want to be embroiled in negotiations with landowners or affected by evictions. They are quite happy with temporary rental arrangements. Some of them have also moved to a particular community because of emotional attachments, i.e. their boyfriends live there. These are often transient relationships and the flexibility to up and move is seen positively.

The poor depend on a large number of informal support networks. These might be in the form of family and friends living in the same community, which appears to be one of the major reasons for choosing to stay in a particular community. Access to credit from local businesses for daily food items or access to other businesses for the products or know-how necessary to run their own businesses all form part of crucial support networks necessary to survive in the city. These networks influence how secure individuals feel living in a particular community vis-à-vis another.

LAWFUL SECURITY OF TENURE AS A PRIORITY

Poor communities can often continue to live for long periods of time on land plots thanks to the patronage of, or protection by, another individual or group of individuals rather than any lawful tenure arrangement. In the case of lawful rental contracts, most communities accept this as a temporary tenure arrangement. Whether the patron–client relationship sees an exchange of remuneration or services or simple control over individuals varies. However, for poor communities this arrangement affords a large degree of security.

The importance of secure tenure for improvement in housing conditions is well established, but how much or what kind of security low-income communities think necessary, varies (see Box 15.4). With access to basic services and protection by the patron–client relationship, the issue of legal tenure is not a high priority with most low-income communities unless they are under the threat of eviction. Many of them have stayed under the existing circumstances for a long period of time. Most residents feel the quality of their houses is adequate, but would like to extend them in terms of having more space. Those who 'sold' reserved plots within the community did so without any exchange of documents or receipts (although they would have had no legal status). Those who rent houses do so without any contractual documents or rent payment receipt. Oral assurance is considered adequate for these transactions and most would be reasonably happy if the status quo prevailed.

Box 15.4   Tenure arrangements and their priority for individuals

Khun YP is a labourer with a construction company and has rented a house in the Samakee Pattana community since 1995:

'I came to live at Samakee Pattana after being evicted from KlongToey. I rent a house because I don't want to get involved with reserving land and evictions. I know there are some negotiations going on with the landowner. It all started when there was a rumour about eviction in 1997. Before that we had no problems. A few repairs to the house would be good, as also cheaper water and electricity, but otherwise it's a good place to stay for Bt500 (US$11) per month. No, the owner does not give me any receipt, but that's not a problem.'

Khun SG is a housewife who has 'sold' two houses in the Samakee Pattana community each for Bt25 000 (US$555) and has lived in the community since 1992:

'Yes, I knew when I sold the houses that the land was not mine and it was not legal to sell the houses, but every one was doing it. If we get a contract with the landowner it will be good but we have lived here for a long time and it would be difficult to move all of us out. Many in the community also know important people.'

Where the poor choose to stay is based on a number of factors, both economic and social. These factors have different significance for different households at different times. Legal security of tenure is a factor that is weighed against these other economic and social factors and its priority for households and communities may vary with circumstances and/or time.

DIFFERENT CONDITIONS BUT SIMILAR PROBLEMS

The Nong Chok community

The Nong Chok community is a small community of 48 households on the outer suburbs of Bangkok. Originally a farming community occupying 160 ha, the community has occupied the land for 80 years. The original owner donated approximately 100 ha to the Clergy Foundation. The Clergy Foundation has leased approximately 80 ha to a private company for the construction of a golf course. The community now leases approximately 20 ha from the Clergy Foundation.

The contract with the Clergy Foundation is renewed every three years and has now been in effect for nearly ten years. The rent paid by the community members depends on the individual size of the plot they occupy, at a rate of US$4.5 per year/rai.[8] Individual contracts exist between the residents and the Clergy Foundation and stipulate that while the land belongs to the Clergy Foundation the house belongs to the individual. If at any time the Foundation wants to acquire the land, it has to pay the cost of the house to the individual. The community has to inform the Clergy Foundation of any housing improvements and if any new persons/families come to stay on the plot. The Nong Chok community has limited electricity and no water supply. They do not have any NGOs working within their community. While they are aware of the NHA as an organization, they have never thought of approaching it for improving the infrastructure and living conditions of their community.

The Samakee Pattana and Nong Chok communities have a landowner, which by nature is a special kind of institution. However, while the issue remains security of tenure, the conditions for the Rom Poon community are quite different.

Rom Poon Community near Rama III

Rama III is the new business district of Bangkok and is experiencing large-scale development. Nestling on the swampy banks of the Chao Phyra River in this area of Bangkok are about six slum communities, of which the Rom Poon community is one. Made up of 63 households occupying an area of 1.6 ha, the community has been living on the swamp since 1990.

Each of the resident families paid a land broker US$200[9] and a monthly rent of US$12. In 1999, the families were informed that they were trespassing on private property and 17 families were served with an eviction order. At this time, the land broker disappeared and the community was informed that the land belonged to a particular individual. With the help of a local NGO, the community sought intervention from the NHA. The owner wants the land back because property prices in the area are spiralling. The district office is also not supportive of the community, as plans for a waterfront development near the land occupied by the community and other adjacent communities are under way.

With the support of the NHA and the Rama III network group (formed by low-income communities in the area) the community has negotiated a contract of six years, in which they will pay the owner a monthly rental of US$4.5 or Bt200 per family. In that six-year period, the community and the landowner will try to identify a land plot for resettlement. At the end of the contract period, the community will leave the current land plot and be resettled on the new land plot. Further details on how and where the community will be resettled are still to be determined.

The land plot where the community lives at present is a swamp. Rough wooden planks join together to form rudimentary pathways a metre above ground level. The community draws water and electricity from surrounding businesses. They pay at a rate of Bt20 per unit, which is more than twice the official rate for domestic consumption. Initially, the NHA was hesitant to commit to infrastructure development as the contract period was fairly short and the NHA policy previously stipulated at least a ten-year contract period for improvement in infrastructure. However, the NHA is now committed to improving conditions in the community. Details of the extent and type of infrastructure improvements are still to be determined. The negotiations and the outcome of the negotiations are critical not just for the Rom Poon community, but also for the surrounding six low-income communities, some of which are settled on land plots belonging to the same owner as the Rom Poon community. The successful resolution of the negotiations is also important for the NHA as it encourages the shift in policy towards providing infrastructure and improving living conditions of communities with shorter rental contracts.

POLICY RECOMMENDATIONS

How the poor perceive security of tenure is related to numerous factors, criteria and social dynamics within and outside low-income communities. Security of tenure also has variable priority for low-income communities. The right to occupy land legally with statutory documents is one extreme, which may not always be a feasible or even necessary option for all urban poor households.

The heterogeneity of low-income communities is significant when considering solutions for secure tenure. Not all people want a freehold title; many are renters and wish to continue to be so for a wide variety of reasons. For many, a rental agreement for a specified period of time is highly acceptable. With location playing such a crucial role in where the poor live, security of tenure at a given place may not be extremely important when weighed against opportunities available at another location, while for poorer families the downpayment to obtain a freehold title may not be feasible.

Any policy move to increase security of tenure in Bangkok for low-income communities under a legal framework would encourage occupation of vacant plots, dissuade landowners from renting out their land on a temporary basis and therefore remove a major housing delivery system. It would also advance the threat of evictions as landowners try to regain their land ahead of such a policy measure taking effect.

To improve security of tenure for low-income communities, one has to accept the temporal quality of land-rental slums. If the land-rental arrangements could be formally recognized so that the obligations and commitments of both parties, i.e. the community and the landowner, are clearly stated, especially with regard to time, and supported by law, security of tenure for these communities would be greatly improved. The NHA should then adopt a more flexible stand with regard to improving infrastructure. For short-tem rental arrangements it can provide low-cost temporary infrastructure and basic services such as water and sanitation. While for longer-term rental leases land fill, reblocking of plots, rebuilding structures and other improvements for the layout can also be considered. This would remove the exploitative forces within and outside a community and allow the landowner to feel secure about regaining his property. It would also allow for organizing the community with regard to savings and credits schemes, skills training and health education, without eviction or the threat of eviction being the binding factor.

NGOs play an important role in increasing awareness about security of tenure, as well as equipping communities with the skills and knowledge to negotiate with landowners and other agencies. It would serve local authorities well to encourage this supportive and reconciliatory role that NGOs

Figure 15.1   With access to basis infrastructure, house expansion and improvements are the next priority for the people of the community of Samakee Pattana. Credit: Aman Mehta

play. Negotiations for determining rental contracts are a long process and there is a lot to do in terms of establishing trust and confidence among the community members themselves as well as explaining legal issues. NGOs that have worked at the community level are suitable partners to fulfil this role.

As indicated by the case studies, each land-rental community situation is different. Each community has different needs and negotiating capacities, and landowners have different perspectives with regard to low-income communities. There are no blanket solutions. The role of the local authorities is crucial and quite different from what it has been used to. It needs to be a negotiator and facilitator and should be vested with the financial and regulatory power and capacity to take and implement such decisions. Centralized and hierarchical bureaucratic systems do not function well and it is imperative to make local authorities and institutions more flexible and adaptable to changing circumstances and better equipped to lead by persuasion and incentives aimed at empowering citizens. Some of these changes can be brought about through internal measures; others require fundamental reforms in the national administration and political support.

With the stress on partnerships to improve security of tenure for low-income communities or resolving other urban issues, local governments have to understand the motives of each of the urban actors. The equitable and holistic view for the city is what should drive local government, but all other partners will be driven by their own, narrower interests, whether they are private-sector companies, low-income communities, NGOs or middle-class interest groups. The ability to understand each partner and the ability to give and take are of vital importance for today's local authorities.

In the developing world, especially Asia, where there are many problems as well as large numbers of people; where the lines between legal and illegal blur; where issues are influenced by politics, culture, values and an accepted way of life, a middle path, in this case not looking for freehold land titles, but lease arrangements of varying time periods, can be far more successful in solving problems. Land-rental slums offer an opportunity, if the authorities play a facilitating role, to improve security of tenure for the urban poor for a given period of time.

Conclusion: the way ahead

Geoffrey Payne

ADDRESSING COMPLEXITY

This book has sought to demonstrate that tenure is central to the development of urban land and housing markets that promote economic development, and also enables the urban poor to benefit from the process and obtain shelter on terms and conditions they can afford. However, while secure tenure is an essential condition, it is not sufficient, in itself, to achieve these broader policy objectives. In this respect, it needs to be seen as part of an integrated package of policy measures that recognize the positive role played by the poor in developing urban and national economies. Measures that seek to remove the poor to the fringes of urban areas and urban society impede not only the efforts of the poor to lift themselves out of poverty, but also the social and economic development of society as a whole. They also raise the question of whether or not globalization and the commercialization of land associated with it, offers any place for the poor in urban areas.

Fortunately, the poor have not remained passive recipients of whatever governments or the private sector have offered them, but have evolved ways of obtaining land and a range of tenure options that go some way to meeting their immediate needs. The question facing policy makers therefore is how these options can form the basis of a more efficient and equitable future for urban areas, or what alternatives can be introduced.

The book has also shown that tenure and property rights is an extremely complex issue. In many countries, legal pluralism exists in which there are officially recognized statutory, customary or religious tenure systems, not to mention myriad forms of non-formal categories, each serving the needs of different social groups.

Tenure also means different things to different people. For the very poor, it is primarily a matter of being able to access any space where they can obtain a basic livelihood, such as street trading, without fear of eviction. Location is therefore more critical than the form of housing they occupy and long-term security of tenure may be less important than the ability to move when livelihood opportunities change. The approach adopted in Bangkok (see Chapter 15) illustrates a practical way in which communities of poor people have come to an arrangement with landowners to occupy land in central locations which would otherwise be far too expensive for

them, and which also puts unused land to socially and economically efficient use. While the approach depends on a social contract, which may be
peculiar to Thai society, it shows that imaginative approaches exist which
can form a way forward.

Longer-term forms of tenure become increasingly important for households with some degree of disposable income, from which they can invest
in improved housing. For these groups, perceptions of security may vary
considerably. As Chapter 14 on South Africa demonstrates, the denial of
rights to land, which the majority of black households suffered under
apartheid, means that only freehold tenure, once the exclusive preserve of
the white community, will be sufficient to make them feel secure. At the
other end of the spectrum, residents without any form of title in the 'pirate'
subdivisions of Bogotá, Colombia (Chapter 6), already feel so secure that,
for many, tenure is not a priority or even a subject of concern because the
threat of eviction is minimal and legislation entitles them to receive public services, such as water, sanitation and electricity, on the simple condition that they can pay for them. Chapter 5 shows that a similarly relaxed
attitude prevails in the informal settlements of Cairo, Egypt. In Benin,
Burkino Faso and Senegal (Chapter 7) and Turkey (Chapter 9), security also
increased over time through the efforts of local communities or civil society groups. For all these groups, tenure is a means to an end, rather than an
end in itself.

The vast majority of low-income households in urban areas fall somewhere between these two extremes and seek a more public recognition of
their rights to the land or dwellings they occupy, especially where they have
paid large sums in good faith. For them, the case studies show that any
form of tenure that protects them from forced evictions and legitimizes
them as citizens will invariably be sufficient to encourage them to invest
what savings they have in improving their homes and local environment.
Some of the innovations have evolved informally, as in Benin, Bolivia,
Burkino Faso, Colombia, Egypt, Senegal, Thailand and Turkey, while others
have been the result of governmental initiatives, as in Botswana, Brazil,
India, Kenya, Peru and eastern Europe. Yet others have been initiated or
expanded through the efforts of NGOs and civil society groups, as in Benin,
Burkino Faso and South Africa. Some are adaptations of traditional or
customary tenure arrangements, while others are recent innovations.

In some cities, formal tenure is required to obtain access to public services and facilities. This presents a major barrier to all households lacking
such status and increases pressure on the formal tenure system, which may
not be necessary and which invariably cannot be delivered by the authorities, at least in the short term. The evidence of this book confirms that
when people are able to obtain public services irrespective of their tenure
status, settlements improve through individual and collective action as
soon as people can afford it. Once perceived security is achieved, the constraint on progress by the poor is not a lack of commitment, but of
resources. The key point is that by providing a form of tenure that meets the

needs of residents *and* permits access to public services, people invest not just in their buildings, but in their local economy. As Benjamin and Bhuvaneswari (2001) have shown in the case of India, such incremental local investments by the urban poor also make a significant contribution to the development of the urban – and therefore national – economy.

THE CONTEXT OF TENURE POLICY

So what is the way ahead? First of all, it is important to locate tenure policy within a wider policy context. The ability of central or local governments to effectively manage their own land portfolios is often poor, so there is little prospect in the short term that they will acquire the capacity to manage urban land markets in general. However, it is vital that steps be taken to increase the supply of officially sanctioned urban land. To do so at a rate equal to the total scale of demand is rarely achieved, yet even this would be only sufficient to maintain existing living conditions and stop them deteriorating further. To get ahead of the game requires that planned supply is actually greater than existing total levels of demand. One way of achieving this is to tax all land at its present market value to encourage landowners holding plots for speculative future development to bring them into the market more quickly. For the poor, property taxes need not be a barrier if the forms of tenure provided yield market values, which are in turn reflected in lower tax rates – and the poor receive a benefit from making payments, as in Bogotá (see Chapter 6). In this way, tax and tenure policy can combine to increase security and revenues, while granting full citizenship rights to the poor and facilitating more efficient land markets.

Second, governments must create a legal framework that protects the rights of all citizens, especially the poor, and enables them to obtain secure shelter on terms and conditions they find acceptable. As McAuslan showed in Chapter 2, in too many countries the law operates to the benefit of the affluent few rather than the poor majority.

However, the Habitat Agenda, which all countries have now adopted, requires measures to accord all citizens equal rights and responsibilities. The process of creating such a legal framework must itself include civil society groups and the book provides ample evidence that they are already active in promoting innovative approaches in many countries, including Benin, Burkino Faso, Senegal, South Africa and Thailand. Within urban areas, land rights are often unclear and measures are required that can resolve disputes and clarify rights in ways that can avoid conflict in future. This need not result in increased litigation if community-based forms of dispute resolution can be established. At the same time, land registries need updating and computerizing, so that as new land is urbanized, rights can be recorded to provide certainty for all parties involved. A central feature of all law, including land law, should be the equal treatment of women and men.

Third, a major reason why people resort to unofficial ways of occupying and developing land is that the costs of entering the legal system are too high. Planning and building regulations and standards, together with administrative procedures, commonly represent barriers that many people are unable to overcome. It is therefore vital that governments undertake regulatory audits to assess options for reform, which can facilitate access to legal and affordable land and shelter. Such reforms will require tackling strong vested interests in both the public and private sectors, but are vital if the growth of unauthorized urban settlements is to be reduced.

Fourth, agencies providing public water, sanitation and electricity should be mandated, as in Colombia, to service all urban areas, irrespective of their tenure status, providing that residents are willing and able to pay connection and user charges. The provision of security will not, in itself, improve the quality of life of the urban poor, whereas a clean water supply, electricity, and local schools and health facilities certainly will. Related to this is the need to strengthen innovative financial instruments, so that low-income households are able to obtain credit on terms and conditions that meet their needs. Invariably, this will require the option of small loans without the necessity to offer titles as collateral.

Fifth, as Fernandes demonstrated in Chapter 12, tenure policies are more likely to succeed when they encourage the social and spatial integration of urban areas operating in conjunction with physical planning policies designed for this purpose. Options that enable low-income groups to remain in areas that might otherwise be too expensive can help reduce social tensions and stimulate the diversity which is the hallmark of dynamic cities and healthy societies. Communal tenure systems, as reviewed in the Brazilian and South African chapters, provide evidence that these can be effective options.

Finally, and perhaps most importantly, it is imperative that tenure policies recognize the links between tenure status and livelihoods.

For all – or any – of these objectives to be realized it will be necessary to strengthen the capability of public sector agencies to perform their roles more effectively. However, this should not mean acting as a supplier or developer of land, as history shows that this is not a role that governments have discharged with distinction. Instead, it requires urban authorities to make greater efforts to achieve good governance through decentralized, democratic systems of administration in which decision makers are held accountable to their local constituents and act as enablers of development by others. While the public sector can no longer aspire to control markets, they should seek to influence and regulate them by ensuring that private investments generate a benefit for the wider community, and especially the poor. Public–private partnerships can contribute to this process, providing the public sector recognizes the legitimate need for investors to make a profit, while being able to negotiate the best deal for the public. This requires public officials to have a good working knowledge of land market operations and the flexibility to negotiate terms that reflect the unique nature of each project within working procedures that are administratively consistent – no easy task even under benign conditions. Partnerships should also include civil society groups, suggesting that multi-stakeholder partnerships (MSPs) are more likely to succeed than the more narrow public–private partnerships (PPPs).

Related to public sector capability is the need to encourage professionals in both public *and* private sectors to adopt multidisciplinary working practices. At present, different professions, such as architects, engineers and surveyors and their professional institutions, tend to compete rather than co-operate, to the detriment of both the professions as a whole and the public interest they profess to serve. These sectional interests are then imposed on successive generations through the validation of vocational courses in academic institutions. Encouraging collaboration between professions and making it easier for public sector staff to work for periods in the private or community sectors without losing seniority could also promote holistic, innovative approaches.

TENURE POLICY FOR EXISTING AND NEW URBAN DEVELOPMENT

Tenure policy also has to distinguish between ways of improving security and land management for the residents of existing urban settlements and the need to facilitate access to legal land and shelter by new households. Existing residents of unauthorized settlements invariably had to fight for many years to obtain secure forms of tenure and in many cases it is their children who have inherited the increased assets created. The key point for the poor is the low initial investment required. Since freehold titles impose a premium that they are unable to pay, this suggests that incremental tenure options of the types reviewed in this book, such as the Certificate of Rights in Botswana, Community Land Trusts and Temporary Occupation Licences in Kenya, or other forms of starter title, can be effective in enabling the urban poor to avoid both illegality and the high costs of conventional titles.

Once new areas are settled using such 'intermediate' forms of tenure, incremental improvement can be facilitated by:

- registering all new plots and the details of their residents
- providing basic services
- allowing a period for resolving land disputes
- allocating property rights to recognized claimants (e.g. to occupy, use, develop, transfer, etc.)
- allocation of formal tenure (e.g. statutory, customary, religious).

SHORT- AND LONGER-TERM POLICY OPTIONS

Within tenure policies as such, it is important to distinguish between short- to medium-term options and longer-term objectives. Any tenure policy must be based on existing realities, needs and resources if it is to command popular acceptance and social legitimacy. It must also be recognized that at present the resource base and administrative capabilities of most government urban development agencies are grossly inadequate for the task of managing the processes of urban growth and balancing the competing interests of landowners, developers and the increasing number of poor households seeking shelter. Progress in Sri Lanka under the Million Houses Programme, and in Peru under the COFOPRI land-titling programme, both depended on the personal commitment of the head of government of the day and, despite major advances, lost momentum when they were replaced. In the vast majority of countries, such high-level commitment cannot be assumed and the institutional infrastructure is invariably weak.

Given its importance and complexity, it is vital that tenure policies avoid the temptation to adopt what appear to be simple solutions, such as providing the poor with individual titles. Arguments claiming, or implying, that this can of itself reduce poverty are not supported by evidence. There is no silver bullet that can solve diverse problems and, as in most aspects of life, things that appear too good to be true are usually just that. This is not to deny that the more formal tenure systems found in developed countries facilitate transparency, transferability and more efficient urban management. Moves to more formal tenure systems are undoubtedly advisable, but should be made at a rate consistent with social and cultural norms and institutional capacity. Legality is important, but legitimacy is all.

In most developing countries, urban land is generally held under private or customary tenure and is often transferred and developed for urban use without conforming to official regulations or procedures. This renders it officially illegal, even though it may only be a procedural technicality. Under these conditions, the ability of government to control development or change tenure status is restricted. Inaccurate and incomplete records of who owns what, and what rights exist over land, are compounded by limited professional staff resources, which weaken the state's ability to clarify existing tenure systems, let alone to introduce and manage new ones.

Under such conditions, progress on the ground can best be made in the short to medium term by adopting pragmatic approaches of the type reviewed in this book. Many of these enjoy a high degree of social legitimacy, are simple to administer and are already in widespread use. To replace or remove them will inevitably confuse people and could undermine existing systems without providing socially, economically and administratively viable alternatives. With a large number of tenure categories existing in most cities, radical changes will impose unpredictable consequences on urban land markets and the position of the poor. For some, such as tenants in unregularized housing, it could result in their displacement and a subsequent increase in unauthorized settlements, which policy presumably seeks to avoid. It could also result in the strict implementation of formal land tenure systems whose costs of entry preclude access by poor households.

All the evidence suggests that it is therefore advisable to identify what options exist in a city and increase the de facto security of those categories that appear to be serving the needs of the poor without inhibiting other productive development of land and efficient land markets. The key is to avoid putting all one's eggs in one tenure basket and instead spread them around to see which basket or baskets are most appropriate. Diversity should be encouraged until sufficient experience is gained and administrative capability in strengthened, at which point emphasis can be placed on a selected number of more formal options. Such an approach will also provide time for reflection and the testing of options appropriate to cultural, institutional and economic conditions.

In this respect, the key to success is to offer a range of options that provide adequate levels of security *as perceived and defined by the poor themselves.* All such options should be offered on terms and conditions that create a 'level playing field' and do not involve hidden incentives or distortions, such as selective access to subsidies. Where individual titles are offered, recipients should be made fully aware of the consequences of ownership in exposing them to property taxes and service charges and the responsibility for property maintenance. In addition, they should realize that the value of property can go down as well as up, as many households in Thailand, Hong Kong, India and the UK, among others, can testify to their cost.

FROM POLICY TO PRACTICE

How can this policy objective be achieved? The simplest approach is to establish or strengthen local administrative structures within which the views of all those involved, including landowners, developers, government officials, and particularly the poor and their representatives, can find a voice. These can help to identify the full range of formal and non-formal tenure categories that exist locally and their role within the urban land and housing markets. Where appropriate, local universities and colleges can be invited to undertake surveys of sample communities as a means of providing valuable information and exposing students to the realities of urban development with which they will have to deal on qualifying.

Having identified the existing functions that specific tenure categories are serving, it will then be necessary to identify ways in which they can be strengthened or modified so that they more effectively meet the needs of the groups served and improve access to livelihoods, services and credit, together with the functioning of land and housing markets. A good starting point, which requires modest institutional capability, would be to distinguish between settlements that it may be possible to regularize or upgrade and those that are in environmentally hazardous areas, or sites that may be needed for a public purpose. This approach would provide residents of the former with protection from the fear of removal and encourage those in the latter categories to seek alternative sites. Even for these groups, however, it will be important to give reasonable notice and offer alternative locations that offer similar benefits.

Where existing tenure systems are found to be inadequate, it may be necessary to adopt and adapt innovations from other countries. This is where some of the approaches reviewed in this book may be of assistance, if only in terms of encouraging innovation.

Before more formal tenure systems can be considered, it will be necessary to strengthen the capacity of existing land administration structures required to deliver and manage them. As Patrick McAuslan showed in Chapter 2, a legal framework that recognizes the right of the poor to equal treatment and access to land is a precondition in this respect. In most countries, he considers it will require primary legislation at the national or state level and fully costed budgets for implementation, for which secondary legislation may also be required. Consultation will also be essential at this stage if new laws are to achieve social legitimacy.

On a technical level of land administration, land surveying standards need to be reviewed to ensure that they are appropriate to local conditions. Levels of accuracy appropriate for high-value commercial areas may be unnecessary for the upgrading of informal peri-urban areas, and impose costs which militate against widespread application. Since a large proportion of land surveying is undertaken within the public sector, where resources are limited, this constrains the rate at which land can be surveyed prior to tenure being regularized in *any* form. It also encourages unauthorized payments as an incentive to process applications. In most residential areas, full surveys are unnecessary and simple 'intermediate' surveys can be undertaken with sufficient accuracy for regularization purposes. Examples of suitable techniques are presented in Davidson and Payne (2000: Technical Notes 2–8).

What longer-term systems of urban land tenure and property rights are likely to satisfy the diverse requirements discussed in this book? From the evidence available (e.g. Oswald, 1999), it seems that even in countries where formal titles are the norm (e.g. throughout Europe and the USA), a wide range of options is the most likely way forward. Obvious options include individual home ownership, leasehold, private rental, public rental, housing co-operatives, housing associations, condominium associations, equity sharing and homesteading, among others. A range of these can ensure that each tenure system is efficient and responsive to the needs of those who use it, since people will choose another option if it becomes more appropriate. The more restricted the choice, the less incentive there is for those controlling any one option to respond to the needs of those using it. A key requirement in achieving this objective will be for governments to resist the temptation to favour one form of tenure over another.

Tax incentives or other forms of subsidy may have attractive short-term benefits for selected groups, but will inevitably distort land and housing markets in ways that are unpredictable and invariably counter-productive.

It is not claimed by any of the contributors to this book that the examples of innovative approaches presented have resolved all the problems of insecure tenure in their respective cities, or that they are applicable in other cities or countries without modifications. What *is* claimed, is that they have provided greater security and official recognition than existed before and a breathing space for the urban authorities to explore options based on local traditions and needs, rather than concepts imported from outside.

As the capability of urban administrations is strengthened and they become more responsive, and as access to legal land and housing markets becomes easier for the urban poor, so the need for non-formal or unauthorized settlements may be reduced. Incorporating various non-formal systems of urban land tenure and property rights into formal systems will, however, take many years. That is why it is important to start immediately, but to proceed with caution.

Contributors

Cecile Ambert is an associate at Development Works, Johannesburg. She holds a Master of Science degree from the University of the Witwatersrand. She specializes in the fields of housing and urban land reform and integrated development planning. Other areas of interest are government institutional and fiscal systems and the impact of HIV/AIDS on development dimensions. Her recent publications include: Development, the State and its leadership in Malawi and Madagascar: the neoliberal paradigm revisited, *Africa Insight* (1997) no. 1; Alternatives to traditional development policies: acknowledging the links between security and development, *African Security Review* (1997) no. 3; Participatory planning in post-apartheid South Africa, Urban Futures Conference 2000 (http://www.wits.ac.za/urbanfutures/papers/ambert.htm).

Nora Aristizabal graduated from Pontificia Bolivariana in 1979, and has a Masters degree in urban settlements design for developing countries from MIT (1980–82). She has been in private practice since 1983. In 1989, she created her own firm with Andrés Ortíz Gomez, and has worked there since, except in 1998 when she took a sabbatical year and went to work as director of Bogota City Planning Office. She worked on the formulation of the new city land plan, as well as public space regulations. She has worked on at least 130 projects in areas such as urban planning, urban standards and regulation, low-income settlements, low-income typologies, research on formal and informal settlements, public and private space, land tenure, and many urban and architectural designs. She has presented papers at conferences on urban city planning and is a visiting lecturer for seminars and conferences in graduate programmes.

Alan Bagré is an engineer and surveyor specializing in urban land management, tenure reform, land records and information systems. He was involved in the implementation and redefinition of the Agrarian and Land Reorganization Programme, Ougadougou, Burkino Faso, where he is currently attached to the Ministry of Infrastructures, Habitat and Urban Planning.

Murat Balamir is affiliated to the City and Regional Planning Department of the Middle East Technical University (METU) Ankara, Turkey. He has degrees in architecture (from METU and the Architectural Association, London), town planning (University College London), and political sciences and public administration (Ankara University). He is a founder member of the METU Housing Research Centre.

Alain Durand-Lasserve is a research director at CNRS (Centre National de la Recherche Scientifique), France. He is currently attached to the SEDET Research Centre, University of Denis-Diderot, Paris. During the past few years he has been involved in a series of research studies on urban land tenure policies and the regularization of informal settlements in developing countries for bilateral and multilateral aid agencies in African, Asian and Latin American countries.

Fabian Farfan Espinoza was born in Sucre, Bolivia, in 1968. He qualified as an architect in 1995 from San Simon University, Cochabamba, and was awarded degrees in international construction management (1997, Lund, Sweden) and scientific research (1999, Bolivia). He teaches at the School of Architecture and is a researcher and lecturer for Promesha's programme (Programa de capacitacion para el Mejoramiento Socio-habitacional). He is also a member of the CYTED (Ciencia y tecnologia para el desarrollo) Program within the Transfer Technology and Capacity Building network and has done several research projects in the housing field, most recently 'Transfer technologies for low income groups' (Cochabamba, Bolivia) and 'Transfer technologies outlines, a Bolivian approach' (Montevideo, Uruguay).

Edesio Fernandes (Bacharel em Direito, Minas Gerais Federal University, Brazil; Especialista em Urbanismo, MGFU; LM in law in development, Warwick University, UK; PhD, Warwick University) is a part-time lecturer at the Development Planning Unit (DPU) of University College London and a senior research fellow at the University of London's Institute of Commonwealth Studies. His research interests include: urban and environmental law; planning and policy; local government and city management; and constitutional law and human rights in developing countries. He has worked as a city planner and a lecturer in Brazil (1980–86) and as a legal adviser during the national Constitution-making process (1986–88). He has also been a consultant to many governmental and non-governmental organizations in Brazil and elsewhere.

Andrés Ortíz Gomez is an architect. He graduated from Universidad Javeriana in 1985 and gained a Masters degree in urban planning in developing countries from Oxford Brookes University in 2000. He has been in private practice since 1986. In 1989, he created his own firm with Nora Aristizabal and has been working there since. He has worked on at least 100 projects in a variety of areas such as urban design, low-income housing, urban standards, low-income formal and informal settlements, land tenure and many architectural design projects. He taught on the Design School undergraduate programme at Universidad de los Andes, and is now lecturing on the urban planning graduate programme, with emphasis on real estate, at Universidad Javeriana.

Richard Grover is the deputy head of the School of Real Estate Management at Oxford Brookes University. He is an economist and chartered surveyor. He has undertaken a number of projects in Russia, Bulgaria and Romania aimed at developing university education in real estate management and putting in place the institutions needed for an efficient property market.

Moussa Gueye is a private consultant in urban planning. He specializes in land management and housing in Dakar, Senegal, where he has been involved with the German Technical Co-operation agency (GTZ) in the implementation and monitoring of the Dalifort settlement upgrading project.

Ayako Kagawa (kagawa@itc.nl) is a lecturer in the Division of Urban Planning and Management at the International Institute for Aerospace Survey and Earth Sciences (www.itc.nl), The Netherlands. She studied the COFOPRI project in 1999 on a summer fellowship from the Peruvian Government, and for this DFID-sponsored research visited Peru for three weeks in November 2000. She is currently engaged in follow-up research on land tenure in Peru.

Amitabh Kundu obtained his doctoral degree from Jawaharlal Nehru University, New Delhi, and did post-doctoral work as a Senior Fulbright Fellow at the University of Pennsylvania. He has been a visiting professor at Maison des Sciences de L'homme, Paris, and the University of Kaiserslautern, South Asian Institute Heidelberg, Germany. He has undertaken international consultancies for UNESCO, UNCHS, ILO, Government of Netherlands, University of Toronto and the Sasakawa Foundation.

Patrick McAuslan is professor of law at Birkbeck College, University of London. He specializes in land law, land tenure and land policy issues, and has worked as a consultant on land policy and land law issues in Africa, Asia and the Caribbean for over 25 years. He worked in UNCHS (Habitat) in Nairobi for three years as land management adviser to the Urban Management Programme from 1990 to 1993. He has drafted many laws on land tenure and land use planning, most recently the new land laws in Tanzania and Uganda. He spent one year in Uganda between 1999 and 2000 as the senior technical adviser on a DFID project to assist the Government of Uganda begin implementing the new Land Act. He was awarded the MBE in 2001 for services to African land tenure and the environment.

Radhika Savant Mohit is a programme specialist with the Urban Management Centre at the Asian Institute of Technology, Bangkok, Thailand. The Centre serves as the urban and environmental planning and management outreach unit under the School of Environment, Resources and Development at the AIT. An urban planner by profession, she has been involved in capacity building, advisory services, research and information dissemination, and management, in partnership with various bilateral and multilateral agencies. Radhika has worked closely with government organizations, NGOs and other stakeholders, both at a regional and local level, on various urban issues. A PhD candidate with the University of Wales, UK, her research interests are urban governance and the impact of globalization on cities.

Paul Munro-Faure is a chartered surveyor who has worked widely in the transitional economies of Central and Eastern Europe on the development of real estate markets. He recently joined the Food and Agriculture Organization of the United Nations in Rome, where he is chief of the land tenure service.

Geoffrey Payne (gkpayne@gpa.org.uk) is a housing and urban development consultant based in London. He has undertaken research, teaching, training and consultancy assignments in most parts of the world for more than 30 years and contributed to numerous international workshops and conferences. Consultancy assignments include housing sector reviews, professional training needs assessments and urban project design. Recent research has included land tenure and property rights, public–private partnerships in land for housing and regulatory frameworks for affordable housing. He has published widely and recent books include *Urban Land Tenure and Property Rights in Developing Countries: a review* (ITDG, 1997) and *Making Common Ground: public–private partnerships in land for development* (ITDG, 1999). He is an external associate adviser to the British Council and a Fellow of the Royal Society of Arts and the Royal Asiatic Society.

Lauren Royston is a principal at Development Works, an urban development organization based in Johannesburg, South Africa, which provides a service to mainly public sector clients in the fields of urban land management and integrated development planning. She obtained a Masters in development planning from the University of the Witwatersrand, Johannesburg, and began her professional career at Planact, an urban sector NGO, which assisted community-based organizations in the struggle against apartheid. She undertakes research and policy studies and advises government departments in South Africa including Land Affairs, Public Works and Local and Provincial Government. She has published on the issue of community struggles to gain access to the city and in the field of urban land management.

David Sims is an economist and urban planner who has 25 years' continuous experience as a consultant/practitioner in the developing world. Most of his work has been in Arab countries, South Asia, South-east Asia and Africa. Although of American nationality, he has made his home base in Egypt. Currently he is the team leader for the Participatory Urban Development of Manshiet Nasser Project, an upgrading effort of Cairo Governorate and German Technical Co-operation (GTZ).

Mikhail Soloviev is a member of the Russian Academy of Sciences Institute for the Problems of Information Transmission. He holds professorial appointments in real estate management at the Higher School of Economics and Academy of Privatization of Business in Moscow, and is a visiting professor at Oxford Brookes University.

José Tonato is a private consultant in urban planning, housing, urban land development and local development. He is currently deputy director of the cabinet of the Ministry of Environment, Habitat and Housing, Cotonou, Benin, in charge of the monitoring of urban projects. He also teaches at the École Africaine des Métiers de l'Architecture et de l'Urbanisme in Lomé, Togo.

Jan Turkstra (turkstra@itc.nl) is a senior lecturer in the Division of Urban Planning and Management at the International Institute for Aerospace Survey and Earth Sciences (www.itc.nl), The Netherlands. Since 1988, he has been involved in an educational programme on urban management in Lima, Trujillo and Arequipa, with an emphasis on urban land administration and urban applications of Geographical Information Systems.

Saad S. Yahya is principal of Saad Yahya and Associates, a Nairobi firm of land economists and city planners specializing in land and urbanization issues in east, central and southern Africa. He is a former Dean of the University of Nairobi Faculty of Architecture, Design and Development. He has published numerous books and scientific papers in the fields of land policy, housing and real estate.

Notes

CHAPTER 1

1. The author gratefully acknowledges comments on drafts of this chapter from other contributors to the book and participants in the Workshop 'Securing land for the urban poor' at the UN meeting in Fukuoka, Japan, October 2001.
2. Granting the right not to develop or refusing other parties access to or use of the property.
3. Benefits that accrue due to value increases in property even if these are due to external factors.
4. United Nations data (1998) indicate that the world's urban population will double from 2 billion in 2000 to 4.1 billion in 2030. Since most of this growth is expected to take place in developing countries, the built up area of towns and cities will continue to increase rapidly.

CHAPTER 2

1. The Development and Planning Commission established by the DFA has produced a resource document and a manual on The Chapter One Principles of the Development Facilitation Act (Pretoria, 1999), which discuss and explain the principles and show how they can be used in specific cases.
2. '"*Beneficial occupier*" means in relation to the occupation of land in a land development area where land development takes the form of upgrading an existing settlement, any person who has been in peaceful and undisturbed occupation of such land for a continuous period of not less than five years.' Section 1 DFA.

CHAPTER 4

1. From the Ministry of Presidency it was later transferred to the Ministry of Transport, Construction and Dwellings and is at present under the Ministry of Justice.
2. There is a question about the number of titles registered in RPU: how many are those that were titled and registered following all the processes from Process 0 to Process 2 by COFOPRI? This question arises as there are substantial numbers of titles that have been transferred from RPI, the traditional registry, to RPU, but its extent and procedures have not been revealed in this investigation.
3. COFOPRI Internal Statistics (March 2000).

CHAPTER 5

1. The most important source of information were the investigations commissioned or carried out in 2000 by the Institute for Liberty and Democracy (under contract with the Egyptian Center for Economic Studies and funded by USAID) on informal residential property in Egypt. Also used were studies carried out in 1999–2000 for the GTZ-supported Participatory Urban Management Program. Knowledge of informal tenure in Egypt also comes directly from the author's experience in a number of urban projects, the most recent of which is the ongoing Participatory Upgrading of Manshiet Nasser Project (Cairo Governorate, GTZ, and KfW). None of this material has been published. The author thanks Mona El-Shorbagi in many aspects of this paper.
2. Following the 1996 military decrees, individual cases of demolition and eviction have become more common, but these follow lengthy court procedures.
3. The process of planning and distribution of public desert land for urban development in Egypt is a textbook case of weak land management.
4. However, Article 874 of the Civil Code, which specifies this right, is said to be cancelled.
5. Census of Egypt, 1996, volume on Housing Conditions for Cairo Governorate.
6. The Cairo ring road project is an interesting case. This massive undertaking, now more or less complete, required significant demolition of informal housing on agricultural land (and some on desert state land). Although the Ministry of Housing could have used police powers for eviction and demolition, it chose to compensate building owners, based on a formula of LE3000–5000 per inhabitable room.
7. This situation is not always the case. In some subdivisions where plots are untitled, land prices can be much higher than in similar subdivisions where land is fully registered, for the simple reason that in the former the building permit regime does not apply and thus there is no limit to the degree of exploitation (height and plot coverage), whereas in the completely formal area, building regulations are fairly strictly enforced.
8. Another reason that the proposed mortgage system will not be popular is that, according to World Bank estimates, only families with steady incomes above LE1500–2000 per month are likely to be candidates. (Note that the median urban family income in Egypt is estimated to be in the LE550–700 per month range where US1$ equals LE3.85).
9. The rate of natural increase in Egypt has been brought down to almost 2 per cent per annum, whereas family formation continues to grow at over 3 per cent per year.

CHAPTER 7

1. Due to the state monopoly on land, prohibition of private land and housing development until the late 1980s, lack of any appropriate regulatory framework, weakness of mortgage credit.
2. The rate of urbanization in Benin has risen from 27 per cent in 1979 to 36 per cent in 1992. About 50 per cent of the country's urban population is concentrated in the capital city of Cotonou, which had an estimated population of 810 000 inhabitants in 2000. The second and third largest cities are Porto Novo and Parakou. The rate of population growth in Cotonou decreased from 8 per cent between 1960 and 1980, to 5 per cent in the 1990s. There are two main reasons for this: first, environmental constraints (a large part of the city is exposed to flooding twice a year), and second the urbanization of a new area to the west

of the city in the Abomey Calavi district, which has reduced population pressure on the city. Population growth has led to an accelerated spatial extension of the urbanized area: in the mid-1990s, it covered more than 10 000 hectares, of which only 1500 had a proper sewerage and drainage system.

3.   The rate of urbanization in Burkina Faso (population living in towns and cities of 10 000 and more) has risen from 6 per cent in 1960, the year the country became independent, to 17 per cent in 1996. If we look at the towns of 5000 inhabitants, the rate of urbanization is around 25 per cent. Between 1960 and 1996 (date of the last census), the number of towns and cities with a population of 10 000 inhabitants and more has increased from 3 to 13. As in other countries of the subregion, population tends to be concentrated in the two main cities: Ougadougou, the capital, where the population jumped from 173 000 in 1975 to 752 000 in 1996, and Bobodioulasso (115 000 inhabitants in 1975 to 312 000 in 1996). The urban growth rate in secondary and small towns is much less.

4.   Senegal has a population of 8.5 million (1996 data). Its rate of urbanization is 45 per cent. About 55 per cent of the urban population live in the Dakar metropolitan area, which includes the twin city of Pikine. Dakar contributes 80 per cent to the GDP. Population pressure on Dakar, combined with poverty and insufficient provision of land for housing by the public and private formal sectors, has accelerated the expansion of irregular settlements. In 1996, about 30 per cent of the population of Dakar was living in informal settlements, 60 per cent of the population of Pikine, and 65 per cent of the population of Rufisque.

5.   The term informal settlement, or 'spontaneous' settlement, refers to the following situations: (i) traditional villages where customary tenure still predominates, but where rights have not been registered; (ii) slums that have developed in vacant, squatted or rented land within the densely urbanized areas; (iii) squatter settlements on public land (usually public domain of the State) (Gueye, 2000).

6.   Such as the Burkinabe Movement for People and Human Rights (Mouvement Burkinabe des Droits de l'Homme et des Peuples, MBDHP).

CHAPTER 8

1.   The Master Plan stipulates that a large number of migrants, because of their 'impoverished rural background' and dependence on the agro-based activities, often create serious environmental problems in the heart of the city. The plan, therefore, recommends relocation of these people and diversion of fresh rural migrants towards the 'urban villages' outside the city limits, where they can engage themselves in their traditional activities.

2.   The cost and price estimates of various items in the text are given in Indian rupees. One may obtain the equivalent in US$, by taking one dollar to be worth Rs50 at the time of the surveys in 2000.

3.   This would enable the local authority to avoid dealing individually with a host of landowners.

4.   The MCD has been reluctant to service these areas due to structural deficiencies and the standards of development here being less than the norms of the Master Plan. Further, these generate little revenue for the local government.

5.   In practice, however, those who could produce evidence of being employed by any private or public agency before 1990 or had given birth to a child in Delhi or even received a letter in Delhi were given the identity cards.

6.   Many among them worked in connivance with the employees of Delhi Development Authority, which had the responsibility of relocation.

7. *Pradhans* are considered to be the leaders of the whole or a part of a slum colony.
8. Unfortunately, only a few – about 5 per cent – among these had a legal connection. The remainder took connections by paying a fixed amount to households with meters.
9. Tigri Khurd and Papankala are the other resettlement colonies that have been included in the larger study conducted by the author.

CHAPTER 10

1. In Cochabamba, and possibly elsewhere in Bolivia, they have a method of payment called *anticredico* (pronounced anti-CRE-dee-co). Anticredico works like this: you give someone a large sum of money (invariably in US dollars) to use something, then when you are done with that thing they give you the money back. When we told people we were looking for a house, they all told us that anticredico was a great deal, the way to go. After all, you get your money back! It costs you nothing (but the interest you forgo). Travel diary, June 1999.
2. Around 2500 Cochabamba's citizens applied for a new passport to travel abroad. The most common foreign countries visited by these people are EU, Argentina, Chile, Spain and Italy. The Migration Department Statistics showed that between December 2000 and January 2001 and 26 344 people got a personal passport and 3761 a sheet passport (groups). In relation to the country's population 0.38 per cent of people left the country just from Cochabamba city. (*Los Tiempos Journal*, 27 March 2001)
3. Current regulations stipulate that the property's user is the one who has to pay the taxation fees, but as shown in this example, both parties can reach an agreement in order to share the expenses.
4. *Los Tiempos* (Newspaper) Economy, 18 January 1999, Cochabamba, Bolivia.

CHAPTER 11

1. US$1 = P3.5.

CHAPTER 12

1. The case study of Porto Alegre was conducted together with Betania de Moraes Alfonsin.
2. For an account of the process of urban development in Brazil, see Fernandes (2000b) and Fernandes and Rolnik (1998).
3. For a more detailed discussion on the process of formation of *favelas* and *loteamentos*, see Fernandes (1997).
4. For an analysis of the constitutional chapter on urban policy, see Fernandes (1995).
5. For a general critique of the regularization programmes in Brazil, see Fernandes (2000a).
6. For a more detailed discussion of this topic, see Fernandes (2000a).
7. For a discussion on the implications of the Civil Code, see Fernandes (1995).
8. For a more detailed analysis of Belo Horizonte's PRO-FAVELA, see Fernandes (1995).

9. For a general discussion on the CRRU, see Weigand (2001); for more information on the utilization of the CRRU in Diadema, see Afonso and Liso (1998).
10. For a general account of Porto Alegre's 'popular administration' agenda see
Allegretti (2000); for a discussion of the city's participatory budgeting process,
see Abers (2000); see also Santos (1998) and Goldsmith and Vainer (2001).
11. Although no specific research has been done in either Porto Alegre or Recife to
assess the impact of the AEIS legislation on the land market, an original and
detailed study with this objective was conducted between 1992 and 1996 in
Diadema, where the AEIS legislation has been combined with the CRRU in
public land. The study's main finding confirms the hypothesis that the creation
of AEIS has a decisive impact on the dynamics of the land market, thus
enabling the municipality to undertake its social housing programme; see
Hereda et al. (1996).
12. Both Porto Alegre's municipal administration and the state government's Special Housing Secretariat have formulated comprehensive programmes aimed at
legalizing tenure conditions in *loteamentos.*
13. The *usucapiao* sentence in Jaboatao dos Guararapes is even more original
given the fact that the case was brought to court collectively by a group
of residents; the city's ground-breaking tenure policies have been discussed
in several master's dissertations presented at the Federal University of
Pernambuco's Urban Development Department.
14 . An important legal development in Porto Alegre consists of the 'Projeto More
Legal' (Live Legally Project) that has been conducted since 1996 by the judicial agency in charge of supervising the local land registry offices, aiming to
facilitate the legalization of *loteamentos* and *favelas.*
15. For an analysis of the regularization programmes in Recife, see Assies (1994),
Rabaroux (1997) and Maia (1995).
16. For a detailed evaluation of the first ten years of PREZEIS, see the report jointly
published by the local NGOs FASE, ETAPAS and Centro Josue de Castro (1999).
The survey focused on PREZEIS's political and organizational aspects, concluding that despite the programme's significant achievements, there is still
room for improvement in managing capacity and reach, requiring further
resources. A fundamental problem is the need to provide faster responses to the
communities' needs through more effective upgrading works and legalization
strategies. The survey's main conclusion is that a more productive system
would enable the replacement of councils existing in areas properly regularized
with a monitoring system, liberating the scarce technical and financial
resources for other, still neglected, areas. It is interesting to note that the survey
failed to give any special treatment to the nature and implications of the legal-
political fundamentals of the tenure legalization programme. This implies that
the impact and importance of the choice of legal-political instruments adopted
in terms of the programme's direction, problems and successful development
is not sufficiently recognized. The interviews conducted with many such people confirmed this perception. For a detailed report on the residents' view of the
regularization process, see FASE, ETAPAS, Centro Josue de Castro, DED and
GTZ (2000).
17. For a discussion of this issue in Coronel Fabriciano and other settlements in
Recife, see Souza (2001). It should be mentioned that a wealth of educational
material has been distributed over the years by governmental agencies and
NGOS. The particular issue of the nature of the CRRU was dealt with, for example, in a special leaflet prepared for Coronel Fabriciano's residents back in 1983.
The legal-political history of the area is told in fascinating verse, including several remarks on the superior importance of possession rights over individual
property rights.

CHAPTER 14

1. For example, the nationally binding principles for land development, contained in the Development Facilitation Act of 1995 establish that: 'Land development should result in security of tenure, provide for the widest possible range of tenure alternatives. . .' (3[1][k]). Similarly the Housing White Paper of 1994 asserts that: 'Secure tenure is a key cornerstone of Government's approach towards providing housing to people in need. . . Subsidy policy will therefore be designed to provide for the fullest range of tenure options. . .' (section 5.3.3).
2. At the time of writing the US$ was 7.7 to the South African Rand.
3. Chapter 2 also refers to the Development Facilitation Act. The Act will be repealed if the Land Use Management Bill is enacted. The intention is to replace the multiple land development laws and associated procedures with a single route to township establishment.
4. Cope Housing Association is a Johannesburg-based co-operative housing institution active, since the early 1990s, in the promotion of co-operative housing models. Cope's activities are defined both in terms of the projects it is involved in, and in shaping the nature of the housing legislation, policy and programmes pertaining to housing delivery. The Norwegian government has provided financial and technical support to the organization.

CHAPTER 15

1. Klong Toey is an informal settlement built on land belonging to the Port Authority of Thailand. In 1979, evictions were carried out before the community, supported by a local NGO and under pressure from the community the Port Authority, agreed to a land-sharing scheme.
2. US$1 = Bt45, May 2001, Thai Farmers Bank.
3. The Thai measure for land is 1 wah^2 = 4 m^2. 1 Rai = 1600 m^2.
4. US$1 = Bt25.61, 1996.
5. US$1 = Bt47.25, 1997.
6. US$1 = Bt25.61, 1996.
7. US$1 = Bt45, May 2001, Thai Farmers Bank.
8. US$1 = Baht 45, May 2001, Thai Farmers Bank. 1 Rai = 1600 m^2.
9. US$1 = Bt 25.29, 1990.
10. To protect personal identities of respondents, individuals are referred to by their initials.

Bibliography

CHAPTER 1

Abrams, H. (1966) *Housing in the Modern World – man's struggle for shelter in an urbanizing world*, Faber and Faber, London.

Angel, S. (Ed.) (1983) *Land for Housing the Poor*, Select Books, Singapore.

Angel, S. (2001) Comments on Hernando de Soto's 'The Mystery of Capital', contribution to roundtable discussion, Interplan, June 2001 (http://interplan.org).

Barnes, G., Land tenure issues in the Third World, *The Canadian Surveyor*, vol. 39(4), 1985, pp.437–39.

Baross, P. (1983) The articulation of land supply for popular settlements in Third World cities, in Angel, S., *Land for Housing the Poor*, Select Books, Singapore.

De Soto, H. (1989) *The Other Path: the invisible revolution in the Third World*, I.B. Taurus, London.

De Soto, H. (2000) *The Mystery of Capital: why capitalism triumphs in the West and fails everywhere else*, Basic Books, New York.

Doebele, W. (1983) Concepts of urban land tenure, in Dunkerley, H., *Urban Land Policy: issues and opportunities*, Oxford University Press, Oxford.

Doebele, W., The evolution of concepts of land tenure in developing countries, *Habitat International*, vol. 11(1), 1987.

Fernandes, E. (2001) Comments on Hernando de Soto's 'The Mystery of Capital', contribution to roundtable discussion, Interplan, June 2001 (http://interplan.org).

Gilbert A. (2001) On the mystery of capital and the myths of Hernando de Soto: what difference does legal title make? Paper presented at the European Science Foundation/Network-Association of European Researchers on Urbanization in the South (N-AERUS) International Workshop, Leuven, Belgium, 23–26 May 2001 (www.naerus.org).

Mabogunje, A. (1990) Perspective on urban land and urban management in sub-Saharan Africa, World Bank Africa Technical Infrastructure Department mimeo.

Malpas, P. and Murie, A. (1999) *Housing Policy and Practice*, Macmillan, London.

Malpezzi, S. (2001) Brief notes on housing tenure and development indicators, notes prepared for Cities Alliance meeting, Washington, D.C., September, mimeo.

Mangin, W. (Ed.) (1970) *Peasants in Cities: readings in the anthropology of urbanization*, Houghton Mifflin, New York.

McAuslan, P. (1985) *Urban Land and Shelter for the Poor*, Earthscan/International Institute for Environment and Development, London.

McAuslan, P. (1989) Land law, tenure and registration: issues and options, paper presented to the Urban Land Management Seminar, World Bank, Washington, D.C.

Oswald, A. (1999) The housing market and Europe's unemployment: a non-technical paper, working paper available at www.andrewoswald.com

Oswald, A., Buying: why it's bad for you, *Guardian*, 4 August 2001.

Payne, G. (1989) *Informal Housing and Land Subdivisions in Third World Cities: a review of the literature*, Oxford Polytechnic (now Oxford Brookes University), Oxford.

Payne, G. (1997) *Urban Land Tenure and Property Rights in Developing Countries: a review*, IT Publications, London.

Payne, G., Urban land tenure policy options: titles or rights?, *Habitat International*, vol. 25(3), 2001.

Persaud, T. (1992) *Housing Delivery System and the Urban Poor: a comparison among six Latin American countries*, World Bank, Latin America and the Caribbean Technical Department Regional Studies Program Report No 23, Washington, D.C.

Turner, J.F.C. Lima's Barriadas and Corralones: suburbs versus slums, *Ekistics*, March 1965, pp.152–55.

Turner, J.F.C. Barriers and channels for housing development in modernizing countries, *Journal of the American Institute of Planners*, vol. 33(3), 1967.

United Nations (1973) *Urban Land Policies and Land-use Control Measures*, vols 1–5, UN, New York.

United Nations (1996) *An Urbanizing World: global report on human settlements 1996*, Oxford University Press, Oxford.

United Nations (1998) *World Urbanization Prospects: the 1996 revision*, UN Population Division, Department of Social and Economic Affairs of the United Nations Secretariat, New York, Table A3, p.97.

World Bank (2000) *A Strategic View of Urban and Local Government Issues: implications for the Bank*, World Bank, Washington, D.C. (reference to the November 1999 version).

World Bank (1993) *Housing: enabling markets to work*, World Bank policy paper, World Bank, Washington, D.C.

CHAPTER 2

DFID (2001) *Strategies for Achieving the International Development Targets: meeting the challenge of poverty in urban areas*, DFID, London.

Durand-Lasserve, A. with Clerc, V. (1996), *Regularization and Integration of Irregular Settlements: lessons for experience*, UMP Working Paper Series 6, Nairobi.

Fernandes, E. (1995) *Law and Urban Change in Brazil*, Avebury, Aldershot.

Fernandes, E. and Varley, A. (1998) *Illegal Cities: law and urban change in developing countries*, Zed Books, London.

Kombe, W.J., Regularizing housing land development during the transition to market-led demand in Tanzania, *Habitat International*, vol. 24, 2000, pp.167–84.

McAuslan, P. (2002a) Land in the city: the role of law in reforming urban land markets, in *Bringing the Law Back In*, Ashgate, Aldershot.

McAuslan, P. (2002b) Land tenure, the urban poor and the law in Bangladesh: implementing the Habitat Agenda, in *Bringing the Law Back In*, Ashgate, Aldershot.

McAuslan, P. (2002c) Men behaving badly: a narrative on land law reform, in Jones, G. (Ed.) (forthcoming).

CHAPTER 3

Andrusz, G. (1992) The Soviet Union: an introduction, in Turner, B., Hegedus, J. and Tosics, I. (Eds) *The Reform of Housing in Eastern Europe and the Soviet Union*, Routledge, London, pp.237–44.

Basle Committee on Banking Supervision (1988) *International Convergence of Capital Measurement and Capital Standards*, Basle.

Bessonova, O. (1992) The reform of the Soviet housing model: the search for a concept, in Turner, B., Hegedus, J. and Tosics, I. (Eds) *The Reform of Housing in Eastern Europe and the Soviet Union*, Routledge, London, pp.276–89.

Bulgaria (2000) Country note: Bulgaria, *Workshop on Housing Finance in Transitional Economies*, Paris 19–20 June, Organisation for Economic Co-operation and Development

Centre of Economic Analysis at the Russian Federation Government (1994) *Russia – 1994: economic situation*, Moscow.

De Soto, H. (2000) *The Mystery of Capital: why capitalism triumphs in the West and fails everywhere else*, Bantam Press, New York.

EBRD (1999) *Transition Report 1999*, European Bank for Reconstruction and Development

Grabmullerova, D. (2000) Country paper of the Czech Republic, *Workshop on Housing Finance in Transitional Economies*, Paris 19–20 June, Organisation for Economic Co-operation and Development.

Grover, R.J. and Soloviev, M. (2000) *Real Estate Management*, Academy of Privatisation and Business for the Russian Federation Ministry of State Property Management, Moscow.

Hardt, J. and Manning, D. (2000) European mortgage markets: structure, funding and future development, *Workshop on Housing Finance in Transitional Economies*, Paris 19–20 June, Organisation for Economic Co-operation and Development.

Hegedus, V. and Varhegyi, E., The crisis in housing financing in Hungary in the 1990s, *Urban Studies*, vol. 37(9), 1999, pp.1619–41

Hoffman, M.L. and Koleva, M.T., Housing policy reform in Bulgaria, *CITIES* August 1993, pp.208–23

(IMF) International Monetary Fund (1998) *Romania: statistical appendix*, IMF Staff Country Report no. 98/123, Washington, D.C.

Jakobson, I. (2000) The housing sector in Estonia, *Workshop on Housing Finance in Transitional Economies*, Paris 19–20 June, Organisation for Economic Co-operation and Development.

Lawson, D., Social climbers, *Property Week*, 9 June 2000.

Lithuania (2000) Country note: Lithuania, *Workshop on Housing Finance in Transitional Economies*, Paris 19–20 June, Organisation for Economic Co-operation and Development.

McCrone, G. and Stephens, M. (1995) *Housing Policy in Britain and Europe*, University of London Press, London.

Moscow Government websites, www.mos.ru, www.md.mos.ru

Munro-Faure, P. and Evtimov, V. (2000) *Urban Property Market Study*, World Bank Bulgaria Real Estate Registration and Cadastre Project, Sofia.

National Commission for Statistics (1998) *Romanian Statistical Yearbook 1998*, National Commission for Statistics, Bucharest

OECD (1998) *OECD Economic Surveys 1997–1998: Romania*, Organisation for Economic Co-operation and Development, Paris.

Romania (2000) Country note: Romania, *Workshop on Housing Finance in Transitional Economies*, Paris 19–20 June, Organisation for Economic Co-operation and Development.

Rose, L., Thomas, J. and Tumler, J. (2000) *Land Tenure Issues in Post-Conflict Countries: the case of Bosnia and Herzegovina*, Deutsche Gesellschaft fur Technische Zusammenarbeit Sector Project Land Tenure in Development Co-operation.

Slovak Republic (2000) National report on funding housing construction in the Slovak Republic, *Workshop on Housing Finance in Transitional Economies*, Paris 19–20 June, Organisation for Economic Co-operation and Development.

Stephens, M. (2000) International models of housing finance, *Workshop on Housing Finance in Transitional Economies*, Paris 19–20 June, Organisation for Economic Co-operation and Development.

Szilagyi, K. (2000) Country note: Hungary, *Workshop on Housing Finance in Transitional Economies*, Paris 19–20 June, Organisation for Economic Co-operation and Development.

Vecvagare, L. (2000) Housing finance in Latvia, *Workshop on Housing Finance in Transitional Economies*, Paris 19–20 June, Organisation for Economic Co-operation and Development.

Yasui, T. (2000) Housing finance in transitional economies overview, *Workshop on Housing Finance in Transitional Economies*, Paris 19–20 June, Organisation for Economic Co-operation and Development.

CHAPTER 4

Baross, P. (1990) Sequencing land development: the price implications of legal and illegal settlement growth, in Baross, P. and van der Linden, J. (Eds) *The Transformation of Land Supply in Third World Countries*, Avery, Newcastle-upon-Tyne.

Calderón, J. (1990) *Las Ideas Urbanas en el Peru (1958–1989)*, Instituto de Desarrollo Urbano (CENCA), Lima, Peru.

Calderón, J. (1998) Regularisation of urban land in Peru, *Land Lines*, May 1998, Vol 10(3) Newsletter, Lincoln Institute of Land Policy, Cambridge, MA.

COFOPRI (1999) *Annual Report 1998*, COFOPRI, Lima.

De Soto, H. (1989) *The Other Path: the invisible revolution in the Third World*, Harper & Row, New York.

De Soto, H. (2000) *The Mystery of Capital*, Bantam Press/Random House, London.

De Souza, F.A.M., Land tenure security and housing improvements in Recife, Brazil, *Habitat International*, vol.23(1), 1999, pp.19–33.

Government of Peru (2001). Crean las Comisiones Provinciales de Formalizacion de la Propiedad Informal, Decreto Supremo No. 005–2001–JUS, *El Peruano: normas legales*, 4 March, Lima.

Mangin, W., Latin American squatter settlements; a problem and a solution, *Latin American Research Review*, vol. II(3), 1967.

McLaughlin, J. and de Soto, H., Property formalisation: the PROFORM solution, *South African Journal of Surveying and Mapping*, vol. 22(5), 1994.

Molina, U. (1990) Bogota: competition and substitution between urban land markets, in Baross, P. and van der Linden, J. (Eds) *The Transformation of Land Supply in Third World Countries*, Avery, Newcastle-upon-Tyne.

Payne, G. (1997) *Urban Land Tenure and Property Rights in Developing Countries, A Review*, IT Publications/ODA, London.

Riofrio, G. (1991) Producir la Ciudad (popular) de los '90, Centro de Estudios y Promoción del Desarrollo (DESCO), Lima.

Siembieda, W. (1994) Land and housing in parallel markets: how self-help planning functions, in *Manejo del Suelo Urbano*, Programa de Gestión Urbana, Quito.

Turner, J. (1976) *Housing by People*, Marion Boyars, London.

UNCHS (1996) *The Habitat Agenda: goals and principles, commitments and global plan of action*, Habitat II, UNCHS, Istanbul.
Werlin, H., The slum upgrading myth, *Urban Studies*, vol.36(9), 1999.
World Bank (1997) Implementation of the National Formalisation Plan, Annex A5, Peru – Urban Property Rights Project, World Bank internal paper, World Bank, Washington, D.C.
World Bank (1998) Project Appraisal Document, Report No.18245PE, Peru – Urban Property Rights Project, Washington, D.C.

CHAPTER 5

Abt Associates Inc. and Dames and Moore Inc. (1982) *Informal Housing in Egypt*, USAID, Cairo.
Eiweida, A. (2000) Egypt's Experience with Participatory Upgrading – lessons learnt and not learnt, first draft, for the Participatory Urban Management Programme, GTZ, Cairo.
Government of Egypt, Social Fund for Development (2000) Multi-Donor Review of SFD – final report, Cairo.
Sims, D. (2000) Residential Informality in Greater Cairo: typologies, representative areas, quantification, valuation, and causal factors, for the Egyptian Real Estate Formalization Study, Egyptian Center for Economic Studies and the Institute for Liberty and Democracy, Cairo.

CHAPTER 6

Agreement 6 (1990) Bogotá's regulation from 1990 to 2000.
Alcaldia Mayor de Bogota (2000) *Desmarginalizacion* managerial report.
Alcaldia Mayor de Bogota (2000) *Metrovivienda* concept and starting procedures.
Caja de Vivienda Popular (2000) 'General diagnosis about land tenure for Bogotá'
Caja de Vivienda Popular (2000) Programme Titular, Bogotá.
Colombian Civil Code.
Corporacion Minuto de Dios (1999) Institutional document, Bogotá.
Decree 1052 (1998).
Decree 161 (1997) Public Land Tenure.
Decree 619 (2000) 'Bogotá's Urban Plan'.
Defensoria del Espacio Publico (2000) 'Managerial report', Bogotá.
Departamento Administrativo de Planeacion Distrital (1997) Bogotá's population report, The Municipality Planning Office.
Departamento Administrativo de Planeacion Distrital (2000) Legalisation document, Bogotá.
Gilbert, A. (1998) *The Latin American City*, Latin America Bureau, London.
Jimenez, L. (1998) Low-income housing study, Bogotá.
Law 9 (1989) Colombian urban reform.

CHAPTER 7

African NGO Habitat II Caucus (1996) *Citizenship and Urban Development in Africa. Popular Cities for their Inhabitants*, prepared for Habitat II, Istanbul, June 1996.

Africities (2000) *African Charter of Partnership between Inhabitants and Local Collectivities*, Windhoek, Namibia, 23 May.

Annales de la Recherche Urbaine, Special issue on: Régularisations de propriétés. March, No. 66, 1995, Plan Urbain, Ministère de l'Equipement, des Transports et du Tourisme.

Bagré, S.A. (1999) Land management and tenure security in Burkino Faso, paper presented at Tenure Security Policies in South African, Brazilian, Indian and Sub-Saharan African Cities: a comparative analysis, Centre of Applied Legal Studies, Johannesburg, 27–28 July,

Bagré, S.A. (2001) Systèmes de sécurisation foncière au Burkina Faso, contribution to the research project on Innovative Approaches to Tenure for the Urban Poor, Geoffrey Payne and Associates.

Becker, C. (1990) *L'aménagement des quartiers d'habitat spontané à Ouagadougou, Burkina Faso*, University of Amsterdam.

Benton, L., Beyond legal pluralism: towards a new approach to law in the informal sector, *Social and Legal Studies* vol. 3, 1994, pp.223–42, Sage, London.

Comby, J. (1998) *Étude préparatoire à la réforme du droit foncier au Bénin*, ADEF.

Durand-Lasserve, A. (1993) Conditions de mise en place des systemes d'information foncière dans les villes d'Afrique Sub-Saharienne Francophone, Programme de Gestion Urbaine, PNUD-Banque Mondiale, document de travail no. 8.

Durand-Lasserve, A. (2000) Security of land tenure for the urban poor in developing cities. Home ownership ideology v/s efficiency and equity, paper presented at the Global Conference on the Urban Future, Urban 21, Berlin, 4–6 July.

Durand-Lasserve, A., assisted by Clerc, V. (1996) Regularization and integration of irregular settlements: lessons from experience, Urban Management Programme, Working Paper Series No. 6. Nairobi: UNDP/UNCHS(Habitat)/World Bank UMP.

Durand-Lasserve, A., in collaboration with Tribillon, J.F. (1995) *Urban Land Management, Regularization Policies and Local Development in Africa and the Arab States*, Urban Management Programme, Research and Development Division, Nairobi.

Durand-Lasserve, A., Sall, C. and Ndaye S. (1993) *Simplification des procédures pour une régularisation à grande échelle à Dakar*, Ministère de l'Urbanisme et de l'Habitat, DUA-GTZ.

Environment and Urbanization, Funding community level intiatives: the role of NGOs and other intermediary institutions in funding and supporting low-income households to improve shelter, infrastructure and services, vol. 5 (1), 1993.

Farvacque, C. and McAuslan, P. (1992) Reforming urban land policies and institutions in developing countries, Urban Management Programme Policy Paper no. 5, World Bank, Washington D.C.

Fernandes, E. and Varley, A. (Eds) (1998) *Illegal Cities: law and urban change in developing countries*, Zed Books, London.

Fourie, C. (2000) *Best Practices Analysis on Access to Land and Security of Tenure*, United Nations Centre for Human Settlements (Habitat), Land Management series no. 8 (forthcoming).

Gueye, M. (2000) Note sur la politique de régularisation foncière au Sénégal, 1986–2000, contribution to the research project on Innovative Approaches to Tenure for the Urban Poor, Geoffrey Payne and Associates.

Guiebo, J., Bagré, A., Belemsagha, D. and Kibtonré, G. (1994) *Gestion foncière urbaine, politique de régularisation et développement local en Afrique. Étude de cas: l'expérience du Burkina Faso*. Ouagadougou.

Groupement de Recherche INTERURBA and Association Internationale des Techniciens, Experts et Chercheurs (AITEC) (1995) Cities in developing countries. integration of irregular settlements, *Current Questions in Asia and Latin America*, Pratiques Urbaines no. 12. Interurba, Paris.

Hernandez, A. and Tribillon, J-F. (1994) Projet de Réhabilitation et de Gestion Urbaine (P.R.G.U.), contribution à un état du droit et des pratiques d'urbanisme et d'aménagement foncier. Rapport soumis au SERHAU-SEM, Cotonou.

Imothep-Planurba (1997) *Étude de la stratégie de l'habitat urbain au Bénin.* Rapport final.

Institut des Sciences et des Techniques de l'Equipement (ISTED) (1998) *Dynamique de l'urbanisation de l'Afrique au sud du Sahara,* sous la direction de Michel Arnaud, Groupe de Travail Mécanismes et Logiques de l'Urbanisation en Afrique au sud du Sahara, Ministère des Affaires Etrangères – Coopération et Francophonie.

Mabogunje, A.L. (1992) *Perspective on urban land and urban management policies in sub-Saharan Africa,* World Bank Technical Paper No. 196, Washington, D.C.

Mathieu, P., Delville P. and Ouédraogo H. (2000) *Sécuriser les transactions foncières au Burkina Faso: étude sur l'évolution des transactions foncières au Burkina Faso,* Rapport de Synthèse, GRET.

McAuslan, P. (1998) Urbanisation, law and development: a record of research, in Fernandes, E. and Varley, A. (Eds) *Illegal Cities: law and urban change in developing countries,* Zed Books, London, pp.18–52.

Ndoye, D. (2000) *Le droit des terres du Domaine National et du Domaine de l'Etat au Sénégal,* Les Editions Juridiques Africaines, Dakar.

Oloude, B. (1999) Land issues in French-speaking sub-Saharan African countries: the experience from Benin, paper presented at Tenure Security Policies in South African, Brazilian, Indian and Sub-Saharan African Cities: a comparative analysis, Centre of Applied Legal Studies, Johannesburg, 27–28 July.

Payne, G. (1997) *Urban Land Tenure and Property Rights in Developing Countries: a review,* IT Publications/Overseas Development Administration (ODA), London.

Payne, G. (Ed.) (1999) *Making Common Ground: public–private partnerships in land for housing,* IT Publications, London.

Platteau, J.P., The evolutionary theory of land rights as applied to sub-Saharan Africa: a critical assessment. *Development and Change,* 1996, p.27.

Rakodi, C. (1994) Property markets in African cities, draft, mimeo, provided by the author.

Rochegude, A. (1998) Décentralisation, acteurs locaux et fonciers; mise en perspective juridique des textes sur la décentralisation et le foncier, Ministère Délégué à la Coopération et à la Francophonie.

Shelter Forum (1999) *Security of Tenure in Urban Settlements,* Shelter Forum Annual Event Report, Nairobi.

Tonato, J. (2000) Accès au foncier et sécurisation de l'occupation en milieu urbain au Bénin, contribution to the research project on Innovative Approaches to Tenure for the Urban Poor, Geoffrey Payne and Associates.

Tribillon, J-F. (1992) *Instruments d'aménagement et de gestion foncière urbaine africaine. Manuel à l'usage des techniciens, des administrateurs et des élus locaux,* ACT Consultants, Paris.

Tribillon, J-F. (1993) *Villes africaines. Nouveau manuel d'aménagement foncier,* ADEF, Paris.

Tribillon, J-F. (1995) Contourner la propriété par l'équipement des villes africaines, in *Régularisations de propriétés. Les Annales de la Recherche Urbaine,* No. 66, Plan Urbain, Ministère de l'Equipement, des Transports et du Tourisme, pp.118–23.

United Nations Centre for Human Settlements (Habitat) (1993) *Améliorer les systèmes d'information foncière et de reconnaissance des droits sur le sol dans les villes d'Afrique sub-saharienne francophone,* Série Gestion Foncière no. 3, UNCHS, Nairobi.

United Nations Centre for Human Settlements (Habitat) (1996) The Habitat Agenda. Goals and Principles, Commitments and Global Plan for Action, United Nations Conference on Human Settlements (Habitat II), UNCHS, Nairobi.

United Nations Centre for Human Settlements (Habitat), The Habitat II Land Initiative, *Habitat Debate*, vol. 3(2) 1997.

United Nations Centre for Human Settlements (Habitat), Towards securing tenure for all, *Habitat Debate*, vol. 5(3) 1993a.

United Nations Centre for Human Settlements (Habitat) (1999b) *Implementing the Habitat Agenda: adequate shelter for all*, Global Campaign for Secure Tenure, UNCHS, Nairobi.

United Nations Centre for Human Settlements (Habitat) and Burkina Faso Government (1999c) *Aménagement foncier urbain et gouvernance locale en Afrique sub-saharienne. Enjeux et opportunités après la Conférence Habitat II*, Rapport du Colloque régional des professionnels africains, Ouagadougou, Burkina Faso, 20–23 avril, Série Gestion Foncière No. 7, Nairobi.

Urban Management Programme, Nairobi, Ministry of Foreign Affairs, France, GTZ, Germany (1995) Urban land management, regularisation policies and local development in Africa and the Arab States, Abidjan, 21–24 March 1995. Lessons from the study and the seminar. Land Management Series No. 4, UNCHS (Habitat).

World Bank (1991) *Urban Policy and Economic Development. An Agenda for the 1990s*, World Bank policy paper, World Bank, Washington, D.C.

World Bank (1993) *Housing: enabling markets to work*, World Bank policy paper, World Bank, Washington, D.C.

CHAPTER 8

Acharya, S.K. and Parikh, S. (2001) Slum networking in Ahmedabad: an alternative paradigm? In Kundu, A. and Mahadevia, D. (Eds) *Poverty and Vulnerability in a Globalising Metropolis – Ahmedabad*, Manak Publications, Delhi.

Dutta, S, with Batley, R, (1999), *Urban Governance, Partnership and Poverty – a case study of Ahmedabad*, IDD, School of Public Policy, University of Birmingham.

Joshi, R. (2001) Integrated slum development – case of Pravinnagar-Guptanagar, in Kundu, A. and Mahadevia, D. (Eds) *Poverty and Vulnerability in a Globalising Metropolis – Ahmedabad*, Manak Publications (forthcoming).

National Sample Survey (1998) *Housing Conditions in India*, Report No. 429, Government of India, New Delhi.

Payne, G. (2000) Urban land tenure policy options: titles or rights? Paper presented at the World Bank Urban Forum, Westfields Marriott, Virginia, USA.

Risbud, N. (2000) Policies for tenure security in Delhi, presented at the International Workshop on Tenure Security Policies: a comparative analysis, Johannesburg.

Tripathi, D. (1998) *Alliance for Change: a slum upgrading environment in Ahmedabad*, Tata McGraw-Hill, New Delhi.

CHAPTER 9

Bademli, R. (1987) Forms of housing in Ankara: segmentation in the domain of housing in a segmented city, in Keles, R. and Kano, H. (Eds), *Housing and the Urban Poor in the Middle East: Turkey, Egypt, Morocco and Jordan*, Institute of Developing Economies.

Balamir, M. (1969) 'Spread of ownership fragmentation in rapid urbanization', unpublished dissertation proposal submitted to University College London.

Balamir, M., 'Kat Mülkiyeti ve Kentlesmemiz' (The process of ownership fragmentation in the urbanization of Turkey), *METU Journal of the Faculty of Architecture*, vol. 2(1), 1975, pp.295–318.

Balamir, M. (1982) 'Kentlesme, Kentsel Süreçler ve Kent Yapısı' (Urbanization, urban processes, and urban structure), in Gülöksüz, Y. (Ed.) *Türkiye Birinci Sehircilik Kongresi*, vol. 1, pp.13–54, METU Faculty of Architecture, Ankara.

Balamir, M. (1992) Türkiye'de Kentlesme ve Kat Mülkiyeti (Flat Ownership and Urbanization in Turkey), unpublished research report, Yunus Nadi Social Sciences Award.

Balamir, M. (1996) Making cities of apartment blocks: transformation of the built-environment in Turkey by means of reorganizations in property rights, in Sey, Y. (Ed.) *Housing and Settlement in Anatolia: a historical perspective*, pp.335–44, prepared for the occasion of Habitat II, The History Foundation, Istanbul.

Balamir, M., Formation of private rental stock in Turkey, *Netherlands Journal of Housing and Built Environment*, vol. 14(4), 1999, pp.385–402.

Karagözoglu, K. (1986) Formation of unauthorised high-rise apartment blocks as a distinct aspect of Turkish urban growth, MSc thesis submitted to the METU Graduate School of Natural and Applied Sciences.

Keles, R. and Kano, H. (1987) *Housing and the Urban Poor in the Middle East: Turkey, Egypt, Morocco and Jordan*, Institute of Developing Economies, Tokyo.

Meral, D. (1996) The shared ownership process in urban development, MSc thesis submitted to the METU Graduate School of Natural and Applied Sciences.

Payne, G. (2000) Urban land tenure policy options: titles or rights? Paper presented at the World Bank Urban Forum, Westfields Marriott, Virginia, USA, 3–5 April.

Payne, G. (1978/9) *Ankara: housing and planning in an expanding city*, 3 vols, research report submitted to the Social Science Research Council.

Uzel, A.L. (1987) *Imara Iliskin Bagıslamaların Gelisimi ve Degerlendirilmes* (An Evaluation of the History of Public Responses to Unauthorized Developments), Konut'85, Kentkoop, Batıkent Konut Üretim Yapı Kooperatifleri Birligi, Ankara.

CHAPTER 10

CYTED Program (1999) Toward a housing diagnostic in Ibero-America, data before discussion, Asuncion, Paraguay, p.30.

Dale, P., Land tenure issues in economic development, *Urban Studies*, vol. 34(10), 1997

Farfan, F. (1999) *Transferencia Tecnologica y Vivienda Popular*. Instituto de Investigaciones de Arquitectura, Programa Promesha, Cochabamba, Bolivia.

Government of Bolivia (1996) *Bolivia: the community participation. Towards Habitat II, Istanbul, Turkey*, Community Participation Ministry, La Paz,.

Navajas, S., Schreiner, M. and Meyer, R., Micro-credit and the poorest of the poor: theory and evidence from Bolivia, *World Development*, vol. 28(2), 2000, pp.333–46.

Payne, G. (1999) *Making Common Ground: public–private partnerships in land for housing*, IT Publications, London.

Ramirez, L. and Bazoberry, G. (1997) *Outlines for a National Housing Policy*, Human Development Ministry, Government of Bolivia, La Paz, Bolivia, pp.15–17.

Solares, H. (1997) *Housing Policies and the Developing of Low-income Habitat in Latin America*, Promesha, Cochabamba, Bolivia.

Vargas, H. (1997) *The Law of Community Participation, and its Habitat in Bolivia*, Cuaderno de Analisis N.1, Promesha, Cochabamba, Bolivia.

CHAPTER 11

Government of Botswana (1982) *National Policy on Housing,* Government Paper No. 2 of 1981, Gaborone.

Government of Botswana (1983) *Report on the Presidential Commission on Land Tenure,* Government Printer, Gaborone.

Government of Botswana (1985) *Government Policy on Land Tenure,* Government Printer, Gaborone, Botswana.

Government of Botswana (1997) *Review of the National Policy on Housing,* Government Printer, Gaborone.

Government of Botswana (1987) *State Land Act,* Chapter 32:01, Government Printer, Gaborone.

Government of Botswana (1993) *Tribal Land Act,* Chapter 32:02, Government Printer, Gaborone.

Mathuba B.M. (1993) Land institutions and land distribution in Botswana, paper presented at the Conference on Land Redistribution Options, Johannesburg, South Africa.

CHAPTER 12

Abers, R.N. (2000) *Inventing Local Democracy. Grassroots Politics in Brazil,* Lynne Rienner, Boulder, Colo.

Afonso, M.R. and Liso, C.H.(1998) A concessao de direito real de uso na regularizacao fundiaria, in Fernandes, E. (Ed) *Direito Urbanistico,* Del Rey, Belo Horizonte.

Allegretti, G. (2000) Informality as a culture of dialogue: three Mayors of Porto Alegre face to face, in *Plurimondi/PluralWorlds,* Dedalo Libri, Bari, Vol II(3).

Assies, W. (1994) 'Reconstructing the meaning of urban land in Brazil: the case of Recife (Pernambuco)', in Jones, G. and Ward, P.M. (Eds) *Methodology for Land and Housing Market Analysis,* UCL Press, London.

FASE, ETAPAS and Centro Josue de Castro (1999) *Uma politica inovadora de urbanizacao no Recife – 10 anos do PREZEIS,* FASE/ETAPAS/Centro Josue de Castro, Recife.

FASE, ETAPAS, Centro Josue de Castro, DED and GTZ (2000) *PREZEIS: O olhar dos moradores,* FASE/ETAPAS/Centro Josue de Castro/DED/GTZ, Recife.

Fernandes, E. (1995) *Law and Urban Change in Brazil,* Avebury, Aldershot.

Fernandes, E. (1997) Access to urban land and housing in Brazil: 'three degrees of illegality', Working Paper WP97EF1, Lincoln Institute of Land policy, Boston, Mass.

Fernandes, E. The legal regularisation of favelas in Brazil: problems and prospects, *Third World Planning Review,* vol. 22 (2), 2000a, pp.167–87.

Fernandes, E. (2000b) 'Law and the production of urban illegality: urban development in Brazil', in Faundez, J., Footer, M.E. and Norton, J.J. (Eds) *Governance, Development and Globalization,* Blackstone, London.

Fernandes, E. and Rolnik, R. (1998) Law and urban change in Brazil, in Fernandes, E. and Varley, A. (Eds) *Illegal Cities – law and urban change in developing countries,* Zed Books, London.

Goldsmith, W.W. and Vainer, C.B. Participatory budgeting and power politics in Porto Alegre, in *Land Lines,* January 2001, pp.7–9.

Hereda, J.F. et al (1996) O impacto das AEIS no mercado imobiliario de Diadema, mimeo.

Maia, M.L. (1995) Land use regulations and rights to the city: squatter settlements in Recife, Brazil, *Land Use Policy,* vol. 12(22), pp.177–80.

Rabaroux, P. (1997) La regularizacion en Recife, in Azuela, A. and Tomas, F. (Eds) *El acceso de los pobres al suelo urbano*, Centro de Estudios Mexianos y Centroamericanos/Universidad Nacional Autonoma de Mexico, Mexico City.

Santos, B. de S. Participatory budgeting in Porto Alegre, *Politics and Society*, vol. 26(4), 1998, pp.461–510.

Souza, F.A.M. de (2001) The future of informal settlements: lessons in the legalisation of disputed urban land in Recife, Brazil, Geoforum 32(4), in press.

Weigand, V. (2001) A concessao de direito real de uso no direito brasileiro, in Fernandes, E. (Ed.) *Direito Urbanistico e Politica Urbana no Brasil*, Del Rey, Belo Horizonte.

CHAPTER 13

Aiemwa, B. (1991) *Socio-economic Survey on Tanzania Bomani Settlement (Voi Municipality)*, MLG/GTZ Small Towns Development Project, Nairobi.

Etherton, D. (1971) *Mathare Valley: a case study of uncontrolled settlement in Nairobi*, University of Nairobi Housing Research and Development Unit, Nairobi.

Gitau, S.K. (1998) *Land Buying Companies for Urban Housing Development in Eldoret, Kenya*, University of Nairobi, Nairobi.

Githongo, J. (1997) Interior land related conflicts and violence, research paper for the Conflict and Conflict Management in the Horn of Africa Project, USAID, Nairobi.

Government of Kenya (1995) The Local Government (Adoptive Byelaws) (Building) Amendment Order, Legal Notice No. 257, Government Printer, Nairobi.

Kiarie, P. (1990) The performance of land buying companies in Central Province of Kenya, MA thesis, Department of Land Development, University of Nairobi.

Malombe, J. (1997) Conflicts in urban settlement in Kenya: access to land and services in unplanned settlements, research paper for the Conflict and Conflict in the Greater Horn of Africa Project, USAID, Nairobi.

Opiata, O. (1999) Security of tenure – a human rights perspective, in *Security of Tenure in Urban Settlements*, Shelter Forum, Nairobi.

Yahya, S.S. and Agevi E. (1997) *Seeking The Standard Bearer*, ITDG, Rugby.

Yahya, S.S. et al. (2001) *Double Standards, Single Purpose: Reforming Housing Regulations to Reduce Poverty*. ITDG Publishing, London.

CHAPTER 14

CSIR (Centre for Scientific and Industrial Research) (1999). The state of human settlements: South Africa 1994–1998, draft report prepared for the Department of Housing, Pretoria.

Development Works (1999) Urban tenure policy research: report 1: recommendations on R 293 towns and conditions of unregistered and informal tenure, unpublished report for the Department of Land Affairs.

Republic of South Africa (1994) *White Paper: A New Housing Policy and Strategy for South Africa*, Government Gazette, Pretoria.

Republic of South Africa (1995) *Development Facilitation Act, Act 67 of 1995*.

Rust, K. (2000) The contributions of co-operatives to shelter development in South Africa, unpublished report prepared for the International Co-operative Alliance and the United Nations Centre for Human Settlements (Habitat).

Social Housing Foundation (1998) *Current Status of Social Housing in South Africa*, Report to the Minister of Housing.

CHAPTER 15

Angel, S., Benjamin, S. and DeGoede, K.H. (1977) The low-income housing system in Bangkok, *Ekistics*, vol.44(261), pp.79–84.

Bijl, J., Janssen, E., Meijer, M. and Willemsen, E. (1992) *Slum Eviction and Relocation in Bangkok*, TUDelft , Delft University of Technology.

Government Housing Bank (1997), *Annual Report 1997*, Government Housing Bank of Thailand.

IMF (1998) *International Financial Statistics Yearbook*, International Monetary Fund.

JICA, BMA and the Govt. of Thailand (1997) *The Study on Urban Environmental Improvement Program in Bangkok Metropolitan Area*, vol. 2, Master Plan, Pacific Consultants International Suuri-Keikaku Co. Ltd.

Pornchokchai, S. (1985) *1020 Bangkok Slums: evidence, analysis, critics*, Bangkok, School of Urban Community Research and Actions.

UCDO (2000) UCDO update, No. 2, Urban Community Development Office, Thailand.

Van der Linden, J. (1977) The bastis of Karachi: types and dynamics, Amsterdam, PhD thesis, Amsterdam Free University.

Yap, K.S. (1992) *Low-income Housing in Bangkok: a review of some housing sub-markets*, Bangkok, Asian Institute of Technology.

Yap, K.S. and Mohit, R.S. (1998) Reinventing local government for sustainable cities in Asia, *Regional Development Dialogue*, vol. 19(1), UNCRD, Japan.

CONCLUSION

Benjamin, S. and Bhuvaneswari, R. (2001) Democracy, Inclusive Governance and Poverty in Bangalore, Working Paper No 26, International Development Department, School of Public Policy, University of Birmingham. Accessible at www.bham.ac.uk/idd/activities/urban/ubgov.htm

Davidson, F. and Payne, G. (Eds) (2000) *Urban Projects Manual*, 2nd edn, Liverpool University Press, Liverpool.

Oswald, A. (1999) The housing market and Europe's unemployment, a non-technical paper available at andrewoswald.com

Index

Namibia 36
sub-Saharan Africa 115–16, 117–21, 122,
    128, 131
Tanzania 34
Uganda 35–6
Czech Republic 44–5, 48, 49, 51

Dalifort, Senegal 125–7, 129–30, 133
De Soto, Hernando 9–11, 12, 57–8, 70–2
dead capital 10, 55, 231
decentralization 30–1
    Peru 73–4
    sub-Saharan Africa 117–18, 120–1, 123–4,
        129, 130–2, 135
Delhi, India 136–57
Demetevler, Turkey 166–7
demolitions
    Egypt 82, 86, 93–5
    exploitation 27–8
    India 146, 147, 150, 155–6
    Kenya 236, 251
    Turkey 175
Department for International Development
    (DFID) 14–16, 23
Durand-Lasserve, Alain 18, 114–35

Eastern Europe 17, 41–56
Egypt 18, 79–99
El Mounira el Gedida, Egypt 91–2
El Porvenir, Trujillo, Peru 61–2
elites 27–8
Estonia 44, 45, 48, 53
Everest Court, South Africa 268, 269–72, 273,
    274, 276, 277
evictions 296
    Brazil 210, 212, 215, 225, 229
    Burkina Faso 124
    Colombia 18, 105, 109
    Egypt 82, 93–4
    India 9, 19, 138, 139, 146, 148, 150, 155–6
    Kenya 236
    Senegal 121
    South Africa 271, 272
    Thailand 278, 281, 282, 284, 286, 287–8,
        291–2
    Turkey 159, 175
    see also demolitions
exploitation 27–8
Ezbet el Haggana, Egypt 87, 88–9

family title 265, 266–7
Farfan Espinoza, Fabian 20, 181–92
favelas 209–13, 216–26
Fernandes, Edesio 21, 209–32
Fixed Period State Grant (FPSG) 20, 194–5,
    197–8, 199, 204
freehold tenure
    Benin 122
    Botswana 193, 195
    Brazil 212–14, 217, 220–1, 225–6, 228–30
    Colombia 100, 104–5, 106, 108, 109

Egypt 81, 83–4, 85–6, 89–90, 93
India 138, 139–40
Kenya 233, 259–60
Senegal 130
South Africa 264, 301
sub-Saharan Africa 115, 116
transitional economies 42
Turkey 158–9, 160, 162, 167, 170–3
Uganda 36

gender 7, 8, 302
    Botswana 200–1
    Brazil 214, 218–19, 221, 228
    Egypt 98
    India 137–8
    Kenya 234–5, 237, 242, 246
    Peru 65
    South Africa 269
    Thailand 294
    Turkey 175–6
Global Plan of Action (GPA) 23, 24–6, 33
Grover, Richard 17, 41–56
Gueye, Moussa 18, 114–35
guided land developments 60–3

Habitat Agenda 23–8, 302
hekr land rent system 84, 92
housing associations 47–8, 64–5
housing loans
    Benin 122
    Bolivia 183–92
    Botswana 195, 199
    Egypt 97–8
    Kenya 243–4, 247
    Peru 74
    Senegal 125, 129
    transitional economies 47–52, 55
housing permits 115, 116
    Benin 18, 118, 122, 133
    Burkina Faso 119, 123, 128–9
Hungary 45, 49, 50, 51

identity cards 142–3, 146–7, 150–1, 155
illegality 28–30
India 9, 11, 19, 136–57
Indira Camp behind Safdarjung Hospital
    (ICH) 145, 146, 150
Indira Camp in Srinivashpuri (ICS) 145, 146,
    149, 150–1
informal settlements
    Bolivia 181–92
    Botswana 195
    Brazil 209–32
    Burkina Faso 123–4, 128
    Colombia 100–13
    Egypt 79–99
    illegality 28–30
    India 136–57
    Kenya 236–47
    law 30–8
    Peru 57–75

www.ingramcontent.com/pod-product-compliance
Lightning Source LLC
Chambersburg PA
CBHW060024030426